T0064441

POWER OF THE UNIVERSE
LIES WITHIN YOU

POWER OF THE UNIVERSE
LIES WITHIN YOU

PRADIPTA KUMAR DAS

PARTRIDGE
A Penguin Random House Company

To order additional copies of this book, contact
Partridge India
000 800 10062 62
orders.india@partridgepublishing.com

www.partridgepublishing.com/india

Dedicated to fond memories of my late
elder sister Minati Das whose loving
inspiration has carried me all along….

The author's proceeds from this book will be used to
support the Charitable Trust in the name
of the author's mother,
*"Biraja Rani Trust for Education,
Health & Culture"*, Odisha.

CONTENTS

FOREWORD xv

PREFACE xvii

ACKNOWLEDGEMENTS xxiii

CHAPTER 1:   APOLCALYPTIC WHISPERS **1**

Midlife crisis 1

The aftermath 11

The eternal questions and the quest for answers 13

CHAPTER 2:   TEENAGE DREAMS **16**

It is natural to dream at a young age 16

Attributes of parents manifest themselves as expressions of God 18

Values of honesty and integrity 19

Lessons on self-esteem and challenge 20

Lessons on non-violence 21

Lessons on unconditional love and respect for others 23

Lessons on simple living 24

Dreams and desires of the teenage years have inherent divinity 25

My parents are my best teachers 29

CHAPTER 3:   SARMA – SIR MODEL **34**

Selective(S) Attention (A), Retention(R), Modification (M),
  Absorption (A) – Satisfaction(S), Internalization (I) and
  Realisation (R) Model 34

Reflection of the Soul's image in oneself 39

Less than one hundred percent satisfaction 41

How the SARMA-SIR model actually works 42

Glimpses of a miracle or a mere coincidence   45
Painful sight giving a burst of positive energy   47

CHAPTER 4:   POSITIVE, NEGATIVE & NEUTRAL
EMOTIONS   **50**

Fundamental attributes of self   50
Imbalances in life's inbuilt system and the problems
   thereof   52
Ambivalence can lead to real problems   53
Fear of death or fear of loss of prestige   55
The three components of human intellect   58
Superstitions and their effect   60
"Karta Feeling" and its relevance   65
Obstacles and their solution   66
Failures are actually the pillars of success   67
Mistakes are not committed at all levels in one go   68
Negative vs. Positive thoughts   71
Bizarre thoughts Vs. Yogic action   74
Sensuality vs. Sexuality   76

CHAPTER 5:   WAIT A MINUTE! AREN'T WE
ALL SEEKING HAPPINESS?   **78**

Life changing scene   78
The Goal Post   80
Bliss is very real   86
Stress, happiness and spirituality   90
Happiness online   94
Happiness and pain do not go together   97
Work is a need, whether for the body or the mind   98
Deep scar on the soul can act as a large bowl to contain joy   100
Kindness to one's own self is a necessity   101

The Wall Clock; life's metaphor   103

Happiness lies in giving   104

Distance between sadness and happiness is just twelve inches   106

Happiness is a journey and not the destination   108

The binary code of happiness   111

Bits and bytes of happiness: Cracking the Code   114

Happiness is just one thought and emotion away   120

Was it real or illusory?   121

CHAPTER 6:   UNIVERSE, EARTH AND SOUL -
**   AREN'T THEY ALL EXPANDING?   124**

The Big Bang and the Universe   124

Expanding Universe   126

Expanding Earth   126

Search for Truth is not illusory   129

Infinite to finite   133

Instincts, Actions, Emotions & Spirit   134

Expanding soul   137

CHAPTER 7:   OUR INTERNAL UNIVERSE;
**   NEURONS & NEURAL NETWORK   139**

Neurons, Neurotransmitters and Neural Networks   139

How many stars are there in the Universe?   141

Influence of the Sun and its planets vs. that of all stars in
    the Universe   143

Neuroplasticity and its significance   144

Power of neurons and neural network   146

We own hundreds of complex machines but still hanker
    after petty ones   148

Dreams and their meaning   150

Source - Sink phenomenon   152

Childhood memories can be handy during midlife crisis   155

Independence, interdependence, conscience and social
    conscience   157

Sound is more powerful than light   159

Emotions and their influence on our bodies   161

**CHAPTER 8:   GOD AND HIS SEVEN BILLION
              CHILDREN   163**

Faith can move mountains   163

GOD lies within each cell of you   166

Evil does not exist   168

God's letter to a soul about to take human form on the
    planet Earth   172

Hindu belief of thirty-three crore Gods   176

**CHAPTER 9:   MUSINGS ABOUT HUMAN
              EVOLUTION AND SATYA YUG   180**

Musings about human evolution   180

Dashavatara and its relevance to human evolution   185

Bhagawat Gita: three dimensional internal reflections
    inside a diamond triangle   191

The Dawn of Satya Yug   193

Playing spoil sport with God   202

Tenets of Satya Yug   204

Does consciousness reside within or without?   211

CHAPTER 10: PURPOSE OF LIFE   217

Encounter with a White Light with golden edges   217

Who is swinging my leg?   219

Look deep inside you and meet your own God   220

We have to protect our own good self from destruction by
    the environment 222

We are the highest species, let us together justify that 225

Our goal is to spread peace, love and compassion 231

CHAPTER 11: WHAT ARE THE TOOLS THEN? 233

Are there any skills or tools, and do we need to practice them? 233

Accept the problem, the responsibility and the reality 236

Take a break 238

Do not consider it to be 'the only life' 241

Get help from every possible quarter 244

Together you win 246

Let go 248

Don't be angry or guilty; have faith in the greater design
    of God 249

You are already a winner! Just maintain the status 252

Discern and Discriminate 253

Feel content and feel grateful 264

Adapt & adopt Halt-Rewind-Meditate-Grow (HRMG) model 265

Power of the Universe lies within you 270

Engage yourself till you make it a habit 271

Go back to your hobbies 273

Turn around to the Nature 274

Be aware that weakness is not always a burden 276

Learn and relearn constantly 277

Immerse in Awe 279

Get involved and make others involved 280

Pour love & affection and make the small family the best
    teacher and boss 283

Believe in infinite happiness 288

Prioritise through Child-Adult-Parent Continuum 291

List out long, medium and short term goals and mark the
    calendar   296
Choose the path to happiness   298
Revisit the fundamental scripture   303
Engage in some holy rituals   306
Live in Hope   307
Create a safety network and nourish it for your own help   309
Relish the speed breakers   310
Add just one more layer to your soul   314
Have a two-way switch ready: from within or from without   317
Look from the end to when it all began   319
Never allow your soul to feel like a burden   322
Follow a healthy diet and a healthy exercise regime   325
Breathe your way to life   326
Cultivate laughter into your life   329
Heal through meditation and visualisation   330
Rewire and recover   332
Activate the dormant feel-good old circuits in the brain   333
You may not like everybody but you can certainly love all   336
Recollect and reinforce all your successes of the past   341
Keep challenging your own bias and widen the horizon   343
Give and Live   346
Leave your legacy: Dad, Mom and You   347

BIBLIOGRAPHY   **353**
ABOUT THE AUTHOR   **361**

FOREWORD

I first met Pradipta Kumar Das (PK) in 2000. He was presented to me with what appeared to be a depressive disorder, and his General Practitioner had started him on an antidepressant (paroxetine). After the antidepressant dose was increased, he developed an acute psychotic reaction which resulted in him being admitted into a mental health unit of a General Hospital. There he was treated with antipsychotic medication which successfully treated the psychosis. He was only in hospital for a few days, but after a few weeks at home, he began to suffer from severe panic attacks. He continued with his medication and also had regular supportive and cognitive therapy to which he responded well.

PK had come to Australia to do his PhD studies with his wife and small child. Whilst here, they had another child. They were well supported by the university community and also by the local neighbourhood. They made good friends and, despite missing their family in India, were managing very well.

Following his psychotic episode, PK became intrigued about his experience and felt that it had changed his life. He felt that not only had this been a chemical reaction to his antidepressant medication, but it also reflected a deeper spiritual truth for him. The ongoing panic attacks continued to challenge him to find other strategies to treat these. He began to realise the power of relaxation and meditation and how he could influence his symptoms by changing his thinking patterns. He also started to concentrate on how balanced his life was and on the spiritual aspects of himself.

After PK had returned to India, he would regularly email me to discuss his progress and for reassurance that he was using the correct strategies to treat his panic attacks. Over time, these attacks subsided and contact became infrequent.

He had discussed his wish to understand all of this better and that, with this knowledge, he might help others. This then became the origin of this book. As can be seen from the book, he delved into every aspect of mental health issues. He researched widely and emphasised the areas which were most significant to him. His hope is that others who read this will be able to use aspects of it to understand what has happened to them, and to help themselves, using the different strategies he has outlined.

What happened to PK in 2000 changed his life in a positive way. It led him on a journey of self-discovery which has resulted in his personal growth and has had a positive impact on his family and friends. Mental illness can have a devastating effect on a person's life, but it can also be the challenge that brings about change and growth. It can build resilience and lead to exploring oneself. This is what happened to PK and has resulted in the writing of this book.

It has taken PK fifteen years to write this book and I know that it has been a task that has cost him a lot in terms of emotions, time and energy. My wish is that this book will positively touch many people and that it will be a great success. I have found it to be a moving account and am sure that others will be moved also by it.

I hope that this book will be read by large number of people from all sections of society and that it will make a difference in their day-to-day life.

Dr Jo Lammersma MBBS FRANZCP
Consultant in Psychiatry
Honorary Secretary RANZCP 2001-2007
Awarded Medal of Honour RANZCP 2009
Adelaide, Australia

PREFACE

Three incidents in my life spanning more than half a century triggered nearly four decades of focused work on the subject of 'Human vs God Power, Knowledge vs Ignorance, Destiny vs Free will, Traditions vs Modernity, Science vs Religion, Love vs Hate, Self-gratification vs Self-sacrifice, Single life vs Many lives, Happiness vs Madness, Separateness vs Togetherness, Reality vs Illusion and Disease vs Well-being.' This book is the result of that work. The title of the book has been chosen according to my perception about the *well of life* - the depth of which most of us fail to measure because of our superficial understanding about the infinite expanse and vastness of *soul power*.

I must have been in class VI or VII, a boy of just eleven or twelve. I was returning from the school, about one and a half kilometers away from my home, in the town of Keonjhar, Odisha. It was just in front of the children's park, hardly two hundred meters away from home, that I saw a herd of cows being goaded back to their respective homes by a cowherd coming in the opposite direction. Those days, it was the practice even in small towns of Odisha to hire a boy or an adult who would go in the morning to collect all the cows and calves from a few residents of a particular locality, guide them to nearby a field where good grass and green leaves would be available for them to eat, and bring them back in the evening to their owners. I was casually walking past the herd that afternoon when a cow with large horns suddenly started charging towards me. It was very sudden and scary and actually shocked me quite a bit. By that age, because of my pious upbringing at home (both Mom and Dad being very religious and pious individuals) I had started having strong belief in God. But at the same time, school education had also developed in me a scientific mind that questioned everything in this world and always tried to find a logical answer to each and every problem facing me as an individual and perhaps the world at large. I thought to myself that if God was in charge of the world, and if there were about thirty-three crores Gods (three hundred and thirty million Gods, as believed in Hindu philosophy) and if the world population was about three hundred and fifty crores at that time (year 1972 or 1973), then each God from heaven must have been looking after the welfare and controlling every movement of around ten individuals on Earth - which was okay because God, being very powerful, can of course control ten people on Earth!

It baffled me; I had not done anything wrong to the cow, nor had I done any misdeed on that particular day at school. So why then did the cow come charging at me? I moved away from its horns in the nick of the time and saved myself from any serious physical injury. But why on Earth did God want to assault me through this cow? This was perhaps the earliest memory I have of my continuous research on interaction between mortal man and invisible God.

The second incident happened while I was walking on the bridge over the River Levin, near the town of Ulverstone, Tasmania, during one beautiful morning of February 2001. I had gone to present a technical paper as part of my PhD work at a two day international conference on Earth Sciences. While walking over the bridge, I had a subtle flash of feeling inside me, a kind of urge to jump into the flowing river beneath the bridge!

I was not hundred percent fit those days in terms of my own mental health condition and was under medical treatment. Too much of anxiety driven stress on whether I could complete my PhD within the stipulated period had already caused depression in me and the fear of loss of face, due to the likely failure, had created a subconscious urge to escape!

The third incident occurred sometime in mid-2004. I was at a week-long spiritual training workshop at Jorhat, Assam, conducted by one of the teachers under Sri Sri Ravi Shankar, the founder and head of *Art of Living Foundation* in India. It was the penultimate day of the course, popularly known as the *Foundation Course*. Being very true to what I was being asked to do, I was following each instruction carefully, following what the recorded voice of Sri Sri Ravi Shankar, coming from a tape recorder run by his disciple, Mr. Samir Jolly, was saying. The participants were being trained on a specific but most important part of the course: *Sudarshan Kriya.* I had been thoroughly enjoying the training course over the last few days and was very attentive to the detailed procedures given to perform the *Sudarshan Kriya* and actually did it in a meticulous manner without any prejudice. After nearly twenty-five or thirty minutes of the exercise, a simple yogic breathing exercise, when the routine was in the waning phase, so to say, I felt a sensation of complete nothingness - something that amounted to a clear case of loss of my own existence as I knew it so far. I felt as if 'I', in the normal sense of the term, lost its meaning, my existence, and that I was sort of in communion with the entire Cosmic Universe, within an energy field, under its influence and yet nowhere as a separate entity. This feeling lasted for a few minutes. The teacher on that day, Mr. Samir Jolly, when queried by me on what this feeling could be, explained curtly, 'It could be a feeling of *Samadhi!*' I had never gone through such an experience ever before, but literature says *Samadhi* refers to a blissful state where the yogi is absorbed into the One. This incredible feeling has never been replicated in the last ten years of my life. Perhaps that's because I have never been able to sit down, concentrate and truly and sincerely practice *Sudarshan Kriya.* While being engrossed in my mundane daily routine, I have never focused on a deliberate journey along this specialized spiritual path to attain *Samadhi,* but the feeling which I experienced for a few minutes that day remains within me as vivid as I experienced it. It was an exalted feeling wherein ordinary emotions associated with vibrations of mental thought processes were completely gone and my separate existence was merged with the all-pervasive God, if we have some meaning for it!

Right from my early childhood, I have been asking myself questions, about the possibility of the existence of God, and His relationship with man or woman. Questions like how nature has brought us into existence, how nature deals with us and what nature expects from us have always fascinated me. Who chose my parents, or how I chose my parents, or if my parents had a hand in choosing me and, if so, how and why the same parents chose completely different characters for their other children. Why one child is born into poverty and deprivation while another is born with a golden spoon in his mouth. What or who decides this phenomenon of simple discriminatory difference in the present day world and why.

Questions like who I am, where have I come from, where I am going and why I decide on certain things in a particular manner etc. have always bothered me. Questions about religious tenets, rituals of which there are so many. The age old tussle between Science and Religion. Is there any one *right* path? Why so much violence in the name of religion? Are we all doing okay as a single human race? Is reincarnation real or a figment of imagination? Are we deep in *Kali Yug* or have already entered the early part of *Satya Yug* - two of the four eras of the *cycle of life* in Hindu philosophy.

The journey of my life so far has been phenomenal with hundreds of successes, small and big, and with failures in equal number - if not more. The constant longing to learn new things, to enjoy new things, and to be able to help and serve humanity has always been intrinsic within me. Obstacles have been there, but they have been overcome finally in each case. Moments of glory and triumph, as well as moments of utter desperation and helplessness have all been there. However, somewhere, pure intentions have helped in guiding me to grow with love and break barriers.

Recalling very small incidents and really big events both in my own life as well as on a global scale, I have tried to imagine some sort of Universal Law or Unified Theory which can be easily understood by ordinary souls like me. The fruits of my experiential existence through several crises and a similar number of exalted highs have continuously haunted me, urged me to put down my story in the form of a book so that the zest that I have been able to extract can be summarized thus: *'To be human essentially means to be spiritual'* and every human being represents an *'Infinite Spirit within finite body'*. The very fact that we are born as human beings having a Conscience in the truest sense of the term, separates us from the animal world in a distinctive fashion. That our souls have made a tremendous journey and taken the costume of human being points out to the infinite possibilities that lie ahead of us. It is as if the total Cosmos is captured and coded in the miniscule entity of our souls which actually represents the Power of the Universe waiting to be explored and experienced.

This book's intent is to work like a bridge between what is easily comprehensible and that which is seemingly incomprehensible with a subtle aim to help those who have momentarily lost track and touch of reality and pushed themselves too far in the world's rat race so as to even contemplate *'quitting life'*. I have reached the bottomless pit once, seen it all, and have a very clear memory of the sequence of events (all orchestrated by me though!) that pushed me into a mental hospital for a week followed by frequent and intense *panic attacks* over a long period of almost a year and half that brought me so much pain and suffering. As a normal human soul yearns to serve his brethren through his own experiences of life, this attempt of mine is hoped to help those sweet children of God who for their innocence never tried to measure the power that lies within their own souls and who, while running after the illusory world, finally got stuck up and stranded at a crossroads of life, just like I once did. The tools I have outlined are the ones which I resorted to; some very ancient and time-tested ones and some which evolved through my own experience as I moved along. These are the very tools that helped me overcome my crisis. I am sure any reader who faithfully approaches the nuances of life along similar lines, with his or her own adjustment, can certainly tide over the worst crisis of his life and enjoy again the beauty of life that this mysterious Universe has to offer.

Depression, Anxiety and *psychosis* are a very common phenomenon these days as are the resultant *panic attacks* that can appear deadly and be very painful. But there is ample hope and scope for anyone on this planet to just reorient his thinking, make a few changes in his lifestyle, not hesitate to ask for and get help from whatever sources, adopt some ancient but proven practices of healthy living, and easily come out of the crisis.

There will be passages in the book which might appear insane, purely hallucinatory, awkward, illogical, utterly stupid and even shameful. And some will appear as boisterous. But I can honestly claim that, right from my childhood, I have always had this yearning in the very core of my being to be of some help to humanity. My close family and friends are the best guardians of the veracity of my claim. But one thing is absolutely certain; there is not an iota of untruth in any of my words, sentences or feelings as I perceived. Nothing that has not resonated with my mind and heart has been included in this book.

While writing these words, it alerts me pretty clearly that I am no big star or any great leader in a particular field. I am neither a great scientist nor a great sportsperson or a great philosopher for people to emulate. However I have always tried to carry out my own experiments with spirituality ever since I was a teenager, be it through my physical passions, sensual observations or be it through my intellectual rumblings. These experiments are so very human and down to Earth that I am confident that it will be of some value and guidance to those who seek Truth and enjoy the beauty of Truth in its myriad dimensions. If distressed souls somewhere in the world derive some benefit from this book, it will give me immense satisfaction and, hence, I would consider that all my hard work has not been in vain.

The use of words like 'Hindu' and *'Bhagawat Gita'* in many places of the book might dissuade some readers by making this seem as an overtly religious book. I must emphasise that it is not a religious book and that I am quite confident that it will appeal to people of any religion around the world. Quite a few Sanskrit-based words which are a popular part of the Indian cultural milieu have also found a place in the book although their meaning and purpose have always been universal. I have given notes in relevant places that while some of the words and concepts are based on the Hindu way of life (finding mention so profusely in my book because of my cultural background) they are just pointers to a general theme. Any individual belonging to any other religion can find something very secular in the ideas and concepts and may find resonance in their own scriptures as well.

ACKNOWLEDGEMENTS

Writing a book based mainly on personal experience at different stages of my life so far would not have been possible unless, at each stage, I got the support and encouragement of many people. The list is very long. Topping the list, obviously, is Dr. Jo Lammersma, my mental health doctor in Australia during 2000-2001. She was the key to helping me pull myself out of the deep morass of my mental health crisis - not only through her cognitive therapy sessions, but also by her suggesting that I stay away from diverting my energies to write a book at the peak of my PhD research work. She knew full well how such patients behave and what was good for me at that time. She encouraged me to concentrate mainly on my PhD work while writing only points for the book, helped me achieve my primary goal in Australia i.e. obtaining my PhD degree, and at the same time helped me keep the flame of authorship of a book burning in me. Failure to achieve the primary target would have certainly changed my life for the worse! This is my way of saying thank you Jo. My special thanks to Jo for acceding to my request to write the Foreword for the book.

Next in the list would be Joan Harris, my next door neighbor at my residence at 1/21 Ballantyne Street, Thebarton, South Australia. She was the one who gave me and my little family the much needed intimate company for four full years. Without her warmth, compassion, help and support, my stay at Australia would not have been so enjoyable and successful. I am thankful for my stimulating discussions on philosophy with her.

I would like to acknowledge the help rendered by my daughter Amrita and son Kaushik, in spite of their busy schedules, in typing the entire Bibliography. My sweet wife Snigdha, son Kaushik and daughter Amrita have been deprived of my time and attention for numerous weekends and weekday evenings. As a father, I had to struggle with myself to remain free from guilt because at the critical time of my son's Board examination, I committed to my publisher to complete the book. My sincere thanks and gratitude to my sweet family for bearing with my selfishness without too much nagging and for the exemplary sacrifice they have made for more than a year to just help me get the book into final shape for publication.

Dr. K. Guru Rajesh, my junior colleague at the workplace who at such a young age shows extraordinary talent in many diverse subjects, and is a celebrated author himself, always stood behind me during the last year of writing my book. I had a series of enlightening discussions with him on Indian mythology and on the subject of astrology which enriched me immeasurably. He was always prodding me to write a few pages every day so that I could complete the book on time. My sincere thanks to Rajesh.

A word of appreciation to the excellent work done by the editorial team of Notion Press who actually took up the editing job and delivered right on time. But for their editing, quality of the book would not have been the same.

Views expressed in the book are purely personal and do not in any way represent the viewpoints of any particular organization, institution, religion or social group. However, many ideas that have been reiterated in the book might resonate with many other authors of the past and present and they all have my sincere respect for having cared enough to express themselves in different ways so that I can now generate a sense of vindication. On the other hand, a few of my concepts might seem controversial, but my intention is more academic; my intent is espousing those ideas rather than vouching for them. However, the central theme of the book is aimed at helping people tap their full inner potential so as to solve their own problems in some specific cases of mental health issues as well as in other general issues.

Apart from those who directly helped make me what I am today, there have been a great many people including some outstanding teachers in both academic as well as spiritual fields who have contributed indirectly to my inner growth. If I were to name them all, the list would be endless, simply because I have actually learned something or the other from innumerable individuals. I have been inspired sometimes by their kind words, sometimes by their own examples and sometimes by the challenges and criticisms they threw at me. And this has happened right from my childhood till today, and the learning is still continuing.

I have included many discussions on various subjects which have been adapted from several public sources like Wikipedia, Newspapers, News magazines, Internet searches etc. I wish to acknowledge with greatest sincerity and gratitude the original authors of such articles, some of which were anonymous.

Finally it was because of Gemma Ramos from Partridge Corporation (a Penguin Random House Company) who so politely used to remind me about the final draft almost every fortnight for more than last six months. But for her repeated reminders, this book would not have seen the light of the day. A Big Thank You Gemma!

CHAPTER 1

APOLCALYPTIC WHISPERS

Midlife crisis

During my stay in Australia, on the sixth of July 2000, I had my weakest day, possibly due to drug overreaction.

I was there on 'study leave' from one of the national oil companies of India, to work on a PhD project at what was then the National Centre for Petroleum Geology and Geophysics (NCPGG), University of Adelaide, Australia bagging a prestigious Overseas Postgraduate Research Scholarship offered by the Government of Australia. There was an official constraint in terms of the duration of my stay, or the time during which the project had to be completed. I had to complete the PhD within three years (July 1997 – July 2000), but this was officially extended later on for another year, both from the University's side as well as from the side of my parent organization.

Around the time I completed my first two years of the PhD study, I felt as if the progress of the research work was not going that well, and hence, projecting my anxiety and fear, I had perhaps a false perception building in my subconscious mind that the project might not be completed on time. This made me very anxious and worried. Continuous anxiety about the successful completion within the stipulated leave period started creating stress which further reduced productivity in my research work. This vicious cycle of worrying about progress on one hand, and lack of productivity on the other, slowly led me to a state where even the birth of my second child - a very cute looking and lovely son - in July 1999 failed to drive me, to give me the energy and vigour to give my best for my research work.

1

In spite of the marvelous medical facilities available to us in the beautiful city of Adelaide, and to the surprise of many of my Indian friends in Australia, we had planned for the delivery of the child back in India, simply because of the abnormal rise of nationalistic feelings in me around that time. In hindsight, perhaps the 24/7 media coverage of the Pokhran II nuclear blasts in 1998, the Balkan war in 1999 and the Indo-Pakistan Kargil war, which I was absorbing while being stationed in Adelaide, thousands kilometers away from the events, had together helped create a surge of such intense nationalistic feelings in me that I decided for my son to be born in our own motherland!

There were clear signs of loss of vigour, no zeal to work and complete shadow of fear and anxiety which made me feel as if I was totally stuck without any tangible progress. Even after my family joined me back in Australia in November 1999, about four months after the birth of our son, I was still feeling thoroughly exhausted and energy less and did not observe any signs of improvement.

This ultimately led me to look for some medical help, which I naively thought could catapult me back to feeling normal and energetic and hence help me make good progress in my research work. Towards the later part of May 2000, I first consulted a general practitioner whom I was quite familiar with. Listening to my problems intently and perhaps because of a word from me about my *'depressive feeling'*, the general physician prescribed for me, without much hesitation, a popular anti-depressant drug called 'Aropax'. But he suggested that I should simultaneously see a mental health specialist also. Although Dr. Jo Lammersma, the mental health doctor I consulted soon afterwards approved of the continuation of the said anti-depressant drug, she said that I would start seeing some results only three to four weeks after starting the medication.

Contrary to expectations, I was not feeling anywhere near out of that depressive feeling even after four weeks of medication. I decided to go for a pre-emptive increase in daily dosage (after a casual consultation with Dr.Lammersma over the phone) believing that it might help in faster recovery. I had been prescribed with the anti-depressant Aropax (serotonin re-uptake inhibitor). And instead of one tablet a day, I took two. I had been on this increased dosage just for two days. On the third day, the sixth of July 2000, by the time I went home from the NCPGG at 5 p.m., after a day's PhD work, I felt so tired both physically and mentally that I could not even stand properly, I felt so low, totally drained of energy. I went into sleep at 8.30 p.m. and got up at 11 p.m. I had not slept so soundly in nearly two months, but I woke up with a strange experience…..

I was having a very sound sleep and at some point of time during the sleep, almost through a dream like fashion, I felt as if my heart was completely drying up. But this was simultaneously accompanied by a feeling of blissful pleasure coming from the top right corner of my forehead. The feeling was very real. Subconsciously, I felt as if I was deriving energy through that side coming from Heaven or so. I felt I was getting some sort of cool energy into my heart which had felt almost dried up! After few minutes, I did not want to continue drinking this *'nectar-like honey of joyous feeling'* any further as it would have amounted to "greed". I got up with a jerk and immediately told the story to my wife - saying that I'd almost died and had woken up only through some Heavenly intervention! I had felt as if I'd reached death, as if my soul had dried up totally. And I felt as if I'd gotten my "life" back only through the beautiful sensations. It was as if God had intervened by providing the cool light energy we see in the pictures of some of our Hindu Gods and Goddesses - those beams of light energy spreading from their palms…..

I triumphantly declared to my wife; 'The title of my book will be *"The Story of a Bizarre Indian to Reincarnation of Christ!"'* This feeling of triumphalism perhaps emanated from a thought deep down that I had defeated death and got back to life after being dead once…..

My wife immediately countered; 'No, the title should be *"The Story of a Bizarre Geophysicist to…"'* She replaced the word 'Indian' with 'Geophysicist', but she agreed to the rest. She must have her own reasons for saying so.

There was one very intriguing part to the story. Normally, I used to go to sleep with the lights turned off. But on this particular evening, when I returned from the research institute, I was feeling so tired that I thought of relaxing on the bed for a while with the lights still on. There was a tungsten light bulb in front of my forehead which was on while I was sleeping. When I woke up, the bulb went out with a sound. It got fused at exactly the same moment I woke up! There cannot be any scientific or logical explanation to this, but it happened this way for sure.

I went to sleep again at around 12 p.m. but when I suddenly woke up again at 4 a.m., I thought I was dying, as if my *'Soul' (Atman)* had dried up inside, making me quite nervous about it. Once I felt that *death was inevitable*, I woke up my wife who was sleeping in the adjacent room and, holding her hands, I told her to do certain things, about my inner desires, so that I could die peacefully. At that very moment, it felt as if I was being taken away by the *agent of death*, and that I should let go of my wife's hands to protect her from the wrath of the *agent of death*, or else the children would be left without parental support at such a tender age. Few moments later, I started having continuous terrible sensations inside my whole body. It felt as if I had normal warm blood flowing inside my whole body one moment, and cold water the next. This cycle repeated itself several times, all happening as if controlled by an on-off switching mechanism. I am not so sure whether it was similar to an *NDE (Near Death Experience)* - a term quite well known since mid nineteen seventies in scientific studies and medical research in the field of human brain and its dying process. Based on the overall experience I had during that day spread over a span of few hours, I can safely claim it to be an NDE. Because as per the *Greyson scale*, as described by Dr. Sam Parnia in his book, *'What happens when we die'*, my experience can be rated with a score of about eight or nine when according to Professor Bruce Greyson who actually devised this scale, the minimum score of seven was needed to classify any such experience as an NDE.

While trying consciously to stabilize the awkward internal feeling by fast pacing steps/jogging on the same spot inside my home in order

4

to get away from the scary feeling of my 'Soul' trying to escape from inside my body, a thought flashed suddenly from the right side of my brain which worked amazingly for me. This thought that cropped up out of nowhere was; 'Hey, I am still breathing and hence I am alive. The very fact that blood is flowing from my heart to different parts of the body, sensed through the hot-cold feeling of circulation of blood inside me, means that I am perhaps okay'.

This single thought was so powerful. I cannot say whether this thought of well-being was a conscious or a subconscious thought, but it happened. Most likely it was a subconscious thought and I had no conscious control on that thought. I now believe strongly that we are all instinctively endowed with such power of thought within our souls which are part of the subconscious brain.

How this thought got into my brain will remain a mystery, but this single thought made me take another quick rational decision – calling for an ambulance and go to Queen Elizabeth Hospital at Adelaide, in the middle of the night, to get immediate medical attention. Since we knew our neighbor, Ms. Joan Harris, an old lady of over fifty, had been visiting this hospital for her own treatment; perhaps the idea to call this hospital came automatically to my mind. My wife was watching all these developments with complete consternation, but she was wise enough to call our neighbour who she thought could provide some help, support and necessary advice at such a critical moment.

The moment Joan entered our drawing room, where all this drama was going on, without batting an eyelid, I threw both my hands around Joan and embraced her very tightly murmuring some words in her ear; 'Joan, you are Mother Mary and I am Jesus Christ.' While I was still embracing her, another strange feeling coursed through me. I felt that some sort of very mild electric current fluxes from the Universe around me were charging me when my body was in close contact with Joan's. I actually started feeling quite stable in just a couple of minutes of staying this way. It was as if my body, which just moments ago were feeling totally devoid of energy, was getting filled with energy through these fluxes of mild and pleasant current. Joan got a bit disturbed by seeing my condition and, with my wife's help, called for the ambulance immediately.

Once inside the ambulance, I tried to look and behave normal by talking with the nursing staff, and later to a doctor I saw in the emergency ward of the hospital. Just to prove to the resident doctor in the emergency ward that nothing serious or abnormal had actually happened to me, I started talking absolutely normally with him for a few minutes. At the same time, I had an uncanny feeling of extrasensory or supernatural power within me. This paranoid thought made me even express my willingness to extend some sort of help that the doctor might need to attend to another patient, for whom his services were being called for while I was talking with him. The doctor, quite expectedly, declined my help and went to attend to the other patient. When he came back to me, I behaved and interacted with him as if I was absolutely okay and, with his permission, came back home in a hired taxi.

By now, I know that mentally ill patients have an initial tendency to thwart any idea that they are actually not in control of their minds. Although my internal feelings during the night alerted me that something was seriously wrong and hence needed medical attention, but over a period of an hour or so, through my sensations running across my body while in close proximity with Joan and later through overtly normal conversations with the ambulance staff, I developed a false sense of mental stability. All this was behind the decision to call for the ambulance, go to the hospital, see the doctor and rush back home as if everything was okay.

Unfortunately, I did not contact my counseling psychiatrist Jo Lammersma about all these developments that had happened in quick succession over the preceding twenty four hours. On the other hand, I had ventured to take my morning dosage of antidepressant (doubled only two days back) without even giving thought to the fact that the entire problem could be due to adverse reactions to the medication.

Later that day, after just a few hours, the problem resurfaced with a vengeance. I started behaving totally paranoid with thoughts like the total destruction of mankind, the end of the world, saving humanity from disaster using the power of wisdom and so on running through my mind. I actually started feeling quite stable in just a couple of minutes of staying this way. Although I attended the research institute that day, wrote one or two emails to some friends and then came back home for lunch, I could not even go to school to bring back my daughter - a daily routine of mine until then. My wife had to leave me on the roadside, where I was looking at the Sun, pacing my steps to and fro, murmuring incoherently. I can clearly recall even now how I was looking at the bright Sun with unaided eyes and could see the Sun's disk spinning very fast in two directions - clockwise one moment and then anti-clockwise the next. During those moments, when I was staring at the fast-spinning Sun, an interpretation was also getting generated simultaneously at the back of my brain that perhaps the Sun was attracting the Earth towards it in such a way that the distance between the Sun and Earth was reducing! After picking up our daughter from school, my wife came back home and somehow forced me inside the house because I was wandering outside making weird gestures. In hindsight, it is heart wrenching to imagine the scene of an Indian housewife all alone in a foreign land, seeing her husband behaving completely paranoid, sitting on the roadside, often walking along the road looking at the Sun – and that while worrying about bringing back a little girl of six who was stranded at school after school hours!

In the last few hours preceding this incident, I knew very well that my conscious brain had completely malfunctioned. The capacity to think logically was completely gone. But my subconscious brain was working on overdrive. A few basic human survival instincts were still working. This was clear because my memory cells were all very active and recording everything that was happening inside me and around me. Once inside my house, I began doing another strange thing - I was looking at the wall clock, and the hands of the clock appeared to be moving in an anti-clockwise direction, very fast, as if *Time* was going backwards, to the *Origin*. I was definitely hallucinating, but somewhere in my brain, I felt as if I was being guided back to the origins of Earth and hence the Universe! I was saying repeatedly; 'Look at the Sun, look at the clock.'

I looked at the Sun (light as the source of the wisdom which would save the earth as always) and emphasized the essence of the number zero and how everything finally turned into zero through the word 'OM' which has the syllable 'O' in both its English and Sanskrit versions. The Zero represents in form, shape and size, everything that exists in this material world both at a minute level (atoms, molecules, sub-atomic particles) and also the gross things (planets like the Earth and stars like the Sun). All these are almost shaped like an 'O'.

I shall write about one interesting incident where the concept of zero hit the sanest of sane minds simply because of its deep philosophical significance. I recall one dinner party held sometime in 2010 to mark the superannuation of one of the highest ranking executives at the Board level of our company. The concerned Board member in his farewell address said; 'Life is ultimately a zero! You excel in your studies, get into a profession, excel there, move up the ladder and reach the highest position in the Company and then finally a time comes when you are asked to go. So life is finally a zero.' Imagine; such a highly intellectual person, superannuating from a full term on the Board of a multibillion dollar multinational company, saying such words in the public!

Seeing my behaviour, my wife called for help from the hospital and I was literally pushed and forcefully sent to The Queen Elizabeth Hospital at around 5.30 p.m. in an ambulance. Reaching the hospital, I had all sorts of strange experiences of 'time', 'clock', insecurity that I may be poisoned.

I can also vividly recall that, when I was requested by medical staff to take some medication, I spontaneously pulled myself close to the nearest wall and made a strange drama of putting my hands and legs back to the wall to look like Jesus crucified. I then allowed the nursing staff to put some tablets in my mouth by sticking my tongue out, thinking that I was being poisoned, similar to Crucifixion!

Seeing my behavior, I was asked questions inside the hospital on whether I was having any special powers. Asked several times by medical staff attending me there but declined to comment. At the same time, I was skeptical whether the medicines were being used as poison in a bid to take my life, remembering what happened to Jesus on the Cross! But then another thought flashed in the back of my mind. The only way to survive was to swallow the medicines offered by the hospital (perhaps the subconscious mind working perfectly at the time my conscious brain was worried about possibility of being poisoned!). There were few other thoughts that kept coming which included the importance of 'time', 'clock', 'zero', 'going backward and forward in time' and 'origin and destruction of mankind and earth unto Sun'. These thoughts were perhaps a sequel to the thoughts generated that same afternoon on the roadside while I was looking at the Sun and felt the spinning Sun was attracting the Earth towards it so as to swallow it altogether. There were some other thoughts related to human survival, like heat/energy and water being the two most important elements for survival on Earth rather than so many other things.....

In hindsight, I can safely say that deep down within ourselves, we have that divine spark which represents God, whether it is of a Christian or any other belief system. And, whilst under stress, this spark flies out from inside the body. Perhaps, this is experienced by each soul on Earth at that critical juncture when the soul is squeezed out of the body under extraordinary stress affecting both the conscious and sub-conscious parts of the brain. I grew up in an environment of the Hindu belief system, entrenched with its customs, rituals and traditions, but the feelings related to Jesus and the Crucifixion came from what society had taught me. These teachings can go so deep into our souls that, during extreme conditions, peculiar conscious thoughts like these can always crop up.

Immediately following hospitalization at the detention centre of The QEH, Adelaide, after some initial treatment at the emergency ward, I started feeling better and better. The feeling of heaviness was still there though. Antidepressants were stopped immediately because of the adverse reaction of my brain to them and instead, I was put on a mood stabiliser (Respirodon). The heaviness in my brain started to ease up slowly. The sight of patients much more ill than me in the hospital not only alleviated my pain considerably, but also gave me the inner strength to write my story so that someday people wouldn't lead themselves into such mental health conditions by their own follies. And even if it happens by chance, there is always the '*Hope*' for a better life, with a little bit of conscious effort. The seed of this book was born inside the precincts of The QEH, Adelaide, way back in second week of July 2000. I know it has been a long time, but the reason for making the story public has been deliberate and purposeful.

For about five days in July 2000, I lived the life of a mentally ill patient inside the mental health wing of the hospital. My wife visited me with a small, play school going kid and an infant on her lap every evening. One Good Samaritan, an Indian born surgeon (Dr. Bimal Bose, who had been in Australia for the last thirty years by then, and had become very close to my family during my stay there) provided daily help by going to my house and picking up my wife and two small children so that they could come see me at the hospital during visiting hours. When I could spend five days without any major problem in the hospital, when I could start thinking much more logically and started feeling like a normal human being in a true sense of the term, I tried to convince my consulting doctor at the hospital (coincidentally another young Indian born doctor working in the hospital!) that I was doing quite well and hence could take care of myself. Thus, I could finally persuade the hospital authorities to release me and send me home.

This one week changed my whole perspective of life. Total mental breakdown leading to hospitalization created a severe dent on my physical capacity also. This event was later followed by my struggle with *panic attacks,* which were very intense and frequent for the first one and half years and continued in a milder form for another three or four years, less frequently and much less intense. I was thirty-eight years old when my severe mental breakdown happened. Obviously it appeared to me that it was what many people refer to as a *midlife crisis*. From my own background knowledge and internet searches, I was quite convinced that I had been in a state wherein my brain chemicals had faced some serious imbalance and the body's natural mechanism to release the stress was manifesting through *panic attacks*. I also knew that this imbalance of brain chemicals had to be neutralized as soon as possible to get me back to normal health by whatever means. I knew subconsciously by then that the entire problem arising from my serious midlife crisis had its roots in my own thinking process, and that I had to undo the mistakes and untangle the knots that were clearly causing stress hormones so that I could liberate myself from the impending danger and start enjoying my life again.

The aftermath

The journey of rebuilding my life began in right earnest through monthly counseling sessions (cognitive therapy) with Dr. Jo Lammersma, my psychiatrist for as long as I was in Australia, while continuing just one capsule of Respirodon a day. Readjusting my priorities, changing my internal thought patterns, intense self-counseling and bringing in some deliberate relaxation mechanisms like watching movies on videos which I hired in bulk from friends, spending more quality time with family, visiting friends etc. in the first few months helped me slowly improve productivity in my PhD research work which had reached rock bottom. Connecting to my inner core of total faith in God, the Unknown, the Supreme Power, and total surrender to Him helped me heal very fast. My approach to life - which had gotten slightly derailed by my exuberant and ecstatic experiences during my first two years of "Oz Life" (especially after coming from the background of a developing country) on one side, and anxiety and stress subconsciously building up about the successful completion of my PhD on the other - was consciously remodeled by a carefully crafted routine and anchoring around my spiritual being.

A lover of sleep, I was a person who never had problems while going to sleep up until that period of severe mental breakdown. It so happened that after my release from hospital, for the first two days, I could not sleep at all. It seemed strange to me. How could my body sustain itself going without an iota of sleep for forty-eight hours? I was averse to take sleeping tablets (a personal inhibition), but after consultation with Jo and after getting assurances that it was not harmful to use them temporarily, I resorted to sleeping tablets and tried to bring my body clock back to its normal routine. I never had to use sleeping tablets after that except for one other time, for just another day, while I was still in Australia.

I used to go through the very bitter experience of frequent *panic attacks* during this period of one and half years. One evening, about three weeks after my release from the hospital, I had a *panic attack* so severe that I started feeling again that I was going to meet my end in few minutes. The feeling inside was so horrible that I always pray to God not to inflict anyone else with that feeling. But doctors would know as well as the patients who suffer from such *panic attacks* just how bitter and ugly the feeling is. I immediately contacted Jo over the telephone and she advised me to go to a quiet corner of the house, relax, and try to sleep taking a sleeping tablet.

Although initially it was very tough to follow even these simple instructions from my doctor over the telephone, the willingness to surrender my whole self at the altar of God, sometimes referred as the *collective consciousness* – and of which my doctor, Jo, was like an angel to me in those days – helped me compose myself a little and move to the quietest corner of my bedroom and try to relax there. This worked for me and reinforced my confidence and faith in the counseling regime and the mild medication I was going through.

During one of the several rounds of counseling sessions, I mustered enough courage to ask Jo about the *apocalyptic whispers* of the night before my hospitalization. It took her no time at all to tell me that not everything in this world can be explained by *chemical and electrical energy* alone. There is definitely a role of *spiritual energy* and that inexplicable indications helped, at some level, to heal me faster because intrinsically I was a strong believer in God and spiritual energy myself, right from my childhood. And her statements, coming from a doctor of a completely different background and culture, resonated with me very well.

On another occasion, I asked my doctor why I would have to go through so much pain and suffering when I knew I hadn't really committed any major crime or mistake in my life so far. Again her reply was quick in the coming: *'Sufferings are good for the Soul.'* I personally believe that this single sentence from my doctor, at this critical juncture, was the key to my continuous healing and growth. It allowed me to return to normal health by anchoring me on the fact that even these sufferings were ultimately going to benefit me! This was an outstanding innovative thought for my healing from the deadly crisis, particularly the horrible and painful *panic attacks*; to think that there is separateness between the physical body and the soul, and what appears to be sufferings to the body might even help the soul learn and grow further!

This resulted in a very dramatic and interesting turnaround in just seven months. One of the research articles based on part of my PhD work which was presented in an international conference at Ulverstone, Tasmania got the Best Student Paper Award in February 2001. Moreover, I could complete my PhD work well within the officially sanctioned time of four years, submit my thesis for examination and return happily with my family back to India in August 2001 to resume my normal official duty at my parent organization located at Dehradun.

The eternal questions and the quest for answers

So what are these apocalyptic whispers? Where did they originate? Why at all would a normal, healthy mind brimming with energy and enthusiasm just a few months before, fall into a self-created trap and spiral downwards into a morass where the only savior ultimately turns out to be that all-pervading God? How and when do we as normal human beings make the mistakes that lead us down this path? Is it totally pre-ordained? Or has there been an element of *free will* operating all through? What is the fine distinction one has to make between his or her free will and what is charted by the Maker? Do all of us at some point of time in our lives face a similar crisis? What controls the nature, timing and the intensity of such a crisis that befalls on us? Are there any common roots to such problems that could have common solutions - just the way we tackle fever with paracetamol, and infection with antibiotics, or hypothyroid with altroxin, anywhere in the world? Or could there be some common tools one can use as self-help tools to handle such midlife crisis?

Is it wrong to have desires? Is it wrong to have expectations from ourselves and from the world? Where should we draw the fine line between expectation and reality? Who brings us to this Earth and why? Do we actually decide our own fate and destiny? Who takes care of us, apart from our parents, during our journey of life? How do our emotions pan out and what is their origin? We all know that some of our desires get easily fulfilled both in terms of time and labour taken to realize them and some get fulfilled with much difficulty after tremendous efforts and consuming lots of time. Some of the desires fail to materialize but if we closely look at our own past history, we would notice a pattern. There is obviously a clue to such a phenomenon which many great authors and thinkers have noted in their work. Maharishi Patanjali's words about how the Universe conspires to ensure the fulfillment of a pure desire which takes root inside the mind and heart of a human being finds echo in the works of Stephen Covey, one of the greatest modern inspirational leaders. How does the Universe conspire to finally make one realize what is the purest form of desire? How are desires going to be fulfilled? And, in the process, how do individual souls learn about the divinity and interconnectedness that all beings have to experience on this beautiful Earth? Since one of the most important sources of stress experienced by people these days is caused by desires born out of ambition, it is important to understand what would be the purest form of desire that can be goaded by the forces of the Universe towards fulfillment - as is indicated by both Maharishi Patanjali from ancient history and by Stephen Covey from modern school of management.

It is when a person reaches the state of utter hopelessness and helplessness that his dwindling soul wavers between two extremes. The progress while moving towards such a state could be either deceptively slow or very dramatic and sudden. But if one can somehow manage to hold on to the belief that an all pervading God who was instrumental in bringing the soul into existence on this Earth as a human being will take care of him, thereby following the path of total surrender to Him; it definitely won't be very long before that person is slowly brought back to rails by the divine power from within and from without. I am living proof of this as thousands have been before me and whose wisdom is available to us in the form of vast literature on the subject.

Each one of us has a story to tell. But to complete that story, we need to have patience, perseverance, faith in ourselves and faith in Ishwar, God, Allah, the Almighty - the Collective Consciousness which has helped millions of souls come to this Earth before us and has made our life much easier, be it through their knowledge and wisdom or through their scientific discoveries and technological inventions.

The common thread running through the remaining chapters of this book is a single coin which gives *Hope* when tossed on one side and *Faith* when tossed on the other. And this common thread has brought humans from being forest wandering, cave dwelling *Homosapiens* to modern day *Global Citizens* in an increasingly interdependent and interconnected global village.

CHAPTER 2

TEENAGE DREAMS

It is natural to dream at a young age

Right from birth, till we reach our teens, we are physically and mentally dependent to a large extent on our parents or caregivers. While interacting with family and friends in the neighborhood, we start making distinctions about what is good and what is bad in the world around us. Similarly, and also through interactions with school friends and teachers, we develop a sense of the world we live in. Depending on our mutual interactions, we are flooded with thoughts on how to dream for a wonderful future for ourselves. In today's modern world with television, internet and smart phones in every household, the volume of information that is easily accessible is sometimes beyond imagination. From gross to very minute details of anything that one can aspire to see or have, everything is readily available. Naturally, our minds will be exposed to countless possibilities of careers and professions at a very young age. Added to that is the peer pressure, influences from family and social influences which stir up young minds and sometimes make us decide on careers and professions which are not in alignment with our inner core or internal grain.

At some point of time in my school days, I recall having dreams of becoming a very powerful administrator upon joining Indian Civil Services because we used to see the respect and awe with which the Collector and District Magistrate of the district used to command. I used to sometimes dream of pursuing a career in banking and commerce so that one day I could head the Central bank, the Reserve Bank of India (And my signature as the RBI governor would appear on each currency note in circulation!). Sometimes, I used to dream of being a very renowned space scientist exploring the frontiers of space. The news of India's space missions, with the launch of satellites into space in the late seventies and early eighties, used to excite us and naturally had an influence on our minds. The interesting thing though was that nuclear science and technology - which was also in its growing stages in India during the early seventies and eighties with nuclear tests and development of nuclear reactors for harnessing nuclear energy - could not catch my imagination as strongly as space science and technology did. The root cause for such dislike could lie in the very facts that I read in history books; about the deadly destruction brought by the atomic bombs dropped during World War II. Perhaps my natural inclination towards the peaceful use of science and technology overshadowed my interest in the likely use of the same for mass destruction.

Sometimes I dreamt of becoming a national level sportsman - a highly acclaimed cricket or badminton player, two of my most favourite sports in my early days. When one beats his opponent in local games, such dreams are bound to fly, even though the level at which state and national games are being played is far beyond our reach. To top it all, my mind used to wander sometimes to becoming a very powerful politician, either heading a State Government or even the National Government. Sometimes I used to think of becoming a very active and compassionate social worker serving masses of people while, at other times, I used to dream of being a great philosopher. These were some of the practical dreams that I used to harbor as a child.

Dr. Abdul Kalam has written in his book *'Wings of Fire'* how he originally wanted to be a fighter pilot and how, on his failure to achieve this, he approached one of the saintly spiritual masters, Swami Sivananda, at Haridwar who said to him with love; 'Do not get disheartened my boy, maybe you are destined for far bigger and greater things in life'. The words were so prophetic that the same prodigal son of India went on to become a missile scientist and headed several top level defense organisations in the country. He went on to win national honors like the *Padma Bhusan, Padma*

Bibhusan and finally *Bharat Ratna* - the highest civilian honor India can bestow upon someone. It is of great significance that the same pitiable failure at the job interview for fighter pilots moved on to become the President of India later in life. He had dreams of being a fighter pilot, but God fructified his dreams in a much grander manner.

Every child harbors great dreams in his mind. It is crucial how the family and the immediate society around the child respond to such dreams. The more positive the response, greater is the likelihood of those dreams being fulfilled at a later stage. The flip side is how much intent and faith a child can punch in his dreams. Whether he can pursue his dreams relentlessly in spite of the odds that may come his way will determine how far one can succeed in life.

Attributes of parents manifest themselves as expressions of God

Children see their parents as role models and this is true for each child. Parenting is therefore very important because children get their influence in a direct one-to-one exchange of interactive feelings, expressions and communications. Children, from a very early age, develop internal skills to adapt to situations and adopt the new parental guidelines inside an effective and functioning social unit. The best way to inherit, extract and internalize the positive attributes of both father and mother is through one's own logical analysis. Although capacity or efficiency varies from individual to individual, the natural procedure and social customs that one needs to fulfill while maintaining the new models of administration at home are evolving with the rapid advancement of modern technology and means of communication.

No parent can be a hundred percent perfect. However, strands of high ideals, principles and values can easily be discernible and available for a young mind to emulate. In today's world, delivery of wisdom by parents through actual habits and actions has a far greater impact than mere words of advice. This has been the truth from time immemorial. *Example is better than precept.* If there is some fine wisdom to pick up from parental action, even if it is not perfect, it still can get registered in the mind of a growing child. All of us can recollect little experiences from our own childhood. The vulnerability of children at a very young age forces them to take each parental action of protective nature as something similar to the grace of God. Although there will be elements and strands in their actions which could be very irritating or disturbing to the children, generally the parent-child blood relationship has an inbuilt power to forgive those aberrations.

Values of honesty and integrity

How parental influence can leave an indelible impression on a young mind can be understood from the little story here. My father, a renowned advocate in the town we lived in, one among the top three as it was popularly believed those days, once shouted at a client (who he knew personally as well) because he tried to bribe him by bringing a few large bags of rice (which cost fortune those days) to our door in his jeep (I remember the scene very vividly still). My Father yelled; 'Get out. How dare you come to my door trying to bribe me?'

This happened when the case of the defendant was on trial and my father was the advocate representing the government against the accused. This was a lesson that I would never forget and was the guiding light for me because I knew that my father, with a large family to support, did not have huge income, but he never sacrificed his ideals and values for a few bucks. What better opportunity to learn these values than from such a parent?

The other aspect of our father which I used to be amazed by was how he helped the poor people who came in large numbers to him with legal cases. Since they were poor, they could not afford even the minimum amount that was prevalent as the fees for an advocate. The basic minimum consultation fee in the first round used to be five rupees those days, and some other advocates in the town used to collect even ten rupees from clients. But our father never grumbled when he got only two or three rupees instead of his own fixed charge of five rupees. It was an eye opener for me because he knew that poor people did not have the capacity to pay and always considered it his duty to help even if they could not meet his minimum consultation fee. There are going to be many readers who will try to rationalize the facts and events, saying that my father was perhaps scared that if he did not accept the two or three rupees from these clients, they would have gone to some other advocate who was willing to work for them. 'He did not want to lose clients,' some may argue. I have a different view. I think he felt; *'If I do not take these clients, then they will approach crooks and get consultation not worthy even of whatever they can afford. These poor clients will be left open for exploitation'*. And this perhaps came from deep within his soul, though I never discussed the matter with him.

I can now visualize these matters in a more holistic fashion than I could have done in my immature young days.

Lessons on self-esteem and challenge

A rich trader once came to my father with a case from a far off town. He had a business running in our district and hence had cases in the local court where my father used to practice. I clearly remember how my father was quite old by then and never spent much time on studies or preparation for his cases. He relied more on his own knowledge and experience rather than on any deep studies those days. At the time, one fine morning, when this rich trader with a perfect white dhoti and kurta presented his case, my father went through it and found nearly fifty percent chance of winning from his own intuition. All this I can describe because I was very close to my father and with my own inquisitiveness, used to follow his daily activities closely. After going through the details of the case, my father proposed an unusual offer: he would not charge any fees if the case was lost and the client would pay my father one thousand rupees *if* he won. This deal offered by my father was quite unusual in two ways. Professionals like advocates and doctors do not normally charge fees according to whether the case was lost or won or, in the case of medical practitioners, whether the patient is relieved of his disease or not. They normally charge their fees upfront, immediately, after their consultation as a pure professional charge for their professional advice. The other reason why it was unusual was because of the so-called exorbitant fees my father asked for this one case. Those days, my father's total monthly income used to be just about two thousand rupees and he used to earn this money through dozens of cases every month. (I must add here that my father won the case and I think the rich client paid two thousand rupees instead of thousand rupees because he was very happy, and thrilled by my father's style of functioning – which was creating a challenge for himself and meeting the same!.)

Lessons on non-violence

My father never ever lost temper to beat us - me or my seven siblings. Although I recollect him using strong, unparliamentary words when his frustrations with our wrong doings reached demonic proportions, he never raised his hand. This habit of his has left an undeletable impression on me and my own research to life says that violence is unnatural and can be driven out of earth if we follow some great ideals of Mahatma Gandhi and Jesus. Even most of what we see in our own parents can be easily perceived as love and peace oriented - except when we provoke strong reactions from our parents with our mischievous acts. And such a peaceful approach to life can be taken as a benchmark for the later part of our lives.

Only once in my childhood, my father took a small stick and - being very angry - ran behind us one afternoon when my younger brother and I, his two youngest children, were fighting with each other for some petty reason. My father could not tolerate this and ran after us holding the stick, but we both escaped unhurt! Because of the age difference of more than four decades, and also because he was in a lungi, an informal attire not amenable for fast running, we could easily avoid being hit. And my father's anger subsided very quickly.

Gandhi had dedicated his entire life to the pursuit of Truth & Non-violence, even while being in the thick of a political career during the most tumultuous period of the modern history of the world. A period that witnessed two World Wars in which millions were killed, borders drawn and redrawn, millions displaced from homes, mayhem all around and cruelty of highest order. Pursuit of Truth, to him, meant practicing non-violence in the most fundamental core of our being. Gandhi wrote in *'My Experiments with Truth'*; 'There are some things which are known only to oneself and one's Maker. These are clearly incommunicable.' I have a subtle feeling that perhaps Gandhi's highest ideals emanated from the life of Jesus Christ - who walked on this earth just about a millennium before his own arrival on earth, and who sacrificed His life for mortal men. Although there was at the same time another very passionately religious person in the name of Nathuram Godse who harboured feelings of revenge and retribution against other religious fanaticism who eventually took the mortal life of Mahatma Gandhi claiming to stop Mahatma Gandhi's style of appeasement to the minority communities. But the high and noble ideals of peaceful coexistence, non-violence and Truth which were aggressively pursued and experimented by Mahatma Gandhi in his own way did create an impact on my mind more than the violent medium espoused by religious fanatics. I have always believed that two human beings, Lord Jesus and Mahatma Gandhi, within a span of a millennium, have experimented with self-sacrifice as the highest goal of life for upliftment of society from the veil of ignorance.

Long after these events of my childhood, one morning, when I was doing my morning Pujas (Prayers) before the domestic deities sometime in 2004 at Jorhat, Assam, my daughter (aged eleven) and my son(aged six) were fighting for some reason while playing on a bed nearby. I became furious and was about to beat them both and tell them to stop so that I could perform the Puja rituals peacefully. But something from within struck me as a whisper and I asked myself; 'What are all these Pujas for if I cannot control my anger and pass on the habit of violence?' (Beating children for their minor misdemeanors actually sows the seed of violence in their minds and hence perpetuates violence in society). Why could I not control myself for a few moments and rather concentrate on my Pujas? It was great sight for me! In just a few seconds, the two siblings started enjoying each other's company, cuddling each other, playing and having fun where, just a few moments ago, they were indulging themselves in some sort of aggressive behaviour, fighting over some small thing and my blood was boiling to discipline them!

This taught me two things. First, we as parents are responsible in inculcating these dangerous habits of violence in our children's minds unnecessarily, when we resort to such punishing tactics. And second, our own temper is so unstable that even while engaged in the holy activity of doing Puja, we tend to be inadvertently attached to our very basic animal instincts.

Lessons on unconditional love and respect for others

My father used to love everyone - his own children, his sisters and their families, all his cousins and their families, his own juniors and peer fellows in his legal profession and his subordinates. He loved them so deeply that it was fascinating to see. I learnt so much from this, the ability to love everyone on earth and, more importantly, to be compassionate towards all of them. He used to love the workers who helped with our domestic chores, and our agricultural cultivation activities, and other carpentry or gardening activities. It was amazing to see how he commanded deep love and respect from each one of them. I can't forget those beautiful days of love and peace pervading through our household.

Is it not worth emulating a father who had so much love and affection for everyone including the opponents in his profession? I remember him saying how he digested, with a pinch of salt, the unparliamentary words one of his professional opponents used against him in public even though he felt he could have easily retorted in the same vein.

This example of my father has helped me in controlling myself during a few occasions in my professional life too. On one occasion,

I could check my anger and frustrations at the bad and loose words thrown at me in public by some senior boss at my workplace. I did not retaliate on the spot, but made it a point to let him know later that I did not accept his bad words and did not approve of his ugly style of administration. I made it a point later on to convey my resentment, in no uncertain terms, and succeeded in extracting an apology from him. This was a greater victory for me than using loose words against my boss and humiliating him in public, which I could have done as well in retaliation to his misdemeanor. It was not a fear of professional loss, but the ability that was ingrained in me by my parents' exemplary behavior decades ago that came to my help.

Lessons on simple living

My father knew how to lead a very frugal life and this helped me learn to be content with very little. This not only gives us peace of mind, but also fulfills our own responsibility towards nature and the environment by means of proper conservation. Our constant demands on resources destroy the environment and if we all learn to live within our means and to not run after material prosperity alone, the world will start becoming a wonderful place to live.

Here, I would like to recall an interesting incident. In one of the public meetings organized at Hyderabad in 2004, I had a chance to question Sri Sri Ravi Shankar. Being constantly worried about the problems of deprivation, hunger and war at one end, and affluence, the constant race for more and more acquisition of material prosperity and wastage of natural resources at the other, I asked; 'Swamiji, at a famous public meeting in Australia, in 2001, where the felicitation ceremony after the completion of a human genome project was happening, the Director of the Project mentioned that the Earth had sufficient resources to sustain only about two billion people with the current standard of living of the USA. We know that the earth's population has already crossed six billion. We also see that in every corner of the globe, there is a constant longing to improve one's quality of life, which is based on material prosperity. With both the people and their respective governments engaged in such an endeavor, how can we sustain the pressure of more than six billion people trying incessantly to have the same quality of life that American citizens do until and unless we eliminate four billion people from Earth?'

Swamiji replied to this question thus; 'We have to understand that people's needs in different nations are different, depending on the climatic conditions they are in. And by imagining that the Earth, Sun and all the other planets have a life of their own, we can think of the future as having the ability to take care of itself.'

I knew that I was not very satisfied with the answer in one corner of my brain, but to that I had my own internal answer. Why can't we make our own little efforts to live within our limits, to try to put less pressure on the environment and the global ecosystem? Why can't we make collective efforts to reach a proper balance of distribution of global resources relatively more equitable between nations, and achieve a similarly equitable distribution of national resources between people of different strata and different states through a conscious approach so as to help humanity in general?

Dreams and desires of the teenage years have inherent divinity

Stephen Covey has suggested the concept of *'Begin with the end in mind'* which finds its root in the scriptures rather than in modern books. Generally, this process of thinking is likely to take concrete shape in adult minds only. However, we know that it is mostly the latent desires and dreams that originate in the teenage years that hold the potential for fructification, through consistent hard work, in our adult lives. Human civilisation urges its own survival and for the survival of the species just like how every tiny individual gets alert and looks for a means to survive when threatened by impending danger to his or her life. Therein unfolds a possibility where we fit in by doing things that help us individually and collectively.

As growing adults, we continue to receive impulses from our surroundings, generate our own responses to them and modify some of them through the process of an internal feedback mechanism and then try to act upon the established foundation of the core thoughts within us. For example, if at a point of time some particular impulse has set off a thought within us that we need to own a home or a car, then we start working towards achieving that. Whether we are in schools or colleges, the moment such a thought takes root, the subconscious mind records it and gets activated. While apparently being dormant, the subconscious brain has its own role over the conscious brain and keeps directing it from time to time through its representative in the world of ether - the inner voice or inner whispers. First we make up our mind to do well in studies and then either get a job or start a business and try to make money or save for the purpose of either building a house or buying a car as the case may be.

Similarly, if a thought comes to mind in terms of scoring the first position in the class, or taking the first position in some race, or scoring a century or take five wickets in the next cricket match, then what happens is we tend to get started by first recording this desire in our hearts and subconscious mind. And then, from time to time, we get helpful signals that propel us towards achieving our goal by making conscious efforts and finally attaining the desired result. Take the case of Sachin Tendulkar, the legendary and iconic Indian batsman, one of my contemporary heroes and youthful idols. He ultimately went on to score a century of centuries in Tests and ODIs, but at the beginning of his cricketing career, he had a dream of surpassing the record of thirty-four Test centuries set by another legendary Indian batsman, Sunil Gavaskar. For a teenager taking up professional tennis, obviously the record of seventeen Grand Slam titles currently held by the legendary Swiss tennis player, Roger Federer - one of my all-time heroes - will be a target that will always motivate him or her to perform.

During a victory speech after the women's singles tennis championship at Wimbledon, a certain Grand Slam winner said that while cycling to her school and the tennis court, she had this dream of holding aloft the Wimbledon trophy and how she had achieved her long cherished dream that day and felt ecstatic about it. Quadruple Formula One world champion Sebastian Vettel said in December 2014 that he was living his boyhood dream after completing his first weekend at Maranello, Italy as a Ferrari driver. He said; 'Looking back at when I was eleven or twelve, trying to look over the fence to catch a glimpse of Michael Schumacher on the track, well today I was on that track.'

At one place in a recently published book, *'Maa Mun Collector Heli'*, Rajesh Prabhakar Patil, while informing his mother immediately after achieving the ultimate success of becoming an Indian Administrative Services officer which he had dreamt during his childhood, mentioned clearly his inner feelings in the following words, "I was always addressing my mother as the mother of a Collector during my childhood and this childhood dream has finally been fulfilled. I was filled with utter joy and I later informed about it to my father also". Although the book describes the strenuous struggles, hardships, sufferings Mr.Patil went through during his entire childhood and teenage years leading to finally succeeding in one of the toughest competitions in India, the fact that his subconscious expressed the above words clearly point to the fact that childhood dream can hold immense potential. These are just few examples from the sporting and professional arena which speak volumes of how our teenage dreams can be pursued with single minded focus and finally achieved.

These sort of conscious desires keep coming to our mind and try to take root in our conscious brain first and then get passed into our subconscious brain through a delicate link which is hardly understood in totality even after very advanced brain research. It is during the teenage years that such things happen because, when we are kids, we are guided more by feelings and less by reasoning. Whatever appeals to our sensory organs, we try to either possess, or achieve, or want to experience in our own lives. This raw love or attraction to worldly things, or people, or even ideas all happen in our teenage years.

As time progresses, we either delete some of the latent desires, or reshape some of them depending on the amount of mobility in our lives. Finally, we tend to narrow down some of the latent desires and work towards achieving them. Sometimes, it may so happen that, in our own way, we tend to remember and record some of the events in our lives so well that a distinct pattern can be observed linking all those thoughts, desires, goals of life, words of advice, words of excitement at stepwise success and words of encouragement to empower ourselves for our continuous journey to ultimate success.

The practical approach to achieve the above paradigm is by just reminding ourselves of the oldest of the old sacred desires that one day took root in our mind. It may have been for a fraction of a second, for may be a few days, or a few weeks or months or even a few years. We might have discussed those ideas or pondered over them, deliberated on them with friends, relatives and well-wishers. By simply remembering, we can easily see that there has been a pattern in our approach to arriving at that goal we set for ourselves all those years ago.

An example from my own life: I recall my eldest brother's friend, who used to live in the US and work as a professor of computer science at The University of Texas, visiting our family during his holidays to India. He used to wear a triumphant look and pleasant personality in front us, bubbling with confidence. He had a sort of strength of character that gave me a kick from inside - why not try to go to America, study further and achieve what he has achieved, and of which my own parents even were so proud! I used to see my parents treating him to a fantastic meal with so much love and affection every time he visited India and his family at Keonjhar. That personal bias, based on the apparent external appearance of someone who I perceived to be such a high achiever, had been ingrained in me as a sort of inspiring goal that I decided I had to achieve one day in my own life. Whether a school going boy like me judged his charming and confident personality correctly or not, the memory of him still resides in my mind and it is as old as my early conscious thoughts which shaped my future professional career.

This latent desire got an opportunity to fructify nearly twenty-five years after the day that it first took shape within me during my teenage years. I could achieve the same desired result, albeit little differently, and fulfill my long cherished dream by going to Australia and completing my PhD before coming back with some honors. It was not a very mean achievement for a boy from my background. They say; *'Don't ever lose sight of the target.'* This is where the eternal success mantra comes in. The mantra of having infinite patience, of discipline, of forbearing, of wisdom, of love, of surrendering so that God can open His door of infinite power and energy to help us achieve the desired result. Maharishi Patanjali has experienced and propagated this on earth for us to savor, and to experience for ourselves the Truth that is latent in his discovery nearly five thousand years ago. The same has also been experienced by the eminent author Paulo Coelho and Stephen Covey in our contemporary times.

My parents are my best teachers

Some of us may be tempted to find fault outside of us and list dozens of reasons why we think our parents were deficient and how they ill-treated us and how it is because of their follies that we are currently leading wretched lives. Unless checked at an early stage, such thought processes can magnify into very dangerous proportion that it can start affecting the normal day to day life. Everything in the world will feel bitter and the nagging blaming tendencies which start from parents can spread to each sphere of activity and can ultimately lead to serious depression, psychosis and other mental health problems. Although while growing up or even at adult stage, we may be exaggerating some deficiencies that we see in either or both parents, but in hindsight, more often than not, we realize how foolish we were or how foolish we are. Mark Twain had said; 'When I was fourteen years old, I could not stand having my old father standing around me due to his ignorance, but when I was twenty-one years old, I was amazed to see how much my father had learnt over the last seven years.' This anecdote summarises what we are and what our parents represent. Our parents are our eternal connection to divinity, both at the root stage and also at a much later stage when we can embolden them as our doorway to heaven.

From an early age, I could see that every possible good thing to be found on this Earth was there in my parents, along with a very few minor shortcomings. These shortcomings were not appealing to me since, from childhood, I could sense what is good and what is bad for human lives. As powerful divine souls during childhood, perhaps each individual is endowed with these insights. A child is born pure, powerful, unadulterated and carries all the sanskars from previous births. The simple procedure that I was mentally applying was to convolve the resentment and grievances of one parent towards the activities of the other. The net result that came out was something that remains as one of life's eternal lessons to me. For example, I used to witness strong resentment and frustration in my mother whenever my father, who was past his prime at that time, was engaged in his habit of addictive gambling. On one hand, he was one of the top three lawyers in the town those days, the darling of the common man and a sports champion in his younger days. On the other hand, he was addicted to gambling and used to spend nights together playing cards with people belonging even to lower strata in terms of profession and occupation. This was strange to explain and also, when my mother shouted and felt totally aggrieved by my father's intransigence, I could convolve her feelings with my father's behaviour and easily come to the conclusion that gambling was just bad.

Although I was very young, I could still feel proud that my father passed with full hundred percent marks when I weighed all his other attributes - his love for his children and grandchildren, his love for his kith and kin, his professional excellence and his standing in the society, his outlook towards the world and society at large from his utterances and his anguish towards anything apparently bad in people, his democratic values, his outstanding sportsmanship, his great love and faith in God and above all his faith in himself. It was simply amazing. However, on one front he showed fallibility, as I could sense from my mother's frustrations. I then consciously and subconsciously decided that gambling in any form is just bad. At a later stage in my life though, I could sense I had a genetic propensity of my *being* in the form of a weakness for gambling, and I lost once in 1985-86, huge amounts of time over a period of six or seven months playing cards in a field camp with all sorts of people just the way my father used to do. I observed within myself an inherent craze for stock trading. But the lessons learnt during childhood help me, every day, to desist from my genetically codified urge to go overboard. I try to make conscious efforts to abstain from addictive gambling even when I see some of my close friends engaged in such acts during holidays.

On the positive side, the sight of my father's ability to sit down with all types of people and enjoy the nuances of life gave me the power of being uninhibited in so far as my dealings with anybody from any strata of the society is concerned. I was as friendly to an office cleaning professional in Australia as I was with the famous professors, doctors and lawyers there. And so it is in the case of my dealings in India as well. The saying *'No risk, no gain'* is generally exemplified by one's ability to experiment and gamble with life. The fact that my father extended this micro-scale attitude in him to his ability to take risks in so many different fronts of his life also had an impact on my mind. I have an inner sense of belief that to achieve anything in life, one needs to be prepared to take risks, and hence in some way gamble, if not in the literal sense. I believe that this knowledge can be attributed to my own childhood learning from my father.

There is another side to the above story. Since I was born very late, the seventh child out of a total of eight, I could see only very little of his talent for tennis at a nearby tennis court in Keonjhar. And I could never actually witness his hockey or football prowess in which he was a champion material too. How could a sports champion indulge in petty gambling at a later stage of his life? It was perhaps due to the fact that my father was bored - which can be expected of a sportsperson once he's past his prime. There are plenty of modern examples of international sports champions failing to adjust to changing lifestyles after the peak of their career. One example that comes to mind is that of one of my all-time heroes, Ian Thorpe, the great swimming champion from Australia who went into depression at one point of time in his life. These things happen unless we are armed with proper coping strategies to handle the strong emotions following our active and exuberant life.

The other aspect, I could judge by my father's reactions to any follies done by my mother. But these were very rare. My mother was a pious lady. Due to the number of children born from her, and perhaps due to many chronic diseases and malnutrition, she lost most of her capacity for doing hard domestic work. But she could manage things that were vital to any family. She could cook and she could take care of all the internal management through maidservants and helping hands. I could imagine that she had everything in her.

I tried to learn everything I could from these two personalities. I tried to bring myself up by teaching myself about every good quality they possessed, and I found that I was getting stronger and stronger every day - in my own capabilities with regards to studies, in my extracurricular activities, in my dealings with friends and also in my overall vision of life. If through his inner eyes and subtle feelings a child can see the abundance of everything good that life has to offer, just by observing his parents, the minor shortcomings of the parents could act as some sort of reminder for the growing child to abstain from these and lead an even better life than his own parents.

Many may argue that there are examples when children lose both parents or at least one parent during childhood, or even after birth. How then can they gain from the role model system that we are talking about here? A child, when born, is genetically predisposed to many great things of life including the very basic survival instinct. This survival instinct is in its purest form and the child tries to learn all that good he can see in his surrounding, irrespective of whether he has lost one or both of his parents, because *soul consciousness* is a fundamental attribute in each human being. The most powerful and creative phase during the growing up years is mainly guided by the *soul consciousness*, which gets slowly overpowered by *ego consciousness* as one gets older. There are thousands of stories about the great achievements of those who lost either or both their parents at a very young age. This attests to the fact that human beings, when born on Earth, have the intrinsic potential to attain great heights. And it becomes possible for the souls who emulate anything worthwhile that they observe in their immediate surroundings. The unfortunate thing is that we adults, whether as parents, or neighbourers, or relatives, spoil the environment in such a way that the child gets a hazy and fuzzy picture about the rudiments of life.

CHAPTER 3

SARMA – SIR MODEL

Selective(S) Attention (A), Retention(R), Modification (M), Absorption (A) – Satisfaction(S), Internalization (I) and Realisation (R) Model

If we look back at our lives, no matter what stage we are in now, we would notice that certain things are embedded in our minds quite clearly, and we can easily pluck these out of our memory banks at will. However, certain other things are not so well embedded. There are classifications and different levels for such memories. With some prompting and effort, we can retrieve certain memories even if we could not recollect them easily at first. And sometimes, certain events can be completely erased from our minds even.

The reason this happens is because scientifically there are tiers in our memory. There are short term, medium term and long term memories. Most long term memories have their roots in links with the heart or the emotional feelings associated with a particular event. Whether they are of a pleasant or positive experience or a hurtful, unpleasant, or negative experience, such memories would be deeply entrenched in our minds as long term memories. The human species has this automatic mechanism of recording such sensitive memories for its own survival and growth through an influence of the subconscious brain.

Most of the medium term memories can be easily traced to professional learning and the utilization of the same. These are basically mental or intellectual activities that can be memorized with bit of practice and utilized whenever the requirement arises to carry out day to day functioning in the workplace or otherwise.

And lastly there are the short term memories which are basically sensual memories and can help an individual charter his day-to-day life. However, these memories can be converted to medium term memories and even long term memories depending on how deeply we feel about them and how often we recall such memories in our daily lives. People who believe in *Karmic philosophy* will understand easily the cause and effect relationship of all our deeds whether reflected in the same birth or accumulated over one lifetime for re-enactment in future births. The inborn tendencies of any human being are generally decided based on the *Karmic Account Balance* the particular soul carries from previous births. During all our activities in the present lifespan, we create and use the said different categories of memory depending on the level of development of the mental faculty or intellect in collaboration with our memory power. This way, we prepare our own bank account of *Karmic lessons, Karmic values* or *Karmic exchanges.* The basis for such an observation is that different siblings born to the same parents quite often charter totally different paths in life in spite of the fact that, genetically, they are born from the same parents. Even sometimes the twins do manifest totally different traits.

How our sensory organs respond to events or activities in our daily lives is dependent on our genetic makeup, our upbringing and the immediate atmosphere that has surrounded us from the time of childhood and our conscious efforts to train our composite system consisting of body, mind, heart and soul. The *SARMA-SIR model* is the ideal model that encapsulates the entire picture of how our body, mind, heart and soul combine to generate themselves from nowhere – or, as some say, from Heavenly ether - and take the shape of a physical human body, lead a full life cycle packing up a barrage of memories along the way, leave the body and decide to descend again, either with a time-break or immediately afterwards, to complete another full life cycle here on earth. Although there are conflicting concepts within Hindu philosophy about the possibility of one form of life venturing into another form, I personally feel intuitively that it is perhaps only one way traffic. When we take the form of a human being once, we do not go back to another lower form of life during our repeated cycles of birth and death unless the concept of split souls is invoked. Although the scriptures talk about such a possibility, it is difficult to believe such a notion propagated by our ancient scriptures which were prepared at a time when human intellect was far less developed, science was in its infancy. However, the reverse process involving a lower form of life evolving into higher form of life including the highest i.e. human form may be true. It is still a far cry to prove from modern scientific methods about the veracity of such statements. But deductive logic points to such a phenomenon nonetheless. When I enjoy intrinsically the association and interaction of different forms of life, there is perhaps a possibility that the path from lower forms of life to progressively higher forms is possible, but the path is irreversible. This means that a human soul will be born again in another human body, although it may choose a different parents, place and culture to be born into. An evolving branch of neuro-psychiatry which takes cognizance of the ideas of after-life and reincarnation, utilizes these concepts in the healing methods which are popularly known as *Past Life Regression Therapy.*

We do receive signals from the environment continuously, but only some of the signals come to our notice and are captured by our senses depending on our own internal makeup. These signals can be trigger for physical, metaphysical and imaginary thoughts. Our minds are conditioned, based on several criteria as discussed, including genetics as well as Karmic debts or credits, to *selectively receive* only some of the signals from a total flux of such signals from around us - which actually stands for our acronym *Selective Attention (SA)*. These physical signals can be the input for any sensory organ. We see only what we want to see, hear only what we want to hear and so on. The most prominent of our sense organs are our eyes and ears although the others do play a role in our memory bank. Smell, taste and touch also behave in similar fashion, but discretion is less vigorous. The impact of different sense organs on our memory bank can vary greatly, but the extreme long term effect is generally associated with sense organs related to sight and sound. The next part is *Retention(R)*. Whatever is *retained* from what is selectively sensed by our sensory organs, again depends on our conditioning and is only a part of what is received in total.

There is an interesting twist to the next activity, the *Modification (M)* part, which happens both consciously and sub-consciously. What we receive and what we choose to retain is again not going to remain totally sanguine because of the dynamic world and dynamic nature of any living being, especially the living human soul. The constant flux that is driving the *Universal Soul* will have an impact that would lead to a change in whatever has been retained. This modification occurs due to certain influence of each subatomic particle in our own bodies. These impact each of the other subatomic particles in the Universe and vice versa. There can also be scope for *Modification* of what has been already stored.

The next step is the final one which remains within the inner core of the soul, i.e. *Absorption (A)*. There is no more change. This is what is finally absorbed into our psyche. This entire process is something which is valid for about the period of one generation before the influence of the next generation's new inputs start transforming the entire perspective, unless one feels very rigid and orthodox about his standpoint. Genetic makeup, upbringing, the influence of the regional or national or even international environment, and our conscious efforts to follow some ideals or principles, all combine to help formulate what we bring into our inner core through the above SARMA model.

In the next round, there is the overwhelming influence of a new generation in all aspects of our lives. We may start feeling that the things that have gone into our deep memory banks in one generation time are not helping us anymore. This is when we are challenged by our own offspring because they come with a quantum leap of generational change in every area of life. Science and Religion both get influenced by these generational paradigm shifts and teach us all, both individually and collectively, in a manner that is decipherable to an alert and conscious mind.

The next level is the interaction within one unit made up of body, mind, heart and soul. Whatever the stimulus-response-feedback cycle that our sensory organs provide to our psyche through SARMA model, now goes one notch higher. Retaining what is *Absorbed* gives us a kind of permanent *Satisfaction(S)* leading to either bliss or pain. If it is giving us Satisfaction, then it goes to the next step of *Internalization (I)* within our body-mind-heart-soul unit and then progresses to the highest level of *Realisation (R)*. This entire process is actually the path towards enlightenment. The part which our pure conscience plays for Eternity is the part which gets recorded in our ultimate *Karmic Account Balance* (KAB) - and this decides our soul's fate in the next birth. These residuals are sometimes referred to as *Sanskars* in Sanskrit terminology and get carried forward in cycles of birth and death. During the above process, the negative feelings do get recorded, but, as it appears, each soul on Earth longs for betterment in every lifespan through the learning and experiences gained. The power of the soul to convert all negative experiences as part of the feedback mechanism for its own growth lie intrinsically within each soul. The so called 'evil' which appears evil to its contemporaries in one lifespan will generally tend to improve upon its own experience during future births irrespective of who the reincarnated souls come to share the life journey on Earth with.

The tendency of human mind and heart combination is such that certain stimulus is aligned to our minds and hearts in such a way that we try to enjoy its sensual response. These again vary considerably for different individuals. The individual *Karmic Account Balance* decides which path the soul would charter. One single stimulus from environment can have multiple responses in different souls and that is the clue what and how each soul filters information from environment and then moves along its own chartered path to its ultimate destiny. The fortunate thing about human souls is that, at the most fundamental level, we tend to understand each other very easily. The only requirement for such an understanding is a perceptible time frame and a level of understanding between two individuals such that one can read the message of the other's heart and mind. People who have reached great heights, such as self-realized souls, can communicate with each other at a very personal level, but in a theoretical sense that personal level is actually a Universal level because no other human soul can participate in the conversation unless he elevates himself to the same level. Certain fundamental principles, fundamental laws of nature have faced centuries of denudation, but they have remained intact. The reason is simple. They are the truly fundamental attributes of every human being, howsoever ordinary he may be. To illustrate the concept by an example, writings of Mahatma Gandhi clearly suggest that from whichever angle he might have looked at happenings around him, be it British colonialism and associated exploitation, caste and class division in society with associated exploitative tendencies in his own people of the land, racial prejudices and subversion seen around the globe of his time, or even personal experiences including attraction of sensual pleasures, he never budged from his stand for freedom, truth, love, compassion and non-violence. It is safe to conclude that his soul was such a realized soul that the same very attributes in human beings have never been dislodged from their idealized positions since dawn of human civilisation.

Reflection of the Soul's image in oneself

Since all human beings have the same number of genes - although some may have some defects - one person can sense the feelings of another if he puts himself in that person's shoes. For example, when we read or hear about an outstanding person, and if we succeed in retaining any of his qualities at least in the form of 'quotations', without ever actually acting in the same way ourselves, it means that in some corner of our heart, mind and intellect, we can visualize our own ability to imitate the same qualities. It is because of our lack of discipline and readiness to work hard that we sometimes fail to translate such ability into reality. It is of course a fact that everyone is endowed with different capacities and qualities, but at a very fine and subtle level, we are definitely the same.

If we read about all the great people throughout history, we find they believed that everyone had the same capacity as themselves.

Mahatma Gandhi once said; 'I am an average person with less than average abilities and whatever I have achieved in life, I have no doubt in my mind that anyone else can also achieve that.'

Similarly, contemporary Yoga Guru Maharishi Swami Ramdev also thinks the same way. Having been born into an average farmer's household, he ascribes whatever he has achieved to the teachings of great people including his mother.

Our soul actually works as a magnetic mirror and anything it catches from another soul, it reflects in the inner mind of the soul and hence is visualised. And when this ability of the soul is properly utilized, it can produce the same results for us as the original person. Measure of success may vary, but that can be attributed to the mysteries of nature. By and large, one can really replicate, almost totally, what one sees in another's soul. Mahatma Gandhi has written in his autobiography how the stories of Sravana, the devoted son of blind parents, and those of King Harischandra influenced him so strongly that he thought of copying their attributes in his own life. We all know by now how Gandhi not only copied the attributes of these great souls, but perhaps went far beyond that, to reach extraordinary heights. But at the time, he intrinsically considered himself to be ordinary.

If I am appreciating or highlighting certain qualities of Mahatma Gandhi, Swami Vivekananda, Rabindra Nath Tagore, Leo Tolstoy, George Washington, Subhas Chandra Bose, Albert Einstein or Thomas Alva Edison – all of whom are from older generations, then it is a simple truth that part of its own reality exists within me. Just the way children carry genetic influence from parents which manifest quite visibly in physical features as well as behavioural traits, the fact that our parents and grandparents not only inherited their genes from their ancestors, that they acquired much learning themselves during each lifespan and obviously passed on their subtle influences through their genes to their progenies. Thus the inspiring influence one derives from leaders of the past and the present is generally possible because of the potential that each soul has, to be able to copy such attributes just the way Mahatma Gandhi could copy the attributes of Sravana and King Harischandra. Similarly, I might feel inspired by certain qualities of Sachin Tendulkar, Roger Federer, Amitabh Bacchan, Dr.A.P.J. Abdul Kalam, Steve Jobs, Bill Gates or Stephen Hawking, all of whom are from recent generations. This indicates the propensity of my soul to long for further growth by copying such high achievers' contributions to the society in different fields. I may not be able to achieve what any of these great leaders in their respective fields did in their lifetimes, but certainly there is a very good chance that I can achieve a good measure of what these global leaders have achieved - if not in terms of a measurable gross scale outside, at least in terms of an immeasurable finer scale within me in terms of mental resolve as well as intellectual hunger ingrained in my soul such that the tendency gets carried through to next birth. The more important thing is that, in the journey of the soul, as espoused by the *Bhagawat Gita* (Chapter 3, verses 21, 22), one can steadily pick up such power by owning up to the great inspirational attributes of leaders from previous generations.

Less than one hundred percent satisfaction

It is sometimes very apparent that, when we get into the details of someone's character, either by observing the person closely or by reading about him or his life, we aren't satisfied even if we greatly admire that person. For example, Mahatma Gandhi wrote in his autobiography that for him to be able to call anyone his real *Guru* or spiritual master was very difficult even though he has hinted about how some great souls came close to falling into that category for him. This indicates a very fundamental human urge to be satisfied one hundred percent but it does not happen because he or she is just a representative of *Infinity*. Many cultures talk of God in terms of *Infinity*, and this simply means that human beings are endowed with souls that are infinite in expanse. *Human beings are just infinite beings within finite bodies.* The great spiritual leader, mystic Jaggi Vasudev, explains how during several occasions he experienced such feelings of inseparableness from the Cosmic Universe, a form of *Yogic Samadhi.*

This attribute of a human being helps him to continuously strive to attain perfection, even after so many thousands of years of our civilization. We all know that when we fail at something, we try to blame it on circumstances or situations. This simply means that we are still prisoners of our own environment. The highest form of realization is to go beyond that, but it is not easy and needs years of dedicated searching with patience and conviction.

If we get into analyzing some contemporary leading character, or one from history, we would find that even though ninety-nine percent of their attributes satisfy our inner quest and satisfies our notion of ideal behaviour, there would still remain one percent, in terms of attributes of the same individual, that would not appeal to us and either we take it as human failing (the oft-repeated sentence; *nobody is perfect*) or start searching for a new soul that is a hundred percent perfect. This is simply a reflection of the fact that since humans are infinite beings and that infinity can never be satisfied by any finite permutation, combination or comparison however hard we try.

How the SARMA-SIR model actually works

Mahatma Gandhi has explained in his own works (*'My Experiments with Truth'*) how he was influenced by the writings of Leo Tolstoy (*'The Kingdom of God lies within you'*) who lived just about a generation before him. If we go through Tolstoy's work closely, at one point he has clearly mentioned that *it is futile to take oaths upon oneself.* Perhaps he was writing from his own experience of life. Mahatma Gandhi, who literally modeled his life after the great teachings of Tolstoy and the ideals of other greats like King Harishandra and Sravana, the mythical son of blind parents, once took an oath not to consume cow's milk. As part of his personal philosophy, he wanted to experiment on himself thinking that it was not correct from a moralistic point of view to consume cow's milk perhaps considering that it was meant for its own calves!. But once when Gandhi was very sick, the attending doctor advised him to drink cow's milk which was the only option at the time to help him get better. But Gandhi could not break his oath! Then, as an alternative, someone close to

Gandhi suggested goat's milk and the doctor reluctantly approved the suggestion - which Gandhi agreed to as well. He recovered soon after. Gandhi has however mentioned in his autobiography that his desire and inner urge to somehow survive was paramount during several such occasions.

There are two lessons here. Although Gandhi experimented very well with his own oath, and disproved Tolstoy here in a literal sense by sticking to his oath of not touching cow's milk, at another level he had to break his own oath (Tolstoy's findings and advice seem to have worked) because, logically, we should not differentiate between two domesticated animals i.e. a cow and a goat. Both are mammals and if Gandhi believed that cow's milk was not meant for consumption by humans but for its own calves, then the same logic holds for goats and definitely Gandhi would not have differentiated these two animals by the standard of his own ethics and ideology that he had set for himself. Since cow's milk was an established dietary habit culturally, Gandhi took such an oath to experiment on himself. Goat's milk has never been a normal dietary supplement and that was the reason why Gandhi never had to include goat in his ambit of experimentation. Perhaps God's invisible Hand was working all along to promote Gandhian as well as Tolstoy's philosophy in the world by coming to the rescue when it seemed humanly impossible!

On hindsight, it appears that Leo Tolstoy is perhaps right when he cautions us against *oath taking*. It is right because of the scientific reasoning that no two moments in the history of the Universe are identical and situations are changing constantly. The earth is spinning around its axis while at the same time moving around the Sun in its orbit; the earth's crust is mobile, the crustal plates are moving with respect to each other, earth and universe are perhaps both expanding and hence to imagine that two moments in history can be identical will be wrong. And hence, the oath taken by a small entity of the whole universe, (i.e. a *conscientious man*), no matter how powerful and godly his soul, is likely to fall flat at some point of time because of the very nature of dynamic life and interstellar space-time continuum. Many people might dispute this concept, but the fact of the matter is that absolute morality might not be easy to achieve though there is no harm in pursuing it.

As far as SARMA-SIR model is concerned, Mahatma Gandhi, while literally absorbing Tolstoy's teachings on non-violence, missed Tolstoy's cautioning with regards to oath-taking (Selective Attention caused Gandhi to miss this). But it caught my attention since we in India read a lot about Gandhi. Similarly, the entire episode of oath taking by Gandhi, forced to circumnavigate the crisis during sickness caused by his own oath and using goat milk instead of cow milk, is engraved in my memory (SARMA-SIR model working full circle here for me!).

Gandhi's conviction in Truth and non-violence as another face of God, which he probably imbibed from Tolstoy's work *"The Kingdom of God is within you"*, made him declare in a very confident manner that Truth and non-violence would stand the test of time, irrespective of what stage of development the world is in. We know historically that events started unfolding during Tolstoy's time that were contrary to his ideas - both in his country and around the world, culminating in the Bolshevik Revolution and the First World War - but the essence of what he wrote struck a chord with Gandhi, who was born and brought up in a totally different environment. Gandhi held on to Tolstoy's beliefs while experimenting with non-violence, but once again, global events unfurled leading to the Second World War in the later years of his life. If we analyse these events objectively, the SARMA-SIR model just reinforces the belief that the path towards Truth or God cannot be anything other than non-violence. The permanent learning of the human soul about the efficacy of non-violence is thus along the same path that was first shown to us by Jesus Christ, decoded a millennium later by Tolstoy and practiced by Gandhi only a generation later - in this very stage of the world, to attain immortality.

At a very basic level, each of us will recollect some of our oldest memories, even from early childhood. There are generally three major situations that trigger our memory cells in such a fashion that the record what is happening gets engraved in our memory for almost a lifetime. First is the extraordinary negativity that affects us - they can be visual scenes, sounds of words, some tragic emotional events or some accidents which impact us in a deeply negative way. For example, a very hurting sentence from someone will be recorded so deeply that unless we try very hard, it will keep popping up. Similarly, on the other extreme, extraordinary positivity gets recorded as well. This can come from great success, from highly inspirational interactions or simply some great humanitarian help that we receive or give somewhere. The third situation is when something very different from our mundane and routine activity hits us. By this I mean some unusual scenes, unusual sights, unusual interactions, unusual nature driven catastrophe etc. These will always be recorded deeply in our memories. The SARMA-SIR model catches these situations and creates specific wiring or neural pathways inside our brains to be retrieved later at regular intervals, further reinforcing them and hence become a part of our indestructible and imperishable eternal soul.

Glimpses of a miracle or a mere coincidence

Towards the end of my PhD work in Australia, I was going through severe depression and was under medical supervision by a psychiatrist for about 15 months during my later part of the stay. I was struggling almost every day, even with professional support and the support of my beloved wife and two very young children. I was not able to sit down and carry on with the writing part of the PhD thesis even after many attempts. I tried all sorts of visualizing and self-counseling mechanisms to inspire myself to go through the tribulations of putting together all my work into a presentable thesis.

One morning, during this period of trials and tribulations, I remember how my little son, hardly one and a half years old at that time, suddenly caught hold of my finger and started slowly pulling and guiding me towards the master bedroom where our TV was kept. It was morning time, and my son was by then pretty conversant with the technique of switching on the TV. I followed my son with a bit of curiosity. Nearing the TV, he suddenly switched on the TV and the visuals of an ongoing horse race broadcast at that particular time in the channel appeared on the TV screen. I saw the name of the horse being drawn by the jockey: *"Live In Hope"*. I vividly remember that moment, and I did not share it with anyone then. Not even with my wife. I thought that it was perhaps some kind of divine discovery for me, and that I should be guarded about it lest it be construed as insane or hallucinatory by ordinary mortals!

On later analysis, I could see that something extraordinary was happening here. The Cosmic Intelligence, the Collective Consciousness or God, was sending me a message through my son. Small children are generally full of divine instinct and hence God chose the medium available and was basically using him to point me in the path, to tell me to continue to *'Live in hope'*. I was depressed during those days about whether I would be able to submit my thesis on time. It appeared to be a Herculean task. Such small inspiring thoughts, generated by whatever means, however, can bring immense power when we are in deep trenches of self-doubt and helplessness. Each sentence of this book is written with complete hope turned faith, and both interchanging seamlessly. I must add here that there is no inclination to distinguish my son's action as something prophetic, as something distinct from what any other child of any other parents can do. I am more than sure that God provides clues for every soul on Earth to experience such miracles - if not in exactly the same fashion, then definitely in some other form. The discernible manner in which it happens for different individuals is yet to be scientifically established. The beauty and warmth when one consciously thinks about such incidents, they appear mysterious and unbelievable but the inspiring sensations one gets from such stories need not always be necessarily attempted to reject or be suspicious about. Such anecdotes carry immense power within subconscious mind.

Lord Krishna (One of Lord Vishnu's incarnations as per Hindu belief) manifested Himself totally on two different occasions: once during his childhood to Yashoda Maya (His mother) and once to His warrior friend Arjun at Kurukshetra, the battlefield of the Mahabharata.

People familiar with Indian mythology and culture know how God revealed His Universal Self to Yashoda Maya through the inside of His own mouth! Similarly, Arjun was shown the Universal Form when he demanded it from his charioteer friend Krishna, during the discourse on the battlefield. It is generally referred to as the *Biswarup Darshan*, God's revelation of His Universal Form (*Bhagawat Gita*, shlokas 11.9 to 11.31). Some authors (reference - internet searches) try to interpret this image of Lord Krishna as something similar to what modern physics describes as the phenomenon during creation of the Universe through the concepts of Black Holes and Big Bang.

If anyone looks back at his or her life, similar stories of personal encounters with such miraculous experiences can be easily traced. Skeptics will term the miraculous event that I went through that day with my son as a mere coincidence or chance, but is it not bewildering to see the magnitude of at least the probability for a one and half year old to stage manage such an event? Is it, therefore, some unexplained occurrence that we normally ascribe to be God's or divine influence?

Painful sight giving a burst of positive energy

Two interesting incidents are etched in my memory, and strengthen the idea mentioned above. During the same period, while I was struggling with my anxiety driven depression on a daily basis, I was trying to point out mistakes every now and then in my beloved wife! Failing to control my own emotions, I tried putting all the blame on her, as if her absence from me in Australia for those six or seven months she'd gone back to India for the birth of our son was the root cause of all evils! One day, I even suggested that my doctor counsel my wife so that I could have a free run at home. I naïvely believed that all my problems would then vanish!

On the day of that appointment, I recall how I had described my problems to the doctor, putting all the blame on her. During the conversation with the doctor inside her chamber, unwittingly I had a cursory glance at my wife who was sitting with our small boy – only about a year old - in her lap. She was totally out of sync with what was going on! The fact that I was dragging her into my distorted world of depression was clearly casting a serious and painful frown on her face. She looked extremely innocent, but indignant. Her frown suddenly caught my attention and got me concerned! "Hey, what am I doing, dragging her to the doctor for no fault of hers and making her face this humiliation!", I thought to myself. This single thought dramatically changed my perspective about the whole problem. I understood that I had to own my problem and take full responsibility for that. It was 'I' who had created the problems all by myself, and I was going to have to solve it alone. I decided then and there that come what may, it would be solely by my efforts that I would come out of this vicious circle and reestablish myself in society without humiliating any one of my family and friends.

On another occasion, during one of my monthly counseling sessions, my doctor enquired about the rate of progress in the writing work for my PhD. She had tried to enthuse and inspire me through cognitive therapy sessions every month and was perhaps expecting that her efforts as a doctor were bearing fruit. However I told her, point blank, that it was not going at all well and that I was almost at the same place I was about a month back. This brazen declaration by me created a perceptible disappointment in her which my subconscious brain-guided inner eye could easily sense. The interesting thought which got generated in my mind at that very moment was to wholeheartedly put all my efforts to bring out the best of me, work intensely and aggressively and bring out some result so that, during my next visit, I could tell her about the progress I had achieved. This would please my doctor, which was the least I do for her in return for the extraordinary care she was taking of me, through the cognitive therapy sessions which had been ongoing for several months by now, and all with absolute sincerity and thorough professionalism. Another coincidence was that Jo suggested that I see her after a gap of about eight weeks now instead of four weeks saying that she had a busy schedule. Perhaps it was God's invisible Hand again!

My senior research colleagues at NCPGG (all of whom had got their PhD degrees already), prescribed about a year of writing at least to fully synthesize all the research work carried out during the previous two or three years. I knew I had only eight weeks to show some tangible results that would please my doctor. And so I sat down over the next couple of days and wrote a detailed plan in my notebook. It was my *'to do'* list and in it I gave myself specific time durations, in days, both chapter-wise and even sub-chapter-wise. I was very determined and carried my business of writing the thesis from then on in an almost clinical fashion. The good thing was that a few research papers out of my PhD work had already been presented at some international conferences held in Australia. I made a valiant effort, collated all the work, joined the dotted lines here and there and came out with the final draft - which was later appreciated first by my supervisor, Professor Nicholas Miller Lemon, and then by two overseas examiners from highly reputed universities of the UK.

And thus the spark or the inner urge that was created at the Doctor's clinic that day helped me muster enough divine power, strength and energy in the eight weeks that followed to put together my entire thesis and submit it even two or three days ahead of my internally defined schedule! The sense of achievement to my mind was thrilling and incredible. During my next visit, when I triumphantly declared the news to my doctor, I could see the elation and ecstatic joy in her face! It was pure bliss both for me and my doctor. The memory has been ingrained in me as product of SARMA-SIR Model without doubt.

CHAPTER 4

POSITIVE, NEGATIVE &
NEUTRAL EMOTIONS

Fundamental attributes of self

Each of us is born with almost all the human attributes possible during birth, in varying degrees, according to our past Karma. How else can we explain the very many different qualities of different siblings born from the same parents although the DNA of both parents remains the same for all the siblings? Although parents act as a medium for each soul to come to Earth according to the theory of reincarnation and rebirth, to claim that children born from us are owned by us is wrong. As the great spiritual leader and mystic Jaggi Vasudev often says; 'Do not be mistaken. Your children are not from you but through you.' It is easy to conceive such a concept if the passion and emotional attachment that comes with the parent-child relationship is viewed with objective detachment. Parents are important anchors for each one of us. The connection between past, present and future that is ingrained in the theory of Karma tells us that all attributes will manifest in every human in the beginning, but also that there will always be a part that will be different from ordinary human attributes and that is purely divine material. The entire development of a person sustains only one critical ingredient and that is this divinity. Everything we do today is going to ultimately be weighed against and measured in terms of its human content and the divine content.

Human beings are endowed with all kinds of attributes; greed, fear, anxiety, frustration, jealousy, hatred, anger, aggression, violence and destruction on the negative end of emotions, and contentment, courage, calmness, satisfaction, empathy, love, peace, affection, competitiveness and inquisitiveness on the positive side. The instrument or tool which we are endowed with to realize the driving ambitions arising out of the above human attributes is our intelligence or intellect, and its direct interaction with our mind or brain. The other tools given to us are our ability to sense the underlying divine attributes, the positive attributes. Although they are apparently connected to human intellect, they come from far deeper level i.e. the *consciousness* or *super consciousness*.

The great balancing act we do to achieve the fine balance between the negative ordinary human emotions and the positive divine emotions is delicately linked with our destiny, and the connection between our past Karma and our destiny which takes us to ultimate divinity. Our past Karma brings us to the present day world, and this life's Karma helps us proceed further towards the ultimate goal of *salvation*. The beauty lies in our ability to understand the inherent human nature that tries to leave the path of negativity in preference for the path of positivity, sometimes incrementally in steps and sometimes by quantum jump during one cycle of birth and death alone. The understanding and realization helps us to either delay or hasten the process for our soul to get trapped in this worldly cycle of birth and death or get liberated from this bondage to ultimate divinity. Our thoughts, actions, habits and attitudes all originate from this intricate relationship and our intellect provides us with a realization through which we satisfy the needs of ego and our divine quest for salvation.

The profound statement *'From the philosophy of survival of the fittest to a philosophy of survival of everyone'* is actually the hallmark of this current civilization. But unfortunately, the speed with which this realization, in ordinary humans and in the collective consciousness, would help transcend obstacles is difficult to imagine. Perhaps, in each generation, there have been definitely realized souls who showed the path to the larger community allowing humanity to sustain and grow so well, and into the present day. The ancient scriptures from various faiths all point in this direction and provide a good check and balance to our collective souls. There is no reason to fear about human species' ultimate survival. The only thing we can do is perhaps to speed up the process for ultimate realization of our soul's journey and hence attain salvation, or liberation from this bondage of cycle of birth and death.

The speed itself is the only variable here since all the rest have always been there and will remain forever. Speed is related to time. We all know now the details of the Earth's creation, and its connection to the universe; we can visualize the origin of the human species and its ultimate path. The ultimate path is liberation from bondage and it can't be violated. However, the speed of the journey is in our hands and we can definitely hasten things up for ourselves. This quest is nothing but the realization of the simple truth, which will lead to ultimate happiness and bliss.

Imbalances in life's inbuilt system and the problems thereof

Happiness is a state of mind and is closely linked with different parts of the total human system including the body, mind, heart and soul. We, as humans, always need our most basic needs fulfilled before we can go on to look for satisfaction of our higher needs. Abraham Maslow's hierarchy of needs and the progressive journey of any man, as an individual or a group or a society or a nation, fall into the same category and follow the same path. The needs may be defined in slightly different ways.

In case of individual human beings, the most basic need is food – even ahead of shelter and clothing. It is followed by other needs which are sought to be fulfilled in successive steps. Fulfillment of basic sexual needs finds different expressions from a very young age. This expression in an adult is seen when one first seeks to satisfy his sexual urge and then, in the next stage, when he longs for procreation. The need to leave one's imprint on earth by producing another human being (procreation) is paramount when we reach the adult stage. This longing is of course preceded by a need for social recognition as per the Maslow's hierarchy of needs. Now all this is so delicately and intricately woven into the human system that unless we carefully study ourselves, we will miss the target and beat around the bush to find ultimate satisfaction in worldly things.

Once the body's requirements are fulfilled, one then follows the needs of mind. The key here is the total synergy maintained amongst the various arms of the human system. If proper balance is not maintained by a continuous feedback mechanism amongst the various arms of the system, be it the body, the mind, the heart or the soul, then the imbalance will throw the system out of gear and disease will set in. The normal growth would be disturbed.

When we grow in a healthy environment, we develop healthy needs and healthy systems. The immediate physical needs will be quickly fulfilled and then the other higher needs will long for their fulfillment. When I was growing in the safe, secure environment of a happy family, I developed certain desires in line with my inbuilt character. I always felt that a sound body and mind is the primary requirement. The body's requirements are finite whereas the mind's requirements are almost infinite. Unless we carefully analyse ourselves time and again, we will not be able to visualize the situation comprehensively.

Ambivalence can lead to real problems

I went to do a PhD which was a need that I had long felt within me. I wanted to achieve some higher educational qualification from an internationally reputed University in a developed country, and that was fructified when I got the admission and fellowship. This was definitely in line with my need for greater recognition - a social need after I'd fulfilled all my other basic needs. It was right for that moment because I'd relegated my lower order needs to the backstage and brought my higher order needs to front. There was a hidden agenda too. I said to myself, if possible, I would like to stay back in Australia, if I was given due recognition and opportunities to work there and if I found the atmosphere congenial for me to work.

Few things I saw during first few weeks of my arrival in Australia triggered intense mental churning. I was not very happy to see the condition of the aboriginals in Australia and also the treatment of Indian immigrants, and other Asian and European immigrants (apart from the British and Americans) at the hands of so called European settlers. This triggered the question in my mind as to why we as human beings behave exactly in a similar manner in every corner of the world and how we land up in similar problems everywhere. We in India, historically, through the centuries of being one of the oldest civilizations and a continually evolving one, have been witnessing all kinds of problems that emanate from a lack of fulfillment of human needs. Caste, religion, race, state boundaries and language all seem to have created artificial divisions in Indian society to such an extent that, as a child, I had felt the agonies and pain caused by this division in public places where the impact of them was actually felt. After few months in the exquisitely beautiful city of Adelaide, I started to believe that things were exactly the same even in a very developed nation like Australia. However, there are some finer points that lie within the core of human souls that are still glowing and shining everywhere in the globe. And I found traces of them right through the four years I spent in Australia.

The mistake I made was to divert so much of my attention towards understanding general human problems that I earmarked less and less time for my PhD - and so my internal feedback system started creating stress on me. I gave highest preference to my spiritual needs without fulfilling the requirements of my other needs at this time. For completing a PhD within three or four years, I needed to concentrate more on my studies, but I allowed myself to drift towards finding solutions to other social problems even though they all emanated from my spiritual need, the highest need.

I ended up in trouble. The subconscious feedback mechanism did not succeed in preventing me from the ominous danger that was coming. However, when confronted with the crisis, I relied mostly on the same feedback mechanism to get me back on track. Here, I took all the help that I needed from both extraneous sources as well as internal sources. It was a great struggle I went through before I fully succeeded in overcoming my problem. And the whole exercise would demonstrate how one might inadvertently land in a problem, and how one can come out of the crisis if he can find his inner voice, listen to it, follow the highest spiritual alignment and act according to what it dictates to him at that time. And if such a situation occurs in anyone's life, we will be able to find clear reasons for it and also solve the problem by resorting to the connection of our soul with the other dimensions of our systems i.e. the physical, mental and emotional.

Fear of death or fear of loss of prestige

Fear of death or fear of loss of prestige and social status are the two basic and fundamental reasons for all our miseries and unhappiness or lack of balance in our lives. And they could be caused by numerous factors. Lack of good health causes fear of death, lack of proper security leads to fear of death, lack of trust on others particularly doctors or lack of proper resources can cause fear of death and so on.

I will recall an incident which was shown in Indian national TV footage. There was a terrorist attack on the Indian Parliament. On the thirteenth of December, 2001, five terrorists infiltrated the Parliament House in a car bearing Home Ministry and Parliament labels. While both the Rajya Sabha and Lok Sabha had been adjourned forty minutes prior to the incident, many members of parliament (MPs) and government officials were believed to have still been in the building at the time of the attack. More than a hundred people, including major politicians, were inside the parliament building at the time. The gunmen used a fake identity sticker on the car they drove and thus breached the security around the parliament complex. The terrorists carried AK47 rifles, grenade launchers and pistols.

The TV footage showed an intense gun fight between security personnel and the terrorists. What I vividly recollect from the TV footage is the sight of a couple of the terrorists running for their lives when there were literally no way they could escape the barrage of fire from the security around the Parliament complex. The human instinct in its primordial form manifested when confronted with sure death. These terrorists were running for their own lives! And these same terrorists had come there to terrorise and cause destruction and mayhem! This goes to show that in spite of all the training and experience, even a terrorist is first a human being - whose inbuilt survival instinct will always make him try saving himself when almost certain death confronts him.

I will describe another very personal incident. Just about sixteen hours before my mother's death on the sixteenth of August 2002, I witnessed the human survival instinct in its combative action. I had taken leave from the office at Assam where I was posted then. I got telephone calls from my two elder sisters who knew that our mother's health condition was very bad (She had not been keeping well for the past one year or so and was almost completely bed ridden when I had seen about four months ago, just prior to my transfer to Jorhat, Assam from Dehradun in Uttarakhand). I was advised by both my sisters to try and go see her if I could. And so I decided to take at least two weeks leave from my office in Assam to be with my mother. My daughter's mid-year exams were underway, but the Principal of her school was kind to grant her leave as well.

On the night before her death, my mother had been complaining about serious pain in her abdomen and stomach area. At day break, we three brothers who were near her at the time decided that urgent medical attention had to be arranged. I personally called upon one of my relatives, who was a doctor by profession, by phone and described my mother's symptoms. He suggested that it could be the start of multiple organ failure. I had a hunch that what he was saying might be true because, being in the same town, he was quite aware of my mother's health condition. My mother was eighty-one years old at that time, and had pulled herself well for about fourteen years after my father's demise in March 1988. But for some reason, my relative doctor (who was actually an ENT specialist) suggested that we should ask a famous medicine specialist in the town, whom we all knew, to come and have a look. He came along with one of his assistants and after having a close look, decided to administer an injection on my mother. I was not very familiar with critical care medication at that time, but he explained that my mother's condition had actually worsened. She was also severely dehydrated and the only way to improve her condition was by administering this injection. My elder sister-in-law and I then tried to convince our mother to allow the doctor to administer the injection. She was not very sure, and when we both tried to help the doctor and his assistant administer the injection by holding her hand, she murmured loudly while forcefully trying to take her hand away; 'Leave me, or else I will die.' It was a tough moment for me and my sister-in-law. Neither I nor my sister-in-law could do anything except listen to the doctor's advice. We thought the medication was more important than her fearful cry, because that was the only way we could ensure she got better, if at all. Our forceful administration of the medication immediately caused the area to become swollen and we got panicky. She survived less than sixteen hours after that fateful administration of the injection. Was her survival instinct cum intuition telling us that the injection could prove to be fatal, which we missed? Maybe, but in our desire to see her get better, we gave in to the doctor's advice and even used a bit of force when the injection was being administered.

There is another type of fear which emanates from projected worry about loss of prestige. This is another great source of fear. As humans, our body consciousness or ego always tries to establish its supremacy over others, if not in a vocal manner then certainly in a subtle manner. Ever since we, as social animals, adopted our social image to be one of the most important parts of our being, the attachment to this image causes fear in us if we are threatened with any loss or damage to it. This has been one of the major causes for suicides, if the physiological health of the victim otherwise was normal. There can be still another kind of fear, an unknown fear, which is basically nonexistent, but is caused by our apprehensions of a dreaded future. Fear *(False Evidence Appearing Real)* is actually the cause of all human sufferings and we fall into the vicious cycle of fear and anxiety if we are not vigilant enough and do not analyse everything with a true perspective.

The three components of human intellect

One of the oldest spiritual texts of Hindu belief, the B*hagawat Gita* illustrates clearly three divisions of every aspect of human life: the highest, the middle or average and the lowest. The *Sattwic, the Rajashik and the Tamashik.* Human beings are endowed with these three qualities in every aspect of life and the degree one possesses such qualities depends on the Karma he or she carries from the previous birth and the tendencies he thus manifests in the present birth to proceed towards the next birth. Agility and alertness, desire for doing good and divine work and pure and benevolent desires emanate from one's *Sattwic* attitude and are the highest qualities. *Sattwic* people are peace-loving, loveful beings who are clean in mind and heart and full of wisdom. These qualities are aimed more towards intellectual satisfaction than bodily pleasures. Their food habits are also different (vegetarian with juicy fruits, sweets and fresh food). *Rajashik* qualities stem from worldly desires, attachment, hunger for power and dominance and greed. Such people are engaged in the pursuit of gratification of physical pleasures. The *Tamashik* qualities are exemplified by ignorance, laziness, dirty tricks, lies, treachery, thinking ill of others etc. *Tamashik* people love to eat meat; sour, salty and spicy food, and even foods which are not fresh. The *Bhagawat Gita* says that all the sense organs of humans are actually meant to derive *Sattwic* pleasure, but it is our ignorance which comes in the way. It is possible for any human being to raise his or her awareness and slowly raise up the ladder of virtuous qualities, from the lowest *Tamashik* form to the highest *Sattwic* form in everything he or she does. Instead of being stuck up in the basest qualities, one can easily ascend the order if he is determined to adopt the highest form of divine life by transcending the different levels. The *Bhagawat Gita* has enumerated in extreme minute details, the full dimensions of these three components of human intellect, *Sattwic, Rajashik* and *Tamashik*, how they are reflected in individual's character and how one behaves under the influence of such tendencies with which one is born and how one can transcend these qualities through his thoughts and actions (Shlokas 2.45, 7.12-7.14, 9.13, 9.25, 14.5-14.22, 17.1-17.22, 18.7-18.39).

The fact that human qualities classified in these three divisions have been given maximum coverage across the above six chapters out of a total of eighteen chapters in this great scripture speaks about its vital importance. One needs to understand that irrespective of the fact that one is born with certain tendencies, by the help of sheer will power and devotion to God, one can really transcend in every dimension of life from the basest *Tamashik* qualities towards higher qualities, i.e., *Rajashik* and *Sattwic* qualities.

We will slowly realize, as we proceed in life, that perhaps hardly anything is controlled by us in this vast world. This is reflected in the yearning of Mahatma Gandhi to subjugate and suppress his own *ego* to such a level that it was lesser in weight than a small particle of dust. What this means is that our internal *ego* makes us believe that we are doing this, and that this is happening in the world because of this act of mine and that act of mine. When Gandhi aimed higher, towards the liberation and salvation termed as '*Moksha*', which is nothing but communion with God, the all-pervasive Consciousness, he knew very well that the '*Karta Feeling*' is illusory. Except in a very miniscule way, we cannot control any major aspects of our lives or change the course of life on this earth. This simple fact has given rise to the vast science of *astrology*. Although there has always been conflicting argument between the proponents of the *free will* of human beings and this overpowering influence of stars and their positions during our birth and in life charts, the *Karmic Life Principle* speaks of the inherent influence of free will as separate from stellar influences. They say, 'Shallow men say it is luck, but great men believe in a cause and effect principle.' Of course, the state of our happiness is in our hands because happiness is a state of mind and perhaps each and every mind is endowed with the capacity to remain happy right from the moment of birth. The ultimate realization of such a state of happiness would come from the understanding that, in our birth, we played no role. It was God's desire - which is inbuilt in each human soul, the *Conscience*, and when this is understood properly, one can remain in a state of eternal happiness. We ordinary human souls fail to achieve this state for various reasons; the most important one being our belief that we can actually control the happenings in this world.

Scientists and technologists create ideas, make discoveries and inventions not because they feel they can change the world but because they feel they can fulfill their inner urge to serve humanity in their own way. Even some scientists argue that Einstein, who was instrumental in manufacture of the atomic bomb, might have been influenced at a very personal level by the then-current global geopolitical atmosphere and was motivated to stop the human sufferings caused by atrocities wrought by Nazi Germany. This understanding, that they can ultimately serve God by serving humanity, lead scientists to work hard and move towards achieving scientific or technological marvels.

Superstitions and their effect

There are instances in India where I have seen how our belief systems can go to such extents that we can be misled to believe what is scientifically not feasible or possible to imagine. For example, few weeks after my marriage, I was told that, close to my in-laws' neighbourhood in Bhubaneswar, Odisha, there was a weekly evening programme when the Goddess would enter the body of a pious/ devoted daughter of a particular Odisha Government employee and that she would be able to bless the devotees who thronged the place seeking solutions to their personal problems. I had also heard about another such case in Ranchi, Jharkhand, where one of my elder sister-in-law's relatives, a young woman, had experienced similar episodes and contributed to the belief that persisted in those days. These incidents are about three decades old now.

I was invited by my wife and mother-in-law to go and see, with my own eyes, how these things happened in the modern world. I did not believe much in these things, but out of scientific curiosity I went along with them to the place where the Goddess was to come down to earth and enter the body of this girl! I held my breath and the said girl's father, a working state government employee invited or invoked the Goddess, amidst the chanting of hymns and the sounds of bells and conchs etc. But the girl whose body the Goddess was supposed to enter into was sitting unfazed and nothing happened even after two rounds of psychic invitations. Then a bizarre thing happened suddenly. A man in the prime of his youth was sitting in a corner and we found him suddenly developing signs of hysteria which attracted all our attention. This man was one of the expectant visitors that day. The girl's father who was trying his best to invoke or invite the Goddess down to earth could perhaps sense (in his make believe world) that Goddess was not happy that evening and hence chose not to enter the body of the girl, his own daughter, but tried entering the body of the man sitting nearby instead. But what it appeared like to me was a purely psychological problem at the time; one caused by the atmosphere of total belief of all the people there including my own wife and her mother.

The only skeptic and non-believer was perhaps me. It later transpired that the gentlemen who was conducting the ritual as a weekly practice so far, either due to his own wisdom, or by virtue of past experience and knowledge, declared to the anxious group; "The Goddess was not happy because there was one non-believer in our midst and hence she did not think it proper to get down to earth and enter the body of her daughter as she does usually!". I could feel that all the people there were of the same wavelength, and that there was a weak chord running amongst all of us, perhaps including me, to believe in the supernatural power which was what got reflected in this fashion. Such belief systems can appear to be rampant in many rural and smaller towns even in this modern world of digital age. Another example is nicely described by an author of a very popular book *'Maa, Mun Collector Heli'* (Mom, I became the Collector) Rajesh Prabhakar Patil. Coming from a rural agricultural background from remote part of Maharastra, Patil struggled with abject poverty and backwardness of his family and surrounding and made it to the highest public service position in the country, i.e., Indian Administrative Service, a very prestigious and coveted job in India. He has written in his autobiography how in his village, a very similar system of God and Goddesses entering the body of villagers existed and how he himself was witness to week long celebrations during which God was supposed to enter the body of a villager. The custom in the village was to take sick people to such Godly influenced beings for advice and relief from serious diseases. In one such incident, when one of his own relative succumbed to the disease even after consulting such a Goddess, that his blind faith on such matters was removed from his mind. This suggests that such things can play truant with lives of ordinary people anywhere in the world. Odisha and Maharastra are two states, one in the extreme east and the other in the west! There would be hundred such examples in all over the country.

There are other stories based on beliefs about how people can do damage to others, out of jealousy, and destroy other's prosperity through some *Tantric* practices. This belief is prevalent in many parts of India. Such beliefs go deep into the subconscious part of the brain. The conscious part of the brain is the one which tries to decipher meaning from the environment and sometimes events of coincidence so as to feed and strengthen such entrenched beliefs. It needs some skeptics and their scientific outlook to look at things more objectively and logically to challenge and remove such superstitious belief systems existing in the cultural milieu. In terms of social cost, people's superstitious belief in Godly men and their power can sometimes be exploited by the same revered so-called pseudo spiritual Gurus. Modern stories of spiritual leaders from almost every community involve child sexual abuse, murder, corruption, deceit, money laundering, tax evasion, illegitimate sexual offences and other such crimes. These happen in almost every part of the world and suggest that putting blind faith in any spiritual leader can have very dangerous repercussion when the superstitious beliefs of millions of minds are exploited and cheated.

Here, how strongly we develop our belief also is a factor. For example, when I was going through my own severe psychological crisis of depression, anxiety and panic attacks in Australia, I kept my scientific mind wide open although I was also keen to observe all that happened during those months with regards to the superstitious beliefs built up in me during my mind from childhood. It also transpired in my mind that I was perhaps being subjected to such ill effects because of other people and even things like a ghost entering my body etc. I experimented intensely on my own body and observed my own mental health closely during the lunar system, during the full moon and new moon. I must add here that, except for some very minor changes in my behavioral pattern, all of which are easily explainable by science, none of these things had any effect on my mental health during those days. People have done extensive research on the effects of such things on lunatics (perhaps the word "lunatic" is derived from the phenomenon in which the moon has an effect on psychological patients). I closely watched my own behavior, my thought processes and how it went up and down during those times. I could sense that, although there *was* a very mild effect caused by such large scale variations in the gravitational pull of moon on the frail mind that was under the siege of mental illness, and which is also scientifically explainable, it was never so powerful as to thwart my inner core and hence could be easily guarded against with proper cognitive therapy and medical intervention.

There is easy escape route for the human mind which is to blame others for the things happening in our lives as far as psychological problems are concerned. To avoid being ridiculed, we try to blame others' jealousy and their wrong doing on us. I don't believe it is true. It is to the extent that we harm others that harm comes back to us in a cause & effect relationship. If we do good to others, it will come back to us also. Nothing more, nothing less.

The greatest teacher is our own self-awareness and conscience. When our ego is blown up and we are blind to its ill effects, all these problems start happening. We need to realize that our ego can be as damaging to us as it can be helpful. It can be helpful only to an extent; for survival perhaps and nothing more. Ego can overpower our total system of mind-body connection and lead us to disaster, if it is allowed unbridled supremacy.

There is however another interesting side to superstitious beliefs. Most sportspersons and even politicians, who often manipulate human emotions to their advantage by rhetoric or false promises, are generally found to be superstitious. Some businessmen are also very superstitious. But this side of superstition has some positivity attached to it. Sachin Tendulkar, the legendary cricketer, would not allow certain things in his cricketing arena if it violated his beliefs. He has candidly mentioned several stories in his autobiography about the influence of his superstitious mind. During one innings in which he scored an unbeaten double century in Australia, he had been going to the same restaurant, sat at the same table and ordered exactly same dishes consecutively for four days to invoke good luck gracing him! As long as we are happy to be within our resources, and to maintain our beliefs without causing public disorder, there is no reason why we should not be allowed the luxury of holding such beliefs. Because at a subconscious level, one derives divine strength and energy from such a belief or faith.

The interesting thing about human nature is that both positive and negative attributes behave in an almost similar fashion, if they are left to it, and particularly in the absence of any proactive indulgence or proactive engagement.

Fear of failure is a negative attribute, and normally it is unfounded. When we make mistakes that lead us to apparent failures in life, there is the likelihood that the whole experience will generate some neural networks inside our brains, connecting specific neurons, and will be recorded as a memory. During any future attempt towards achieving something, unless we are careful, the negative emotions that are attached with the memory of the apparent past failure will get triggered and pose a challenge to us. The brain always tries to find small reasons to strengthen that superstitious belief system, and a sign of weakness is its giving too many reasons. Here, the courage to take risks comes into play. If the goal is driven by pure desire and pure intention, then there is no reason why one should fail to achieve it, irrespective of obstacles on the way.

Maharishi Patanjali said; '*Whenever any great desire with pure intention takes birth in someone's mind, the entire Universe conspires such that help and support arrives from all directions & all dimensions to help fructify such pure desires.*' Divine power and divine grace come into play whenever such pure intentions create any desire for fulfillment. Successful results become certain. This fundamental law of life is so true in the annals of Cosmic Intelligence that two persons of completely different backgrounds from Patanjali, Stephen Covey and Jack Canfield, two of the most famous modern day inspirational leaders have experienced the true meaning of this statement by the pioneer of Patanjali Yoga Sutras.

"Karta Feeling" and its relevance

It is our "Karta feeling" which is the root of all problems. Who are we? We did not have any role in our birth? Why shall we have no control over death and how then we are responsible when things go wrong in the first place?

We are born into this Earth after a series of evolutionary stages, so far as our physical body is concerned, because we inherit the genes of our family including immediate parents to great grandparents or even more ancestral lineage. In this way we get our physical body and our mind; what we get is guided to a large extent by what we supposedly inherit. We as individuals never had any role per se to play in the affair of making ourselves. And yet, though we tend to differ when it comes to the close details, we will agree that how we spend the time between our birth and death, how we make most of it, depends on us to a large extent. It is a strange conundrum.

The Spirit is not something in which we have a say. It is that all pervading entity which some call God, some call collective consciousness, some call it infinity and some call Allah, Jesus, Iswar and so on. We are all living beings and just one part of a Big Whole. How the Spirit takes birth, and when and where it does so, are mysteries and will remain mysteries forever, as is propounded by the *Bhagawat Gita*. Recent research into *Past Life Regression Therapy*

(Hypnotic Therapy) have started unfolding these mysteries to some measure, and how the human beings are born repeatedly into this world, suggesting that we are all immortal. This essence has been known to mankind for quite some time now. This part, which is a fraction of the Holy Spirit that we inherit apart from our physical bodies (which we get through family lineage as mentioned above) is actually the main driver of everything. To think that we are doing everything all by ourselves can be a root cause of mental health problems.

Obstacles and their solution

Obstacles of all kinds come up when the time is not in our favour. But it is not to deter us from our life's goal or objective, but rather to reorient us and strengthen our inner resolve and character so as to mould us for the greater ordeals lying ahead. One needs to set broad goals in life (thinking backwards, from the end) and also be prepared to keep accommodating and adjusting to the small setbacks that come up on the way. The success lies in visualizing and adjusting the thought processes of one's own brain to what is likely to be the thought processes of God. Generally, there would be very subtle indications and revelations about the Greater God's (the Collective Consciousness') designs. These are the signs which should be accepted as the Holy Grail.

Questions will arise in our minds when our expectations are not met exactly the way we wanted them to be, but one needs to realize that everything has either a decent end or the sort of end we wanted most. There could be obstacles which are very small - physically, mentally and spiritually - and it will be easy to overcome them or avoid them or circumvent them or even smash them. Just like kicking a football on the way. But there could also be bigger obstacles which need little bit of bending and pushing as part of the maneuvering. Then there could be still bigger obstacles and these may require real strength or help from friends, and family - if not in physical terms, then in terms of moral support. This will help in many fronts; in building permanent relationship with those well-wishers and also by way of making it easier to overcome the problems and obstacles on the way with others' support.

Sometimes, obstacles along our way appear so overpowering that we tend to succumb to the pressure. We fail to get an inkling of what could be the greater design of God when such obstacles come on our way because everyone in this world loves to see life as a smooth journey. But this has never been the case. *Success is ninety-nine percent perspiration and one percent inspiration.* To achieve any of our goals, a simple 3-4-5 principle based on a few important attributes are essential. They are the three P's, four C's and five D's. Passion, Patience &, Perseverance (the three P's); Commitment, Concentration, Confidence and Courage (four C's); and Determination, Diligence, Dedication, Deftness and Devotion (five D's). All these attributes are available to each and every individual in varying degrees. Whenever a pure desire takes root in our hearts and minds to work towards a goal and achieve something, it is through these attributes that we can easily overcome any obstacle that might come in our way and achieve the desired result.

Failures are actually the pillars of success

Kalpana Dash from Kumbhar Sahi of Dhenkanal, became the first Odia to climb Mount Everest. Kalpana made her first attempt to climb the world's highest mountain in 2004, but had to turn back at an altitude of seven thousand meters due to health constraints. Her second attempt in 2006 also ended in failure due to hostile weather conditions. But on her third attempt, Kalpana left Dhenkanal with a strong determination to succeed. And she finally made it on the twenty-first of May 2008 by scaling the eight thousand eight hundred and forty-eight metre high Mount Everest and making Odisha proud. While departing from Odisha, her last words to the reporters were; 'I am taking along with me the blessings of Lord Sri Jagannath and wishes of all my brothers and sisters in Odisha. I will definitely succeed this time.' And she did. *'The glory is not in being successful, but in being able to rise up from failures and move on.'*

'Failures are failures only when we do not learn anything from them. Otherwise, failures are actually the source, inspiration, gateway and food stock to success.'

Mistakes are not committed at all levels in one go

We create an imaginary problem by thinking that we made this mistake, made that mistake and so on. Yes, everyone makes mistakes and perhaps we are punished for them by circumstances, family, friends, relatives, government, and society and so on. But everyone makes mistakes. So what? The feeling that "we" make mistakes is wrong. It is just a fraction of our whole being and never our "Full Being" which makes mistakes. We have our bodies, our senses, our mind, our intellect and then finally our Spiritual Consciousness - in that order. And saying 'we make mistakes at all levels in one go' every time we make a mistake is just wrong.

Because, those actions executed at the time when we are fully awake, aware and conscious, are guided by particular intention or desire from within. Actions do not happen just like that. Although there could be a long personal history behind a particular action, it cannot be denied that even the hardest criminal moves with a defined intention to carry out his action resulting from the thoughts in his mind. At the time of such actions, intentions are known only to us, but our actions may or may not find acceptance with outside world. Our actions may appear as mistakes by someone else's standard.

Nathuram Godse writes in his autobiography *'Why I assassinated Gandhi'*, "If devotion to one's country amounts to a sin, I admit I have committed that sin. If it is meritorious, I humbly claim the merit thereof. My confidence about the moral side of my action has not been shaken even by the criticism levelled against it on all sides, I have no doubt that honest writers of history will weigh my act and find the true value thereof someday in future". This goes on to prove how composed and confident a well learned person like Godse can remain to be, even after taking law into his own hand while assassinating a person of such stature and influence as Mahatma

Gandhi. Researchers may argue in many different ways about the fallibility or infallibility of such statements of a well-educated man being viewed as a killer in the eyes of law of the land. The entrenched belief systems that we carry as *sanskars* in our souls from several previous births can motivate us to take some extreme actions as it happened in case of Godse because of his strong religious feelings. The growing religious hardening of stance of Muslim leadership apparently not stopped by Gandhi perhaps created an adverse reaction in Godse's mind which he could not filter objectively before taking law into his own hand. Sometimes, larger events in society can act as silent provocation for individual anger and hatred and unless, one is very clear about the root of such thought processes, one is likely to commit mistakes. Godse has indicated in his presentation during his trial, how he fell flat against his own mentor and guide Veer Savarkar whose constitutional and democratic means did not appeal to Godse anymore because by that time, his mind had taken a militant path itself. But from the letters exchanged between him and son of Mahatma Gandhi, it is crystal clear that Nathuram Godse was a very sensible and sentimental person. He was extremely poised and knew what he had done and why he had done. He was a very well read person, knew at least the literal meaning of the scriptures quite well and in spite of the ghastly act he had committed, he remained humble till his end which is clear from his words, 'Let the disciples of Gandhi satisfy me that I have acted wrong; I shall declare my repentance without asking for any reward for it and go to the gallows'. This amply proves that human beings carry the divinity at one level even moment before their execution in spite of any ghastly act that might have been committed by them.

If we do something that appears to be a mistake to some, then we are chastised for it. There are many prisoners languishing for several years in jails across different parts of the world, but a few remain strong within because of their pure intentions in the first place. Particularly in the case of political prisoners. This clarity helps them remain calm and give them strength and power to fight for freedom from prisons. A parent beating a child in order to force discipline can be considered outright brutal even in the eyes of the law of some countries. But at a very subtle level, when I discuss such issues with some of my close friends who faced such strict disciplinarian parents during their childhood, they neither show any grudge against their parents nor do they feel guilty about themselves following a similar path of repeating such acts with their own children!

Mistakes can be the result of wanting to satisfy lower level desires like bodily/sensual needs. But that does not corrupt our entire Being in the beginning itself. As we commit mistakes at the lowermost level and get away with it, without doing an equal amount of good/ noble deeds to compensate for our wrong doings, the accumulated mistakes then move on to corrupt the next higher level, and this trend, unless checked, will cause harm in the end. Our entire Being is said to be involved in the mistake when our *intentions* are corrupted. This does not happen easily. Hence, if somebody is accused of making a mistake, and that too in the initial level, then there is plenty of scope for amends and this is where our upbringing, cultural background, knowledge, experience, understanding, family support etc. come into play. We can certainly overcome mistakes with concerted efforts. There is an important saying that goes; *'Saints too have a past and Sinners too have a future.'* This is the reason why we see prisons or jails are beginning to be called correctional homes in different parts of the world.

This world is neither perfect nor ideal from a human perspective and hence one needs to be vigilant when he is likely to face problems. He may need to patiently work towards a cleansing act so that he can overcome the ill effects of past mistakes. Sometimes, mistakes can be ascribed to our surroundings, circumstances etc. A terribly corrupt environment is likely to entice a fresh and pure person to fall into the trap of making such mistakes. Sometimes, when such mistakes are revealed or come to light, we may quickly slide into depression and anxiety which, if not tackled, can cause permanent damage. If this had been a perfectly clean environment, then most of individuals would not act in this manner. This applies to any kind of wrong doing; economic offence, political offence, criminal offence, technical offence, social offence or any such offence. The environment plays a big role. The best way to come out of such problems is to have faith in God, the all-powerful, all-pervading God, and by surrendering one's ego at His altar.

Negative vs. Positive thoughts

It is a fact that we have been bombarded by this age-old concept of the impact of positive thoughts in our life as against that of negative thoughts. We have been told time and again the benefits of maintaining a line of positive thinking, but somehow we tend to fall prey to the habit of negative thinking. There must be some means to explain this behaviour.

There are very fundamental aspects that are ingrained in our genes. One is related to *survival instinct* - from survival in its most basic form to a form where we talk of corporate survival, market survival or even a nation's survival. These ideas are all linked at different levels to the basic human instinct of survival. Next is the instinct which is related to the *aging process*, but this process has some indirect links related to the nature of human beings to leave a legacy - be it in its primordial form of leaving behind an offspring, or by way of leaving behind an idea, or gained knowledge, or understanding of natural processes, or some kind of scientific invention to help humanity etc. This very approach to the human thought process (Stephen Covey's four L's: Live, Love, Learn, Leave a Legacy) is very similar to Abraham Maslow's model of human behaviour with its five stages leading from the very basic instincts of food, shelter and clothing to the highest form of self-actualisation or even self-transcendence. In both models, there is a tendency of positive growth towards achieving a state wherein unraveling the missing link between action and purpose, the thread of human conscience, resides. The greatest power that lies in the conscience is its ability to ensure its own survival and growth having seen many cycles of life and death and many generations and even evolutionary jumps from one species to another, starting from the very basic unicellular animals to the highest forms of animals in the animal kingdom including humans.

We would sense the beauty of the impact of positive thoughts on our lives if we are open, stress free and relaxed, and watch the inner thought processes which have been studied by saints, rishis and great thinkers of the past as well as many leading authors in the modern era. We tend to derive some sort of sadistic pleasure when we criticize others behind their backs or even directly because, by belittling them, we try to elevate ourselves. There is a kind of sadistic pleasure that one gets by doing such things openly in a very public manner. This process of self-aggrandisement, of trying to create a feeling of self-satisfaction by establishing one's superiority over others, is core to human nature. However, if we watch closely, the hormones we secrete from such a negative approach to emotional behavior, by criticizing or chiding or trying to prove our superior thought process or power to others, would be detrimental and lead to deterioration of health both internally and hence externally. The traditional processes in education, health, culture or social systems have all been very solidly based on the internal purification mechanism and that leads to enrichment of the soul rather than only of the body or mind. These systems are central to our scriptural texts. The very idea that it is the soul which is going to survive much longer than the body or mind has given rise to such a thought process in our ancient wisdom. Leaders of our spiritual heritage, including today's Jagat Guru Kripaluji Maharaj, Swami Jaggi Vasudev, Swami Ramdev Baba and Sri Sri Ravi Shankar and many others, are preaching these facts of life to humanity.

Western education has been built upon producing outward results rather than inner transformation for the simple reason that our five sense organs comprehend things much more easily and understandably for the ordinary human. Only very rich souls, however, can understand the processes of nature more intrinsically through inner transformation and wisdom. The erosion of the ancient Indian form of education was caused by this apparent failing of man. But, even with the delay, the western form of medicine is catching up with the earlier achievements made by our ancient Indian wisdom through scientific processes, documentation, research and experimentation in ways that any ordinary man can understand.

A word of assurance, a word of encouragement, a word of appreciation or a word of inspiration can energise our internal system much more strongly and effectively than any alluring or temptation to achieve something. Many people like to link the habit of continuous positive thinking to super human ability, but perhaps we fail to understand that each one of us actually have a powerhouse within ourselves which is nothing short of superhuman ability. Two of the greatest human beings of the twentieth century, Albert Einstein and Mahatma Gandhi, have both remarked about this. They always believed that they were average people - an intrinsic feeling of any human soul - and sincerely believed that whatever they achieved in their lives could be achieved by any other ordinary soul. We need no further proof than these two great human beings of the twentieth century.

Our minds are prone to storing both negative and positive examples about situations, people and places. The balance between the two decides how well we tread in life. For example, some of us are more prone to quote negative examples whenever a situation arises, suggesting thereby that we are being influenced more by negative thoughts - which normally drain us of our energy. And so are more scared and concerned than we should be in terms of simple safety and security for our daily lives. Apart from acting as warning signs, negative thoughts like fear, hatred and anger towards people or places affect our personality also.

On the other hand, positive thoughts can trigger excellent hormones which have a cascading effect on human psyche and can easily elevate the mind and thought process to a higher level. This can lead to improved productivity. It is possible to watch, feel and sense such a process within ourselves if we surrender ourselves completely and find unison with God, our Creator. It is neither easy nor quick, but it is possible for every person on earth to live such an experience. This is the beauty of human Conscience. One positive thought can set off a chain reaction which gives rise to greater productivity than the many negative thoughts that arise from trying to belittle someone else directly or indirectly.

Bizarre thoughts Vs. Yogic action

On two different occasions, a thought crossed my mind which may not find resonance with anybody so easily. But it crossed my mind nonetheless. During the midlife crisis whilst in Australia, I was going through my mental health problem and dealing with it on a daily basis. It was the later part of 2000 or early part of 2001. One day in the morning, as a part of the routine, I was brushing my teeth and washing my face in front of the mirror in the bathroom. Normally, our minds behave in such a fashion that we keep thinking, planning, imagining, calculating inside our brain consciously while subconsciously we might be doing something else. In this case, I was brushing my teeth but perhaps thinking about some other things simultaneously. A strange thing happened all of a sudden. Just when I was finishing the routine by washing my face off for the last time around while looking at the mirror, a sudden chilling thought mixed with strange horror feeling crossed my mind. What I was seeing in the mirror! Two bright eyes of a snake (paradoxically my own eyes) were staring at me! It was as if a snake was looking at me from behind the mirror with its ferocious eyes! I got terribly scared. I don't deny that there could be a reason for this particular hallucinatory (?) thought. In Indian society, people make fun of others and ridicule them by saying; 'You are a two-headed snake; you say one thing at one time and just the opposite the next moment!' My own eldest brother had said this to me once earlier in life, and my wife had said it several times during our routine home conversations on issues which generally do not carry any serious weight otherwise. The other reason might have come from the mental churning that was going inside me, at a conscious as well as subconscious level, about the Hindu Gods, their *vahanas* or associates, their symbols, their meaning etc. Particularly about the snake around Lord Shiva's neck and Adi Sesha with Lord Vishnu. As per Yogic wisdom, the snake also stands for the power of *kundalini,* which is described as a coiled serpent lying dormant in the *muladhara chakra* of all human beings and ascends upwards when one starts his spiritual journey and becomes increasingly oriented to the divine. After going through some literature regarding *kundalini,* and the symbolic meaning of the snake around Lord Shiva's neck etc., it is quite easy to visualize how such religious symbols came into cultural folklore of India and have carried on through the ages!

On another occasion, I was having sound sleep at a geophysical camp we had set up to carry out seismic data acquisition operations for hydrocarbon exploration in the Silchar area of Assam. It was a beautiful camp site with several huts made up of bamboo structures and thatched roofs in serene rural backdrop. It was during December 2002 or early 2003. One night, at around 1.30 a.m., I had a dream in which I felt as if a Ghost entered my body and I suddenly woke up with a strange sensation in my stomach. I started feeling very strange and started behaving a bit paranoid. I was worried about the Ghost inside my body and hence I was feeling totally unsettled, I felt like running towards the central area of the camp in the middle of the night and then outside, but somehow I checked myself. I decided to knock on the door of my closest neighbor in the camp, Dr.Animesh Dhar. And when he opened his door and turned the lights inside his hut on, I told him; 'Dhar Saheb, I am feeling sick. What should we do?' He invited me inside and asked me to sit in a nearby chair and drink a glass of water. Surprisingly, my paranoia went away while I sipped water and I started feeling better in just a few minutes. Together we decided to go back to sleep, in our respective rooms.

Contrary to the weird and bizarre thoughts that I experienced, when I went through the wonderful book by Paramhansa Yoganand, *'The autobiography of a Yogi',* I was amazed at the depth and power of Yoga. He has described in his autobiography how he could create a beautiful palatial building out of nothing just to satisfy the latent desire of one of his follower and how he could bring a very recently departed soul back to Earth. Similar such Yogic power is also described by Sadhguru Jaggi Vasudeva in a few of his lectures. Those souls who get disturbed by what goes on inside them in terms of the bizarre thought processes created during the time of a mental health crisis, should keep their spectrum of imagination as large as possible to maintain sanity. Our Yogic experiences can be a big help. It is now obvious how the human mind can create thoughts varying between such extremes. On one side conscious Yogic thoughts are powerful enough to create apparent matter from nowhere (or invisible energy fluxes). The same power can also be invoked to bring a departed soul back to Earth in a new body. It can also go extremely wild. Weird thoughts without any scientific or logical basis can surface in a temporarily derailed mind.

Sensuality vs. Sexuality

We are all products of sensuality as well as sexuality. However, they are not same. Raw sensuality expressing itself in the form of basic sexual acts can be very different from the subtle sensuality in every activity we undertake to enjoy the beauty of life. Sensuality can be viewed in the realm of love and beauty, whereas sexuality is just the instinctive manifestation of bodily needs. Love here can encompass various dimensions of life including love for profession, love for nature, love for family and friends, love for motherland, love for society, love for knowledge and wisdom, love for God and so on. It is a question of the level of emotional expression. When we cuddle a cute looking, smiling child, it is predominantly sensual satisfaction of love that we derive and in turn provide the same to the child for his or her complete emotional growth. Sometimes, due to ignorance, these very acts can degenerate into barbaric sexual acts. In adulthood, sensuality can be expressed through romantic poems, romantic prose or even simple sweet flattering words. However, sexuality is a very raw thing. Depending upon one's level of mental and spiritual growth, these two emotions can widely vary.

Sometimes we make mistakes by thinking that any visual or any other sensual pleasure that is obtained by looking at the opposite sex or interacting with them should be construed as a call for sex. Actually, in such cases, it is the internal chemical reactions inside the body and mind, due to higher libido, which is the cause for such distorted thoughts inside the mind rather than anything to do with a true exchange of love. The unchecked emotional urge can lead to serious errors of judgment. These can later on lead to mental health problems. The careful analysis of one's own bodily reactions to the different stimuli one gets from the environment can help distinguish and separate the wheat from chaff. One thing that is certain, however, is that, irrespective of what happens, there will be scope to take steps to mend our ways and get back to a normal routine even if some punishment is meted out to the erring individual for mixing up sexual urges with sensuality. The author Rajesh Prabhakar Patil has beautifully described in his book '*Maa, Mun collector Heli*' about his own experience with regard to his feelings about a girl during his student days. How he was literally mad after the girl and was for few months totally oblivious of his acute responsibility of focusing on his studies, build some career to help his family meet the grinding challenges of poverty and deprivation. He goes on to outline in his book how he could overcome the disturbing influence of such libido driven thoughts by coming face to face with the reality of his difficult life! Mahatma Gandhi has also written some of his own experiences in this context in his autobiography and how he came to terms with it.

CHAPTER 5

WAIT A MINUTE! AREN'T WE ALL SEEKING HAPPINESS?

Life changing scene

The year was 1996 and I had just concluded an important official meeting at Nazira, Assam. This meeting was one of our Regional Exploration Board Meetings, where important decisions about identification and prioritization of drilling locations to find hydrocarbons were normally taken, and I had gone to attend the meeting from our headquarters in Dehradun where I was then posted. I, with few colleagues, had just finished our lunch after the meeting was over. Before taking a taxi to the Airport for our return trip, we were walking towards a betel shop for our customary dose after lunch (taking a leaf of betel with a few ingredients that work as digestive and mouth freshener is an age old practice almost all over India). We were walking through one of the crowded market places in the town of Dibrugarh. Suddenly the sight of a man without any legs and arms, rolling around along the road to make him move, while at the same time begging for alms from passersby, sent a chill through my spine.

Hey, wait a minute! I thought. *What is going on here?* Here was a man of average size, but looking much smaller because he had no limbs. He was moving around by rolling, without any help from his arms or legs - which of course he did not possess. I was too embarrassed to even pause a little and stare at him, think about him, to ask him what actually was the cause for his condition, whether it was inborn or if any mishap had befallen him in later years, whether he had any family and whether he had any other support system other than this horrific means of survival. The reason why this scene struck me and is etched into my memory is something else.

The face of the man was far from depressed or sad. He wore a cheerful smile which brightened his overall appearance even though he was obviously conscious of his severe disability. The extraordinary shock I felt was on account of the condition of the literal rolling of this handless and legless body along the street of an Assamese town, but what was on offer was a great sight of God's design. The memory was etched in my mind such that I could always measure my pain and suffering in a calibrated scale to what I saw that day. Aren't we living and continuing to enjoy lives far better than that of this poor soul? The bright face of the man always reminds me that, whenever someone goes through pain and suffering for some reason, he can rest assured that there are poor unfortunate souls in the world who live in far worse conditions than most of us. Is it not worth then to continue the struggle in this world, so that our hard work can bear fruit both for ourselves and for our fellow countrymen and our fellow human beings who are less fortunate than we are? Instead of always feeling condemned over what we don't have in life, for what we have not been able to amass in terms of wealth, position and power, can't we all pause to think of the poor unfortunate souls living in abject poverty and inhuman conditions across different parts of the world, sometimes just across the street? Almost every human being on Earth would have had such a moment in his or her life wherein the sensitivity of the heart, in the creation of which God has invested so much, would not have witnessed and recorded in the memory such heart touching moments. Whether it is of a polio or leprosy stricken person, or a blind person, or a severely physically or mentally disabled person, such a sight will certainly create a chill at least in those moments when our minds are not overburdened or stressed out. Howsoever momentarily such a sight comes our way, it would definitely be recorded in our latent memory and we need to reorient our lives and see the world from this perspective, in this rat race of the modern age.

The Goal Post

Those who have played football will know very well the experience of the 'ultimate happiness' - the ultimate excitement or thrill we get at the time of scoring a goal. Whether it is the individual player scoring the goal, or the team, or whether it is the supporters of the scoring team who are either directly watching the game in the football ground or following it from a distant land through radio or television, all become exuberant, reaching a momentary state of bliss at the very moment the goal is scored. Hence, the *Goal Post* is a symbol for that against which we test our skills, amidst heavy odds, to score the goal. A lifetime of hard work, dedication and sharpening of the inborn talent of the players concerned are the measure of the skills. The odds are measured along similar lines and they are the degree of opposition that is raised against the very act of our scoring the goal. Both the odds and the skills are two elements of the same system that cause happiness to one set and sadness to another when the goal is scored.

In the same way, the goalkeeper experiences ultimate happiness when he manages to stop the opponents scoring a goal. All the others in the field weigh their level of happiness during the game depending on how effectively they manage to exhibit their skills. The ecstatic feeling of the striker when he finally scores a goal, and of the keeper when he manages to save a goal, is visible in any game anywhere in the world.

We, as ordinary human beings, experience a tinge of happiness or sadness when faced with the results or outcome of any activity in which either we are directly engaged in or are even remotely connected with through an emotional link. A success or failure leads to happiness or sadness. Life's journey is a composite of activities, small and big, short-term and long-term, expensive and not very expensive, tough and easy, personal and collective. All of us aspire to achieve success at the end of every activity we undertake. Can we see a parallel between our lives and the football player working his way across the ground towards the goal post to score the goal i.e.

to achieve the ultimate success? All of us basically enact the role of this football player in our day-to-day affairs as we plan, prepare and make targets and try to achieve them. We tend to approach life as a playing field. Some will criticize the term *'game playing'* by hinting at some sort of devilish political connotations, but if we can detach ourselves from such a wrong interpretation as *true realized souls*, we can see how beautifully it can capture the imagination.

For people struggling with the material aspect of happiness, each loss or victory would make a big difference. But for realized souls, it would be just another experience of life to learn from and they will proceed on the path of the eternal journey. If we manage to detach ourselves from the outcome or result (as the Lord teaches us in the *Bhagawat Gita*), the very game of football can be a journey to reach perfect bliss as the entire process consists of hard work, determination, dedication, devotion, diligence and sacrifice apart from inborn talents or qualities.

If we can envisage accurately the entire gamut of skills and resources that are in harmony with our own selves, and how much more we can manage to extract from the available skills and resources in the environment and support system outside of us, we tend to reach the goal of ultimate happiness in our attempt to score the goal in any field of activity of our lives. And even if we concede the goal, we can still remain in a state of bliss since we can satisfy ourselves, our own souls, with the knowledge that we have not left any stone unturned, having put our best efforts into making use of our God given talents during the time and process of preparation for scoring the goal.

Expanding on this a little further, we can see how the ultimate goal of happiness perhaps lies in our ability to control our own selves. This control comes from an understanding that it is not what we do with our capacity to control others or our surroundings or nature, which brings us lasting peace and happiness but it is our capacity to achieve *total inner self-control*. Normally happiness results from the capacity to achieve success in its numerous forms, and if analysed in the subtlest way, true joy comes from *the victory over oneself rather than over others*. It is the victory over our sense organs, including the mind and ego, which provides us with permanent happiness, and which some people term as a state of self-actualization or self-transcendence. If we are sensitive, we can visualize how victory over others (the victory that world understands i.e. victory in material terms) actually leads us to misery. Emperor Ashoka had such an experience after the great war of Kalinga where, even after he vanquished his vast and powerful enemy, he was surrounded with sorrow and pain. Circumstances on the battlefield brought about a kind of transformation in him and later converted him from ill the infamous *Chanda-Ashoka* (Chanda means cruel, useless and devilish) to the eternally popular and adored *Dharma-Ashoka (Dharma here denotes religious, pious and divine)*. In a very subtle form, therefore, human beings are most satisfied when they see others happy by their actions and it is not the other way round.

Victory over others means humiliating the opposite party, and defeating them and subjecting them to misery, which actually brings pain to us. All of us must have experienced this and know how pertinent it is. The sense of guilt or sadness that one experiences when his act of politicking, or of inflicting physical or mental pain on someone to meet his selfish needs, in however miniscule a manner, meets with success - and at the same time leads his opponent to misery. The consequential feeling of pain dawns on us when we realize the innocence of the opponent, just as the inner eye of the soul reminded Emperor Ashoka that the true essence of joy lay not in the falsehood of victory over his enemies but rather in mitigating the sufferings of his fallen victims.

The Lord has bestowed everyone with such an inner eye, but our follies often lead us to wrongdoing. The tendency of people with *scarcity mentality* makes them rush madly after material acquisition, but scholars of all ages have established how futile it is to aspire for eternal happiness through material acquisitions alone. After a certain point, we bring in more botheration and mental agony by our yearning to acquire material wealth alone. The same is true for social position and power. Many of us try to rationalize all our acts in this direction through subtle lies to our *inner conscience*, the ultimate compass for our soul's progress. We still do things foolishly contrary to what acts as our guiding light by way of whispers from our subconscious minds and hearts, and search for happiness in the world by acquiring material wealth, social position or power.

The world, particularly in this age of digital revolution and extraordinary scientific and technological progress, constantly bombards us with heaps of information. Some of it is pure garbage and it becomes difficult for us to separate the diamonds and pearls from the grains of sand. When we think of the goal post and attempt to score a goal, we take into account our total strength, our support, the planning of the moves, the outsmarting of the opponents and only then moving towards the goal post to finally score the goal. Sometimes, the forward player needs a pass from the midfield or from the back and then, once the ball reaches him, it is his initiative to move ahead amidst the surging opponents who try to take the ball away from him. Whether he does manage to force his way through the barricade of opponents in a flash of speed, agility and tactics, or he just goes a few steps ahead and then passes the ball to another forward player positioned beside him, or to the back or in the front, to help the ball move faster towards the goal is a critical decision that he takes on the spur of the moment.

Life's teachings, similarly, are the diamonds and pearls we collect from the ocean of knowledge that has been built by our predecessors. The pearl or diamond is the ball we receive from our co players in this stage of the world and it is our duty to either carry the pearl to its destination (the goal post being Heaven) or to pass the baton to another co-player so that he can carry it further towards its destination.

The human journey if analysed can actually tell us how we, as social animals, simply follow our predecessors, their wisdom and their knowledge, and take on the strings they leave behind to move forward in our own journey. We face obstacles, impediments, along the way in the form of natural disasters or problems caused by unscrupulous elements in the society, uninvited diseases, or sometimes our own weak genetic makeup and, sometimes, environmental degradation caused by our collective follies. In this way, we have to constantly pass through the obstacles in our way. Maneuvering ourselves through the journey of life depends on how strong our will is and how powerful our wisdom is. The wisdom of rishis, seers and philosophers is timeless; they are in fact the same principles which today's management thinkers are exploring and discovering. Eternal Truth manifests itself in realized souls who spread the message amidst humanity through their teachings and we ordinary beings need to pick up those pearls of wisdom during our journey. These pearls can be in the form of even scientific theories, technological skills, management principles, life's golden virtues taught by religious leaders or philosophers or wisdom-filled ideas generated within our own souls (these are sanctified if they come from the deepest part of our own souls; the part which can stand the test of time and space).

Each of us is endowed with almost all the possible human attributes at the time of birth, in varying degrees, according to our past Karma. How else can we explain the very many different qualities of different siblings born from DNA of same parents? Although parents are via media and are divinely important for each one of us, the connectivity between past, present and future that is ingrained in the *theory of Karma* tells us that attributes would manifest very *human* in the beginning but there would always be a part that would be different from ordinary human attributes and that is pure *divine* material. The entire civilisational development has sustained only one critical ingredient and that is the *divinity or collective consciousness, the faith on the human species itself for its own survival.* Everything we do today is going to ultimately be weighed against and measured in terms of its human content and the divine content.

Every one of us is endowed with all kinds of both positive and negative attributes: fear, jealousy, greed, anger, hatred etc. representing the negative side and love, affection, kindness, sympathy, competitiveness and inquisitiveness constituting the positive aspect. The instruments or tools that we are endowed with to realize the driving ambitions arising out of the above human attributes are our intelligence or intellect and its direct interaction with our surrounding. The other tools that are given to us are our ability to sense the underlying divine attributes, the positive attributes. Although they are apparently connected to human intellect, they come from far deeper level i.e., *consciousness*, or *super consciousness*. The Lord teaches us the essence of all this through the divine song of life, the *Bhagawat Gita*.

The rapid development of technology, and the continuous bombardment and brazen display of material prosperity around us tempts us to the brink. This naturally makes us stretch ourselves far beyond our capacities while trying to overtake our immediate neighbours both at our workplace and in society. The constant endeavour to strive for more material gains, to further enjoy the outside world, is the natural fallout. In this rat race, we distrust even our closest neighbours, our closet colleagues at the workplace and even our siblings in the extended family. This is a really tragic development, but the root cause for such degeneration of society can be easily halted and society can be made better and healthier if we, as individuals, make serious efforts to stem the rot.

We tend to be engaged in a constant search for happiness and try to achieve that by *shifting the goal posts* we have set in our lives. If it is a two-wheeler we desire today, it could be a car tomorrow, and then a big luxurious car the next day. If it was a target of a million rupees worth of property today, it could become a hundred million or even a billion tomorrow, when we see someone near us making that kind of money. If it was a promotion to the next higher post we desired first, it could become a longing to proceed up the ladder and reach the very top next. This raw ambition could be justified if it is driven with conscience, hard work based in morality and sacrifice. But if it is driven through manipulation of the system and set up, then it not only pollutes the very being, but the society in general. This *shifting of goal posts* can be harmonious as long as it is tuned and aligned with our innermost virtues and values. If we break a sense of loyalty or commitment in order to reach an excessive limit of material prosperity alone, we are sure to land in trouble and may even be heading towards our doom. Hence, a fixed goal post set through a wise imagination should be the criteria for maintaining a healthy, peaceful and active life.

Yoga Guru Swami Ramdev used to say; 'One single thought can change human lives and even a single moment is enough to transform human lives.' The process of how a chain of thoughts can originate from a single thought and then lead to a total transformation is mysterious. However, in most of our lives, these *"aha!"* moments have been there. The infinite power that resides in the soul sometimes gets activated and ignited by one single conscious thought.

Bliss is very real

SATCHITANAND is a Sanskrit word composed of three parts - SAT (Truth), CHIT (Awareness) and ANANDA (Bliss). To attain a blissful state, we need to make sure these three aspects of life are fulfilled. Soul is Truth and once we become aware of the Truth, Bliss is achieved. Mahatma Gandhi said; *'Happiness is achieved when what one thinks, what he speaks and what he does are all in harmony.'* Happiness is a natural state achieved with the most vital tools of *honesty and integrity* in character. It basically reflects how truthful we are and how we translate the truthfulness in our thoughts into words and actions.

The Truth is actually the only remnant of our past lives which is carried across generations, across the very process of evolution. Truth does not vanish from earth. When we try to orient all our activities to what is dictated by the Truth, then satisfaction automatically dwells in us. Satisfaction is the essence of a harmonious and enriched life, and one derives satisfaction if he does things according to the natural principles of truth, honesty, integrity, and conscience.

It dawned on me how fortunate we really are when I see the world around me, when I see my own small family and my surroundings. We are all born with bodies commensurate with our past Karma. Depending on how we utilize our inborn talents and qualities, how we direct them to the conscientious way of living, we achieve desired results in life. They say; 'First deserve and then desire.' Many might argue, as we have always faced the *chicken and egg conundrum*, by saying just the reverse; 'First desire and then deserve.' Etymological break up of English words holds a key to solution of many of our problems. This is an eternal struggle between *de-serve* (serve..serve… entire humanity and not just your family or creed and then you automatically become *deserving* of anything) and *des-ire* (destroy.. destroy...ire or anger towards anything and you automatically become amenable for germination of pure, divine and Godly *desire*). I have really been fascinated by the infinite number of ways to look at any problem and its solution, either way however, the basics have to be holy and pure intentions, with a broader goal to serve humanity.

I can fondly recollect how Swami Ramswaroopanada from the *Divine Life Society* (DLS), during one of his Satsang meetings in Adelaide, Australia, explained how our desires are realized and how one should not desist from having desires. The key to success or failure is how we strike a good balance between our desires and how much we actually deserve. He said, 'Once I desired intensely about going to Australia because it was the only country I had not yet visited. I have been to North America and Europe, but never to Australia. I wanted to go to Australia and here I am in Adelaide speaking before you all!". We miss the true essence when we run after materialistic goals without setting proper foundations in the spiritual domain. Anything will sustain on this earth if it is built on spiritual roots. The above fact about what the Swami was trying to convey may appear superficial or just a coincidence or even absurd, but I believe that this is *the way* how world operates. However, behind such a desire espoused by the Swami, there was timeless efforts and dedicated spiritual work for several years (he had described to me personally how he had served the society as a very close confidante of the head of the DLS, Swami Shri Chinmayananda), and hence automatically, he had created the congenial environment in this ether world how his desires would get fulfilled.

Regarding our perpetual complaining about what we have not got and what we have not yet achieved, about what others are gifted with but not us etc., we never fail to notice how much Nature has given us already, how much God has gifted us with in the first place. For example, I was gifted with a body that was strong enough to let me carry out my daily duties right from my childhood - education, games and sports, social activities, marriage, children etc. How can I blame God for not giving me a good body? There are millions in this world who are less fortunate than us. It thrills me when I sometimes see less fortunate people - people with disabilities in vision, hearing, speech - and they have much happier faces and a more positive attitude towards life than people who have almost everything life had to offer - good physical bodies, good family atmosphere to be brought up in, good education, good jobs or means of livelihood. What they lack is perhaps that spark of divinity which intrinsically curbs people from being too greedy, angry, jealous, impatient, hateful or discontented. Hence, in this world, looking at such divine souls reminds us of the simple fact that it is not materialistic acquisitions but a sense of gratitude towards God that can bring contentment, eternal happiness and bliss.

There is a tendency in our modern hit and run world (with its cut-throat competition) to forget the true hidden beauty in ourselves and run after materialistic things that might give us momentary pleasure but can never give us eternal bliss. Some people suffer from a perpetual feeling of insecurity about their own future or their children's future. They engage in a mad rush even after stockpiling materialistic things. They complain of a lack of financial security all the time when, just across from the building or across the street, there are ample instances of slums, beggars and destitute struggling with life. These poor people do not even have a day's meal, proper shelter, proper drinking water facilities or anything to protect them from the cold, rains, heat etc. When we look at these things around us, we can easily understand how fortunate we are, and how we can extend a helping hand to mitigate the sufferings of many people around us. Although there is a nice tendency amongst the youth and elderly of the modern world to strive to do social work and social service, it is not enough. The vast disparity among the different sections of society in all parts of the world creates opportunity for all of us to help and opens up the possibility to render selfless service. The old saying 'Service to mankind is service to God' is so very apt.

When we look at our children, we can derive immense pleasure from simply thinking how fortunate we are when compared to the millions who are not blessed like us. But we still put pressure on them to achieve more and keep comparing them with others. On the contrary, we should instill confidence in our growing children that materialistic achievement is not everything. A spiritual dimension should always be given equal emphasis and children should be encouraged to develop their inner souls so as to be helpful elements in the society.

If we think about it, we live mostly on not just borrowed ideas but borrowed bodies also. How have our bodies come to take this shape? Science has taught us about the process of evolution, and our genetic footprint tells us how we managed to get our bodies through generations of living and hard work. Similarly, the world has been blessed with great people whose ideas have enriched lives, and naturally we can simply live our lives based on these ideas. However, there still remains massive scope for addition of new ideas - and this will happen only if we keep our minds and hearts open for the breath of fresh air that is the divine grace. By filtering the good from the bad of what is taught to us by our parents, elders, teachers, friends, peers, past leaders of society, and also by the traditional customs followed in a culture and by imbibing the good in one's life, one is sure to lead a happy and prosperous life.

Happiness is simply a state of mind. I believe that we achieve a true state of happiness when we maintain a perfect balance between our conscious and subconscious mind. The subconscious mind shows us the path (what Stephen Covey terms as true north principle) and the conscious mind follows the path thus chalked out. And if we maintain a good balance between the two, we achieve happiness. The conscious mind derives signals, stimuli, from the environment and sends them to the subconscious mind for processing. The subconscious mind tries to develop different paradigms, sets different goals, devises certain principles, and then asks the conscious mind to operate within the confines of the framework it has created to achieve the desired results. If we go along the set path, we will surely remain happy generally and if we do not, we fail to achieve happiness. Having desires and trying to fulfill them does not amount to greed just by itself but when we get caught up with unending desires, source for stress and hence unhappiness is planted.

Stress, happiness and spirituality

Most of us, including school and college going children, are quite familiar with the word "stress". Sometimes we call it by different names - like tension, pressure, worries and anxieties etc. Although the degree and extent may vary with each individual, all of us can expect to face some stressful situations at particular periods of time, such as on the eve of an examination, on the eve of some meeting where we have to make a presentation, on the eve of an interview or selection process, or during some health crisis or accident, the loss of a job, the sudden loss of a near and dear one or a sudden change of situation like change of place, change of assignment etc. Stressful situations like these generally affect all of us; it is quite but natural. However when stress becomes permanent, when it remains with us for very long unintended periods of time, we tend to fall sick as it manifests itself through various physical ailments like hypertension, migraine, diabetes, heart disease and so on. Modern research invariably tracks the root cause of many present day diseases to the single factor, *stress*.

The fundamental reason why we experience stress in our daily lives is that we expect something from life and then either fail to get what we expected or simply presuppose that we would fail to get what we expect. This means that the original point of stress could either be very real or sometimes be simply perceived.

For example, against the backdrop of the expectations that our parents have of us and we have of ourselves, we might expect to get a score of say ninety-five percent in our final examinations. But after writing all our papers, we might start becoming anxious thinking that perhaps we would not achieve the expected ninety-five percent target we set for ourselves. This is a case of a perceived reason for stress. We create stress for ourselves even though there is a long way to go for the results, a couple of months at least. Similarly, we might put lots of effort into our job life and expect to get an elevation which we believe we very much deserved. But we may not get the promotion we expected. This is a case of real reason for stress. The failure of an expectation to be met, the expectation we had of ourselves or of our family and friends, might cause us to get disappointed and upset leading to mental agonies and stress. These are two simple practical examples for cause of stress.

At a very fundamental though generic level, stress tends to build up in our minds when the balance between our *conscious mind* and the *subconscious mind* is disturbed. These two parts of our mind, according to modern research, work harmoniously as long as we maintain a healthy balance in our lifestyle and a healthy perspective of our lives. The subconscious brain knows full well about the inherent capacity and inherent limitations of our overall personalities, but our conscious brain tries to imitate what it absorbs from our social environment and then falsely projects to us a feeling or dream that can sometimes be much bigger than our capacity. This is when problems start to develop. And this applies to both very small acts and also the much bigger tasks of life that we undertake.

There are two reasons mainly why we get into situations of stress. One is when we fail to reconcile our own mistakes, meaning that our inability to accept how we could have made such mistakes, leads to self-abuse, self-cursing, guilt, a feeling of inferiority, anger, frustration etc. Secondly, when we expect something from others and encounter just the opposite, it gives rise to anger and frustration in two forms. We question ourselves on why we're failing to modify the other person's habits or actions (the other person could even be our own spouse or child) and also on why people who do not conform to our expectations or ideals get to go scot free. They aren't punished and may even get rewarded.

The root of these problems lies in the *"Karta feeling"*. In our assumption that it is we who are doing and controlling everything. This is not true. There are an infinite number of ways that the finite number of people whom we live and work with on earth can think, act and behave. This is not within our control. Sometimes though we do feel that things are happening according to what we planned or worked for. However, if we go a bit higher up in the *plane of realization*, we will understand that all our own past desires, thoughts, words and actions are systematically linked to what is happening today, at this moment of time.

The process of how the cycle of *desire-efforts-success-new desire* operates is actually so subtle that sometimes one lifetime is not enough to fully grasp the finer beauty of it. When we closely analyse a *successful achievement cycle* in our own life, we can easily see how the minutest steps we took in the past, towards the achieving of today's success, look almost like the *small parts of a big jigsaw puzzle*, all fitting together nicely in the end. This is when a pure soul starts believing in the efficacy of God which I define as *Collective Consciousness*.

Whenever a true desire appears and takes roots in our hearts, it gets recorded in both our subconscious and conscious mind. Not all the conscious efforts we make from that point onwards may subscribe to what is apparently in line with what we first desired, but somehow the events of life all occur in such a manner that eventually they bring about a favourable result. One that is in accordance with the purest expectations of our inner desire - which is recorded in our subconscious mind and which again has a subtle link with the heart.

As far as stressful situations are concerned, the cause for them is directly related to our *"Karta feeling"*. We can avoid stress by following the advice given to us by the *Bhagawat Gita*, 'One who has understood the essence of spiritualism never thinks he is the doer (Chapter 3, Shloka 28).' The Lord reiterates; 'The life of one who completely surrenders himself unto me becomes easy and smooth (Chapter 3, Shloka 31).'

The conflict occurs when we see only the surface of what is happening. Occasionally, we see very bad and undeserving elements prospering in society. But if we analyse in detail, there can be no better opportunity to notice that at a not-so-obvious level, the same undeserving people possess great human attributes that ordinary eyes can easily miss. Similarly, if we look at human history, right from prehistoric times, we can easily see how there is an order to everything. Every action of each individual is not free from the *global collective consciousness network*.

Quoting from our ancient scriptures, Swami Chinmayananda said; 'Man's search for happiness is a universal tendency and everyone is searching for lasting happiness in a world of constant change. Hence, permanent happiness must be independent of a changing environment. There is a substratum of permanence on which the changing phenomena rose and fell.' The statement is profound because the very fact that man has an universal tendency to attain a permanent state of happiness amidst a continuously changing and dynamic environment indicates that there must be something deeply rooted in our soul, something whose longing is permanent within! Happiness is actually a state of mind. Even during the worst crisis of life, if we can surrender fully at the altar of the Lord, the Omnipresent, the Omnipotent and the Omniscient, we can be one hundred percent sure to come out of the ordeal unscathed. The *Bhagawat Gita* teaches us (Chapter 3, Shloka 18): 'One who engages himself in selfless pursuits with pure intellect remains in sublime happiness.'

The essence of *Karma Yoga* (Chapter 3 of *Bhagawat Gita*) teaches us to focus only on efforts and suggests that results will take care of themselves. Many people have criticized the apparent connotations of this divine sermon by saying it is a discouragement to aspire for success or higher achievement. But with experience, and steady inward realization, we will ultimately understand the true meaning of this *diktat*. It does not mean we should not look for results. What it means is that, if we are being driven by clean inner desire, and fitted mentally with the infinite possibilities brought forth by the *"Collective Consciousness"*, then when we put in effort, we must concentrate only on our efforts. Dissipation of energy in continuously thinking about results can be checked if such an approach is taken by concentrating only on our sincere efforts. The full energy can be devoted to efforts and obviously result will follow in accordance with what Mother Nature or our Creator has destined for us.

Happiness online

Human civilization has progressed in such a fashion that we can today convert what was the science fiction of yesteryears into reality. During my childhood, we in our household used to get excited when we correlated certain signals to anticipated events in our daily lives. (Events such as the repeated *cawing of crows* inside our compound, or the slipping of utensils/other household items from the hand of someone in the family, prompting our elders to say that someone would soon be arriving at our home or that someone was desperately thinking about us etc.). This had a link with scientific reasoning. When we consciously activate our brain and think about someone, gravity waves are generated by the power of our thoughts and these can be transmitted as very subtle signals. And the interaction of these gravity waves with the *ether world* helps activate the receivers within us, and we manage to pick up the signals if we are sensitive and sensible enough to do. There is a connection here.

However, modern science has now captured this philosophy through sophisticated technology and tools like electricity, electromagnetism, wave propagation theory and other scientific means to convert what was yesteryears' dream into reality today. We can pick up the telephone and communicate with someone in any part of the globe. This is nothing but a means of "Happiness Online". Happiness can be gained through the satisfaction of connecting with different people including family and friends. We can connect to our common Source, the Supreme God, by way of these souls interacting, learning and sharing both sorrow and happiness through love and affection. This way we all get connected and by being part of the Universal Soul, we enjoy the warmth and peacefulness by exploring the infinite dimensions of its existence and the infiniteness of the Supreme God. This is made possible through the advent of modern science and technology. Doctors and engineers can consult over the telephone in a matter of seconds about any doubts or possibilities or procedures and then apply the same to their own work and also derive immense pleasure out of it.

In our personal lives, we might recall how, at the time when we are feeling very low, we become calmer the moment we talk to a trusted friend or confidante. We may be far away from it at first, but through the soothing words of someone who we trust, love or respect, through a telephone call or through emails, we get a boost of energy. I have personally observed this several hundreds of times when I talk to family and friends who are in distress. They get instant relief when I speak to them and this has been possible through long distance communication. My daughter, while being in a hostel in the far away town of Visakhapatnam, away from her parents and extended family, used to get upset for various reasons, but through phone calls and mails from me and her mother and even her younger brother, she used to get enough soothing effect in her mind to carry on. So is the case with my younger brother. Being a sensitive person, he is overwhelmed with joy when I try to explain different causes or the possible reasons for the heartburn or stressful mental conditions that he might be going through for a very long time. This is just to illustrate that humanity is at a juncture to revolutionise the use of technology and use the same to its advantage in all aspects of life. We all enjoy blissful ecstasy through the live TV coverage of our heroes in different sporting arenas winning over their rivals. Of course many will argue about the evil side of the use of digital technology. One can wreak havoc in minutes, through the use of technology, across the far corners of globe. We now know that during the November 2008 Mumbai terror attacks, telephones were being actively used even by gun trotting terrorists!

The power of social media is being seen as a game changer. When leaders in all fields, starting from the international level, to the national level and down to the block and village Panchayat levels, understand what such a revolution can do for the Collective Good, one can easily imagine the bright future ahead. This paradigm shift in the environment is only possible when leaders at all levels in every field of activity - including politics, sports, culture, education, health, religion and science - *think from the perspective of the global society,* when they think that whatever they do today will have an effect on the survival of the entire global society. Many skeptics might dismiss this as a utopian idea, but I must not hesitate to say that those who do it, do so at their own peril. I have seen personally how some misguided youths let their first taste of brilliant success in life get to their heads and then resort to treachery, hypocrisy, deceit, and manipulation. It does not take them too long, then, to meet with their own destruction. Since, as I pointed out earlier, it is the Collective Consciousness which is permanent, temporary thrills experienced by an individual soul is not the barometer for global emancipation.

There is another dimension to the age of internet today. The world is now just a small family. Internet has made this possible. People can access almost anything and everything through internet and can derive information on any matter instantly. Mental anxieties can be lessened tremendously if one knows how to retrieve information on any subject and knows how to use it for his benefit. Shopping through internet has become a global craze. Entertainment through internet by accessing different sites like games, movies etc. have almost replaced conventional media. E-books have become the alternative to conventional books. Man's search for happiness can find a new destination in internet. Online chatting, dating and even marriage negotiations through internet have revolutionized the way we look at our lives. All this indicates the potential of modern communication network that can be harnessed to make this world a much happier place.

Happiness and pain do not go together

Everyone wants to be happy, but do we know the ingredients? Pain and suffering and happiness cannot go together. Pain and suffering may be due to any reason physical or emotional i.e. of the body or the mind. These agonies cannot exist side by side with happiness. Then how do we remain happy? It is simple. We were all born happy. The moment immediately after birth will always be an exciting time for the mother and will hence be ingrained as a seed of happiness. But what happens in the middle? As we go along life's journey, we slowly lead ourselves to unhappiness and then realise one day that we are not happy. Then we long for what we lost.

In September 2009, I had to be hospitalised in one of the hospitals in Kolkata for a fever that was not going away despite several visits to doctors and several rounds of medication. I became so week physically that the anxiety deep within me surfaced as thoughts of God taking me away. In a corner of my mind, however, I clung to the eternal hope of a quick recovery. But to help that happen, I prayed and surrendered to God. Within a week, through the miraculous intervention by a few highly qualified doctors, I became alright again.

During the time, I was feeling awful, and I could not even dream of happiness. The only thing my mind preoccupied itself with was how to overcome the crisis with proper medical care and God's grace. It is not easy to think of being happy when we are reeling under pain, physical or mental. But the beauty lies in the fact that once we surrender during such times to God, and allow everything to take its own course whilst only faintly intervening by converting our subconscious thoughts to conscious actions, God will slowly take us back to safety.

But is there any link with sin and suffering in this birth itself? If we elevate our soul to a great extent, then we can experience how our own actions bring in misery to us. There is always a train of thoughts followed by a train of actions that precede a major crisis. Most of the times, these originate in our present lives, as responses to environmental stimuli, and in the form of what seem to be moral and righteous deeds. If we fail to find answers regarding the cause for such pain and suffering in our present lifetime, then it is all the more obvious that there is a past *Karmic Debt* that manifests itself as our thoughts and actions in our present lifetime. Such negative trains of thought would slowly drain the energy from our soul to such an extent that even though we may be taking all possible precautions (like, in my case, exercises, good food, pranayam etc.) the very seed of the negative emotions of anger, frustration and hatred towards someone in this world will have a boomerang effect and do more damage to us than the persons we hold the grudge against. These will manifest in the form of diseases.

Work is a need, whether for the body or the mind

The human physique consists essentially of four parts. First, the physical body consisting of various internal organs and outer body parts. Then comes the mind with its associated emotions, the power to think, the power to assimilate information from within and from without and its ability to process that information for its own betterment. The third is the intellect, which is actually the part of the brain which discriminates bad from good and helps satisfy the needs and requirements for the survival of a person or a species through imaginative vision and necessary actions. Finally comes the heart, which is the center of a man's sense of wholesome growth including all positive emotions, and is the most important organ responsible for providing a sense of divinity and spirituality to the entire being. Each one of these parts is built in such a way that it needs to work for its growth and needs its own rest to rejuvenate. And all them coordinate their activities in such a fashion that they can collectively propel progress and betterment of civilization.

Idleness leads to devilish thoughts and creates all kinds of negative hormones whereas engagement with a daily routine of work gives positive energy. However, too much work also tells on the health of the body, mind and spirit of an individual. If there is no work for one, he senses a vacuum, but if he is wise enough, he can create enough work to satisfy his body, mind and spirit. The interesting thing is that when one works, he gets maximum satisfaction when there is a collective demand for the work rather than his own individual demand. It is interesting because the work he does for the collective goal earns him recognition, and this is a very vital step for his growth. Sometimes, conflict arises when the individual thinks that the work he is asked to do is not fit for his position and need. As a result, a cycle of frustration sets in. The best solution for such a scenario is to surrender oneself to God, the collective consciousness, and believe that it is ordained by Him. The world is interconnected and all our desires and ambitions are linked to the *global consciousness network*. Some people try to manipulate the system to take advantage of a situation and get some extra benefits out of the system which they may not deserve.

This thought alone can relieve anxiety and frustration from the mind if one is thrown into deadlock because of conflicting demands on his being. The self-satisfaction one gets when he manages to serve others, the parents, the children, the siblings, the relatives and friends, or the larger society, is immense. When the spirit of service is ingrained in each unit of the being, as it happened in Mahatma Gandhi's case, or in Swami Vivekananda's case, it will lead to perfect bliss. Egolessness is actually the state of perfect bliss, and that is possible only when one dedicates himself to the service of others.

Mahatma Gandhi aspired for a state of total egolessness, comparing his ego to be just a grain of dust ready to be easily blown away by the wind of God's desire. It is not easy to visualize what is meant by total egolessness. To achieve it needs disciplining of the mind, body and spirit. Work for body and mind is like food to a hungry being. The system operates harmoniously so long as work is provided to the body and the mind both, in order to keep the spirit active, fresh, and expanding.

During an international conference in 2010, one spiritual session was conducted with the highly respected spiritual leader from the *Art of Living Foundation.* There was a half-hour talk followed by a question-answer session. A gentleman from the audience asked; 'Guruji, in today's corporate world, to achieve anything, one is bound to harbor ego-driven motives in any of his jobs. So is it good to possess such ego?'

The Guruji replied with a smile, making a little gesture in his hand and fingers; 'Only so much of it, just the way we use salt in our food.'

Deep scar on the soul can act as a large bowl to contain joy

There are many cultures which still believe that any pain & suffering that befalls an individual is actually punishment from God for his or her misdeeds in the present life. This belief is easily acceptable in the case of adults, but in the case of small children, people might wonder how God can be so cruel as to punish innocent children with serious illness and even genetic deformities. The Karmic philosophy in Hinduism and Buddhism explains how a soul journeys through such pain and suffering, life after life, depending on its level of growth. The problem arises when one tries to get answers and comprehend everything about the cycle of pain and suffering and the cycle of pleasure and happiness in the span of one lifetime. Christianity takes a slightly different approach by saying that the very fact that Jesus laid down His own life was to teach us that it is indeed a joy and the ultimate bliss to lay down one's life for the benefit of mankind. Hence, pain and suffering can be converted to love and joy if we can relate to the Cross.

When one goes through a crisis, he will of course be suffering and going through a very hard time which only he experiences and truly understands. And when he is finally done with that episode of pain and suffering, when he has completely overcome the crisis, he will typically find his mind's ability has been enhanced. Modern brain research suggests that, by virtue of the plasticity of our brains, our mind would have experienced an amazing degree of expansion because the sorrows, pains and sufferings would have actually helped in stretching the limits of our mental makeup in the negative domain. If we can visualize it as a *swinging pendulum,* whenever the pendulum is swung by applying a particular force, it would first swing in one direction from the static position, to the extreme, and then swing back to the other extreme in the opposite direction. The force with which it swings varies with the quantum of force applied and also on the characteristics of the string, size of the pendulum etc.

The capacity of the human mind functions in a similar manner, if we understand the mechanics behind it. In the aftermath of a painful experience which causes the mind to swing in one direction (obviously in the negative direction) it creates also the space and opportunity for the mind to swing back in the opposite direction, the positive direction, to the other extreme. This process would obviously yield positive results, positive benefits. It is just like the swinging of a pendulum in a *to and fro motion* or in *simple harmonic motion.* The harder and longer the swing in one direction, equal is the creation of the amount of space for swinging in the opposite direction. By the analogy of the swinging pendulum, one can visualize how the hardest crisis in one's life can open up the scope for an equal amount of joy, if faithful processes are adopted. We must keep taking right decisions based on what we learnt from our pains and sufferings. We can then derive the satisfaction and joy associated with the successes that will follow – and which happens because mind has the inherent ability to take positive decisions and actions if some conscious efforts are made in that direction, leaving the experience of the crisis behind.

Kindness to one's own self is a necessity

Researchers have now found the reason why some people can keep calm and stay balanced even during times of crisis and adverse situations when compared to some of their counterparts who are in similar circumstances. They have found the answer in the paradigm of self-pity.

Sometimes, we fail to understand our follies and blame and criticize ourselves even to the extent of chastising ourselves. This causes internal scarring and our mental makeup gets damaged by such thoughts. When we fail to accomplish tasks within a stipulated time or when we fail for some reason to stick to the ethics, principles and laws of life that we have set for ourselves, we tend to do this. We try to think and feel negatively about ourselves. It is human, but to get trapped in such a mindset is dangerous.

The dynamics of life and the ever-changing world both tell us that nothing is static and that everything is bound to change. When we decide to accomplish something, we take into account certain parameters and perimeters for us to act upon and act within. But due to changing scenarios, we notice that the basic framework changes - which puts pressure on our set goals. And hence, sometimes, the results do not reflect what we originally had planned. Here comes the understanding that, basically, we can set goals for ourselves but the results are not in our hands. This is once again the essence of the *Bhagawat Gita* and it teaches us to concentrate on our goals and our actions instead of the results. This realization helps us remain eternally calm and peaceful.

The *day's balance sheet* also helps us slowly settle down into the feeling that nothing is meaningless in life and that every moment is actually an opportunity to learn from, for further progress. The negative feelings, their source, their genesis, their damaging effects, all of this can be assimilated into a system that can help each one of us in different situations. To avoid the feeling of emptiness which arises mainly from our lack of properly planning alternative courses of action and proper goal setting, we need to plan each day of the week, each week of the month and each month of the year. This we must do in such a fashion that we weave all our activities, all our moments, into a necklace of beads that can be offered to our Creator - which is metaphorically similar to offering of a garland of flowers to a deity in Hindu rituals. This means that setting the ultimate goal and weaving each action of ours into it, and planning each day and each moment, all help us achieve not only our daily goals but also our ultimate goal in life which is nothing but to merge with Thee.

Self-pity comes into play when we fail to achieve our set goals and can still manage to tell ourselves that it is okay. It is reconciling ourselves with the fact that only actions and not results are in our hands. This is a form of showing kindness to ourselves, and of not being aggressively critical of ourselves. This helps us maintain our inner peace, tranquility and calm under most circumstances.

The Wall Clock; life's metaphor

Sometimes, if we are quiet and do not have too many thoughts going through our heads, particularly in the early morning time, we can hear the sound of the clock hanging on the wall or the table clock ticking a few feet away. If we close our eyes and try to be in communion with our surroundings, with the birds chirping in the background, we can better hear the soothing sound of the ticking of the wall clock or of the table clock. If we are fully aware and quiet, we will be able to enjoy this blissful state. This momentary flash of peace, happiness or bliss would be relevant if we understood the mechanics involved in such a phenomenon. Here the soul is the silent onlooker, undergoing silent experiences through the blissful state of feeling at one with nature. The soul is the highest instrument available to us to observe and feel the charm and bliss of life. The mind is free from all thoughts which means that there is a direct connection between a person and his soul to the all Creative Source i.e. God, Mother Nature or whatever one may want to call it.

If we analysed the clock, we would see that it is working without stopping even for a microsecond. It is always alert and working so as to be able to tell us the time. The life of the clock is one of service. We feed it through the electric energy that comes from the battery that we put in it. The work that it does is its way of giving back and there is absolutely no discrimination. It will show the same time to a billionaire and to a beggar, to a child and to a centenarian, to the greatest scientist on earth, to the common farmer and to the most powerful politician. A clock does not discriminate. Our souls are meant to view the world in a similar fashion. But our mental training or conditioning deters us and moves us from this ideal position to instead hold a distorted view of the world.

The energy of the battery that we put into a clock cannot last forever and once we see that the battery is getting drained, we put in a new battery. We can visualize our lives in a similar fashion. When we feel that a particular thought or a pattern of thoughts, or some work or a few types of work, are not able to power the internal machine, we should realize that it is the time to replace the existing battery of thoughts with some new and positive thoughts. What it means here is that we should be prepared to change the battery to give new life to the clock. However, the fundamental attribute of the clock does not change i.e. it continues showing the time to us, continues to render the dedicated service it is meant to provide us with. Similarly, nature creates us to render service to humanity and our soul is a representative of God or nature. It should be allowed to decide, on our behalf, the time when the battery needs to be changed.

Happiness lies in giving

Since the Sun is the source of our immediate origin (science has now almost conclusively proved that we all are born from Sun, as are all the planets of the solar system), it means that the inhabitants of the earth can learn immensely from the impersonal philosophy that the Sun represents or radiates. In one small sentence, this philosophy is; *'Burn yourself while giving light and energy to others.'*

I shall describe a small anecdote here. I have been working on my book for quite a few years now and since my writing has been spread over few years, although most intensely in the last two years, I was literally astonished when immediately after the demise of our ex-President Dr. APJ Abdul Kalam, one famous quotation purportedly from his latest book, started appearing in the press, *"If you want to shine like the Sun, first burn like the Sun"*. This was so close to what I had already written as above although I had conceived the idea in a slightly different context. It might be mysterious to many but it is quite easy to visualize how such a thought came to my mind when around the same time perhaps, Dr. Kalam wrote similar words, repeated in this book much later. These are fundamental truths and will always find resonance in more than one human being's mind in this earth just the way many scientific discoveries are worked out in two or three different places at the same time without one group having any knowledge of the other group. When time for any great idea is ripe, it would undoubtedly excite few people's brain waves, in the form of intuition which is essentially the way the Collective Consciousness or God as we call it, interacts with human souls.

We can think of how we can expand our internal emotions to generate happiness. This points us in the direction of internal burning and the associated emission of energy and light. The Sun continuously gives us light and energy through a physical process of heat generation called *fusion reaction*. The process is one of nuclear fusion of hydrogen into Helium. Similarly, all human beings are supposed to experience this kind of internal burning and give off energy and light to others in the form of peace, happiness and joy. This is the ultimate truth. We fail to see this and run after false goals in the modern age and fall into traps, and suffer. We may fail once or twice, but we can keep our internal torch glowing through our connection with spirituality, our connection with God. This can be done by reminding ourselves constantly about our humble background– in the context of individuals or group or organization or society or even nation. We will surely relish this. We miss the target when we fall into the trap of our ego, which keeps a swirling and unreasonable burden on our head, and we get deviated from our divine goal as a result. However, there is always hope in making a course correction.

This is possible if we continuously evaluate our strategy, our goals and our objectives in the short term, but in the long term, our goal must be to serve humanity. It is through giving and giving alone that we reach happiness. That is fundamental. But we can only give what we have. And nothing comes easy. It comes through hard work, suffering, pain and when we share it with others, it gives us joy and happiness. In the same way, all the scientists, engineers, professionals, workers, laborers, educationists, technologists, teachers, spiritual leaders and gurus do hard work, burn their internal energy and spread cheer and happiness through the society.

Distance between sadness and happiness is just twelve inches

One day it struck me that the *'Shortest distance between sadness and happiness is just one foot or twelve inches'* which is the approximate distance between the position of a man's heart and brain. From early childhood, since the time our earliest memories started getting recorded, we remember many things: facts, sciences, mathematics, management, ethics, events, feelings of awe, bewilderment, feelings of frustration, surprise, happiness, gratitude, anger, hatred, dissatisfaction, satisfaction, reverence and respect for teachers, seniors, holy men, great leaders and so on. Even statements get recorded in our psyche and then get retrieved in flashes during conversations, during an encounter with a current problem and so on. There is an inbuilt feedback mechanism in all of us. It is automatic because of the two most fundamental attributes of the human species: the *survival instinct* and the *instinct to love and feel loved.*

The successes and failures that we face during our journey from early childhood can either get recorded in our brains or in our hearts. The "feelings of the heart" are permanent memories and they can either get modified for the better, or remain as they are until our last breath. The modification is normally done through the mechanisms of the mind and through a rational analysis of the events we see in our surroundings and the silent observation of the feelings that we experience inside our minds and hearts.

The moments of happiness that we feel at the time of achieving some success, in terms of meeting our basic needs or some higher needs, is clearly recorded within our hearts and minds. By analyzing it closely, we understand the full meaning of it. Any experience of sadness in the past can be converted to an experience of happiness if we can catalogue it as a part of our own learning experience. The learning here is meant for the ultimate path, the ultimate journey, to reach the state of bliss, the state of eternal happiness.

On many occasions, we might have cursed ourselves for our failures by self-criticizing and naively believing that a few tasks performed in different ways could have perhaps led us to successes instead. In hindsight, when we think about it, we see that our failures were actually critical junctures for our learning and growth. What we consider to be our mistakes can thus be translated into vital experiences that are necessary to build the inner wisdom we require for our further growth. Such positive perceptions can help us come out of feeling imprisoned by our past mistakes and can lay the foundation for designing a better future.

Scriptures tell us essentially the building blocks for leading a healthy, peaceful, happy and divine life and teach us how to progressively grow into a state of self-actualization or self-transcendence. Is it not enough to understand that all this is possible by effectively crossing a distance of only one foot? How much we cover of this distance, and how well, is a matter of personal development. Some may die young, but they have crossed that distance. Great saints like Swami Vivekananda left their physical bodies at a very young age but not before achieving extraordinary heights of spiritual growth and sharing the wisdom with humanity. Ordinary folks like us take a lifetime to reach that state. Just a few months before she died, my mother said of my father; 'Now I realize that I was married to a mythical *Ram-like person!*' (Lord Ram is the protagonist of the Indian epic '*Ramayana*') This statement was profound for me because it opened up new ideas about our cultural conditioning and how it impacts us. Apparently my mother struggled her entire life to find the "*Ram*" in my father (who incidentally had died fourteen years prior to her own demise) and could realize those attributes only a few months before her own death! It meant two things to me, one was that both my father and mother were replicas of Ram and Sita in a sense, and the other was that if we are not careful, then we will fail to realize the true essence of our souls until we are close to our own deaths which will be too late for all practical purposes.

Happiness is a journey and not the destination

'People are just about as happy as they make up their minds to be,' said Abraham Lincoln. Newly born babies communicate their feelings to the outside world through primordial means like crying, gestures, smiles etc. which, as adults, we decode and interpret to either meet the needs of the babies or to simply join in celebration of their blissful smiles! As we grow up however, we learn to communicate with the outside world through words, sentences and some formal structured language.

Happiness is one of the most important words. And it has connotations so profound that, even though we might not like to talk about it, it still keeps coming into our conscious and subconscious brain. It has the greatest influence on the human race because it is what – despite being an abstract concept - drives humanity mostly towards sustainable growth. Material prosperity is the result of the fulfillment of the latent desires of mankind, and these originate from the conscious mind constantly as a longing for a state of comfort, peace, joy and happiness. Inherent in our genes is this *craving for eternal joy and happiness.* And it doesn't matter whether we are in the top or bottom rung of society.

Abraham Maslow studied human behaviour and came out with a pyramidal model popularly known as the *hierarchy of needs* in which he has rightly spelt out our need for food, clothing and shelter as the most fundamental and basic needs everyone tries to satisfy before going up the ladder for the fulfillment of higher order needs. The top of the pyramid is occupied by our need for *"self-actualization"* which many social thinkers now extend to something called *"self-transcendence"*. Although it sounds philosophical, for achieving ultimate success in our earthly lives, something in our genes must keep ticking and guiding us *"true north"*. This guiding force is what is generally referred to as the *"Conscience"*, the divinity ingrained in all of us.

So, what is *"happiness"* actually? Is it something tangible or intangible? Is it some real sense of achievement or success or something else? How long will or should that sense of achievement continue for us to realize that we are truly happy? How long and how far is the journey going to be for each one of us? Perhaps the answers to such questions keep coming to our mind and force us into different positions. Negative answers sometimes bother us and cause anxiety and stress while an affirmative answer, on the other hand, helps us *refine our internal thought processes*. This is nothing but a reflection of the so-called *"soul force"*; the unique attribute possessed by the human species. As earthly beings, we perform all the instinctive acts that all other animals do except we can possess a *conscious thought process towards divinity*. This may be inborn or it may be triggered by different events in our lives at different stages. The thought processes needs to be anchored firmly to a scientific basis and also retain its metaphysical anatomy.

Revisiting fond memories creates a feeling of sublime happiness, but the human mind longs for continuous growth both in materialistic terms and in spiritual terms. While the old adage *says; 'too much of anything is bad'*, science has yet to crack the true and full meaning of *"God"* - *which encompasses infinity*. Our forefathers aptly developed means so that, through rituals, we remember the influence of God on our daily lives. Many suggest that *'work is worship but worship is not work'*. Some have nicely combined the three important paths to salvation as dictated by the *Bhagawat Gita* – *Karma Yoga, Gnyana Yoga and Bhakti Yoga* - by saying that *'Karma with Gnyana is Bhakti'* and that it is through *Karma* alone that we gather knowledge, experience and wisdom. Hence, to do our daily duties with proper knowledge, having an intrinsic attitude of *surrendering everything in the long run as a sacrifice to all-pervading God* is the surest path to success, and sustained happiness.

If we adhere to what our scriptures advise for the four stages of our lifetimes - *brahmacharya, grihastha, vanaprastha and sanyas* - then we would realize that at no point of our lives, except for periods of suffering such as during disease or other unforeseen tragedies, would we be away from the sublime goal of human life which is to attain happiness. Clear cut divisions, in the aforesaid manner, of the four stages not only discipline our lives but also give us full freedom to enjoy our lives in adherence to the ultimate *sattwic goal of salvation*. Our scriptures help us regulate our supposedly adult lives by allowing us to cultivate various means of *dharma, artha, kama* and *moksha*. Although many people get confused while categorising all our activities as being one or the other of the above mentioned four, if we analyse critically, then we can arrive at a wholesome process wherein all four of the above can be integrated in such a manner that one is complimentary to the other and the process becomes all inclusive rather than exclusive of any one of them. Satisfaction of desires (which includes *Artha*, meaning prosperity and wealth, and *Kama*, meaning to love and being loved through procreation) can be done using honest and pure means which helps us reach a holy end (path of *Dharma*) and which ultimately also leads to what is known as *Moksha or liberation*.

Mani Bhaumik, author of *'Code name God'*, grew up in poverty and deprivation, but he had the guidance of his father, who was a freedom fighter, and of his great loving grandmother and another old lady who had been a close disciple of Mahatma Gandhi. The memories of his association with Mahatma Gandhi and with the two ladies mentioned above had a tremendous impact on the brain of Bhaumik. Strong negative perceptions about the contemporary Indian society in which he grew up - a society that was badly caste ridden and poverty ridden - remained a major driving force for his ambition to beat both handicaps and excel in life. But at the same time, fond memories of the love and affection of his grandmother and the other old lady, the disciple of Gandhi, filled him with positive vibes that remained with him all through and gave him a healthy respectful attitude for the reality around him.

The world had already become totally stratified at several macro and micro levels, with pockets of extreme richness coexisting with pockets of abject poverty and Bhaumik's young brain could not come to terms with this. And it triggered off in him a strong desire to run madly after wealth, recognition and social status in American Society. Although he used instruments of science and technology to realise his materialistic goals, he also continued his search for a scientific explanation to what we would otherwise call God.

He begins by saying; 'Classical physics, with its mechanistic view of the cosmos, has cut God off from man's psyche, leaving in its post-operative haste, an open wound of spiritual despair, tyranny and endless war.' In order to teach humanity how to heal that wound, Bhaumik has very lucidly explained the way to look at a convergence of science and spirituality and its view of reality. Working systematically towards the goal of *healing the wound*, he has concluded; 'By severing mind from matter, the Cartesian divide provided a justification for our thinking that we are not responsible for our actions, that our consciousness is merely a passive spectator to events.' Contrary to the tenets of Cartesianism, Bhaumik suggests a convergence between the most fundamental levels of physical reality and the consciousness. Science now shows us that our consciousness plays an active role in determining our actions and in bringing out specific manifestations of nature. He goes on to suggest that we are a part of something much larger - which is referred to as *"one source"*. Perhaps our sense of morality stems from the realization that we are indeed a part of something much larger than ourselves. Therefore, our actions should be in accordance with that knowledge. When we act from this realization, we bridge the Cartesian divide of mind and matter and the wound it caused is healed.

The binary code of happiness

Happiness can be achieved through a simple binary format of 'yes' or 'no'. The mind keeps the whole system of body, mind and soul in harmony depending on the time, space and position of any human being. Happiness is a state of mind; when the mind feels that it is content with what it has and what he has achieved, be it for a moment, an hour, a day, a week, a month or a year. But it always boils down only to a thought created in the mind at a particular moment that points to which state the whole being reaches, whether it is happiness or not. Now, suppose we feel that eating two scoops of ice cream when we enter into an ice cream parlor would be fantastic, but for some reason we manage only one scoop, there is every possibility that our mind will keep harping on the lack of ice cream rather than focus on the only one scoop of ice cream we can still enjoy. Here the role of mind comes into play. In a fraction of a second, the mind can analyse the situation and trigger emotional feelings inside the brain and heart that will suggest that if getting one scoop is enough at that point of time, considering the prevailing circumstances, then there is every possibility that the mind and hence all our sense organs will relish and savour that single scoop. Thus, we can reach a state of ultimate happiness. This is one of the simplest examples. Similarly, we can take the example of our performance in examination, in work projects, in competitive sports, in art or cultural performances, in political contests etc.

We must break down everything into that binary code of 'yes' or 'no'. If we can mentally reinforce the notion that we do have everything we deserve, then there is no reason for the mind not to be happy. If we believe otherwise, it can trigger unhappiness. This state is achievable through maturity. Sometimes, we keep comparing ourselves with others and get frustrated by seeing what we have. And this leads us to a constant comparison of the material gifts that we accrue. Hence, we tend to be happy or unhappy depending on what we analyse and how we analyse it.

Just comparing and arriving at a conclusion is not everything though. The amount of pain and effort one has gone through to achieve the end result will decide whether we are in our sound state of mind to fully appreciate our own gifts from God. Sometimes, if we intrinsically fine tune our souls, we can see that what God gives us is much more than what we could ever dream. This kind of feeling and thought can trigger an ocean of happiness. But it all begins with that simple binary code of 'yes' or 'no'.

Any stress that a man feels causes a state of unhappiness. Disease, accidents or a sudden natural calamity would cause temporary setbacks, which in turn can cause immense agony and stress. But in a normal situation, the state of unhappiness finds its roots within the human mind which fails to achieve a harmonious balance in its thought processes.

We are all born with ambition, ego, inquisitiveness, the zeal to do something worthwhile for ourselves, our family and society, but circumstances and our ability to come to terms with day-to-day happenings decides our ultimate fate. When we compare ourselves with others, and do not feel inspired by their achievement but rather become jealous of it, then the seeds of stress are sowed and hence the state of unhappiness sets in. This is where the binary format comes in. If we say 'yes' to inspiration, we will continue to remain happy and if we say 'yes' to jealousy, we will surely become unhappy.

Research by some American social scientists suggests that we imagine and think that what we like is also liked by others and vice versa. But this means that if we find something contrary to what we expect, there is every likelihood of our inner harmonious feelings getting imbalanced. We may experience anxiety, anger and hatred depending upon the intensity of the bad feeling generated by this imbalance. Sometimes differing views, and rejection of our own views, can cause stress to us. Here, if we can say 'yes' to the fact that every human being has a right to his own opinion, his own thought processes, to the beauty that Nature has endowed the human species with, then we will quickly reach a state of happiness because then the imbalance will vanish and we will be able to respect others and their feelings. As a result, harmony will be quickly established.

If we say 'no' and keep harping on why the other person does not like the thing we like, why he isn't falling in line with what we think is correct, then there is every possibility that we would be inviting agony, mistrust, ill-feelings and hence create stress for ourselves that will ultimately lead to a state of unhappiness. *To remain content with what we have* is a misnomer. Sometimes people think such statements are anti-growth or anti-aspirational. But actually they are not. Working with a goal for higher achievement is possible while remaining content with the result we obtain.

Bits and bytes of happiness: Cracking the Code

For a toddler who does not make any *conscious* attempt to attain happiness, because his focus is primarily on the instincts of hunger and physical comfort, happiness itself could consist of satisfaction of just these two things. If you keep a toddler's stomach filled and keep him in a normal healthy physical surrounding, he will, without a doubt, be the sort of kid who will smile at any person he sees. He is definitely a happy being, even though he is a baby. Just try this, with a newborn, anywhere in the world for a year: provide him with a reasonably happy atmosphere at home and neighbourhood, let him mix with family and friends, feed him properly, and you can see him dance to music in a way that even an eleven year old boy or twenty-one year old adult might fail to match. Such is the power of a *clean soul* who is newly born and only one year into life on earth.

For a growing child who is in kindergarten or primary school, the circumstances necessary for his happiness change slightly. He will be happy if he sees other kids of his size around him, and if he hears kind words from his parents and teachers in the course of his interactions with them at home or at school. And of course the other factors that we saw in the case of a toddler - food, shelter, comfortable environment and other basic needs – apply here as well. And if the child is able to keep learning more about the world - about how to communicate, about the basics of structured language, the essence of how the natural world is functioning around him, about earth and the solar system, the animals and birds, the food we eat, the different modes of travel like cars, buses, trains and airplanes, about the various games that he can play with those around him using sports equipment like balls, bats, rackets, sticks, boards, etc. or even games like hide and seek - and gets love and affection both at home and at school, the growing child will continue his happy journey. Researchers in the field have developed tools to impart education to small children through pictures, toys and miniature objects. These are the ingredients for his happiness; certain things that allow him to adequately and constantly explore his world.

However, once the pressure of parents and teachers start mounting on him to perform better - be it at studies, at games & sports, at music and art, at household chores or at any other activity - through a mode called *competition and comparison*, there is every chance that the basic constitution of the child will not allow him to accept this pressure in a way that his teachers, parents, siblings or friends will be expecting him to. If he is naturally driven to excel in some field and keeps getting stimulated by his environment to continue in that direction, perhaps he will enjoy the thrill of performing well in that particular field and may even enjoy the feedback that he gets from his surrounding in the form of appreciation, awards and/or rewards. As a result, the level of his inner happiness might not get affected. But on the other hand, if the child does not intrinsically take well to pressure, it is almost certain that the seed of unhappiness will be sown in the child very early on in life. At another level, be it a child or a toddler, if he is feeling uncomfortable due to sickness, he will not be happy until he is cured of the illness.

I was talking the other day to an electric contractor who was assigned the job of checking the wiring of my house where we were supposed to move in shortly in Bhubaneswar and repairing the faulty lines. He was also assigned the job of replacing dysfunctional electrical joints and making few new ones as per our requirement. After a long day's work, I offered him a cup of tea and we were chatting leisurely over the cup of tea. He was recounting his experience of working in a north Indian town named Jalandhar where he claimed people had good money mainly because of expatriates. The independent houses there were mostly plus buildings with decorative features. He was trying to express about his joyous feelings while working in those areas since he was having an opportunity to be creative in his craft. He said, "There is a lot of pleasure in such jobs because there was an inherent competitive spirit amongst different electrical contractors working in neighbouring houses to come out with better lighting and aesthetics". At the same time, he mentioned how boring and lifeless it was to carry out same sort of electrical wiring and fittings in a multistoried complex where the promoter-builder provides only one specification for each apartment. The monotonous nature of such job was much less enjoyable for this contractor who derived pleasure out of the competitive environment existing in the area where he had ample scope to showcase his talent in independent houses. Such examples demonstrate that competition that comes to mind naturally and automatically is refreshing and enjoyable than which is imposed by environment.

Let us now see how we meet with unhappiness as an adult. Our needs are all rooted in human aspirations. Depending on the state of development we are in, we long and desire to get something tangible in accordance with our needs. And as long as we keep getting it, we will feel happy both within and outside. Moving on from the very basic needs like food, clothing and shelter, once we step up into the next level of the hierarchy of needs, happiness could lie in achieving a satisfying result during a semester, or getting a position in the class, or getting a place in the college sports team, or captaining the national basketball or cricket team, or getting a chance to perform on stage, or win an art competition, or showcase the painting in an art exhibition or art gallery. Or, at another level, happiness could lie in buying an attractive electronic gadget, a swanky car or a big house. At yet another level, it could lie in stardom in the entertainment industry or in journalism or in literary circles, in corporate ladder or even in political landscape of a state or country. For people engaged in scientific pursuits, it could lie in overcoming the challenges of solving practical problems, or to answer mysteries of nature. One can derive happiness through getting motivated to work harder and inch towards unraveling the mysteries of nature or bringing out a solution for the problems that plague society. To some higher souls, when all earthly needs are fulfilled, there will only be longing for service. Does it not vary tremendously? So then what is the common thread running through all of this? The answer might appear to be very complicated, but in reality we can decode the nuances if we think on it a little more and start joining the dots together.

Even as I write, I can give a personal example of having experienced feelings ranging between two extremes, of feeling wretched at one point and sublime happy the next – and all within just two hours.

I was to board a flight to Delhi, and I left my home in Kolkata to catch a taxi very early in the morning (6 a.m.) of a wintry day. When I asked about his willingness to take me to the airport, the taxi driver welcomed me heartily, and this gave me a kick of happiness because of his readiness, a rarity. Once my luggage was inside, as I was taking my seat inside the car, I was suddenly told by the taxi driver that I should dole out about thirty percent more than the usual taxi fare to airport. I felt very irritated, almost angry (at the driver as an individual) and frustrated (with the culture of materialism and money that we are all getting trapped in, and which this innocuous taxi driver not being spared of). I protested and offered to get down and try another taxi. And all the while I was agitatedly telling him also that he should have placed his conditions before offering to drop me with a smiling face. I had hired a taxi just a little over two weeks back, from the same spot, for the same flight, and I knew what I was saying.

With some argument, and when I insisted in front of another taxi fellow who glanced at us having this conversation, this taxi driver quickly climbed down with a compromising stand, and he said unhappily with folded hands; 'Okay Sir, give me whatever you want and please do not be angry.' The taxi sped off towards the airport and I felt the usual urge inside me to pass some judgmental comments on the driver with regards to my recent experience, tell him about how he was wrong and how he should behave in this world to remain happy. Fighting against the burning passion in me to start lecturing, I tried to stay cool and thought of starting a different conversation. I asked; 'Do you live in the neighborhood and own the taxi or do you just drive it on your owner's behalf?' The taxi driver was a middle aged fellow in his late forties, but the long conversation that I could get him to participate with me in, during the one hour drive, was no less enlightening to me than any other event that has shaped my intellect and thought processes so far.

He had two sons. The elder one had passed his B.Sc. examinations; the younger one was in class IX. The stockily built man had run away from his home in a remote village in Muzzafarpur district of Bihar, at the age of fourteen. That was in the year 1979. For the first four or five years, he'd worked with a *Marwari* businessman for whom he was full of praise. The man had shown him much compassion during his initial years in Kolkata. I prodded further and asked what made him run away as a fugitive, just to probe a bit about the criminal intent in him. I wanted to know if it was in him even at that age. And if that was the reason why he was still using such unlawful tactics to get money out of his gullible customers today, thirty-five years later. What came as his reply was not only totally different to my expectation but also enlightening for me.

He said; 'No Sir, my father was so strict and religious that he would not deviate an inch from his principles, and he would not allow me to work harder either. When I saw this, I wondered how we would be able to feed ourselves if we lived a life based on such cruel principles. How would my three sisters get married? My anxiety about my sisters' marriage forced me to take the risk, and I moved out of the village with one of my uncles and came to Kolkata. I bought my first taxi about twenty-six years ago and since then I've been working very hard, day and night, to bring up my two sons, give them the best education, best food and clothes so that they grow up to be well-educated citizens. My elder son who has just passed his Bachelor of Science degree is surely going to get some government job and I do not have an iota of doubt about that. He is already applying for different positions and it won't be too long before he cracks a good job. I am pretty confident about that.' When I asked about his parents and his home in the village etc., he was equally open and said, "I treat my father as no less than God and he and my mother are very fond of the two sons of my younger brother - who runs a business in the village. My parents visit me often here in Kolkata. They stay with me for some time and then go back to the village. My family and I visit our village every year too.'

While discussing in general, the taxi driver's life in Kolkata, he said; 'Sir, earlier on it was a much better and much more enjoyable life, but it is not so these days.'

I thought I was being clever and said; 'Is it because of the large number of taxis that have come up now? Is the stiff competition killing your business?'

This was his reply: 'No Sir, the number of taxis is never too high. Let the number go as high as it can; there is ample scope for everyone to earn his share in this great city of Kolkata with the vast number of people and infinite opportunities.'

The two profound remarks I heard during the course of this conversation gave me the happiness I'd always looked for - converting my unhappy mood to a very somber and happy one. The reason for this was the idea that such a young village lad from Bihar would think of his responsibility to his family and be adventurous enough to come and try his luck in the difficult world of Kolkata and, even after nearly three and half decades of hard living, still maintain the pristine sanctity of the soul saying that 'Competition is not to be blamed.' The *love for his fraternity* (taxi drivers), *the love for the job he does* (taxi driving), and *the love for the family* he worked for was clearly visible. For me, the two legs of the simple harmonic motion represented by two extremes, from one moment of anger mixed with unhappiness (when the taxi driver charged an exorbitant price and tried to exploit me) to the other extreme of blissful happiness (when I saw and learnt about the vibrant and progressive minded human soul ticking inside the same man), were clearly discernible in so far as emotional feeling in me was concerned. Had I not initiated the conversation with the taxi driver that I finally did, I would not have learnt about some of the great personality traits that the same taxi driver possessed. Such notions can generate appreciation about a person which is essentially positive feeling and that can overcome the earlier negative feeling created against the same person due to some reason. This is an example of how the unhappiness arising from our interactions with people can actually be found to be rooted in our ignorance about the broader canvas.

Happiness is just one thought and emotion away

Depending upon how much aware we are about our own self and surroundings, the reason why a thought crosses our mind is closely interlinked to several facets of life which act as *filters*. The first of these is our *belief system*. This belief system is rooted in our *Sanskars*, which we carry with us from previous births and which keep getting reinforced through the previously described SARMA-SIR model in the present life. Second is the relevant information which is fed into our brain by the environment. Third is the personal experience that we gather along our present journey of life. These three facets of life or *filters* decide the perception which we build about any particular event, issue or matter in our daily lives. This perception then gives rise to a thought. Since the speed with which each of these elements responsible for the generation of a single thought operates is extremely fast, we as ordinary mortals fail to catch the significance of the entire process. Only a true *Yogi* has the heightened level of awareness to watch, in a sublime manner, how a single thought gets to cross his mind. Once this thought is generated, it invariably creates a feeling associated with it. Depending upon the quality of the thought, the emotion that is generated is a happy feeling or the opposite of that.

Generally, happy people are productive people. This means productivity is directly proportional to how happy one is. Disgruntled people may produce more through working extra hours and by forcefully extracting work out of others, but this will never last long because the negative emotions of the unhappy person will have reduced his productivity in the long run. Hence happiness can also be construed as something representing a balanced state of mind, a state in which one can put his best foot forward and also give his best to the job at hand. Circumstances and situations can vary dramatically from moment to moment, but with proper prioritization and goal setting, if one can give his all to everything he does, he will definitely remain happy. Mahatma Gandhi has expressed his guilt in his autobiography over allowing his basal instincts for pleasure to overshadow his otherwise strong determination to serve his parents.

Obviously guilty feelings are contrary to happiness. Similarly, in the priorities and goals that we set for ourselves, if some untoward incident arises due to problems at home or at the workplace, or in a public place, or caused by natural disasters, then our focus is forcibly shifted. It is the ability of maintaining a balanced state of mind and accepting such situations as they come which can create a happy state of mind. Talking to oneself by self-counseling on all such issues can improve sustainability of happy feelings. By compensating for lost time and opportunity through filling the gap with fresh ideas and energy, by trying new avenues and grabbing at newer opportunities appearing on the horizon, one can maintain the happiness budget fairly well.

Was it real or illusory?

I shall describe two incidents, apparently unrelated, but the neural network created and recorded inside my brain during those two incidents suggests there is somehow a connection. This connection is an important one for me and also for the theme of the book. During early part of my professional career, one afternoon after the lunch break, I was casually strolling towards the main door of our office building in Dehradun, India when I was stopped by one of my close friends coming from the opposite direction on a bike. Two of us straightway went into chatting on the roadside! My friend spontaneously commented, "When I saw you coming from the other direction, you really looked so contented as if you have got everything and achieved everything that life has to offer". The time was about a couple of years into my professional life after completion of my basic education and acquiring professional qualification; circa 1987. I was still a bachelor and for a person like me coming from the humble middle class background, from the small town of Keonjhar, Odisha, the taste of 'life with a girlfriend' was out of question either. Many people may debate and try to rationalise the reason why he said so. But seeing the *spontaneity*, I could visualize that I perhaps did radiate in my casual walking style some kind of appearance that apparently reflected inner contentment!

The second incident occurred more than a decade later. I was returning home from the Thebarton Campus of the University of Adelaide, where the then National Center for Petroleum Geology and Geophysics was located. I was actually heading towards my home; about five minutes' walk in the same suburb, returning after a day's work in the PhD research project. I was walking perhaps leisurely without any hurry normally seen in so-called developed world when I heard a female voice calling my name from behind and turning back, I saw one PhD colleague of mine in the same department, who was also returning from work to go to her home. Year was 1998. Normally she used to go towards the bus stop about half a km away from our Research Centre to board the particular evening bus for her home, about one hour drive from that point. The road both of us took was the daily route we used to undertake from the University campus. My home was so nearby, less than a kilometer and perhaps I did not bother to walk fast. Whatever may be the reason at that point of time, she commented something unusual that day, "PK, you look so happy and contented".

It was so spontaneous that it caught my breath. I was a bit baffled because there was no obvious reason for her to comment on me at that particular moment of time. I should also mention that there was no apparent reason at all, neither through the entire day nor through the previous few moments of that particular day, that would have urged her to give such a generalized statement about me which she had never given earlier. I was also surprised why someone, that to a female colleague from a background completely different including different nationality (European) would comment on me like this!!

Was the feeling of happiness and contentment *real* within me in both the occasions as I experienced or was it illusory to two separate individuals, one very handsome young unmarried male friend of mine and another, very beautiful and married female friend of me. One was an Indian Hindu coming from the same state of Odisha to which I belong and culturally almost the same background and another, from Christian faith and hailing from an European nation and thus brought up in a totally different culture.

If we analyse the thought processes involved during the above two incidents, we can have a peep into what human consciousness is and how it works. Both of my friends must be internally hungry for happiness and contentment at the time for their own reasons. Both of them had generated a perception about me from the way I generally presented to them and particularly the way I was walking when they saw me in both occasions, that I must be a very happy and contented person, at least till the time I had been interacting with both of them so far.

But then, long after both these incidents passed, the kind of mental stress and anxiety I went through prior to my hospitalization in Adelaide for the deadly mental health crisis, followed by severe panic attacks for at least one and half years, belie such an interpretation about my overall personality. So what was *real* and what was *illusory?*

At least one thing is crystal clear and absolutely certain. A person who was so happy and content with his life for nearly thirty six years, the fact quite distinctly picked up by two separate individuals from two different backgrounds and at two different geographical locations with a gap of one decade, however, broke all rules of the game and fell utterly sick in just another two years! So while happiness and contentment may not be easy to achieve but certainly not at all difficult to lose!

As I write these words, if I can create a mental picture in you about the whole perspective of what I mean by happiness and how important it is for all of us; I would say, the conscious thoughts I am generating while writing, are powerful enough to have the latent potential to create vibrational energy within your brain's perceptible neurons and associated neural network to enable a proper meaning to be obtained. And this entire chain of thought processes involving four persons, myself, both my friends and you as the reader can together make some sense provided the invisible forces, subatomic particles, particle waves etc. during the respective thought level interactions create a coherent underpinning possible to be coded and decoded with the same meaning I am trying to convey with so long a gap of time in between.

CHAPTER 6

UNIVERSE, EARTH AND SOUL - AREN'T THEY ALL EXPANDING?

The Big Bang and the Universe

A brief discussion about the prevalent concept of an expanding Universe and expanding Earth adapted from Wikipedia is presented so as to lead on to the concept of an expanding soul - which is generally not talked about either in the domain of science or spirituality. It may be difficult to imagine but in spite of the name, the Big Bang did not occur as an explosion, not in the usual way one might think. The Universe did not expand into space since space did not exist before the Universe. Instead, it is better to think of the Big Bang as the simultaneous appearance of space everywhere in the Universe. The Universe has not expanded from any one point since the Big Bang — rather; space itself has been stretching, and carrying matter with it. The whole question about separation of matter and energy at one level may then become irrelevant.

Since the Universe, by its very definition, encompasses all of space and time as we know it, it is beyond the theory of the Big Bang to say what the Universe is expanding into or what gave rise to the Big Bang. Although there are models that speculate about these questions, none of them have made realistic testable predictions as of yet.

The Universe is currently estimated to be roughly 13.7 billion years old, give or take a few million years. In comparison, the solar system is only about 4.6 billion years old. This estimate is generally derived by measuring the composition of matter and energy density in the Universe. This has allowed researchers to compute how fast the Universe expanded in the past. With that knowledge, they could

124

turn the clock back and extrapolate when the Big Bang happened. Obviously, the time between then and now is the age of the Universe.

Physicists believe that in the earliest moments of the Universe, there was no structure to it, so to speak. Matter and energy were distributed nearly uniformly throughout. The gravitational pull of small fluctuations (we still do not know who caused it, why and how) in the density of matter back then, gave rise to the vast web-like structure of stars and emptiness that we see today. Dense regions pulled in more and more matter through gravity, and the more massive they became, the more matter they could attract through gravity – thereby forming stars, galaxies and larger structures known as clusters, super clusters, filaments and walls, with "great walls" of thousands of galaxies reaching more than a billion light years in length. Less dense regions did not grow, evolving instead into areas of seemingly empty space called voids.

Until about thirty years ago, astronomers thought that the Universe was composed almost entirely of ordinary atoms or *baryonic matter*. However, recently there has been increasing evidence to suggest that most of the ingredients that go into making up the Universe come in forms that we cannot see. It is estimated that atoms only make up 4.6 percent of the Universe. Of the remainder, twenty-three percent is made up of *dark matter* - which is likely to be composed of one or more species of subatomic particles that interact very weakly with ordinary matter - and seventy-two percent is made of *dark energy,* which is believed to be driving the accelerating expansion of the Universe. When it comes to the atoms we are familiar with, hydrogen makes up about seventy-five percent, while helium makes up about twenty-five percent. Heavier elements make up only a tiny fraction of the universe's atoms.

It is suggested that the shape of the Universe and whether it is finite or infinite in extent depends on the struggle between the rate of its expansion and the pull of gravity. The strength of the pull in question depends partly on the density of the matter in the Universe. If the density of the Universe exceeds a specific critical value, then the Universe becomes "closed" and "positively curved" like the surface of a sphere. This would then mean that light beams which are initially parallel will converge slowly, eventually cross and return back to their starting point, if the Universe lasts long enough. If so, the Universe is not infinite but still has no end, just as the area on the surface of a sphere is not infinite but has neither a beginning nor an end. The Universe will eventually stop expanding and start collapsing in on itself - the so-called "Big Crunch."

Expanding Universe

Astronomer Edwin Hubble discovered in the 1920s that the Universe is not static, but expanding - a finding that revealed that the Universe was apparently born from a Big Bang. After that, it was long thought that the gravity of matter in the Universe was certain to slow the expansion of the Universe. Then, in 1998, the Hubble Space Telescope's observations of very distant supernovae revealed that, a long time ago, the Universe was expanding more slowly than it is today. In other words, the expansion of the Universe was not slowing down due to gravity, but instead, inexplicably, it was accelerating! The name for the unknown force driving this accelerating expansion is *dark energy*, and it remains one of the greatest mysteries of science!

Expanding Earth

In recent years, one of the controversial theories gaining ground in geology is the Expanding Earth theory. From the earliest classes in school to the most advanced of university geology lectures, we are all taught that the size of the Earth has been constant and unchanging for thousands of millions of years. Obviously when some scientific evidence was presented to support the expanding earth theory, it received usual cold response from scientific community.

Stephen Harrell argues in the book *'Dinosaurs and the Expanding Earth'* that the bones of the larger dinosaurs were too weak to support their own body weight. Their bones should have buckled and cracked because of their huge size compared to their size of the bones. And yet the fossil bones in museums around the world show that these giants thrived in their own world of hundreds of millions of years ago. Obviously a question arises, how can both these things be true?

There is one simple and yet astonishing answer, as they suggest. The size of all life is controlled by gravity. A stronger gravitational force would tend to reduce the size of life whilst a weaker one would allow life to become larger. Dinosaurs might have become so huge because the Earth's surface gravity was weaker in a Reduced Gravity Earth Model. The explanation is beautifully simple in its clarification of the dinosaurs' gigantic size. Using the concept of an increasing gravitational force allows the envisioning of a fascinating new theory in which the gigantic animals of the past were forced, along their evolutionary journey, to become smaller as the Earth's gravitational force increased to the present day level. I am not sure yet, because my field of science is vastly different, whether there has been any research at studying the fundamental building block of life, i.e., DNA of Dinosaurs and Kangaroos and whether they could be correlated. I am pleading this because, during my stay in Australia, the first ever sight of a kangaroo created a strange thought in me, 'I have seen images of Dinosaurs and Kangaroos in India and here I am seeing a kangaroo in real. But it looks so much like it is a descendant of the proverbial Dinosaur!' I can vouch for the non-intentional nature of this thought. It was simply at the reaction to the visual sensory organ's output after seeing the kangaroo, this thought emerged from nowhere. Internet searches after nearly eighteen years past that thought in my mind (when I was perfectly alright, mentally stable and well reasoning), some fringe research has started to be published particularly with respect to cloning attempts. If genetically, it can be seen that dinosaurs and kangaroos are somehow related, then the expanding earth theory will be unquestionably proved beyond doubt. But for this, not only geological evidence but also biological evidence will hold the key.

Dr. James Maxlow also argues that, on an expanding Earth, the surface gravity during the Precambrian Eras would be about one third of the present value, and about one half of the present value during the Mesozoic Era. The Mesozoic Era of course was the Era of the dinosaurs, those very large and very long bodied creatures which could very well have benefited from a much lower surface gravity. For a planet undergoing expansion as a result of an increase in mass over time, the surface gravity during the Triassic Period would have been approximately fifty percent of the present value. This would have then increased to approximately seventy-five percent of the present value during the Late Cretaceous Period.

Considering the large size and length of many dinosaur species, this much-reduced surface gravity would have benefited their existence and mobility immensely. The progressive increase in surface gravity over time may then also offer an additional explanation for the relatively rapid extinction of dinosaur species throughout their long history.

The most widely known geological evidence for Earth's expansion is a simple reconstruction of the ancient continents and of the ancient ocean floor, like a gigantic jigsaw puzzle. The continents are ancient and some regions have existed for more than three thousand and eight hundred million years, but on a geological time scale, the ocean floor is relatively young and ranges from only about two hundred million years old near the continents to areas around the mid-ocean ridges that are still forming today. When the dinosaurs first evolved, none of today's ocean floors existed. It is hard to imagine therefore, that the entire ancient ocean floor fit together so precisely to form the complete sphere that was the ancient Earth. Some scientists believe that if the missing ancient ocean floor had been generated by any process other than the expansion of the Earth, it would be unlikely for the areas to be in the exact shapes required to reconstruct a smaller Earth. It would have been more probable for irregular shapes that didn't fit together to exist. The probability of the expanding Earth forming by chance is so low it seems impossible. It is similar to arguing that a jigsaw puzzle fits together by chance rather than due to any logical reason!

Samuel Warren Carey, an Australian geologist, was an early advocate of the theory of continental drift. His work on tectonic plate reconstructions led him to develop the Expanding Earth hypothesis. Carey was greatly influenced by a book by Alfred Wegener who was one of the earliest proponents of the idea of moving continents (*'The Origin of Continents and Oceans'*). Carey backed the theory of moving continents proposed by Alfred Wegener and decided on the Expanding Earth theory as the mechanism for this, and was the main proponent of this hypothesis. He and a small number of other researchers continued to support and investigate expanding Earth models. Carey developed his expanding Earth model independently of the work done prior by Ott Christopher Hilgenberg, who proposed a similar model in his 1933 publication 'Vom wachsenden Erdball' ('The Expanding Earth').

Carey's expanding Earth bears many resemblances to the current model, including supercontinents dividing and going adrift, zones of new crust being generated in deep oceanic ridges, and other phenomena of a still active crust. His hypothesis gave the mechanisms to back an Expanding Earth Theory, and the more widely accepted model of plate tectonics accounted for it with subduction. Although Carey did not believe in subduction, which refers to heavy oceanic crust going below the lighter continental crust, there is much geological evidence to support the theory of subduction. Few budding geoscientists believe that we could have both the concepts, subduction of crust and expansion of Earth, working simultaneously and complimentary to each other.

Search for Truth is not illusory

We were attending a workshop cum internal brainstorming session conducted sometime in 1998 by what was then the Australian Petroleum Cooperative Research Centre at Melbourne. During the lunch break, all the participants were relaxing on a sandy beach. I was speaking with a middle-aged Australian mathematics research scholar of British origin who was engaged in reservoir modeling work and who suddenly asked me a question that caught me unawares.

He was grappling with the question of whether it was *matter* or *spirit* which came first into the world. Another similar question was put to me, at around the same time, by another gentleman, a Romanian, about whether consciousness exists in animals. These two divergent queries made me aware that what we see in the developed world, the so-called western world, should not be loosely termed as brash materialistic pursuit. The search for Truth and the interest in separateness of matter and spirit has been an integral part of the human quest everywhere in the world, and it is not restricted to geographic boundaries or monopolized by any country, community, sect or culture. With progressive evolution of modern man, from ancestral homosapiens that evolved from homo erectus or homo habilis, or with the mixture of genetic material of Neanderthals even, this eternal quest has always been with a part of man's existence. And it has produced many great masters over different generations. Lord Buddha, Lord Mahavira, Lord Jesus and Guru Nanak in older generations, and Swami Vivekananda or even Mahatma Gandhi in what are relatively more recent generations, have all followed the same path with pure divinity in their hearts and minds.

Going by the origin of the Universe, as physicists would have us believe, there was nothing in the beginning. And hence matter would have to come first before spirit evolved. But it is hard to imagine how the two can be different. Spirit is all pervading and is an expression of what we call God, and I believe that they are just two ways of looking at the same thing. Perspectives may be different, but they are both part of the same system. They cannot truly have any separate beginning or end. The idea is irrelevant because what we see and feel about beginning or end of any event happening in our world before us is very real - and if the Universe exists today or is thought to exist, then there is nothing that can convince us that it will *only* end and not begin again. I believe it is a cyclic process and will continue just like it is said by Lord Krishna in the *Bhagawat Gita* so lucidly. Ordinary mortals cannot understand this simple truth so easily, but in a closer analysis supported by scientific research, results and theories, we can easily understand. Recent ideas about whether time moves only in one direction (creation of Universe following the Big Bang and time just rolling on) or in the reverse direction also are all just pointers to the same conundrum.

Modern science has been unfolding mysteries of the Universe in a manner that is understandable to the common man. Although some people claim that the Vedanta knowledge of ancient Indian culture was full of such wisdom, I firmly believe that modern science and technology have been able to translate that knowledge and wisdom into information that is easily decipherable to us. Yesteryears' knowledge, when challenged, gives rise to new knowledge today. There are various theories regarding evolution, both in the scientific domain and in the religious domain. Life as we know it on Earth today perhaps started taking shape with unicellular organisms and is dated to be around 3.5 billion years old. There is increasing scientific evidence to refine such knowledge as more and more research is undertaken. Both biology and physics are evolving in such a manner that most of the questions that remained unanswered till end of the twentieth century are being explained now.

Few simple examples to illustrate this point: Once upon a time, the Earth was considered to be flat. This has now been disproved beyond all doubt. The idea that the Earth is divided into several crustal plates which are moving over a hot mantle in a conveyor belt fashion has been around for less than a century. Paleontology and anthropology have helped us trace our ancestors back a few million years. As per current knowledge, the Earth is about 3.7 - 4.5 billion years old whereas our Universe is about fourteen to fifteen billion years old. Obviously none of us existed during the ancient history of either the Earth or the Universe. It is through progressive evolution that we have reached this state. Particle physics has been unraveling the smallest of small particles that constitute known matter in the Universe. Knowledge about the existence of Subatomic particles is hardly a century old. Speed of light, which was considered a constant for a century, is now being thought to be varying.

I feel as if I am a witness to how evolving concepts of science are currently progressing. This information can bring forth some interesting insight to the uninitiated. Before moving to Australia for my PhD in Petroleum Geophysics, I was not at all aware of any concept of an expanding Earth although, as a Geoscience student, I was quite aware of concepts like plate tectonics, crustal plate movements, new crust generation at Mid Oceanic Ridges, movement of oceanic crust underneath continental crust, otherwise known as subduction phenomenon etc. I recall that during the first few months of my literature review period, I was scanning the University of Adelaide's Central Library at North Terrace Campus for a few reference books. A book titled *'Expanding Earth by S. W. Carey, Professor of University of Tasmania'* in the reference books' racks caught my attention and I became curious. I immediately borrowed the book and started reading through it in our Thebarton campus although it was not really related to my core PhD project work.

One day, when my guide saw me reading the book, he cautioned me; 'PK, be careful, do not go near Tasmania; Carey will grab you and never let you go!' I asked my Professor whether he agreed to the theory of an expanding Earth. He curtly said; 'Nah! That is not possible; there is a problem according to the theory of physics because it violates the principle of conservation of mass.'

Somehow, this statement from my professor did not resonate with me at all. In some corner of my heart and mind, I felt convinced that the concept regarding expanding earth, which was absolutely new to me at that point of time, perhaps had some truth in it. May be my conviction stemmed from my awareness about the other related concept of an expanding Universe - which was widely accepted by then. The details of the physics of these two concepts were not known to me even though my gut feeling told me that they were both correct. Although I did put forward my argument to my professor, saying that the widely accepted concept in physics of an expanding Universe might entail a related phenomenon of an expanding Earth, and that I did not find any problem in accepting either of the theories, I did not have enough material to deal with the scientific reasoning from the realm of physics at the time. But now, after more than fifteen years, as I write these words, a simple internet search about the concept of an Expanding Earth brings up huge volume of literature, scientific evidence and a complete list of reference books dedicated to this expanding earth concept alone. Some of these books have been written based on material evidence gathered from diverse branches of science including geology and biology. This simple fact reiterates that no idea in this world is permanent as long as human intellect utilizes a scientific method of search and discovery and unravels new frontiers of knowledge that is currently in the domain of completely unknown.

Infinite to finite

Whatever humanity has achieved in terms of material growth and prosperity, there has been some amount of inspiration from somewhere sometime throughout the ages. The human spirit has been involved in all the incremental and revolutionary quantum leaps in progress and growth. Human ingenuity in science and technology has brought us almost to the door of that fantastic position of Heaven-like peace, happiness and tranquility. We make small mistakes when we do not recognize this simple truth and commit follies that drag us down to hunger, deprivation, poverty, exploitations, clashes, war and famine.

The philosophers have to bring a solution to such a problem. Innovation or scientific or technological invention needed creativity and skill of the highest order – which can have roots in the human brain only. The digital revolution and computer revolution have surpassed any growth witnessed before. If we look at it closely, these innovations have happened because of the undying spirit of man, which has resided in human body. To express any kind of innovation, the spirit had to take umbrage in the material form of the human body. The infinite spirit had to house itself within the confines of a physical body to give shape to all that was ever dreamt of or desired or likely to be desired in future. Hence, this tendency of the infinite spirit to house itself into finite form is a necessity. The problem arises when we ordinary souls transgress that simple philosophy and feel that happiness, tranquility and peace reside outside of our human body and try to achieve it all through material acquisition alone.

Although we might try to restrict everything in the form of boundaries, starting from our own walls of home and the compound wall around our plot of land, and may try to generate peace and happiness out of this specific space that is allotted to us, it is obvious that true happiness and bliss do not spring from these. Rather, it all comes from within the body which houses the infinite spirit that generates bliss and happiness. Our senses and sensual feelings try to derive wrong impressions and impose them upon our gullible minds, but it is the spirit within us which is the ultimate and will remain the ultimate even during any kind of destruction that any foul person or group of such persons can imagine or bring forth onto the Earth.

Modern day terrorists believe that if they can kill and destroy, they will achieve their misdirected goals, but it is futile to think that way. Such acts will bring in a new life that will overpower the ugliness. The true direction has to be in alignment with love and compassion of the human spirit and that is the only solution. Terrorism, in various forms have always been there but the failure of humanity to learn from environmental responses caused by follies of one group against another, mostly of exploitation of one group by the other, could also haunt back later making it a vicious cycle. Hence the solution, as Gandhi has put it, if someone hits you in one cheek, show him the other. Although it is difficult to fathom when such a realization would dawn on political leadership, but is certain that unless, people start believing in such a concept and work accordingly, terrorism would keep coming back albeit in a new avatar.

Instincts, Actions, Emotions & Spirit

The sperm and egg coming respectively from male and female may at best be guided through some interventional control by human beings to create a chance of fertilization. But the quality of it, the timing of fertilization, success of conceiving and ultimately the child's growth inside the mother's womb and the delivery cannot be indirectly or directly controlled by human intervention. Although today's IVF technology and genetic modifications have revolutionized these areas such that human babies can be almost engineered to predesigned needs, our civilization is yet to achieve social harmony that is prerequisite to maintaining a peaceful coexistence between different groups.

The moment a baby is born, there is nothing but instinct because, at the very early stage, conscious actions have not yet taken shape in the baby's mind. These instincts are in a way so evolved that human intervention cannot change them even if we wish to do so. Now, the actions based on instincts (the crying of the baby when he is hungry) are actions which the infant does not do consciously. Whereas when I am writing these words, it is very much a conscious decision, and hence a conscious action.

When we grow up, as per the inputs from both the natural and social environment that we experience around us, we develop positive, negative or neutral emotions. And the intensity with which we experience them is dependent upon our genetic makeup, and a bit of human intervention in the form of what our parents tried to make us learn, including natural and social behavioral patterns. The greatest mystery lies here in the fact that we grow up as separate individuals, with unique characteristics, based on the extraordinary combination of the genetic material in us as well as the responses they trigger in us to stimuli from the surrounding environment.

Whatever positive attributes we pick up in our infanthood (purely from sensual images and feelings reacting with our genetic makeup) get reinforced during our interactions during childhood, and into adulthood, with our social and natural environment. For example, great famines, war and natural calamities all have a different impact on the minds of growing souls when they occur. They shape us into different individuals. A good example is that of Professor Amartya Sen who was tremendously influenced during his growing years by the Great Famine of the 1950's in India which caused millions to die and suffer from hunger. Even after growing up later to become an economist of international repute (winning the Nobel Prize in Economics), he never lost sight of *developmental economics.* It was for this that he won the coveted prize. He worked on it all his life and did research on it well into his later years. The inborn instincts of curiosity, sensitivity to human pain and suffering and thinking about solutions to social problems all got reinforced from that recent incident of famine which he personally experienced. He therefore directed his energies towards what he thought he could do best to help humanity. Thus, positive emotions get reinforced in us throughout our lives as we get inputs from environment which are recorded as positive. And on the other hand, the negative emotions can either get reinforced or be corrected based on how we build a society around us. Modern-day terrorism is an offshoot of this complex phenomenon, of how we have built our society until now.

Emotions drive us to positive work or negative work whereas the spirit remains intact even though we get entangled in wrong doing. Here the effect of KARMA comes into the picture. Even if a person dies early for no fault of his, the positive emotions that he might have gathered along his short journey will get reinforced into his soul because that is how the soul evolves according to the *Bhagawat Gita* (shloka 2.13). We have similar ideas enshrined in Jain philosophy that suggest a scientific manner in which a soul gets a sort of layer encircling its fundamental core during each life, and how the composite gets passed to a person's next birth in his journey towards final liberation and salvation.

We must believe that the spirit always remains positive; or else it becomes difficult to explain the extraordinary growth in all fields and dimensions that we see around us. Notwithstanding the great wars that we have fought amongst ourselves, every once in a while, we have emerged victorious in terms of our understanding about human nature, its ultimate purpose and ultimate goal etc. It may appear that the Ultimate Truth has eluded us so far, but, as it is slowly getting evident, almost everything in the ether world is explainable through modern scientific theories and principles. The expanding nature of the soul can be deduced from the very fact that capacity in any dimension of life has always grown with each new generation. An average child is much more intelligent, innovative, stronger and faster compared to the average parent. It is not only the scientific temper, but the loving spirit which has grown tremendously in each generation. Skeptics will point out extremism, fanaticism, violence, killing, terrorism and other such social evils to refute the idea of the expansive nature of the soul's love. But in a population of seven billion, some souls will exhibit raw emotions, suffering from ignorance. And this is also easily explainable if we follow the tenets of the *Bhagawat Gita* (2.13). It says that the soul's journey is similar to the body's journey from childhood to adulthood to old age and decay. A soul, over a period of several births and deaths, moves up the ladder from darkness to light, from ignorance to wisdom, with consistent learning and assimilation in each birth.

Expanding soul

Given the way science and technology is headed today, it is safe to predict that if conclusive proof is available in future about expanding Universe and Earth, then it would not be a fantasy to imagine an "Expanding Soul". The simplest indication for this to be true would be the observation of development of human knowledge and wisdom which is multiplying increasingly over each successive generation. The last five or ten thousand years of human civilization has brought unbelievable data to us about Mother Nature and the Universe. And this is amply reflected in the way new generations are able to cope with the massive expansion and explosion of knowledge and wisdom which is happening all around us.

A five year old child is free and fearless enough to operate electronic gadgets that a fifty year old would be uncomfortable or even scared to use. How is it possible to see a five year old behaving more fearlessly than a fifty years old, if not in terms of physical prowess then certainly in terms of mental prowess? This is true in any corner of the globe. Obviously if the awareness level of a lower animal is less than a human's, with function of spirit remaining the same, due to the complexity of DNA structure of different animals, and if everything else remaining constant, the explosion in human capacity - if not on an individual scale but on a collective scale - is enormous, and this can be visualized in the way that the soul is expanding too. I have always wondered about Olympic records, about how they are broken during every successive Olympic event. Although not all records get broken at one go, in general, none of the Olympic records stands unconquered. Be it the sprint, the marathon, swimming or any other athletic event, the story is the same. This gives us a clue of the increasing power of the human soul. As a matter of fact, if the Earth is expanding and the Universe is expanding, is it so difficult to imagine the power of the brain-heart-mind combine and hence the soul expanding in a commensurate manner? Although we are far from establishing conclusively with the methods of objective science, what happens when we die, but research in these hitherto neglected areas have started telling us something astounding. During times of cardiac arrests, Dr. Sam Parnia writes in his book with the above title, *'What happens when we die'*, some patients have described quite vividly how the entire processes of resuscitation, or sometimes other medical procedures are viewed from above when doctors and paramedics had been working on their body. The *Near Death Experience* and *the Out of Body experience* described by some patients hold the clue to the true power of the soul and the way it decides its journey.

What are the ramifications of such a concept of an expanding soul? The power in the human brain is keeping pace with the speed of modern day developments in science and technology and that bodes quite well for the world and the human species from the standpoint of collective consciousness. It means that we can safely take care of all future problems, irrespective of what doomsday believers might say on the contrary. Moreover, the concept of an expanding soul can be ingrained in the thought processes of each future generation such that the world can be guided towards a more peaceful, loving and beautiful place than it is today – ridden with conflict and violence as it is.

CHAPTER 7

OUR INTERNAL UNIVERSE; NEURONS & NEURAL NETWORK

Neurons, Neurotransmitters and Neural Networks

I present below a brief discussion on the important matter of how our brain functions and responds to stimuli, mostly adapted from Wikipedia. Mental health issues have some roots in these aspects of brain although they may not be totally dependent on them. However, an understanding about such issues would help. Brain cells are called neurons and each neuron has two kinds of projections emanating from its cell body: branch-like message-receivers called *dendrites*, and spindly "fingers" like message transmitters called *axons*. Each neuron's dendrites and axons are intertwined with those of other neurons, and each neuron establishes between a thousand and thirty thousand discrete links with others, resulting in a complex web of interconnection inside the brain.

Neurons communicate through the exchange of molecules called *neurotransmitters* that travel in the microscopic spaces, called *synapses*, between dendrites and axons. Neurotransmitters are behave like three-dimensional "keys" that fit into "locks" called *receptors*. Only a particular neurotransmitter can fit into any individual receptor. However, there are multiple types of receptors, even for a single neurotransmitter. For example, five receptors have been identified for dopamine, while serotonin docks with fourteen receptors.

Axons, the neuron's message transmitters, are packed with tiny sacs, *vesicles,* each of which contain particular neurotransmitters. When the neuron sends the appropriate message, the vesicles release their neurotransmitters, flooding the synaptic gaps between axons and dendrites. A neurotransmitter locating its match attaches both physically, like a key, and electro-chemically - resulting in transmission of an electrical charge to the neuron. These exchanges, from the release of neurotransmitters to docking with receptors, the transmission of its electro-chemical message and the freeing of its receptor, take place in the tiniest fraction of a second and continue millions of times within a group of neurons until the supply of neurotransmitters are exhausted.

The electro-chemical exchange initiated by neurotransmitters triggers the neuron to respond with its own electrochemical reaction. Neurons exchange information in chain reactions of electro-chemical messaging along interconnected bundles of nerve cells called *neural networks*. Neurotransmitters stimulate or inhibit neural firing rates, depending on the type of neurotransmitter. The most common neurotransmitters in the brain are the glutamate/GABA (gamma-aminobutyric acid) pair. Glutamates stimulate neural activity, while its opposite, GABA, depresses it. Dopamine stimulates the brain's reward centre to experience pleasure. Dopamine is also involved in the processes of learning, memory and motivation. Other neurotransmitters which are said to be involved in addiction include: opioids, the body's natural pain killers; serotonin, which is involved in mood regulation; cannabinoids, implicated in appetite regulation among other things; and the corticotrophin-releasing factor (CRF) which helps regulate stress. Thus we see large variety of neurotransmitters inside the human brain and they all perform specific functions and it is a continuing field of cutting edge research.

Neurons are nerve cells that are constantly sending signals to our brain, muscles and glands. We have over a hundred billion neurons in our brain sending signals. The signals help the different parts of our body communicate with each other. Thanks to neurons, we're able to swat a mosquito if we feel it land on our arm or wave to a friend when we see her walking towards us. Neurons send chemical signals called neurotransmitters which help us to react to everything going on around us. At another level, the same neurotransmitters act as chemical signals that can influence such feelings as mood, hunger, anxiety and fear. In the human body, there are billions of little neurons, and they're not all the same. Some have short pitching arms. Some have arms pitching up to three feet long! Some neurons throw neurotransmitters at the speed of one metre per second and others throw them at up to two hundred and sixty eight metres per second! Different neurons play different roles too. Our sensory neurons fire signals to our brain neurons, and our brain neurons in turn fire signals off to our motor neurons. Our nerves pass information about what we see and hear to our brain, which then sends out signals to our muscles so that we can react. So when you see a ball flying through the air, towards you, your brain neurons send signals to your arms to reach out and catch it!

How many stars are there in the Universe?

Just to emphasise the enormity of our Universe, I present a discussion adapted from Wikipedia on the subject of the number of stars in the Universe. The question about how many stars are there in space has always fascinated scientists as well as philosophers, musicians and dreamers throughout the ages. This discussion about the large number of stars is to lead one to think how miniscule we are in the scheme of things and it is sometimes much wiser to simply follow the path charted by this grand design rather than complain incessantly about anything in this world. If we look into the sky on a clear night, away from the glare of street lights, and we will see a few thousand individual stars with our naked eyes. With telescopes, millions more will come into view.

Stars are not scattered randomly through space, they are gathered together into vast groups known as *Galaxies*. The star in our own solar system, the Sun belongs to a galaxy called the *Milky Way*. Astronomers estimate there are about a hundred thousand million stars in the Milky Way alone. And outside of it, there are millions upon millions of other galaxies also! It has been said that counting the stars in the Universe is like trying to count the number of sand grains of all the beaches on Earth!

For the Universe, the galaxies are our small representative volumes, and there are around 10^{11} or 10^{12} stars in our Galaxy, and there are perhaps 10^{11} or 10^{12} galaxies. With this simple calculation, we get a figure rough estimate which is something like 10^{22} or 10^{24} stars in the Universe. No one would try to count stars individually. Instead, we measure integrated quantities like the number and luminosity of galaxies. The *European Space Agency (ESA)* launched the infrared space observatory *Herschel* which has made an important contribution by "counting" galaxies in the infrared range, and measuring their luminosity – a feat that has never been attempted before. Knowing how fast stars form can bring more certainty to calculations. *Herschel* has also charted the formation rate of stars throughout cosmic history. If we can somehow estimate the rate at which stars have formed, we will be able to estimate how many stars there are in the Universe today.

In 1995, an image from the *Hubble Space Telescope (HST)* suggested that star formation had reached its peak at roughly around seven thousand million years ago. Recently, however, astronomers have thought again. The *Hubble Deep Field* image was taken at optical wavelengths and there is now evidence that a lot of early star formation was hidden by thick dust clouds. Dust clouds blocked the stars from view and converted their light into infrared radiation, thereby making them invisible to the HST. But the *Herschel* mission, built and operated by the ESA, could peer into this previously hidden part of the Universe at infrared wavelengths, and it revealed many more stars than were ever seen before during a period of four years, between 2009 and 2013. Similarly, the *Gaia* mission, launched by the ESA in December 2013, will study one thousand million stars in our Milky Way. It will build on the legacy of the *Hipparchus* mission, which pinpointed the positions of more than a hundred thousand stars with high precision, and those of more than a million stars with lesser precision. *Gaia* will monitor each of its one billion target stars seventy times through a five-year period, precisely charting their positions, distances, movements, and changes in brightness.

Influence of the Sun and its planets vs. that of all stars in the Universe

While it is common knowledge through the occult science of astrology, that planetary positions with respect to the position of the Sun and position of the moon at the time of birth of a human being determine, to a large extent, the broader course that his or her life might take, the fact is that the Sun is only one star in our Galaxy, in the Milky Way, and that there are a hundred thousand million stars in the Milky Way. This speaks of the possibility of how these stars can also influence the life of a human being who has more than a hundred billion neurons in his brain, all interacting with each other in tens of thousands of different ways inside the brain itself. The science and art of astrology, based on planetary positions, along with the Sun's position and moon's position at the moment of the birth of a human being, certainly has a major influence, but to disregard or discount the influence of all the other stars in the Universe upon the life of a human being is scientifically and artistically not plausible. We may not be able to account for or estimate these subtle influences on the human mind, but logically they would certainly be there even if their influence could be much weaker compared to that due to closer planetary masses to earth. This understanding creates a window of opportunity to look beyond astrology for those unfortunate souls who get stuck up in such imprisoned thoughts that everything in life is pre-destined. Such understanding helps in loosening up our dogmatic views about the world and help us look for solutions out of self-belief and faith on God who is not dead yet!

Studying the intricate processes of evolution, it is possible to imagine that in the absence of any reliable yardstick, to view the subtle influences of all these stars in the Universe on a human mind, individually or collectively, as working for only the benefit of the human species can definitely be taken as the starting point. It is in the very nature of the human soul to explore newer frontiers of knowledge - whether through deductive logic, an area of the human mind or through purely divine revelations - but one particular area, that of the interaction of the human consciousness with the Collective

Consciousness, tells us that there is infinitely more knowledge and wisdom yet to dawn on humanity. In the case of an afflicted or a diseased mind, it is all the more important to keep these possibilities wide open instead of closing the gates based on the limited knowledge we have on the influence of a few planets and one star. This will allow the positive emotion of hope to continue lingering in the mind - thereby guiding us towards better health in the long term.

For people suffering from ailments like depression and anxiety disorders, hope and faith fade away very fast – and unless this is checked, it can be fatal. While it is important to take medication to restore the chemical balance in the brain, (which generally gets misbalanced in such conditions); psychoanalysis, talk therapy, cognitive therapy etc. can lay the groundwork for improvement in the mind of patients. The fact that millions of stars in the Universe can also have positive impact on our minds at a time when astrologers indicate unfavourable planetary positions is a concept I have personally applied when I was going through the acute crisis of depression and anxiety for nearly an year and half in Australia and for the several months after that until I became fully normal. The very fact that we are born as children of God, and are destined to be liberated and merge with Him ultimately, creates such a vast expanse of possibilities that can be exploited by the afflicted mind itself, using his or her own internal power. Such afflicted persons can also be helped by the mental health care givers including professional doctors and the nursing staff, keeping the spiritual aspect of life in mind. Power of spirit is infinite and it is important to recognize this, believe in it, be in tune with it and act accordingly.

Neuroplasticity and its significance

Neuroplasticity refers to changes in neural pathways and synapses due to changes in behaviour, environment, neural processes, thinking, and emotions, as well as due to changes resulting from bodily injury. The concept of neuroplasticity has replaced the formerly held theory that the brain is a physiologically static organ, and explores how, and in which ways, the brain changes over the course of a lifetime.

Neuroplasticity occurs on a variety of levels, ranging from cellular changes (due to learning) to large-scale changes involved in *cortical remapping* as a response to injury. During most of the twentieth century, neuroscientists maintained a scientific consensus that the brain's structure was relatively immutable after a critical period during early childhood. This belief has been challenged by new findings that reveal the fact that many aspects of the brain remain plastic even well into adulthood. Modern neuroscientific research indicates that human experience can actually change over a period of time both the brain's physical structure (anatomy) and functional organization (physiology).

One of the fundamental principles of how neuroplasticity functions is linked to the concept of *synaptic pruning* - the idea that individual connections within the brain are constantly being removed or recreated, largely dependent upon how they are used. This concept is captured in the aphorism 'neurons that fire together, wire together and neurons that fire apart, wire apart'. If there are two nearby neurons, that often produce an impulse simultaneously, their cortical maps may become one. This idea also works the other way around i.e. neurons which do not regularly produce simultaneous impulses will form different maps. One of the surprising consequences of neuroplasticity is that the brain activity associated with a given function can move to a different location inside the brain. This can result from normal experiences through conscious work and also can occur in the process of recovery from brain injury.

The adult brain is not entirely "hard-wired" with fixed neuronal circuits. There are many instances of cortical and subcortical rewiring of neuronal circuits in response to training as well as injury. There is also solid evidence to suggest that *neurogenesis* (birth of brain cells) occurs in the adult mammalian brain—and that such changes can persist well into old age. The evidence for neurogenesis is mainly restricted to the hippocampus and olfactory bulb, but current research has revealed that other parts of the brain, including the cerebellum, may be involved as well. In all the other parts of the brain, while neurons can die, they cannot be created. However, there is now ample evidence for an active, experience-dependent reorganization of the synaptic networks of the brain involving multiple interrelated structures including the cerebral cortex. The specific details of how this process occurs at the molecular and ultra-structural levels are topics of ongoing neuroscience research. But these latest knowledge as they further unfold, can go a long way to unravel mysteries of the interaction between individual consciousness and collective consciousness. Why death penalties which involve only punishment killing of few criminals in the eye of the law in any society create so much furore and arousal of the soft part of human conscience when during wars, it is the same human brains, either individually or collectively engage in mass murder? Why human brains behave in such contrasting fashion and who decides such a tendency in the first place? These are aspects of social science research which will gather clues from ultra-modern brain or neuroscience research in years and decades to come. Those who claim that we have discovered almost everything that Nature has to offer, need to sit back and rethink themselves.

Power of neurons and neural network

Thomas and Amy Harris have described in their book *'Staying OK'* how the human brain has the power of creating new neural networks to come out of any major mental health problem that might have been responsible for some of the older neural networks bringing feelings of pains and sufferings to us. One can imagine a situation wherein the neural networks that may have been created due to a very bitter experience in the past, by a combination of specific neurons and neurotransmitters in the brain, could potentially face a rerun at the slightest provocation by a stimulus from the environment. This process could lead to a vicious cycle; one that would cause immense difficulty for the patient. But modern research suggests that the human brain retains the ability to create new experiences through positive visualization and positive thinking to overcome the ill effects of such a recurrent problem.

Generally, it is believed that the human brain has around eighty to hundred billion neurons during the time of birth and, with age, this number decreases. Although it is now established that there is a possibility for formation of new neural networks with the help of old neurons, it is still not clear whether human beings can create fresh neurons, as they grow older, during one life cycle itself. The indirect evidence that we get from three possible factors can lead us to hope that it could indeed be so. We have already discussed the concepts of an expanding Earth, expanding Universe and expanding soul. These, along with the hard scientific evidence of the process of encephalisation (discussed in chapter 9) with respect to the human brain in the human evolutionary process, point towards the likelihood that humanity is moving towards a situation of a general increase in the number of neurons in the brain. If this is so, then it is possible to achieve even the increase in the number of neurons on a microscopic scale during one generation itself. Mathematically or statistically, it is quite possible to visualize an incremental increase in the number of neurons in the brain during one life cycle - which add up to a gross increase, over a period of a few thousand years of human evolution, as is observed in the evolutionary process of encephalisation.

Sometimes, one negative thought in the mind can trigger a chain or series of negative thoughts that might finally cause the person to feel overwhelmed and overpowered. During such a process, the brain uses its neurons to create specific neural networks that normally produce unpleasant feelings when recounted. However, there is every chance that, if properly guided by the conscious efforts of the self, one can break the old neural pathway and create a new positive one in its place - through the power of visualization. When I was going through my mental health crisis in Australia, I deliberately created several positive images in my mind regarding all my problems, starting at the root level. At the same time, several options for every eventuality was consciously imagined and deliberated with family and friends. This ultimately helped me create new and fresh neural networks to help me handle my mental health problem. The positive visualization can be based on one's own past experience, or it could even be based on learning from another person's positive experience, or even from a hypothetical situation crafted from our imagination guided by accumulated knowledge bank.

During my mental health crisis in Australia, I profusely used my own understanding of Indian mythological stories so as to bring in positive images of God helping His devotees in all the various ways that are described in our Puranas. I visualized myself as the perfect devotee by completely surrendering myself before God and allowing God help me by removing all obstacles in my way. This process is synonymous with getting rid of ego-driven inhibitions and allows us to merge with God. Conscious building of such neural networks inside the brain through *soul consciousness* rather than *body consciousness* can go a long way in stimulating positive energy to help handle any crisis that may befall on us.

We own hundreds of complex machines but still hanker after petty ones

Modern science and technology has been branching out to cater to the needs, upkeep and repair of even the smallest of small organs in the human body. The technological developments and findings of science everyday can baffle ordinary people. They just pour information into our brains. Whether in perfect condition or not, we all own hundreds of such organs, big and small, and humanity has been investing and continues to invest billions of dollars into learning new things about them. We have come down to the smallest of them: DNA, the human gene and so on. But we are still far away from learning about the intricate way in which they all work for both the good and bad of humanity.

Religious scriptures are all full of facts on how evil and good live side by side. Modern science is deciphering them into bits and pieces, in terms of good and bad organs, and delivering technological solutions to repair them. But there is no progress yet on whether we are good or evil within. It is just a matter of interpreting whether, due to circumstances, human souls can get converted into something that might appear devilish to others. Some of the chemicals that could be available in large quantities within the body, hormones like testerostone etc., could be leading to excessive brain activity which can sometimes lead to devilish acts. The other factor is the demand of humanity in general for flashy, tasty things that appeal to the outer senses much faster and lead us into feelings that aggravate our problems.

Regarding the human machine, is it not a fact that we own the greatest machine of all time? We have brains that can expand in their capacity, their vision, and their power if we consciously try to condition them. Similarly, the eyes, the ears and the nose can all do fabulous things for us. They can help us enjoy the good things in life. Sometimes, owing to the power of our imaginations and memory, we can relive the beautiful memories of our past and in fact once again experience the same feelings, almost as much as we did originally. The fantastic organs we have inside do a lot of great things for us. They digest food and supply us with energy. They give us the strength and power to do all kinds of things. There are limbs that help us do things that can be done by machines in case we have no money to buy them. Isha Foundation chief Shri Jaggi Vasudev often says that ours is such a wonderful machine that it can create human beings out of vegetables, grains, pulses, milk products etc.! In fact, the entire human machine is so nicely built that the food and drink we consume get converted into bones, muscles, flesh and blood so as to sustain human life. Although the same applies to lower order animals, food they eat get converted to their bodies too but they do not have the luxury of creating something new totally different from what God has created so far on earth.

A person who has money and buys various gadgets that will help him do his menial work simply passes on his responsibility to utilize his own body, which was gifted by God, in a proper manner. He gets this work done through machines so as to find more time to engage in acts that lead to further amassing of wealth. We can walk the distance if we want. But we depend on two wheelers or four wheelers for even covering small distances. We can wash our clothes in our own hands but there is hardly any middle class household that does not use a washing machine for the purpose. We can climb up a stair or two but even small kids now wait for the lifts to come to their rescue. They show reluctance to take a bit of pains to climb up few steps to go to their apartments in first floor or second floor. Thus, we see the growing indulgence in petty machines in our daily lives when we know very well that we are gifted with the most sophisticated machine by God to carry out small jobs ourselves to enjoy the true essence of life.

Dreams and their meaning

There have been numerous instances that tell us about the power of dreams. Barenya Banerjee in his book 'Intuitive Creativity' lists several examples of how even great scientists have got glimpses of the solutions they were looking for in their dreams, and have proceeded with the clues they saw whilst deep in sleep. If we analyse closely, and over a very long period, we would realize that every one of us gets to experience such dreams. Some are very important and some are not that important. Some stick to our conscious minds and some do not. We derive meaning from some dreams and just return to our slumber in other cases. Scot.M.Peck has described a dream he had few days before the publication of his most famous book 'The Road Less Traveled'. He was in a dilemma and deeply introspective, thinking about how he would handle his life and fame if his book became very popular, and trying to come up with a solution using his conscious thought process was not getting him anywhere. But he could find meaning in one of the dreams he had one night during those times. In his dream he saw himself as a very small child being driven around in a car by his father, who was long dead by then. He interpreted it as a solution to his ongoing predicament by taking the small child to be him and the driver to be his Father (the Creator). Most of us rationalists would question the veracity of such an interpretation, but realized souls would understand the deeper meaning to what he writes. Human beings are ultimately guided by their inner convictions and these deeper convictions originate from the spiritual being within us - though to a lazy mind they do not mean much except blind faith.

In our deepest crises, our dreams are our best guides and help. It is very important to heed these dreams at any point during the crisis because these dreams originate from our inner spiritual being and hence take into account all our abilities, our fear, our commitment to ourselves, our commitment to others, our lost memories, our strengths and weaknesses, our morality, our ethics, our own background, our faith, everything. These dreams are just like the compass of Stephen Covey and not the clocks. They can guide us to perfect bliss, if we nurture the subtle capacities of the inner being to touch upon our dreams and make us understand their meanings.

Most of us go through such experiences in our lives, particularly during times of crisis. Sometimes, when we experience some intense dream, and get up after it, we feel extremely fresh and full of vivid memories of the dream, and it is up to us to either interpret the meaning of it or reject it, saying that it is useless. For me, dreams seem to be result of intense networking between the very deepest part of our brain-heart connection; essentially the spiritual being within us. The sapping of energy during the final moments of a dream is the result of the energy inside the subconscious brain being consumed. Hence many times, the individual wakes up towards the logical end of a composite dream. The conscious brain tries to come to terms with what happened when the subconscious brain tried to overpower the system by joining the neuronal dots in an attempt to reach finality; because it is the conscious brain that translates the subconscious brain's directives into reality and executes the instructions passed on from the subconscious brain. The conscious brain cuts off the link after it gets enough energy from the entire process of dream either for its survival or for further growth. The Super Consciousness (what we otherwise term as God) which has a direct link with our subconscious brain actually powers us in this fashion, provided we make ourselves amenable to such ideas and feelings. After all, the most important drivers of human beings are their feelings, the emotional being, and this happens in the realm of the conscious brain. But the delicate link of emotions to the Super Consciousness can be the real force that drives each one of us. If we can visualize such a position, there can be answers to everything. Once, Scot Peck got baffled by his observation of how he could know or predict beforehand the name of a big building (and of the office it housed) when he and his wife were strolling along a street one evening in Singapore. This can also be explained by the feelings that are experienced, very subtle, by intimately pure souls who can actually decipher signals from the atmosphere. The interconnectedness between our souls and the Earth which is spinning on its axis while revolving around the Sun can explain the advent of the signals that can be tapped by perfect and pure souls. The fact that the building and Scot Peck both existed physically and had encircled the earth and the Sun several times before hand and the mysterious way human soul can sense the coded information hidden in the energy field around may not be apparent but they simply cannot be denied. I was told by one of my very close friend and colleague how about a month before he was to leave for England and visit some places there in an official trip, he saw in his dreams exactly the same streets, the same trees and same buildings he finally saw on his arrival! This person had never made any overseas trip so far from India! Although conventional knowledge may not be able to comprehend such phenomenon but if we stretch our imagination a bit, it can easily be deciphered that perhaps each so called living and so called nonliving subatomic particle in the Universe registers as a memory anything that it experiences while the normal activities of the planetary motions and movement of stars and galaxies is going on incessantly. There is a subtle link between such subatomic particles within human brain and outside such that flashes of memory can trigger in human brain resulting from interaction between such subatomic particles that may not be apparent to conventional thinking.

Source - Sink phenomenon

The world always moves in a source-sink phenomenon, whether it is water flowing from a higher level to lower level, or energy flowing from where it is generated to where it is consumed, or whether it is money flowing from one hand to another depending on who the source is or who the receiver is. In exactly the same manner, happiness also follows a source-sink phenomenon. When we ask a question to fulfill our knowledge bank's requirement, and when we get the correct answer, we become happy. Similarly, when we need some article, we try to garner our resources to obtain the same and once we manage to get it, we become happy. This is to satisfy our material need. All our needs, physical, mental and emotional, require external sources and their intervention in different degrees for fulfillment. But the spiritual need does not need any external intervention for its fulfillment. The spiritual need is there within every one of us. Due to conditioning, right from the moment of birth, we get distracted to various degrees from understanding the true nature of our spiritual need. If we carefully analyse ourselves and introspect, we can easily see that our spiritual need always existed and that we have been experiencing glimpses of its presence within us right from childhood. Of course, depending upon the degree of education, the knowledge and wisdom that we are allowed to gather from our environment, we experience the true nature of our spiritual need.

We blame Hitler for all his misdeeds. But we forget that what he achieved for humanity is setting an example (though of course in hindsight it proved to be in the negative form) of how one single individual can inspire a whole community against another community. And how this can ultimately lead to mass annihilation and destruction. Although obviously he never believed that he would be leading himself to the sorry state wherein he would have to kill himself after becoming involved in all the mass murder around him. But what humanity learns from this sordid example is that aiming for power and control over all of humanity is such a foolish act. The example of Hitler has also shown how human intellect can all be organized and made to work together, towards achieving a set goal, even if in hindsight we find that it was wrong. But another finer aspect of the man's hunger is perhaps one that we do not know very well, if at all - how the kind of hatred he developed against a major chunk of humanity came into his very being in the first place. There was definitely something in his immediate environment that caused this hatred to develop and to take strong roots in him, and which later grew to dangerous proportions. The other aspect which needs to be researched is if it is really true that one can be "born evil". To my mind no human being is born evil. The degree of evil that we ascribe to him, is actually a reflection of the evil nature inside us. And we try to blame this other person for it. I recall how I once read a newspaper story of the Maoist leader of Nepal. He turned Maoist because of the childhood memories he had of his father being tortured by the landlords in those days. In a similar manner, we will find there will always be reasons that trigger some great leaders to turn to war and violence – and which would actually have been caused by naïve acts of other beings. It is a vicious circle.

To me, evil can exist in the quantum that it is needed to maintain a balance in the world. If we say someone is evil, I would say that God created him to neutralize some other evil and not some other good. *To me, any evil in today's context must be seen as a reference to the past and a projection for the future.* Evil does not really exist so long as we are prepared to believe it doesn't. I do believe in my innermost being that, if there is any evil, contrary to my own theories, then the existence of that evil is not to disprove my theory, but to perpetuate the idea that evil does not exist. This is because the very notion of evil existing contrary to my idea is to accept it as some kind of requirement by the whole system to neutralize the bad effect of evil that was already created by human beings on this earth due to their lack of understanding sometime in the past, during the course of progress of human species from cave dwellers to modern day space explorers! Looking at a snapshot of anything in today's world and term it as evil, as many ignorant political leaders do from time to time to arouse passions in the people they lead, is utterly foolhardy because contemporary history cannot truly justify ancient history nor vice versa.

When we set goals in line with our vision, mission and purpose, we try to achieve them and, depending on our internal resources, we succeed or fail. But the very fact that we try to achieve it, never really attaching too much importance to success or failure, will help us maintain the balance and lead us to happiness and bliss. This is again the essence of the *Bhagawat Gita*. The world is destined to be a happy place and, through our actions, we can create such an atmosphere. But that must begin with our own attempt to cleanse our inner self. Only then can we try to influence the outer world through our collective and individual efforts.

Childhood memories can be handy during midlife crisis

Some of the wisdom which is transmitted to us by our family, teachers in school and our elders in society all get into the core of our brains through various means. The memories remain there and sometimes get opportunities in life to be used in practical manner. For example, we have been taught a mythological story about the birth of Sri Krishna in the prison cell of the demon king Kansha's sister and Vasudeva – both of whom were put into prison because there was a prediction by an astrologer that the child of Vasudeva and his wife (Kansha's sister) would be the cause for Kansha's killing and destruction. Hence, Kansha became fearful and wanted to kill all their children as if to remove trace of any potential killers of him.

The night Sri Krishna was born, Vasudeva got a clear divine message about the arrival of God Himself in the form of the newly born child. Vasudeva, guided by divine instruction through heavy rains and a flooding river crossed over to a different village where he could safely transfer the child to the family of Jasoda Maya and Nand Raja, where he would be safe from the wrath of the demon Kansha. The memory of the picture of Sri Krishna being carried in a basket on the head of Vasudeva, and of a great seven-headed snake protecting the child from the rains etc. was quite engraved in my mind, as in the case of any small child in India.

At the time of my own midlife crisis in Australia I somehow felt that I should try to visualize all sorts of situations wherein I could see myself as a winner, victorious from the deep crisis I was in those days. I utilized all modern and ancient methods and tried to make a synthesis of the two to reach a state of mind that would pull me along.

The birth of Sri Krishna was symbolic for me and it meant that a great soul was born with pure conscience and character – and had to be protected from the fury of nature and the demon king. So I also tried to imagine that the midlife crisis I was going through at that time was perhaps like the pain of labour that would deliver to the Earth a brilliant thought or new idea. Those ideas which were brimming within me, both in the context of my final PhD research findings as well as my ongoing struggle with midlife crisis which produced glimpses of the key techniques to handle such problems, have been cleaned and sharpened by Divinity through my conscious and subconscious efforts and hence needed to be protected. I was trying to position myself as Vasudev and my new thoughts or ideas metaphorically as Lord Krishna. And in the same way Vasudev was protecting Lord Krishna from the wrath of Kansha by fleeing from him and lifting the basket high on the head to save Krishna from the flood waters, I needed to protect my own ideas from getting washed away by forces of disruption I was experiencing during my mental health crisis! How it was to be achieved was the job of God. I tried to believe that every hurdle on the way towards completing my PhD project would be automatically cleared and that the obstacles would go away, just how the newly born Krishna was taken away from the danger of Kansha's wrath to a safe place against all odds by Vasudev. Quite interestingly, as if by a stroke of providence, everything happened in that direction. I could overcome obstacles of all kinds, one by one, and finally could reach my goal of not only completing my PhD but also of surviving so far as to write about my experience so that it could reach readers from across the globe.

Independence, interdependence, conscience and social conscience

We ordinary human beings always try to enjoy our freedom, freedom of our own thoughts, our own journeys and our own successes and achievements. There are times when we give preference to our own enjoyment (in whatever form) over that of others. The reason for such behaviour is simple and easy to find. This is generally connected to our free will, our free thinking process, and when we try to tag someone else or with some group with the same, problems start to occur. Depending upon our capacities, we chart out our ways and means to realize our own dreams. The dreams take root in various forms when we play the role of a simple person or a professional in any field - be it a man, a wife, a child, a teacher a worker, an executive, a leader, a politician, a statesman, a sports person, a scientist, whatever. The dreams take shape right at the beginning, during childhood, and we fail to notice the subtle development of them in our subconscious. And it manifests itself when we try to convert the dreams lying in our subconscious into reality. Turning dreams into reality normally takes a lot of effort at an individual level as well as at an interdependent level. The world is not so simple that it allows us to succeed in making our dreams come true so easily. Those who realize this make adjustments accordingly and perhaps do not face frustrating situations along the journeys to realizing their own dreams. But when we are not mentally prepared to accept such details, problems occur. I normally follow a two-step approach to solve any problem that crops up. First, I give my best to solving any problem that might occur along the way. And when I fail to achieve in the way I would like to, I put it in the altar of God and allow Him to do the job for me the way He wants. Which essentially means after a certain point, which is generally dictated by my *inner voice*, I try to consciously as well as subconsciously accept God's will.

The greatest influence on our being is actually that of *social conscience* - which means that we have developed our own models within ourselves of what the world is and how the world should be. This includes how we see our parents and family members as being, how they should be etc. It also similarly applies to our relatives and friends in school, college, the work place or anywhere else. When there is a mismatch between the world we want and the world that actually is, we get surprised, frustrated, elated or excited, depending upon our own expectations and the reality. This applies to even wife-husband relationships and parent-child relationships. We fail to understand that there can be some gap between the 'world that should be' and the reality. This is the crux of the problem.

There is also the effect of our upbringing; our social model building based on our own interpretation of the environment in our psyche. We fail to realize that when we start with a relationship there can be ups and downs, that there can be unevenness and roadblocks, there can be bumps and diversions and there can be patches when it is extremely smooth and patches when it can be extremely difficult. Only this understanding can release the pain and suffering which we would normally go through when we actually make the journey, and when we come across difficulties.

Any relationship journey can be tortuous and this simple understanding can relieve all of us from great pain when we actually face difficulties. The preparedness of our minds can go a long way in adjusting and keeping balance when we make the journey. No journey is free from obstacles and difficulties. The *social conscience* actually means that we make different assumptions, construct different images of life within our minds, and dream that they should always happen as we imagined. When that does not happen, it causes pain in us. The social conscience is actually built by always taking the good from what we see in the outside world. The bad elements are not ingrained in our model, because we are not prepared mentally to face such bad moments.

The individual conscience however knows very well when one goes wrong, when one speaks untruth, when one creates pain for others, when and where one transgresses his boundaries, when one invites guilt into oneself through some wrongdoing etc. The conscience is the *compass* and always points *true north*. Stephen Covey calls the pointers from the conscience as *'true north principles'*. The individual compass helps one to expand, provided he or she allows the door to stay open and accepts fresh air. The moment we shut the door and windows, our conscience creates further guilt and aggravates the problem.

There has to be a delicate balance between the individual conscience and the social conscience. Social conscience might have many assumptions, some of which could be wrong from a holistic perspective and unrealistic because they are limited by social boundaries of various kinds. But individual conscience has the capacity to expand in any direction. This is the beauty of human life. The expanded conscience can then encompass the frailties, the shortcomings and lacunae in the social conscience that was built years or generations ago. The constant processes through which we can develop an ability to create an interdependent culture, or an independent standing, is linked to a common goal in different situations and in then trying to develop the social conscience through the help of the individual conscience. This process can help us achieve the peace we long for, the happiness that eludes us in ordinary circumstances.

Sound is more powerful than light

Different sensory memories generated by sound (echoic), sight (visual), smell (olfactory), taste or touch (haptic) are said to bypass the logical part of the brain and travel to the seat of instinct and memory - the primitive part of the brain. Close analysis of our past memories as a collective consciousness would tell us that the strongest impact that any emotion can have on our minds are those that are generated by the hearing sense organ - even more so than what are generated by the visual sense organ. These sensory memories can be recalled along with the associated emotions and can be used for therapeutic value or healing effect. An example of how the memory triggered by sound can act as a very potent tool is the way old scriptures of Hindu philosophy that have been passed down from generation to generation. The Sanskrit verses are memorized just by chanting them!

When we open the *Bhagawat Gita*, the first chapter describes blind Dhritarashtra asking Vyasadev about the Kourav Sena (soldiers) and Pandav Sena (soldiers) and their activities on the field of Kurukshetra. Vyasadev gives eternal sight or divine power of vision to Sanjay who in turn describes everything to Dhritarashtra. This story has existed since time immemorial. The beauty is that the story has been passed on from one generation to another, and there have been umpteen number of attempts, in almost every generation, to interpret the story in a way which would be beneficial to mankind. Exact dating of the scripture is debated but if Krishna is supposed to live around 3192 BC as some historians quote, obviously the printing technology had not developed even in the most basic form by then. The only plausible path that it followed for its survival and upkeep is through words spoken and memorized by generation after generation.

The *Bhagawat Gita* that we have today, is a recital by Sanjay to Dhritarashtra. And the interesting thing is that neither of them was present in the battlefield, in Kurukshetra. The immortal song, the divine *Gita*, has stood the test of time for more than a millennium, and it all started with this sacred piece of work being memorized and passed on through several centuries and countless generations because of the power within it. And the way it gets transmitted is through the power of sound rather than a visual sensory effect.

There is another angle to this concept. It is generally believed that one who is careful with choosing his words is always a winner. The reason is that when we generate words from within us to speak to someone, it carries the cumulative effect of the other sensory perceptions of our bodies and minds about our thoughts before we express ourselves through our words. The harmful effect on us when we allow another's words to hurt us is much more lasting than the harmful effect of any unruly or unfriendly visual gesture that is directed towards us. This confirms that the emotional effect of sound is much more powerful than that of visual sight and it is necessary to understand the implications of this in our day-to-day lives.

Emotions and their influence on our bodies

Modern medical research has started to unravel the direct connection between human emotions and manifestation of diseases. Type A personality refers to those people who always look for perfection in everything around them, who expect others to behave perfectly towards them at all times. However, these are the people who are prone to migraine, hypertension and heart disease. Modern scientific research has started revealing facts about how our body organs get affected by the chemical imbalances created by long term negative thought processes.

For example, those who feel suppressed over a very long period of time, resigning themselves to the fact that it is beyond their control to handle the environmental pressures, become prey to a hormonal imbalance problem known as hypothyroid. Similarly, people who have a tendency to only see the negative things and find it difficult to hold any positive thoughts will be prone to heart ailments. We all know that genetics play a big role in determining how our body organs shape up, and in deciding which diseases we would be prone to under normal circumstances. In such cases, when the subjects do not take adequate care of their thought processes - which ultimately lead to the creation of undesirable feelings and emotions, and hence chemical imbalances in the body - they will fall prey to those diseases much more easily. Just like how we choose our food, if we can carefully choose our thoughts from a bucket of thoughts, so that we do not invite negative harmful thoughts, then our whole immune and endocrine system will be protected. There is a connection between greedy behavior and affliction with diabetes.

Some people suffer psychologically from artificial hunger. Even if they have just eaten a full meal, after half an hour or so, they start feeling hungry again. It is not actual hunger, but the dissatisfaction within oneself that causes the brain to look for more food to feel satisfied. This type of behavior will quickly lead to obesity.

In terms of direct correlation between how individual body organs function in response to positive emotions, it is being discovered that, if we have propensity towards peaceful thoughts, peaceful feelings, then the lung functions best. If we are peaceful, our breathing is deep and slow, but when we are in a very irritated state, a disturbed state, our breathing becomes shorter and faster. The heart has a direct connection with love, which we know from time immemorial. The more loving thoughts we can create, and the more love we can hold in our hearts for ourselves and our surroundings, the better our hearts will function. The sensory organs look for pure thoughts to function well. Purity is their strength. The endocrine system looks for bliss to work at its highest efficiency. The digestive system is dependent on how much of the satisfactory feeling we can generate within ourselves. The brain gets its nourishment from knowledge of all kinds, including spiritual knowledge.

It is one thing to be born with the DNA of parents which might leave us genetically prone to certain diseases, but how we protect ourselves from the severity of being thus prone or increase the same during our lifetime is entirely another matter. And we may in the process also pass on, to our progeny, DNA that is much worse. If one already has a dyslipidemia profile, and a family history of hypertension, unless he takes some special care with regards to food habits, exercise habits and even thought habits, it is very likely that he will face problems sooner or later. So instead of resigning to our genetic makeup, if we make conscious efforts to focus on the power of the soul, there is a good chance that our offspring will be born with healthier bodies and minds.

CHAPTER 8

GOD AND HIS SEVEN BILLION CHILDREN

Faith can move mountains

Once upon a time, in a faraway town; there was this young man who had everything going well for him till tragedy struck him. A fabulous job which earned him good salary at the end of each month vanished because the plant, where he was working as the floor manager, had to be closed down. The management of the company decided to stop its operation for several reasons. It was running for almost a year at fifty percent capacity utilization for acute shortage of raw materials and hence accumulating losses. The company had a mountain of debt. Incentives to employees had to be drastically curtailed for lack of revenue thereby causing labour unrest. It was a vicious cycle and to avoid incurring further debt, the company had no option than to close down the plant. On the personal family front, his beautiful wife, who was expecting their second child, unfortunately met with a road accident and succumbed to the grave injuries in the hospital. Both his parents whom he loved and adored so much also departed in quick succession due to ill health and old age. He had no zest for life left within him. Feeling utterly hopeless, depressed and frustrated, he decided to end his own life.

From deep within, however, a very feeble voice whispered something and he thought for a moment and paused. He remembered about a monk, whose name had spread far and wide and he had heard a lot about him from his friends. He thought of meeting him once. He thus slowly headed towards a small bamboo shed inside the nearby forests where the monk lived. When he was approaching the shelter of the monk, a thousand questions were crossing his mind in rapid succession. The most intense thought that was bothering him was,

"Why me? Why out of all, God chose me and is giving me so much pain when in my entire life, I have done no wrong to anybody nor have I caused pain to anyone?"

Inside the hut, the monk was sitting quietly in a contemplative mood. When he saw the man approach the door, he made a gesture by his right hand welcoming the man with a smiling face and asked him what was bothering him.

After paying the customary obeisance, the man asked, "Guruji, I have heard from friends about many miracles you have performed and am told that you have actually seen God and know Him. You can know about some body's ins and outs just by simply looking at him and can tell about his past and predict about his future. Can you please explain to me why God has been so cruel to me? I am feeling very restless."

The monk listened to him intently and then gently responded, "Look around," He said. "Do you see the fern and the bamboo? Do you make out what sort of life experience they have had so far?"

The man got a bit puzzled and after giving a thought for a moment, replied, "Guruji, I cannot actually understand what you are trying to get at."

Then the Guruji tried to explain with a caring voice, "See, God had planted the fern and the bamboo seeds, took very good care of them, gave them light, air and water and the fern quickly grew from the earth. Soon the floor was covered with its brilliant green and was looking really beautiful. Whereas, nothing came from the bamboo seed. But God did not quit on the bamboo". Guruji continued, "In the second year the fern grew more vibrant and plentiful and spread further. And still, nothing came from the bamboo seed. But God still did not quit on the bamboo". "In the third year, there was still nothing coming out from the bamboo seed. But God would not quit. In the fourth year, again, there was nothing from the bamboo seed. God still remained patient because He knew what He was doing", Guruji said.

"Then in the fifth year a tiny sprout emerged from bamboo seed planted in the earth. By that time fern had spread all over and compared to the fern, it was seemingly small and insignificant. But just six months later the bamboo rose to over a hundred feet tall". Guruji went on further, "You can now imagine, the bamboo seed had spent the five years growing roots inside. Those roots made it strong and gave it what it needed to survive. God would not give any of His creations a challenge it could not handle!"

Guruji wanted to reassure the worried man, "God makes human life interesting, challenging and different for everyone. He chalks out for each soul on this earth a different path according to the *Karmic Account Balance* of each individual. All these years, through the pain and sufferings, God has been actually helping you build your mental strength and will power to face adversities".

"God did never quit on the bamboo. He would never quit on you. Don't compare yourself to others because our perceptions make things look different. The bamboo had a different purpose than the fern while both make the forest beautiful. You might be passing through a difficult time but it is not the end of the world. All this will pass, your time will come and you will also rise high!" Guruji assured the man.

Guruji elaborated the philosophy of life a bit further, "God is infinitely compassionate, and He would never give up on anyone. You should never regret any action of yours in your life because we act according to time, space and circumstances. During your journey of life, good days will always bring happiness to you while bad days will give you learning and experiences. Both are essential to life. Life is a mixture of highs and lows, joys and sorrows, successes and failures. This is what makes life more meaningful and worthy. It requires our continuous efforts and creativity because nothing in this world actually happens by chance. Our choices and actions are what matters. Each day we are presented with new opportunities to choose and act and, in doing so, we create our own unique journey of life. Happiness brings you sweet feelings, trials and tribulations make you strong, sorrows keep you grounded and human, failures make you humble, success keeps you glowing, but only the Almighty God keeps you going! So keep going and stay blessed and always remember that faith on God can move mountains!"

The man realized his mistake. His faith on God, which was shaken quite a bit due to all the mishaps, got restored by the wisdom filled utterances of the Guru. He said to himself, "Life is so vast, my life is certainly not the worst in the world. There is still a lot that can be done not only for me and my surviving child but for the whole lot of others in the extended family and society at large".

GOD lies within each cell of you

Some people break the word 'GOD' up into *Generation-Operation-Destruction*. This is in line with the ancient Hindu Trinity *Brahma-Vishnu-Maheswar* which represents the three Hindu Gods depicting the processes of Creation, Maintenance and Destruction. Had this not been the case, perhaps, life would have been dumb and uninteresting. If there is a cycle of *birth-growth-decay* in everything we see around us, then the whole thing becomes very beautiful and exciting. Even at the most fine level, it is enchanting to visualize the fact that everything in this Earth and perhaps in this Universe is subject to the *birth-growth-decay* phenomenon. Physicists have been able to follow similar ideas and propounded theories, crystal clear to humanity as sunrise and sunset, about the origin of the Universe. To those uninitiated on the basics of physics, it may be difficult to comprehend, but modern science has come out with theories about origin of the Universe which suggest the birth and death of a star. The Sun is a specific star of which Earth is a planet that is inhabited by us. We could find out from various scientific studies that many species have evolved and become extinct during the long history of the Earth – a phenomenon that makes experience of life on Earth and the studies thereof so very interesting.

Due to the very fact that we are subjected to the processes of birth, growth and decay, both physically and metaphysically, we can conclude that GOD lies within each cell of man. The process of *birth-growth-decay* is ingrained in every cell of a human being, and for that matter in every cell of all living beings.

The entire gamut of human activities is guided by this phenomenon. Whether it is the birth of a child, birth of a society, birth of a company or birth of a nation, the principle remains the same. Only the scale of observation is different. The question of whether the progress of every entity that is born will enter into the full-blown growth phase, and then eternally sustain, depends on a force normally conceived at a very metaphysical level. To this day, we see the cycle made up of these three processes in entirety only in physical substances. Metaphysically also we can visualize that the eternal or deathless state can occur only in case of ideas and that nothing other than those can really sustain. *The only permanent thing in life is change* is a concept that will hold good for eternity.

God can be easily perceived in each cell of man provided he directs and aligns himself totally with this reality and with the way our destiny shapes our future. This feeling of God evokes a sense of satisfaction and happiness which leads ultimately to bliss, if we can visualize and transform these small facts into the metaphysical plane.

A fully grown tree begins with a sprout from a small seed. Each seed thus has packed within it all the resources needed to help it become a new tree. The cyclic process of a tree giving rise to a seed which in turn grows to be a tree of the new generation is applicable to the animal world (including humans) as well. Even while being fully aware that life is not permanent, humans engage in all sorts of ambitious projects, in every sphere of activity; projects which involve experimentation of the highest degree. The very nature of human soul is to explore and experience and then share the wisdom gained with others before restarting the process again for a new cycle.

Evil does not exist

In many instances there have been descriptions of ideas that refer to the existence of evil and good. A relatively recent example is that of President George Bush's referral to *an axis of evil consisting of three nations: Iran, Iraq and North Korea and their terrorist allies* (The famous *axis of evil speech* in a State of Union address on 29th January 2002 following 9/11 terrorist attacks). I was so disturbed by such pronouncements that I thought I should dedicate a full subchapter to this concept, one based on my own personal feelings on this idea of good and evil and perhaps why we should be careful about such political statements lest we mess up things for the worse.

It was May 2000. Teachers, research fellows and research students of the NCPGG were preparing to leave for Brisbane, for the annual APPEA Conference, where I was to present a Poster paper based on part of the research results of my PhD. I worked the whole of the previous night to prepare that poster. It was only the second time in my life when I put in a whole night of study. The first time I stayed awake one whole night to study was on the eve of another exam, during the M.Tech course I was doing at ISM, Dhanbad.

The next morning, I went to the market to give the poster for lamination. I vividly remember the entire episode.

There was only one particular shop which did lamination for posters of a large size and, normally, all the stuff from our department at the University of Adelaide used to be done there. I went and gave my poster for lamination and the man at the shop said it would take about an hour or so. I did not have anything else to do at that time. The only option was to spend one hour just sitting somewhere in the city, on a bench at a bus stop, contemplating things. An idea struck my mind then. Why should I not step into one of the TABs which I had been seeing in Adelaide but never actually been inside? I have never experienced such things in India, and I thought I should see what actually went on inside a TAB. This is a habit of mine; I allow myself the liberty to explore different places, in my own way, with a free mind. I saw one TAB board just across the road and I thought I could easily spend an hour inside the place. Inside, I saw several people standing in some sort of queue and trading with a person across a counter. There were a few TV screens and there were images of horse races being shown. Although I felt as if they were not real-time or live images, but logically they would perhaps be so. What I could gather from the scene and from the activities of the people inside the TAB was that it was a place where some kind of betting exercise was going on, and that the people who were there were addicted to such betting. I thought to myself that my first experience inside a TAB would not be complete unless I played and betted a little myself. I made a decision after several rounds of thought, and after observing the developments going on in the TAB for nearly half an hour. I approached the man at the counter and asked him very matter-of-factly if he could kindly explain me how the system worked there and how individuals engaged in the goings on at the TAB. The man at the counter got a little surprised and even a little irritated, perhaps because such novices don't usually turn up at TABs. After few minutes, the man at the counter was about to explain to me when a strange thing suddenly happened.

A man who was standing in the queue already, and whom I had seen standing before me, quickly got to his feet and literally forced me away from the front of the counter and dragged me outside the TAB, onto the verandah/footpath. I was a little surprised, but open to what was happening and conscious of the same. The man frowned at me. A mixture of emotions was visible on his face, ranging from a strong urge to caution me to wanting to offer friendly advice. There were signs of deep frustration with himself at one end and, at the same time, an overriding desire and wish to extend a helping hand to me. He looked like a man of Greek or Italian origin and he told me in English how he had become trapped in the bad cycle of betting at the TAB and how he had lost a lot of money already in just the last month. He pulled out a bunch of tickets from his pocket and told me how he had purchased all of them with a dream to win big. His dreams had failed him and he had lost a lot of money. But the faint hope of recovering the lost money caused him to become addicted by now - to the TAB, to the vicious cycle of betting. I could easily see in him the reflection of a pure divine soul and of Godly influence, even though I could sense that his losses had already influenced his mental balance and hence his own family life and behaviour in general. He might have even started doing mischievous deeds to compensate for his losses, which normally people do.

I could sense in just a second how the God within this man was speaking to me about the bad influence of addiction and how easily I could be trapped and lead myself to doom. I had just one year left to complete my PhD and it would have just been dangerous for me to get involved in the bad act of betting now. I could see sense in what he was saying. Initially, of course, I was slightly afraid that this man would do me some harm, when he was dragging me to the outside of the TAB.

I decided to designate this day as the day for my once-in-a-lifetime TAB experience, but in the process I crystallized my own idea, the culmination of a lifelong search. I concluded then and there that *'Evil does not exist on this earth'*. The beauty of such a discovery was that it created a lasting impression on my mind and created certain neural networks which will perhaps be impossible to be erased no matter what.

Who knew there would be an anecdote waiting to take birth with this concept my poor brain had finally arrived at? I wanted to share my realization with two people belonging to a completely different cultural background, but a similar professional background. Both of them shared a first name: Nicholas. One of them was the professor under whose guidance I was doing my PhD and the other was the computer system support man at our research centre. When I described with excitement my experience to my professor, his quick response was; 'Oh! That is nothing very new. Lord Jesus has said that in the Bible.' To this I curtly remarked; 'But Nick, I have never had a chance to go through the Bible.' With a frown on his face, the professor said; 'Then, perhaps it signifies something.'

I was excited further about my new discovery, which had now got the approval of my own supervisor. Who better to endorse it than a very learned professor at a reputed University in a part of the developed world! I wanted to test my hypothesis with another person. This time, I chose a very good friend of mine, someone who I liked very much for his honesty and straightforwardness, the computer system support man, the other Nick. I told him the whole story of my discovery along with my professor's comments. Without batting an eyelid, the second Nick said; 'Okay then; if evil does not exist, then good does not exist either.' Extending our conversation on the matter further, and trying to reason it out, when I asked my professor what made the man in the TAB give such pure, humane advice to a complete stranger, he explained; 'Everyone in this world tries to control other people when he fails to control himself.'

In this way, rational minds always speak of day and night, black and white, darkness and light, good and evil, beauty and ugliness, thick and thin, hard and soft, fast and slow, and many other such opposite concepts. It is not that I was unaware about these opposites, but my addiction to righteousness had one inherent aim in my continuous search to prove that the *concept of evil* was manmade. Although our epics and religious scriptures have mentioned the existence of evil, I could not find any reason as to why and how God, the Supreme and the Almighty, would create evil in this world. I always believed in a distorted perception of the human mind to define evil. Perhaps my personal experience recounted above resonated with my inner search.

Is it not a profound chain of events that capture the fundamental human thought processes? I had to go through severe anxiety-driven depression to reach this realization, but I believe that it is not required for everyone to go through such pain and suffering to realise this fundamental truth. These are *fundamental truths.* If Lord Jesus has said this, and the whole world has read it in the Bible, and if I, who have not read the Bible, have been able to experience this truth for a few minutes in the *divine part of my life,* then is it not a fact that everyone has it within him or her to realise it? It depends on us;

whether we choose to act on such knowledge or keep our blaming eye fixated on finding new targets for all the evils outside of us.

As Washington Post reporters Glenn Kessler and Peter Baker put it in 2006: "Nearly five years after President Bush introduced the concept of an 'axis of *evil*' comprising Iraq, Iran and North Korea, the administration has reached a crisis point with each nation: North Korea has claimed it conducted its first nuclear test, Iran refuses to halt its uranium-enrichment program, and Iraq appears to be tipping into a civil war three and half years after the U.S.-led invasion." To elaborate a bit further why all of us should try our best to redefine our perception about good and evil is because, in less than even a decade and half of waging an international war on terror; and in less than a decade of actually killing the mastermind of 9/11 terrorist attack; there is a much more dangerous terrorist organization that has started making headlines by killing and maiming innocent people, all in the name of religion and politics. It is an irony that the terrorists of any creed inevitably end up killing their own people even though they start with a motive to target people belonging to a different faith than theirs. Until and unless such an idea takes root that 'evil is manmade', it would be difficult to contain. Do we eradicate the so called 'evil' or somehow push some of the 'good' into the territory of 'so called evil' by our misguided policies?

God's letter to a soul about to take human form on the planet Earth

Dear my loving child,

You are a roving *soul* in this ether world, currently in a floating state. Very few on the planet which I am going to send you into very soon really understand what is meant by *soul*. But it is a fact that many are prepared to describe many things about how it looks, how it sounds, how it smells, how it feels, how it tastes and even how it thinks. The simple reason for this continued ignorance is because I am actually always tricking and tweaking a bit each time I send a new *soul* to the planet from this part of the Cosmos. Although some of my own representatives - Lord Krishna, Lord Jesus, Lord Buddha, Lord Mahavira, Prophet Moses, Prophet Mohammed, Guru Nanak, Ramakrishna Paramahansa, Ramana Maharishi, and Swami Vivekananda - were specifically given the same letter at an earlier time, every time I decided to send someone special to the planet, I write to them the way I am writing to you now. Usually, my intentions were specific and all the *souls* who have lived out their lives on the planet Earth enacted the dramas I wanted them to perform. But this time, I am sending you with a new piece of information which all those earlier *souls* were not empowered with, once again for a specific purpose. The purpose is a bit subtle. I have created this new information after getting feedback from all the *souls* who have gone from here and played out their roles effectively, including all those great *souls* mentioned above. This information, although new, is very simple. It is as follows:

It relates to three concepts - *the power of the human imagination beginning with infinity and ending with infinity, the science of the soul in terms of the known and the unknown, and the power to govern oneself which is related to free will, free thought and free action in the framework of true democracy.* Most *souls* failed to realise their true potential in spite of the fact that they all were same when I started with them. But a few could quickly reach the exalted state that I wanted them to reach through their own efforts and without even being empowered with this new information that I am providing you with now before sending you to Earth. There is a caveat however. The information that I am giving you will unfold only when you reach a certain age - which I am not going to disclose to you now. How fast you reach that age is left to you. Let me also assure you that you have the capacity inbuilt in you this time to fast track or slow track or no track your journey in the realm of unfolding your true potential. I can give you few tips though. Some souls attain realization at very young age.

I am loading your internal engine with the power to connect to the eternal sources of fundamental emotional attributes like greed, fear, anxiety, frustration, jealousy, hatred, anger, aggression, violence, lethargy, doggedness and destruction on the negative side. Lest you do not fall into the habit of nagging, complaining and blaming as most people do perennially, I am reassuring you that I am also loading you with the opposites of all those negative emotional attributes. These are nothing but the positive emotional attributes like contentment, courage, steadiness, satisfaction, empathy, love, calmness, competitiveness, peace, alertness, inquisitiveness and construction. I will leave it to you to decide which of these eternal resources you would like to have access to, just the way man these days plugs into a source of power to run a machine or recharge a used battery. Let me also assure you that at no point of time, you will find the Source of everything lacking in providing you whatever you may need, be it positive or negative attributes.

Based on the desire of your last moments in your previous birth on the planet, I have created the complete package for your soul. It was during your dying moments that you harbored a desire of being in total control of your *soul* - something which you did not do during the whole journey of your previous lifetime. At the end of your previous birth, you were literally forced out of your earthly body by circumstances in which you unintentionally had a big role. Because of your lack of awareness, you did not enjoy your dying moments and therefore created a subtle desire that in your next birth you would have total control even of your dying moments. That means you wanted to choose your last moment and also the place you wanted to be in then. You wanted to breathe your last while being fully aware of it, alert and awake with a satisfied mind and heart. It is for this reason that I am equipping you with all the ingredients right from the word go.

I have a few warnings though. You were already carrying a large *karmic debt* when I sent you to Earth during your previous birth. You have neutralized most of it during the journey of your last birth, but due to ignorance at both the individual level and the societal level, you got entangled in unnecessary squabbles with a few of your close relatives including your siblings, had some unwanted fights with your colleagues and had serious misunderstandings with your life partner on petty issues. You indulged in some discriminatory activities towards your fellow human beings due to prevalent social customs. The other great and sinister mistake you carried on with was your penchant for eating meat and other non-vegetarian stuff even though you knew already that animals had just as much a right to live on earth as you. Since you have already reached an exalted status in your understanding about the *karmic principles of life*, I wish that you will fulfill your desire of total control of your mind and intellect and achieve your goal of experiencing the freedom of being a *realised soul* at the end of this new cycle of life.

Having reached an exalted state already, you will be so empathetic that others' pain and sufferings will create a big dent in your mind. Some of your associated *souls* whom I have sent, as per their last desires, with disabilities like blindness, deafness, and other infirmities, will create ruffles in your mind, but you already know the reasons why human beings face such problems on Earth. There are other new developments which I am eager to caution you on. There will be moments when your own physical body could be put in danger by a few of your fellow brothers, those who have already been sent to Earth, mainly because life there has become very complicated, with sophisticated machines taking over many human activities. There will be a danger of accidents, due to the fault of others at the manufacturing level, of some machines including cars, railway engines, airplanes, ships, household equipment. There will be danger due to food and drug adulteration, and even due to some natural calamities which will threaten your dwellings - the sudden bursting of dams, flooding of rivers, earthquakes etc. But all these dangers will pass; except the dangers of excessive greed, anger and passion. These emotions will bother you depending on the path you take. Moreover, the political atmosphere prevalent on the planet Earth will incite further passions in you.

Some souls carry the wrong impression that they are sent by me to just enjoy 'one life', but these ignorant souls pose a greater threat to the human species than anything else. These believers of *'one life only'* will do all kinds of extreme things, some of them very nasty. And some may even influence your thought processes and try to tempt you into the same trap. But I am providing you with all the power to come out of all these dangers if you will continue to keep faith in Me. You will have plenty of opportunities to go up a few notches with regards to the *karmic principles of life*, after balancing out all your previous karmic debts and accumulating much credit to your account during this life cycle. If you judiciously choose, by your own will power, to utilize the opportunities that come to you in a wise manner, your divine desire of having total control on your physical body - on the when, where and how to leave the planet earth to come back to Me - will see fructification.

Yours lovingly,

Your Father God.

Hindu belief of thirty-three crore Gods

When I was young, I remember my parents and elders talking often about subtle concepts in Hindu philosophy. One of these was the relatively strange belief in *thirty-three crore (three hundred and thirty million) Gods*. Mine was a big family in the 1960's and 1970's; our parents provided us, during our early childhood and teens, with a very serene family atmosphere which had all ingredients of peace, happiness, forward-looking ideas and freedom of thought and expression when we were growing up. Naturally there were discussions within the family whenever close relatives or friends of the family visited us with regards to matters of faith. In one sentence this faith can be summarised as '*God is Omnipotent, Omnipresent and Omniscient*'. Being a child, it was beyond the power of my intellect to crack the meaning of what "God" was, what He looked like, how He feels, how He commands the globe and how, in reality He operates and manages the whole world. There used to be dramas, theatre and stage performances called Yatras, in Orissa during cultural and spiritual festivals with themes related to religious ideas, various incarnations of God. There would be stories revolving around these central themes for imparting moral and ethical values to society.

My mother and father were very pious people, religious to the core, believing in all kinds of Hindu rituals and festivities that we in any part of India love to celebrate throughout the year. However, in one corner of my little brain, I always used to wonder how God controlled the day-to-day affairs of each individual on earth and how infinitely powerful He must be to manage such a vast world with a perfect order to everything that Nature has to offer. There were trees, domestic and wild animals, forests, rivers, mountains, the Sun, rains, roads, palatial buildings, people living in them just as there were people living under thatched roofs, buses, cars, bullock-carts, children playing games at a national and international level, and so much more. I used to wonder how God as one person could handle so much and with such ease. I used to be pleasantly baffled by how God managed to control all of it so nicely that there always appears to be perfect order. There was perfect order, in us, as little kids, getting up in the morning, studying a little after breakfast, getting ready for school, then enjoying around six hours of learning and play under the watchful eyes of teachers, coming back in the afternoon and enjoying various games and sports activities for a couple of hours, then performing evening prayer in the Puja Ghar, studying a little after that in the evening and then finally retiring to bed after dinner with the news read-out from All India Radio playing in the background. There was literally perfect order and definitely this was all made possible by God - who surely had to be really powerful to manage all of it.

All this changed one day when I was on my way back home from school. My concept of God had its first significant stirring. Those days, in our small town, people used to hire cowherds to graze the domesticated cows (In our cow shed, our family had at eight or nine cows and a few calves). That particular day, I was walking back from school, taking my usual route, and there were hardly two hundred metres to go before I reached home when a cow from a herd coming from the opposite direction suddenly attacked me with its horns. I was around eleven or twelve years old, studying in either class six or seven, and owing to my flexibility, I was able to run away from the grave danger with relatively minor injuries. With the cow deciding to cause no more harm than this flutter in my little brain about why God directed this cow to hit me with its horns, as if in a prophetic way, my search for God from then on became more intense and all encompassing.

The whole of that afternoon, and perhaps from that very moment to the moment of my writing these words, my mind looks to conceptualise the true meaning of God. In the meanwhile, I have gone through high school, college, university and several years of work life. The evolutionary trend of education in physics, from Cartesian Mechanics to Newtonian Mechanics to Quantum Mechanics, and then reading through the vast literature that exists on modern day concepts of physics which is still evolving and looking for a Unified Field or Unified Theory to explain everything that is happening in this Universe through some fundamental law, my little brain is still grappling with the idea that was set off on that beautiful afternoon.

The statement *'God does not play dice'* and *'I would love to believe in God if you can explain to me how His brain functions'*, both of which are ascribed to Albert Einstein who is perhaps the most talked about twentieth century scientist, were all directed at understanding and explaining the fundamental laws of nature that are behind all that we see in this world.

Most people would love science if it is properly explained to us, and I am one such. Science and spirituality are actually two sides of the same coin and while I have been enthralled by scientific ideas explaining nature, in some corner of my mind, I have not been able to leave behind the thread which binds all of us to that all-pervading God. Many believe in crude interpretation of religion and its tenets, but to my mind it is like Cartesian division of space and matter. The very goal of humanity so far to explain everything through one fundamental Law of Nature encompassing all the different laws of gravitation and electromagnetism etc. is nothing but an eternal quest in giving meaning to life - otherwise termed as spirituality.

If God was an entity of imaginable human form, then how to explain thirty-three crore Gods? My little brain was never prepared to accept this concept. Using logic, however, one can explain how, when such a concept first took root in the Hindu community's universal psyche, the total population of the world was perhaps around thirty-three crores (three hundred and thirty million). Since human beings are sometimes considered to have God within themselves or be representatives of God, the thirty-three crore Gods concept was pointing, perhaps, to the projected human population on earth (there would surely not be well established practices of modern day census). Through such a logical analysis, we would have seven hundred crore Gods today as we can all claim ourselves to be one of the seven billion children of God. Unfortunately however, even today in Indian media or in Indian social circles, the concept of thirty-three crores Gods is prevalent and talked about.

In fact, human beings' belief in God, a supernatural power and the Almighty, was very natural because the human mind and the intellect through which we perceive the world and try to find answers to all the questions that arise have only a limited potential. Whenever we fail to explain anything through scientific logic, we have to bow down and ascribe the mystery to the Supreme Power. The intrinsic beauty of the human mind, which lies underneath the charm and pleasure one gets from life on Earth, is its limitedness in deciphering the whole Cosmos at one go. The day the human mind knows it all, the charm of life will be gone. The mysteries of Universe will keep unfolding, and there will always be more getting added to it simply because the Universe is expanding and perhaps the Earth is expanding too. The delicate balance that a healthy human mind enjoys will last only so long as he does not try to challenge the Power of God.

CHAPTER 9

MUSINGS ABOUT HUMAN EVOLUTION AND *SATYA YUG*

Musings about human evolution

How many of us can truly claim to have asked this question ever in our lives, 'Who am I and where from have I come, where I am going and is it the only birth that I am enjoying or I have gone through repeated cycles of birth and death?' We get so much enmeshed in our emotional hook up to our immediate family, friends and social circles that our vision gets obliterated and becomes very narrow in order to be able to think beyond certain level. The fact that I am born from my immediate parents is now hundred percent established in terms of my physicality both including the gross body and the subtle mind that I inherited from my immediate parents. But as it must have happened in almost every one's case, whenever we face some acute or chronic ailment, doctors ask us this question, who in your family suffers from such an ailment. Why is it that genetics play such a major role in determining who we are in terms of our physicality? We have limited information in terms of genetic record but it will not be difficult to imagine that many of the physical features of our body as well as the psychological traits can be easily traced to have roots not only our parents but even in our grandparents, great grandparents and so on. If we can imagine the family tree, it will be amazing to notice that perhaps such attributes get transmitted generation after generation although genetic mutation at each stage might enhance or reduce some specific attributes of either parent in the family tree.

Thus who decides such a unique process that we carry almost everything of the physicality of our ancestors but still maintain some distinctiveness in our character? We always get to hear that every individual in the earth is unique. So it should be. Going a step further, what happens to the animal world? What happens to the plant world? Do all of them go through a similar process just the way we as humans do. Have we all started from the most fundamental of life forms, the unicellular being? Which is the most fundamental of life form? Broadly speaking, we know now that during Azoic (lifeless) period, now called Hadean Period, prior to the Archean period, very early on after the birth of the planet earth, there was no life form. I get intrigued to see in newspaper articles when latest research discovers that the age when earliest life form came on earth, gets always backwards by few million years! How far can we go in this fashion? Can we reach a point when human beings can imagine that perhaps life as we might decipher one day, and not as we know today, actually began exactly at the same moment when planet earth took birth? The moment we start putting our thought processes in this direction, we suddenly get scared to have approached the realm of madness.

I recall one interesting anecdote. Generally speaking, right from my childhood, I have a tendency to ask questions first within myself and if I fail to get a convincing reply, I try to ask others to explain to me about certain phenomenon that baffles me in this beautiful world. Millions of questions keep coming to my mind always and I keep searching for answers. I get very happy when I somehow get some answers either by my own efforts or through the wisdom of others, whether from literature or verbal communications. I was visiting one of our family friends for a dinner while I was in Adelaide during my PhD research study. Few other families had also assembled for a social get together over dinner. As it stood during July 1997-August 2001, the period I spent in Adelaide, only a handful of Indian families with Bengali origin were living in the city of Adelaide and in its outskirts. Most of them were from science and technology background who had migrated to Australia for few decades by then. In this particular get together, there was one gentleman with Biology background from Bangladesh who was a renowned researcher or professor in one of the Universities of Adelaide. We were all chatting amongst ourselves just before the actual dinner. When I came to know about his background, I slowly started interacting with high degree of intensity and keenness with him simply because I felt some of the most fundamental questions that were bothering me since childhood would now be clarified. Those days, internet was not developed as much as it is today. Questions like origin of life, evolutionary processes etc. were always being carried in my mind. I started asking him questions in a systematic manner encouraging him to explain to me the doubts I had in my mind. At one stage he even quoted about one of the Nobel Laureates of Indian (Undivided) origin, Dr. Hargovind Khorana who was awarded the Nobel Prize for medicine in 1968. When I asked point blank one question to him, "Sir, do you think that the plant life and animal life had one common ancestry and if so, when did it happen that both got bifurcated?" The moment I asked this question, he became a bit restless and murmuring that "Oh, those things are generally dealt by people from faith and they are not the job of scientists", he went away from me breaking the conversation. I remember to this day the scene when I felt slightly embarrassed to have put the gentleman in a quandary. So, at one point of time, we as students of science fail to venture into such domain out of sheer fear of the unknown. It could also be because of the fear that we might invite the wrath of the society which has structured itself in such a way that results of such search might jeopardise the harmonius fabric of the society.

There are some fundamental issues with human evolution. It is obvious from fossil record, modern humans came very late, perhaps less than a million years back. As per published literature on genetic research, modern humans have evolved through a complex evolutionary process. It is now believed that about eighty-five million years ago, in the Late Cretaceous period, primates diverged from other mammals and there is fossil evidence which dates back to the Paleocene, around fifty-five million years ago. It is now a well-known fact that hundreds of such fossils were found in East Africa during the 1960s and 1970s. It is for this reason, Africa is said to be the *cradle of humankind.*

It has been documented now that the species *Homo habilis*, which evolved around 2.3 million years ago, is the earliest member of the genus *Homo*. Stone tools were used by this species. In terms of physiology, the brains of these early hominins were about the same size as that of a chimpanzee. Over the next few million years, a process of *encephalisation* (increase in brain size) began as one of the important step of the evolutionary process. Cranial capacity had doubled to eight hundred and fifty cubic centimetres by the time the species *Homo erectus* arrived and there is fossil evidence for this. Few species like *Homo erectus* and *Homo ergaster* were the first to leave Africa and later these species spread through Africa, Asia, and Europe between 1.3 to 1.8 million years ago. It is now estimated that this increase in human brain size is equivalent to every generation having a hundred and twenty-five thousand neurons more than their parents. It is believed that these species were the first to use fire and complex tools.

Studies have now established that archaic *Homo sapiens*, our ancestors, evolved between four hundred and two hundred and fifty thousand years ago. Non-African populations exhibit several haplotypes of Neanderthal origin which has been indicated by DNA studies. It is postulated that Neanderthals and other hominids might have contributed up to six percent of their genome to present-day humans, suggesting a limited interbreeding between these different species. Many anthropologists believe that the evolutionary transition to behavioural modernity, with the development of symbolic culture, language communication, and specialized lithic technology happened around fifty thousand years ago. It can thus be realized that the power to communicate effectively and comprehensively one's understanding about anything in this world, whether about natural life processes or any such thing to another person has developed in a tiny period of planet earth's lifespan so far.

Our understanding of human origin has been boosted by the extraordinary advancement in science in the last couple of hundred years or so, particularly progress in DNA sequencing, specifically mitochondrial DNA (mtDNA) and then Y-chromosome

DNA. Human Genome Project is one such grand project of research into the total genetic mapping of human body. Genetic sequencing mtDNA and Y-DNA sampled from a wide range of indigenous populations from different parts of the world revealed ancestral information relating to both male and female genetic heritage. Genetic studies have shown a greater diversity in DNA patterns throughout Africa, consistent with the idea that Africa is the ancestral home of mitochondrial Eve and Y-chromosomal Adam.

Although we know that several other characteristics like bipedalism, sexual dimorphism etc. have been associated with the evolutionary process, perhaps the most sophisticated development happened in the most complex part of human body i.e. its brain. The human species developed a much larger brain than other primates – typically it is one thousand three hundred and thirty cubic centimetres in modern humans, over twice the size of a chimpanzee's or gorilla's. This increase in brain size through an evolutionary process known as encephalisation, started with *Homo habilis* which had a brain slightly larger than that of chimpanzees, at approximately 600 cubic centemetres. It continued with *Homo erectus* (eight hundred to one thousand and one hundred cubic centimetres) and reached a maximum with Neanderthals who had a brain which in size averaged one thousand two hundred to one thousand nine hundred cubic centimetres larger even than *Homo sapiens*. There is a difference in the pattern of human post-natal brain growth from that of other apes by which it allows for extended periods of social learning and language acquisition. Similarly, the differences between the structure of human brains and those of other apes may be even more significant than simply the differences in size.

Another interesting thing that is noticed is that the increase in volume over time has affected areas within the brain unequally – the temporal lobes, which contain centers for language processing, have increased disproportionately, as has the prefrontal cortex which has been related to complex decision-making and moderating social behavior. It has also been proposed that human intelligence increased as a response to an increased necessity for solving social problems as human society became more and more complex. The human brain was able to expand during evolutionary process because of the changes in the morphology of smaller mandibles and of mandible muscle attachments to the skull, thereby allowing more room for the brain to grow.

It has been argued that human evolution has accelerated since the development of agriculture and civilization some 10,000 years ago. It is claimed that this has resulted in substantial genetic differences between current human populations across different parts of the world. However, many in the scientific community believe that recent human evolution has been confined to genetic resistance to some infectious disease.

From all the scientific research, it is observed that evolution basically leads to better adaptability of species to vagaries of nature. Science has not yet attacked the problem what many theologians, particularly the Hindu religionists, want us to believe in the theory of transmigration of souls from one species to another. Common sense would demand that if we are products of evolution, many of the genetic imprints of lower primates would exist in human beings and if we extend this further, many of the genetic material of other mammals would also find resemblance with that of human beings. What is the significance of such an evolutionary process, many would wonder. Although in a logical reasoning, one directional progression could be a possibility, evolution happening progressively towards a much more sophisticated being from the lowest form of life but in order to believe that reverse process of migration of human souls into lower forms of life will be almost impossible to fathom at the current stage of modern science.

Dashavatara and its relevance to human evolution

Synthesis of modern science and religion is something which has been attempted by many scholars over the last few centuries when there appeared to be conflicts between religious belief systems on one hand and hard scientific evidence on the other.

The concept of Dashavatara, the ten incarnations of the God Vishnu, is very popular in Hindu philosophy. However, some modern interpreters sequence Vishnu's ten main avatars in a definitive order, from simple life-forms to more complex ones, and see the Dashavataras as a reflection, or a foreshadowing, of the modern theory of evolution.

- Matsya - fish, the first class of vertebrates; evolved in water

- Kurma – tortoise, living in both water and land

- Varaha - wild land animal

- Narasimha - beings that are half-animal and half-human (indicative of the emergence of human thoughts and intelligence)

- Vamana - short, premature human beings

- Parasurama - early humans living in forests and using weapons

- Rama - humans living in a community, beginning of civil society

- Krishna - humans practicing animal husbandry, politically advanced societies

- Buddha - humans finding enlightenment

- Kalki - advanced humans with great powers of destruction.

Keshub Chandra Sen, a prominent figure in the Brahmo Samaj and an early teacher of Swami Vivekananda, was the first Indian Hindu to refer about the connection between Dashavatara and human evolution. In an 1882 lecture he said; 'The Puranas speak of the different manifestations or incarnations of the Deity in different epochs of the world's history. The Hindu Avatars rise from the lowest scales of life, through the forms of the fish, the tortoise and up to the perfection of humanity. Indian Avatarism is indeed a crude representation of the ascending scale of Divine creation. Such precisely is the modern theory of evolution.'

Some scholars suggest that the *Satya Yug* had four Avatars (Matsya, Kurma, Varaha and Narsimha); the *Trettaya Yug* had three Avatars (Vamana, Parasurama, and Rama); the *Dwapar Yug* two Avatars (Krishna and Buddha) and *Kali Yug* one Avatar (Kalki). It is intriguing to note that the first human forms are considered to be living in the *Trettaya Yug*. We have been taught that virtues decreased by one quarter in each Yuga. The *Satya Yug* witnessed a hundred percent virtue, and we can only deduce that when humans did not exist, there was no divide between Satya (Truth) and lie (Untruth) and therefore everything was assumed to be virtuous! It is only when human forms started appearing on this planet (starting with Vamana Avatar), that virtuousness began to decrease. The human mind and intellect began to conceptualise things, started differentiating matter and sprit as separate entities and tried to ascribe meaning to their interpretations in a structured form. This is perhaps the reason why Lord Krishna never once utters anything about the existence of the *Satya Yug* or *Trettaya Yug* in the Bhagawat Gita (of course the one I am familiar with) even though we believe He existed in the *Dwapar Yug*, after two Yugas were already completed! Being the Omnipresent, Omniscient and Omnipotent, it was not difficult for Lord Krishna to describe what had already passed (*Satya Yug* and *Trettaya Yug*) and what was to come in future(*Kali Yug*). Is it possible that when Lord Krishna said that He took human form to come to Earth, destroy evil and re-establish divinity, He was only referring to the good and evil thoughts that get created inside the individual human brain and that it is human intellect and the pure divine spark within each human being that can help identify the evil thoughts occurring within one's mind, separate them from the good and destroy them. Perhaps, Lord Krishna giving sermons in the battlefield of Kurukshetra, point towards a lesser talked about theory and that is, Lord Krishna (representing subconscious wisdom normally dormant in the brain) explaining to the alter ego, Arjun (represented by the conscious brain).

In many a place, the mythological symbols of Goddess Durga with ten arms annihilating the Demon King Mahisasura are interpreted as inherent wisdom i.e. raising our own power of divinity to destroy the devilish attitudes within us that may be starting to cripple our natural divine being. Similarly, on the eve of the battle between the Kauravas and Pandavas in the Mahabharat, the wisdom transferred from Lord Krishna to His best friend and disciple Arjun in the 'Song, the Divine' *Bhagawat Gita*, could also be pointing towards the arousing of that divine spark within each human being so as to kill the devilish thoughts, the lazy thoughts, the depressive thoughts, the escapist thoughts, the egoistic thoughts or simply the inhuman thoughts that get generated within us. Why and how on earth would it otherwise be possible for someone like a charioteer to sit down and start giving sermons to a general - for whom he has taken the reins as a charioteer - on the eve of a battle or a raging war? Lord Krishna himself claims in the *Gita* that He takes birth in human form only to teach people to become involved in the Karmic processes of doing one's earthly duties in a divine and proper religious manner (shlokas 3.22 to 3.24).

Is it possible therefore, hypothetically, to imagine a period of complete sublime happiness, complete divinity, complete peace, which is basically what makes up the *Satya Yug*, when each human being takes birth and comes loaded with the knowledge and wisdom of Lord Krishna Himself? Some people claim that the Bhagawat Gita, which contains verses spoken directly by Lord Krishna Himself, represents the abridged summary of the Veda and Upanishad, the storehouse of Hindu wisdom. Can we imagine a time in future, the so called Satya Yug, when each of the eighteen Yogic paths (starting from first Yogic stance described in the first chapter of the *Bhagawat Gita* where the army of the enemy is right up ahead, similar to the obstacles, difficulties, crises we have to face in our daily lives) to the last Yogic path of attaining liberation or Moksha as described in the eighteenth chapter of the Bhagawat Gita are intrinsically known in the subconscious brain of each human being born on earth? Historically, scholars including great saints, rishis and seers have tried to deduce meaning and simultaneously tried to quote from different scriptures to prove or dispute any point of contention.

Metaphorically, every human being who is naturally born today is born out of the union of a male and a female. Obviously, therefore, none of us can escape the nine or ten months of incubation inside the mother's womb. To make the *Satya Yug* a reality, it is very important that each mother on Earth today learns the intricacies of how children who are born of them should be given the powerful but wise thoughts while still in the womb - so that when they are born, they are equipped with the knowledge and wisdom needed to fight the self-created devilish thoughts within themselves and to conquer them all by themselves, which is what I would refer to as *Satya Yug*.

A senior colleague and friend of mine once said something to me around ten years ago which caught my imagination. He said; '*Krishna*, a Hindu Avatar or incarnation of God, and *Christ* are such similar words in form, structure and pronunciation that perhaps they could be representations of the same God!' Although they represent two totally different religious strands, Hindu and Christian, it still may not be too wild to speculate that the *past life regression therapy* which is taking roots in modern medicine could one day find some link between Lord Ram, Lord Krishna, Lord Buddha, Lord Mahavira, Lord Christ, Prophet Mohammed and Guru Nanak. These above souls who actually came on earth at different times and at different places spoke almost same language when humanity wanted them to share their wisdom. Similarly in contemporary history, we find souls like Leo Tolstoy, Swami Vivekananda and Mahatma Gandhi shared similar characteristics. More research in the field of *life after death*, one example of which we see in the work of Dr. Sam Parnia, author of the book, '*What happens when we die*', may reveal more details about the interchangeability of human souls than what currently meets the eye.

Holger Kersten, in the book '*Jesus lived in India*', has tried to piece together almost indisputable evidence that Jesus lived in India for twelve years. There are full-fledged documentaries on the life and history of Jesus Christ who spent a sizable period of His life in India including Puri, land of Lord Jagannath and one of the four most sacred Dhams in Hindu belief system, and Kashmir where it is claimed that His last remains are buried. If this is found to be true, then the teachings of Lord Jesus would certainly carry the cultural underpinnings and well-entrenched belief system of one of the most ancient civilisations that ever flourished in the Indian subcontinent. One more idea comes to mind: if we look at the symbols of the Hindu Gods, particularly the masculine Gods of the *Trettaya* and *Dwapar Yugs*, we will see that, except for Lord Krishna, all the rest wield some instruments of war or violence. Lord Krishna wields the flute, which many people interpret to mean that the all-pervasive God plays the *music of life* through several sense organs of human beings - represented by the holes of the flute and hence give every human soul to experience the divinity. If we can think a bit further, the symbol of Lord Jesus on the cross says that the ultimate sacrifice is equivalent to complete surrender to the all-pervasive God or Cosmic Intelligence. I do not find any difficulty in correlating this symbol of self-sacrifice of Lord Jesus to the symbol of the image of Lord Krishna playing the flute and not wielding any instrument of violence unlike other major Gods and Goddesses of Hindu belief system, which also suggests in one way allowing the whole human self to be used by all pervasive God or Cosmic Intelligence (symbolically Lord Krishna with His flute) to help us enjoy the experience of divinity in a very subtle manner.

I think that unless the entire world starts thinking in some innovative manner, religious hatred which has been the cause for the maximum violence and killing over the last hundred years or so will continue to bother us. Why can't we take such divine beings as belonging to a global community of *incarnations of God*? Particularly those people who have lived in peace, love and nonviolence always, in any part of the globe.

The escapist tendency in Indian society i.e. to ascribe any wrong doing by anyone to the prevalence of *Kali Yug* is, to say the least, startling. Every sensible human being knows exactly what is good and what is bad by the power of his own conscience. His thoughts and his actions are just a manifestation of sensual responses to stimuli from the environment. Each human being is endowed with sensuality and sexuality. The confusion between sensuality and sexuality due to ignorance is the root of many problems on earth. Every person also knows intrinsically what is good for the human species in the long run and what is not. Killing another human being during wars in the name of religion or expanding/defending state borders or even in self-defense may be acceptable in the eyes of the law. But it cannot be good - as is exemplified by sacrifice of Lord Jesus. The cry for the lifting of death penalties for criminals convicted of heinous crimes in different places and by different groups or individuals is a sign of such understanding. Those ignorant souls who have just begun the epic journey towards salvation by reaching first the human form may not, in one lifetime, be able to understand everything about the ramifications of the effect of karma in one's life. Committing a crime out of ignorance and then ascribing that to the influence of *Kali Yug* is as childish as one can get. The other dimension in this regard is when Ajmal Kasab (convicted and awarded the death penalty for his role in the Mumbai Terror Attacks of July 2008) remained defiant as ever, until his last moment, even though he knew full well what he meant when he uttered his last words; 'Lord, pardon me, I will not make such mistakes again.' There will be different interpretations of his words - which were pure and divine on the one hand, when looked at in one particular way, while dysfunctional and perverted when looked at in another way. It all depends on another human being on earth, who interprets and paints his words in a manner that his own soul thinks fit, and according to the maturity level that he has reached in his life.

Bhagawat Gita: three dimensional internal reflections inside a diamond triangle

I was sitting beside a retired old man from Andhra Pradesh (I do not remember which town this old man hailed from) in the Bali Jatra Ground of the Cuttack District of Odisha where the second international conference on religion and peace was being held under the auspices of the Divine Life Society, India. It was December 2001. Since both of us were at the conference for similar reasons, we began chatting. The topic of discussion was the *Bhagawat Gita.* I vividly remember how the old man reflected on his feelings for the greatness of the scripture (perhaps the most sacred of all the Hindu religious scriptures ever written or compiled). I quote his words: 'Every time you read the *shlokas (verses)* of the *Bhagawat Gita,* you will discover new meaning.'

I can't imagine a stronger and better tribute to any scripture on earth. I have been trying in my own way to understand the depth of his words. I managed perhaps to crack a similar such meaning one morning when I was reading my daily chapter of the *Bhagawat Gita* during Puja and Prayers. The first stanza described the scene wherein the King Dhritarashtra, being blind himself, requested the sage Vyasadev to find some means for him to see what was going on at the battlefield of Kurukshetra. Vyasadev blessed Sanjay with the divine eyes (Divyadristhi) so that he could see everything happening on the battlefield while sitting near Dhritarasthra and could then describe to him what was going on. In modern day society, where rationalistic thinking has gained predominance in all spheres of life, teenagers and even young adults will not be able to take this at face value. They will ask; 'If the gift of divine eyes is so easy to get and if it is so easy to see everything through such divine eyes, even without being physically present at the site, why can't I be the person to get such a gift and which Godly man can gift me such power?' We can't blame them for their skepticism. But as I was reading this stanza on that particular day (I might have read that stanza at least five hundred times or even a thousand times by then), it occurred to me that it made good sense when I understood the inner meaning of it. I felt then that this stanza itself held profound meaning for all generations.

The way I saw it now, the stanza meant that when an actual battle was fought anywhere in the world, there would be millions all over the globe wishing to learn from such a battle, even whilst sitting where they are, if some means of communication about the actual happenings on the battlefield were made available. The way Sanjay could see through his divine eyes the happenings in the battle of Kurukshetra and describe them to Dhritarashtra, and which were later recorded for posterity in the *Bhagawat Gita*, in the modern day communication network, a war raged anywhere in the world can be seen sitting inside the living room in any corner of the globe. Each battle or war produces some historical evidence for future generations. When we attempt to preserve our experiences through such historical records, humanity will obviously gain. Books are a convenient means to do this. Modern day live telecasts of sporting events and even wars are a similar mode of expression. They can be viewed thousands of miles away. This has been made possible through technology.

The Dawn of *Satya Yug*

Two simple words of life have stuck with me since childhood, when I was sensitive enough to pick up these two words. They are *Satya Yug;* and of course, as opposed to two other words - *Kali Yug*. I can recall many in our Indian society, including my own family members, friends and relatives, saying that we are in the *Kali Yug* and that quality of life in this age will further deteriorate till we reach the stage of total destruction - after which a new *Satya Yug* would dawn. This *Satya Yug* would entail everything in the world happening right, good, soft, sweet, compassionate, kind, almost divine. This sort of an expression might find its echo in many other societies and other ancient civilizations – which is why it could have gone into our psyche so deeply that we cannot get it out of our thought process so easily. Every Indian child is fed these ideas by his or her parents, grandparents, seniors, teachers and spiritual leaders from very young age. And hence the ideas are so perpetuating that to think out of this cocoon would be blasphemous. No one today will agree to the simple fact that the *Satya Yug* has already set in. However, I believe there is no reason why we cannot, just by virtue of our thought processes, turn this apparently demonic *Kali Yug* into an age that is purely divine in nature with all-pervading happiness present in mystical proportions, bringing Heavenly peace and harmony.

It is a matter of conjecture whether what is happening around us damages our perceptions so badly that we can never imagine another *Satya Yug*. There are heinous crimes that plague society these days; including dacoity, murder, child abuse, assault on women, cheating, lies, betrayal, communal killings, racial killings, sexual perversion etc. Such things tend to pollute our perceptions and we quickly accept that these are signs of the deeply entrenched *Kali Yug*.

Our ancestors never had access to the kind of technology and scientific progress that modern man has made. Our scriptures depict a cyclic phenomenon wherein evil reaches demonic proportions before good destroys it and reestablishes its dominance in society. And this sort of cyclic development has been there from time immemorial. In today's scientific world, as we can record things that are comprehensible to our sensory perceptions and which are directed towards explaining this cyclic phenomenon of civilisational development, we shall have to believe in the one-way growth of society towards *Satya Yug*. In Hindu philosophy, the entrenched belief is that we had first the *Satya Yug*, followed by the *Trettaya Yug*, then the *Dwapar Yug*, then the *Kali Yug* and that there will be another *Satya Yug* after the full cycle is repeated starting with *Kali Yug* forward through *Dwapar Yug* and *Trettaya Yug*. This philosophy has been in my mind all my life. However, I am never fully agreeable whenever I hear these words from anyone around me howsoever learned and wise he or she might be. I just fail to take it at face value. Rationalists and believers alike will have several reasons to counter me but reason why I say so is based on a beautiful statement, 'You can fool all the people sometime, you can fool some people all the time, but you can never fool all the people all the time'. Whichever Yug it is, we should not try to fool ourselves by saying something which defies logic because for human brain, even though logic is not everything, but it is the minimum requirement both for someone to build his or her ideas to propagate to others or to utilize the same logic to be prepared to receive someone else's logic and accept it.

The standard procedure in which any new knowledge in any field concerning human civilization has arrived is through questioning and reasoning with observations. This questioning occurs only when someone finds his or her inner soul failing to resonate with what has until then been established knowledge. This has happened mostly in scientific studies. Dogmatic religious knowledge generally remains unchallenged. This has happened with very simple concepts, like whether earth was flat or round, whether earth revolves around the Sun or the Sun revolves around Earth. The basis of the fight between Science and religion has always emanated from the power of Church or from the Holy Scriptures coming under threat. Author Dan Brown was inspired to write *'The Da Vinci Code'* mainly because of his bewilderment at the contrasting world views of the Church and what he learnt at school. He could never reconcile himself with the teachings of the Church; such as how God created the world in seven days (which was completely different to what he was learning from his school books). Usually, established social norms, or belief systems built on religious ideas, are not disturbed or repudiated for fear of a backlash.

Why should we have to think that we are deep into *Kali Yug* when deep down, we know that every thought that comes to our mind, arising out of this entrenched belief, can be relooked at with a scientific approach in an attempt to find the veracity of such a belief system. There is no reason why one can't be led to believe the tenets of *Satya Yug* starting to be established already. The utopian view that during the *Satya Yug* everyone in the world will turn pious, noble, truthful, peaceful, loveful and will have no quarrels with their neighbours and so on is a misnomer. This sort of situation would have to first satisfy that the individual who is trying to assess whether the society at large has all the above divine attributes will have to start exhibiting and observing the same attributes himself first. Otherwise, it will be impossible for him to believe that the world is in *Satya Yug*. It is similar to someone praising the taste of a particular dish he just had and wanting another person to enjoy the taste without this other person actually having eaten the dish himself. One who does not exhibit divine attributes himself can never appreciate someone else exhibiting divine attributes - the most fundamental aspect of *Satya Yug*. The moment the individual starts thinking, believing, seeing and sensing the world around him to be one in *Satya Yug* will be the moment when those divine attributes start manifesting in him. *We see in the world what we hold inside ourselves.*

The fact that *Kali Yug* is the prevailing age, and that no one knows how it will come to an end before the advent of the *Satya Yug*, can perhaps be easily realized in the course of one's lifetime if we are allowed the freedom to think without any internal or external binding. When that is not the case, any thought that arises may be biased and therefore have hardly any sustainable value. We can imagine how the path that leads us to visualizing the world is itself a clear indication of the prevalence of *Satya Yug*. In every age, in every generation for that matter, rishis and saints have taken birth and shown the progressive development of this system which takes all of us closer to *Satya Yug*. Though ordinary masses may indulge in conflicts and fights to prove themselves right, realized souls know very well that this is earth, hell and Heaven all embedded in one system. Moreover, what we realize deep within ourselves tells us that for every event that appears to be *Kali Yug*, there is a *Satya Yug*-like counter event that goes with it. The advent of a terrorist attack may appear to be an example of such a so-called *Kali Yug*, but at the same time we can easily find aspects that constitute a *Satya Yug*, such as the explanation of why such an attack took place at all. All our answers would lie vividly in the historical developments and evolution of societal structure. Human ambition, misadventure, exploitation and forceful supremacy are the root causes of today's problems. Moreover, a *Kali Yug* like event of terror attack would surely be instantly followed by *Satya Yug* like event of help, care and service by another bunch of human beings showing tremendous courage and passion for divine service. Though we may apparently be fighting in the outside world against each other, the inside world knows very well where the fault lies, and unless we come to terms with this, there is hardly any chance of any sustainable solution. There are some very fine missing links that will also slowly build on the roots that have already been laid on this earth.

The conclusion that this is *Satya Yug* comes from the trend of all our actions, which are all guided by science and technology now. This is the age of science and technology and so this obviously is the age of Truth. Science pursues Truth relentlessly and we can say that has been around for nearly all of humanity's civilizational history given how we are progressing from cave dwellers to modern day astronomers & astrophysicists. And all this has happened within just the last five or ten thousand years. And the Earth itself is 3.7 - 4.5 billion years old! Many spiritual leaders belittle science and technology due to their ignorance, and their ignorant whispers are full of political lineation (a basic constituent of any human being). They say that spirituality is actually everything; that science does not have any basis and that spirituality is totally guided by God's whims and fancies. Is it not futile to vouch for authenticity, without hard scientific evidence, that the *Kali Yug*, the last of the four *Yugas* going up to 4.5 lakh years as few authors claim? Perhaps it can only be imagined and fantasized in the absence of hard scientific knowledge that the entire period of human existence, which is roughly equal to 2.5 - 4.5 lakh years, as per many paleontological, anthropological and archaeological studies, constitutes the full time duration of *Kali Yuga*. Some authors claim it is a cycle of total twelve thousand years with one *Yuga* accounting for three thousand years, consisting of two thousand and seven hundred years with a transition period of three hundred years. There is also a claim by some authors that *Kali Yug* will end by 2025.

The huge body of literature available based on *Surya Siddhanta,* Indian astronomy and western astronomy also contains many conflicting arguments. Some authors suggest that the original cycle of one full Yuga lasting for twenty four thousand years (ascending and descending cycles of twelve thousand years each), which corresponds within a seven percent margin to recent calculations of the *precession of equinox* (celestial positions and motions) which lasts twenty five thousand seven hundred and seventy-two years, is much more valid than the abnormally high duration obtained by multiplying the figures by three hundred and sixty. Some authors suggest that since virtues reduce by one quarter in each *Yuga*, while moving from the highest *Satya Yug* to *Kali Yug*, they correlate that by managing a figure of 4800 years, 3600 years, 2400 years and 1200 years for the four Yugas starting from *Satya Yug* suggesting a time line ratio of 4:3:2:1. By multiplying 360 (perhaps a figure having some relation to the number of days in a year i.e. 365 days) with 1200 years, some authors also deduce the duration of *Kali Yug* to last 4, 32,000 years! There is a correlation of this 4.32 lakh years to the 4.5 lakh years which is what some palaeontologists and anthropologists claim to be the duration since the arrival of modern day human species, discussed earlier in this chapter.

Each human being is endowed with some genetic influence of imaginary power so as to be able to feel spiritually enlightened when certain things from ancient scriptures are quoted. And faith in traditions helps him or her not only to believe in such ideas but to propagate them further. Somehow, right from childhood, I have believed that the influence of celestial positions and motions definitely have a role to play in our destiny. But at the same time, progression of science and technology (modern day horoscopes and birth charts are now thoroughly computerized; a result of science and technology!) to serve humanity must be accommodated with the traditional views that have been ingrained in us for generations. Geologically, *Milankovitch's cycles of ice ages* have a pretty good correlation with the twelve thousand year cycle of our Yugas. But to demarcate the *golden age, silver age, copper age* and *Iron Age* of human development on the basis of the virtuous cycles of the four Yugas of *Satya, Trettaya, Dwapar* and *Kali* has never been agreeable to me. They are quite separate concepts and should be regarded as such. Traditions have their value, but accepting everything blindly will not help humanity in the long run, more so when we try to justify our wrong deeds done deliberately for some selfish gains and then blame it on influence of *Kali Yug* without pausing even a moment questioning our own motives while committing the mistakes in the first place.

The fact is that everything that has been achieved by society has been made possible only through education and training, which includes modern science and technology. All our past and present leaders would have and will attest to this simple truth of life; that man's progress would have been impossible if we did not embrace these simple facts of life. Hence, the age of science and technology actually leads us to a stage wherein we try to scientifically explain everything that exists in nature. Be it shaping of the Earth through different geological processes, or the origin of the Universe by a few simple laws of physics that are comprehensible to ordinary human beings, or information technology and the extraordinary developments of our modern tools and equipments; we sense the meaning of nature in its expression in the simple facts of life. Science tries to unravel the mysteries of the Universe and though we keep changing our own views and theories with each new development in the technological tools we have in our hands, we manage to build on the old concepts and theories that have stood the tests of time slowly and steadily by fine tuning, or making adjustments, or refining them. This is how we have travelled so far - from a stage where we thought earth was flat and with the Sun revolving around it, to our present knowledge of stars, planets, asteroids, the Universe, the Milky Way, galaxies, supernovas, black holes, the Big Bang etc. We keep changing also. We developed the concept of 'the speed of light' and we thought it was constant, but now the idea is being challenged by the theory that perhaps the speed of light is also not constant. We believed in the supernatural theory of God creating Earth in seven days, but we now know that the planet is about 4.5 billion years old and that the Universe is around fifteen billion years old. In future, science and technology together will allow us to further understand any refinement that may occur in all the theories that are currently in vogue. We could never be sure if we would reach those separated from us by huge differences in time and space, but it is now possible simply through the use of available technology like air wave transmission, satellite technology and so on. We thought the human mind got corrupted by the evil spirit but we now know that it is chemical imbalances that create such problems in mentally ill patients. And that our genetic makeup predisposes, to a great extent, why we get afflicted by certain diseases. We have also made sure that, even if we get afflicted by diseases, we can find cures for them.

This simple reasoning comes from the belief that whatever problems we have created today for ourselves are because of our constant search for happiness, and because we always try to derive means from outside to achieve happiness inside. Although to some extent it was necessary in order to save ourselves from the ravages of nature, creating problems and then trying to find solutions without any introspection is certainly not the true path. The modern problem of terrorism is also a result of the imbalances that exist in society and unless we try at an individual level, a group level, a governmental level or at a Universal level, we will not be able to find solutions to the vexing problems like these which keep afflicting the world. We need to do the best we can at, our own levels, to mitigate such problems and completely erase them from earth.

Satya Yug will achieve this and our lifetimes are just a miniscule part of the path that will help in achieving such results. We can just rule out the possibility of such a true path already being laid out for us by saying that we are in the *Kali Yug*. But that will only be because what we see in our lifetimes is just a small event in the larger scheme of things. It is the scale of observation that is critical.

What *Satya Yug* envisages is reflected in the growth of investigative journalism, growth of information technology, growth of communication science and technology and also in the belief of every individual that there is a scientific solution to all the problems we face in our day-to-day lives. Today's untruth gets challenged tomorrow and a new meaning comes to us even in the most basic of scientific facts. This very process is the indicator of the advent of *Satya Yug*.

In genetic theory, birth of a new born involves mutations of human genes. Similarly, we can imagine mutation of ideas giving rise to newer ideas. Ever since human civilization evolved around a structured form of nation, community, society, group, family etc., plurality and multiple diversity has been the norm rather than the exception. Ideas across geography, nations and cultures have influenced human civilization and have tended to synthesise so as to suit to the needs of any particular place. The very essence that our actions anywhere in the world are bound to create reactions in the Universe and that the impact can be something that earlier did not exist just the way genetic mutations always create something different from the earlier form would tend to make us realize that we are into the *Satya Yug* rather than *Kali Yug*. It is the unfolding of this very knowledge about the mechanics of life, our existence and growth that point towards what we can safely define as advent of *Satya Yug*. There cannot be a permanent Universal Truth because even our science has started believing that we are products of evolution and did not exist earlier, all based on hard scientific evidence. Hence the theory that anything is permanent is flimsy, to say the least. As they say, the only permanent thing is perhaps change. But the *Satya Yug* brings us to the understanding of this basic philosophy in trying to scientifically explain everything to us - to the best of our ability and in our current state of mind at least.

The German philosopher Immanuel Kant had said; 'Two things fill my mind with ever increasing wonder and awe: the starry Heavens above and the moral law within.' One can easily see the balanced influence of the God from within and the God from without on one of the greatest philosophers of the twentieth century.

Many ancient scripts around the world have noticed the cyclic nature of life and existence in line with celestial motions and movements like day and night (rotation of the Earth around its axis), seasonal changes (rotation of the Earth around the Sun), creation of the Universe and collapse of it (concepts of Black Hole singularity and Big Bang Theory of Universal expansion). The Yuga cycle tries to explain this cyclic phenomenon. But the *Bhagawat Gita*, which makes clear mention of the creation and destruction of the Universe, tries to explain this concept only in context of the birth and death of human beings (Shloka 8.19). The warrior prince Arjun gets confused when Lord Krishna says that the knowledge of Gnyana Yoga was told by Him to the Sun God, who in turn passed it on to Manu (shloka 4.1). He asks the Lord to explain how He had talked to the Sun God, who took birth many Yugas prior to the time of Arjun and Krishna. The

Lord explained to Arjun that there were many cycles of birth and death and that Arjun had just forgotten the experience of his previous births. At another place, the Lord again brings in the concept of the Yugas when he equates one human year (three hundred and sixty five days) to one day for God and thousand days of God to one day of Brahma and thousand nights of God to one night of Brahma (shloka 8.17). The Lord then suggests that a hundred years of Brahma is equal to the entire duration of the existence of the Universe and that Brahma's night is the destruction of the Universe (shloka 8.18). But it is very intriguing to note that nowhere in the *Bhagawat Gita*, which has tens and hundreds of sermons about the ethics of life, the morality principles etc. is there any mention of *Satya Yug, Trettaya Yug, Dwapar Yug and Kali Yug*. While it is considered to be the summary of the best of Vedas and Upanishads, that these terms are not mentioned raises serious doubts about the limited interpretation of the Yuga cycle which is discussed in the *Bhagawat Gita*. Although there is mention of the cyclic phenomenon in the case of celestial bodies, it is generally tagged with the progress of the soul and physical body. The tendency of human civilization in this modern age of science and technology is to challenge every new piece of information and knowledge so as to derive and extract newer information and knowledge. This should, in my mind, be construed as advent of *Satya Yug*. Swami Yukteswar, the Guru of Yogi Paramahansa, was the first to challenge the dating and mentioned that we are in the *Dwapar Yug* and not in the *Kali Yug* as it was generally believed. I believe depending on the clarity one enjoys in his or her mind about the mysteries of the Universe and human interpretations of them, rigid ideas about such *Satya Yug* vs *Kali Yug* arguments would not persist for long and may even melt away.

Playing spoil sport with God

There has been no instance on this Earth where there has been one hundred percent agreement between two human beings. Be it a father and a child, a mother and a child, a boss and a subordinate, a man and a woman, two friends, two relatives, a man and his spiritual guru, two scientists, student and teacher, two doctors etc.

The unfortunate fact remains that the differences between two individuals can sometimes grow to such proportions that it causes differences between entire groups or communities or nations and ultimately may even lead to large scale war.

From this and from many other such instances has come my belief that the world's current problems will go away if we take three approaches and steps:

Free flow of information, whether positive or negative, about anything and everything on Earth and the availability of this information to each and every citizen equally. This would help make a person more informed and help him to be a better judge of what is right and what is wrong and also of what is applicable to him and what is not. We sometimes get carried away by what we hear (hearsay) and that is the root cause of all problems.

The ability of each human being to conceive multiple choices and, perhaps even an infinite number of choices. This calls for an entrenched belief in that 'diversity is the key'. There can be an infinite number of ways to look at one thing. My own belief emanates from the fact that, when human beings have been able to formulate the mathematical concept of *infinity*, it is applicable to anything in ordinary life. The beauty is that some ideas get crystallized into universal ideas over a period of time and sustain for hundreds or even thousands of years depending on what we are talking about. Some of the most fundamental scientific discoveries fail to survive for more than fifty years - such as in the case of the theory of a constant speed of light which is nearly half a century old, now being challenged. The theory of the Big Bang and Black Hole to explain the origin of the Universe is now being challenged after just half a century. The most fundamental laws of physics are challenged within a period of fifty to sixty years. So why can't we imagine that everything is changeable in this world and that there is no point in fighting over trivial issues, in proving one wrong. Perhaps we must believe that whatever has sustained, sustained only because it had the internal power and strength to do so, whatever idea or system it is. It could be any system of medicine, as we discussed earlier, since it has helped humanity in its own way and people's belief has been based on actual results. Hence, *unity in diversity* is the only solution for all our problems. To believe that there can be infinite possibilities would make our own position so diluted that our egos would lose their power and we will be able to leave ourselves subservient to a greater power, the power of the Almighty, the God and the Supreme.

This would lead to acceptance of the fact that every human being is a representative of God on Earth. The other concept, the one of an ever expanding consciousness (the part that can be attributed to God), also is a must to sustain the concept of there being as many Gods as human beings on Earth. Being an active student of science, religion, spirituality and divine life, I have a strong belief that the ancient Hindu concept of three hundred and thirty three million Gods can prove to be the basis of a total freedom and acceptance that can revolutionise existing dynamics and lead to a quantum jump and paradigm shift in the understanding of the true meaning of *Satya Yug*. While knowing that many well educated and rational scientific minds will, at first instance, feel jolted because this theory goes against the grain of their internal belief system about a prevailing *Kali Yug*, which has been built over several hundred years, I still believe that pursuing the complete Truth, though it may be hard to obtain, is preferable to just blindly taking a few scriptures at face value.

Tenets of *Satya Yug*

The very basis of someone's trust or mistrust in another starts from his own soul. What he sees in others is a reflection of what is already there in his own soul. This is the reason why I announced sometime in May 2000 that evil does not exist. The story line is already written elsewhere. The western belief or disbelief, as compared to the eastern belief or disbelief, all arise from Truth, but when Truth tries to *paint* the outside world through the follies of human minds, sometimes, falsehood is generated. The very nature of the human mind is the cause of all these problems.

Human beings, in their totality, can contain the highest possible degree of love and the highest possible degree of hatred, which respectively lead to self-sacrifice or forced killing. Jesus stood for the former, the infinite apostle of love and peace. The other extreme, merciless killing is represented by the group that caused Jesus's sacrifice.

In a television conversation telecast by the Isha Foundation, Sadhguru Jaggi Vasudeva answers a question posed by the Bharat Biotech Founder and Chairman: 'Sadhguru, given the violence and disturbances across the world now, it seems that this world was a better place earlier in the past than it is now. How do we bring back the old life of calm and peace on to the world?" Sadhguru replied; "The world is much more peaceful now than it ever was. It is just that now we instantly come to know of any violent killing or suffering happening in any part of the world through television signals containing pictures of blood oozing out and body parts strewn all around, beaming into every bedroom and living room across the world."

His words were so emphatic that it resonated pretty intensely with my theory of *"This age is Satya Yug"*. I am however aware that Sadhguru himself speaks about the *Yuga cycle* which is something bit different. He suggests that position of earth with respect to the Super Sun brings in variation in the etheric substance in atmosphere which determines which *Yuga cycle* we are in. He calculates that by 2082 AD, we would be entering into *Trettaya Yug* because we have already crossed two cycles of *Kali Yug* and now about to complete the *Dwapar Yug*. It is once again interesting to see that since Swami Yukteswar, we have at least progressed few notches ahead in our belief system regarding Yuga cycle.

I feel that when we perceive predominant peace and tranquility, is it not the advent of *Satya Yug*? Those who might be outwardly educated and proud of their knowledge of the Sanskrit language or any other language, like French, German, Arabic, English, Spanish, Chinese, Japanese, Tamil, or may still be proud of their knowledge of the Vedic texts, the Brahminical order, or any subject of modern science like Physics, Chemistry, Biology, Mathematics or Medicine, or even their spiritual knowledge, may not lose a single moment to reject this idea of *Satya Yug*. These people are likely to take new births to experience even newer things.

Sadhguru goes on to suggest that human intelligence can reach epic proportions as compared to a chimpanzee's even though we know that there is only about a 1.2 percent difference in the DNA between the two species. This human intelligence, if not handled properly, can start working against man and will be the cause of all kinds of sufferings - including stress, anxiety, fear, anger, hatred etc. As long as we enjoy the differences that exist in this world, the world will always look beautiful. But the moment we allow ourselves to start discriminating based on these differences - be it gender, physical prowess, skin colour, language, profession, wealth, caste, creed, religion, culture, belief system or nationality - the seeds of sufferings are sown. Obviously, life will then turn ugly instead of being joyful and blissful.

Today, the internet has become a vast repository of knowledge of all kinds. Just a click of a button can open up the door and quench one's thirst for knowledge and remove ignorance to a large extent. The ancient Vedic knowledge, which is claimed to have answers to almost all human questions, now has a much friendlier equivalent in the modern age in the form of the internet which is accessible by each and every citizen of the world, albeit with a small cost. Unlike the Vedic period where the knowledge was restricted to only a privileged few, the modern age has at least laid the foundation for easy, affordable and equitable access to the internet in such a way that knowledge is no more any one person's exclusive property. *Wikipedia* in the modern age is beginning to work as a powerhouse of all knowledge and wisdom in any conceivable branch of science, art and commerce, similar to *Vedas* of the past.

All of humanity, as it stands today, has been growing in all directions - both good and bad. But the focusing of all the positive energies in one direction, in the mould of only a 'giver' and not a 'seeker' emulating what the Sun is doing, would perhaps mitigate the sufferings of humanity. The often quoted statement of Dr.A.P.J. Abdul Kalam soon after his demise, extracted from his latest book, *'If you want to shine like the Sun, first burn like the Sun'* summarises metaphorically the inherent attributes of Sun that humanity should learn to adopt. Branches of science, tools of technology, and hence strands of professions are taking birth at perhaps the same rate that different species of life are going extinct. These professions are taking birth with the sole aim of serving humanity. At the same time man is using this rapidly advancing technology to find newer methods to kill people with innovative modern arms and ammunitions. This is a paradox. Einstein's words come to mind: 'You cannot achieve peace while trying to prepare for war at the same time.' This statement is profound. Because we are engaged in such hypocritical approaches everywhere; nations are developing new weaponry and stockpiling armaments while trying to negotiate for peace with adversaries. Perhaps Mahatma Gandhi's quotation is more appropriate: 'If someone hits you in one cheek, show him the other cheek if you want him to love you.' This kind of situation has been there from time immemorial, be it the *Satya Yug* or *Trettaya Yug*, *Dwapar Yug* or *Kali Yug*. We have seen wars and battles in each Yuga which are said to have been fought to establish dominance of good over evil.

Not very long ago, we had different forms of medicine developing in different parts of the world. Then, by taking the example of modern allopathic medicine, we have developed rapidly in the last hundred years or so into many branches of medicine. First came MBBS, the generalist branch of medicine. Then came the specialization into several branches like surgery, psychiatry, pediatrics, gynecology, opthalmology, ENT etc. Now in the modern age, we have gone into super specialization. The field of ophthalmology itself includes specializations like laser surgery, retina specialty, glaucoma specialist etc. The field of hematology, which deals with blood, has developed perhaps a hundred different tests to know the attributes of blood that may indicate some parameter leading to a health problem. There are so many organs in the body! A single branch of medical science i.e. oncology has now several subdivisions, all of them very specialized branches. Similarly, modern medical research has come to such a stage that we can preserve stem cells derived from the umbilical cord and cord blood during birth and keep it in storage banks such that they can be utilized in future to prevent eighty different types of diseases. These are just a few examples from medical field, concerning just humans. So imagine where we are now if we include animal health, plant health and so on. In a similar manner, there has been branching out in all departments of science and engineering into a variety of applied branches all of which are basically directed towards helping and serving the humanity.

If any knowledge is found to be incorrect, there is ample scope for even an individual to verify from several sources, through internet access, about the veracity of any knowledge or information he or she is dealing with. Scientists are relentlessly pursuing new frontiers. I recall one incident during a meeting of top scientists, physicists, astrophysicists, and biologists etc. gathered at the campus of the University of Adelaide sometime during early 2001. One of the former editors of *Nature* magazine was coordinating the discussions amongst the top scientists. It was a large gathering and I happened to be there. At one point, the coordinator was triumphantly saying that most of the big ticket knowledge, or the broader issues of natural laws and principles, had been discovered by modern science and only the connecting dots of finer tidbits were yet to be discovered. Then he gave one question by himself to the entire house. He asked; 'There are a few issues still unexplored. One of them is that we are still not very clear about how a cat, which attacks a rat, decides that he can actually kill the rat and not be killed by the rat before making the attack!'

To me, it appeared to be a very sophisticated question at that time. But now, after a decade and a half, I don't think it will be difficult for me to add another hundred such questions. For example, do we know whether the frequency of the vibrations in the heart's pumping has anything to do with how the mind senses love or hatred as a separate emotion? Do large hearted people really have a heart which is physically large or it is just symbolic? Do we know why nature has kept the heart and mind in the positions they are in now; was there a better alternative? Do we know why some people have longer hands, larger feet, larger ears, larger nose etc. compared to others? Is it just the genes and the DNA we are born with or is there something still unknown? Do we know if Mars or any such planet in the entire Universe had a similar human (or similar intelligent species) civilization and, if so, what actually happened to it? We are yet to find concrete evidence that life exists in a form similar to that on earth anywhere else in the Universe. Another prominent question that still bothers us is what happens when we die? Still very unclear is why same event triggers different emotions in two different individuals? Hence the horizon of science is unlimited. After making a thorough survey of Near Death Experience case studies and the associated literature while working in Southampton General Hospital, UK, Dr. Sam Parnia writes in his book *'What happens when we die'*, "The problem in science today is where does our consciousness-our free will, conscience, feelings, thoughts and emotions – actually come from and how it is produced?"

I believe that the more we know, the more we will find that we still do not know much. This is a paradoxical situation. And this gap will continue for eternity, so long as human brains maintain their inherent inquisitiveness. Similarly, if we think that *Satya Yug* will dawn on earth and everyone will start behaving like divine entities, then we would be making a mistake. We all know from our *Puranas* that even during the so called *Satya Yug*, different Gods showed and expressed ferocious anger. Some engaged in lust also, as we find in the story of Lord Indra and Ahalya. To avoid such paradoxes, some scholars interpret the story in a slightly different manner, where Lord Indra is said to have converted the virgin or unploughed land into a fertile land. Thus, it seems that almost everything that can be conceived is there already in the power of the human brain. It is when we fail to acknowledge this, because of our deep rooted belief systems entrenched in us over a large number of birth and death cycles in the course of our own *Karmic Life Cycles,* that we fail to fully comprehend the ramifications. To put it in common man's language, if Gods were blinded by passionate feelings, then what is the difference between them and today's common people when we know at least all the facets of anger and understand its emotional ramifications in a scientific manner i.e. what type of brain chemicals and brain areas are involved when too much anger leads to stress and cause imbalance in the brain chemicals. Is it not apt then to suggest that this modern age of science and technology, in all honesty, can truly claim to represent *Satya Yug* more than ever? To me, *Satya Yug signifies the tendency to unravel Satya (Truth) without being tied up or closeted with dogma.* The impediments to the human mind's visualization of the advent of *Satya Yug* can now be removed by this modern tool of internet, by getting all answers to his questions within a fraction of a minute. Human beings know, in their heart of hearts, what they are doing, whether conscientiously or otherwise. The modern criminal jurisprudence system, with its advanced investigative tools, highly advanced IT network and highly professional investigative journalism, can unravel truth from a pack of lies in any field of activity. Great popular spiritual leaders also are not spared from the grip of law and media. If we still do not believe that this is not resonating with the idea of *Satya Yug* in our minds and hearts, it is because we have, traditionally, been taught for centuries about the four Yugas and that presently it is the *Kali Yug* which prevails over us. It would then be hypocrisy to suggest that we worship science, but at the same time we are prisoners of a traditional belief system without any scientific basis.

A recent news report about how the Federal Bureau of Investigation (FBI) of the USA's department of justice admitted to erroneously doctoring forensic lab reports to convict people on death rows is an example of this. As per the news report, out of a total of sixty cases in which the FBI admitted to errors, three defendants were put to death ultimately. The above example establishes one thing loudly. Even if a wrong is secretly committed anywhere in the world today, there is every possibility that democratic forces and conscientious drive inherent in humanity as a whole will be relentless at some level to bring out that to light. These things have happened in many cases.

The help of modern science, technology and journalism to reach this global order is a clear indicator of what I have been suggesting as the dawn of *Satya Yug*. Initially, microscopic hair analysis was the procedure, but it is currently mitochondrial DNA hair analysis, along with the usual microscopic hair analysis, which is put to use in the USA during such criminal investigations and reporting. Classified documents of war crimes have been made public within a hundred years, in a constitutional manner. The publication of these and other such secretive documents by governments across the world, through the power of democracy, is another vindication of the prevalence of *Satya Yug* today. We do not need to wait for thousands of years to expect or imagine a Heavenly atmosphere to reign over us. The period of a hundred years, or fifty years, as it stands today, for any secretive thing happening anywhere to become publicly known is bound to reduce further through the judicial activism and people's movements across the world including in developed, developing and underdeveloped nations. The above examples refer to political events or those having larger ramifications. Similarly, on an individual scale, we have come to such a stage where we intrinsically know our follies very well, even if we keep them secret due to fear of admonition from society or fear of loss of prestige until someone discovers it and exposes it.

Does consciousness reside within or without?

On twenty fourth July 2000, I had attended a public discussion in Adelaide shortly after the launch of the book *'Secrets of mind'* by Graham Cairns Smith in which a well-known physicist Paul Davies was also present. The author had argued in his book that study of human consciousness was more to do with human sensations, feelings, perception, awareness and intuition etc. I recall during the question-answer session that followed, I had raised the question whether it was necessary to look for *consciousness from within or from without*. I had then commented about the possibility that the entire body-heart-brain-mind-soul combine should be the entity looking for consciousness rather than brain alone which unfortunately is the basis of modern science so far. Fifteen years ago, I had this suspicion that the heart has a much bigger role to play than the brain in the domain of feelings and sensations which Graham attributes to consciousness. Any conscious experience of human being perhaps has much to do with his heart first before it is decoded by combination of neurons and neurotransmitter in different areas of the brain. In his book *'What happens when we die'*, Dr.Sam Parnia passionately suggests that brain should be considered separate from mind and consciousness although for any conscious experience, including all our emotions like anger, fear, love, hatred etc., different areas of the brain and brain cells with their chemical and electrical signals are always involved. He has raised an important point that we still do not know how thoughts themselves are generated and my own research from the realm of metaphysics suggests it would be wrong to try to decode everything through neural activities inside the brain alone.

Modern science has discovered that there are broadly four ways in which particles with mass or charge interact with each other; gravitational, electromagnetic, strong and weak interactions. Human body and for that matter, the entire universe is made up of combinations of elementary subatomic particles. We have seen a phenomenal growth in the understanding of how our universe operates. In the last century alone, the quantum physics has discovered large number of subatomic particles including the recent God particle *'boson'*. There are some invisible forces always in play which we as human beings fail to perceive with our normal senses. However, with advancement of technology and with sophisticated instruments, we are able to measure the same invisible forces. Electromagnetic waves which are made up of very basic subatomic particles are one such example which we still cannot see but can be detected with appropriate instruments. Television, mobile phones and radio are products of these very principles.

MRI (Magnetic Resonance Imaging) and PET (Positron Emission Tomography) are couple of latest medical technology used in brain scan to monitor any damage or malfunctioning in someone's brain. We all know that if some part of the brain is damaged due to head injury caused by an accident, specific mental functions may be lost such as memory or even coherent speech and these can be identified and confirmed by use of these above medical scanning devices. Thus relation between brain, mind and consciousness are established but how exactly they function and manifest together is still a mystery to us. Dr.Parnia summarises very well, "Consciousness encompasses every moment of our lives and all our interactions with others. It allows us to know joy or sorrow, happiness or sadness, to feel a sense of shame or pride, to experience a moment of remorse. It gives us higher faculties such as forgiveness, love, compassion and a moral conscience. It is what allows us to sacrifice our comfort and happiness, or even life, for the love of another." He also optimistically suggests that like everything else in the universe is constituted from basic fundamental subatomic particles, mind and consciousness also must be constituted the same way. It is just a matter of time before we have instruments to measure the effect of such subatomic particles one day. In this connection, I quote one of the most eternal assurances of optimism and hope from the *Bhagawat Gita*. Lord Krishna, while showing the *Biswarup (Universal Form)* to Arjun, says, "Whatever you have seen so far in this Universe, and whatever you desire further to see in this Universe, you can see all of that in my Body. Because you do not possess power to see in your eyes, I provide you divine eyes and through those eyes of wisdom, you can see everything (Chapter 11, shlokas - 7 & 8). I have a suspicion that the current string theory in physics involving origin of Universe, the existence and behavior of invisible God particle *'boson'*, and exact frequency with which an individual's heart vibrates in the minutest scale division one can fathom, all have together to contribute to our understanding how that person's thought processes are generated in the mind. Because behind any event happening in the Cosmos, there could be resonance effect between two separate vibrations one involving entire cosmos and the other involving an individual's heart which gives rise to a person's conscious experience.

I am also quite confident that those mysteries of consciousness will be unraveled to humanity in not very distant future. After having gone through the deepest trench of life once, I am more intrigued by *how and why desires are generated*. Although we can find out how thought processes cause a conscious experience, it would be difficult to understand how, when Mahatma Gandhi's each day was dedicated towards experimenting his immortal belief in nonviolence and truth characterized not only by his words but also by his deliberate actions, another human being Nathuram Godse not very far off, was harbouring thoughts to eliminate him. How can such contrasting thoughts be generated in two human beings at the same time? Is there a mysterious process how hatred in one community towards another, cooked up by unscrupulous politicians and utterly selfish leaders generate hatred within a member of an opposite community? Otherwise, how a person who was proud of his knowledge of the *Bhagawat Gita,* the most sacred of texts of the same Hindus whose interests he was trying to protect through his so called brave act of eliminating the Mahatma, decide about undertaking the most heinous of all crimes that humanity knows? Nathuram Godse proudly claims in his book (Nathuram's presentations before the trial court compiled and published by his brother Gopal Godse) to belong to a devotional Maratha Brahmin family and once justifies about his act of murder to Gandhi's son citing the same *Bhagawat Gita* but forgets what the Lord Krishna says outlining clearly the fundamental traits of a Brahmin, "A Brahmin must personify will power, control of senses, willingness to bear pain for safeguarding own conscience (perhaps Nathuram Godse mistook collective conscience of the Brahminical Hindus of the world as that representing whole of humanity?), maintaining cleanliness and sacredness of body, mind and spirit, forgiveness, simplicity, knowledge of history, vedas, scriptures, puranas, love for God" (chapter 18, shloka 42).

Why and how such desires originate in mind? We all know that towards later part of his life, coincident with the then national struggle for India's freedom from the British, Godse was becoming more militant in his political thinking. He was becoming less and less tolerant towards a large chunk of humanity (of course being instigated by the ongoing cruel happenings in the contemporary society with mindless riots, arson, killings, rape and murder around him) and even discarded the path of Veer Savarkar of whom he was a very loyal follower in his formative years.

So this brings us to the quandary. One who was actually having quite a few attributes of a Brahmin failed so miserably in few others of the list as above. Is it then the *Karmic Account Balance* (KAB) effect? Who decided all such things in the multitude of invisible fluxes to create the desire within Nathuram Godse not to go along the path of improving upon his Brahminical qualities a little more to acquire those attributes which were missing during the birth-death cycle we have historical record of both Gandhi and Godse? Who decided that he would take a different path totally inimical to Brahmanism of which he was so proud of? Why did he succumb to the pressure of what was going on around him and he deviated from the Brahminical thought processes that should have come more naturally to him? And he took upon the path of violence and hatred, the most prohibited path of all for true Brahmins. So as Dr. Parnia sometimes fluctuates between truly scientific theories and social constructionist theories, and finds answers ultimately in non-locality solutions of certain invisible forces interacting between particles at a distance, Nathuram Godse also got carried away by prevalent social events more than his personal hatred towards Mahatma Gandhi. This he has very clearly and categorically laid out in his presentation in the court during his trial which later formed major part of the book *'Why I assassinated Gandhi'*. So does consciousness reside within or without?

This brings us to another important question for humanity. Is self-consciousness to be studied in isolation or should it be studied in totality, in league with *Collective Consciousness*? These are questions which modern science has never given any thought to. These have remained in the realms of philosophers, religious and spiritual leaders.

Conscious thoughts work within the brain much later. It is the *desire* that originates first within the entire heart-brain-mind-soul system. And this *desire* is the root of everything that has been driving humanity from time immemorial. From cave dwellers we have now come to such a stage where we are trying to understand with objectivity how consciousness works in human beings and other animals. The journey of individual human soul to ultimately merge with Thee can be tortuous, as we see in case of Godse but it is certain that only the divine and sattwic Brahminical qualities, in true sense of the terms, as espoused in the *Bhagawat Gita*, and perhaps in consonance with the other basic scriptures based on which Gita has been written, are the surest path for such a fulfillment.

CHAPTER 10

PURPOSE OF LIFE

Encounter with a White Light with golden edges

It was as unintentional as it could be. I had just undergone a *phimosis* operation when I was studying in class X. The year was 1977 and I was recuperating at home with a seven days break from school.

One fine morning, I had experienced a sudden bout of pain while not being able to pass urine even though my urinary bladder was full. On hearing this from me, my father took me straight to the Keonjhar district hospital, carrying me in the front of his bicycle, and consulted a few of his doctor friends. I was taken straight to the Operation Theatre, and I vividly remember the sense of total relief and relaxation I felt when I had my bladder clear itself on the Operation Table, even under influence of anesthesia.

At home, I was just recuperating from the operation and perhaps on the third or fourth day, when I got up from the bed in the morning, with my eyes shut and my mind calm and peaceful, something unusual happened. It was some sort of *White Light with golden yellow edges* that I could clearly see even when I had my eyes totally shut. It was a bit baffling to me. How could I so clearly see something when my eyes were completely shut? I was curious. Within a few seconds of opening my eyes, I deliberately shut them again and tried to explore further. Strangely, I saw the same white light with golden edges again. It was sort of an elliptical shaped ring of white light, but with sharp golden edges. And I could see it occurring exactly in between my two eyebrows, on the forehead. This sensory feeling, even with the eyes were shut, was not a fluke then. How is it that I could see this even when my visual sense organs were shut?

I was a normal happy go lucky boy growing up in the very happy environment of a large family of eight siblings in the small town of Keonjhar, Odisha. A bit about my extremely loving and exquisitely beautiful hometown Keonjhar. During my childhood, I used to hear people jokingly criticising that our district was the thirteenth most developed districts of the state of Orissa, now known as Odisha. Orissa was constituted of thirteen districts then and ours was the thirteenth! However, we used to boast of the second largest Jagannath temple in the state, only second to the Puri Jagannath temple. People from across the state used to prefer Keonjhar as a good destination for settling down after their retirement from government jobs. The main reason behind their decision was the fantastic climate Keonjhar has always enjoyed. The serene environment of the town amidst dense forests, hillocks, beautiful water falls, small and big rivers all around it and most importantly because of the predominantly innocent tribal people inhabiting the district, Keonjhar was the darling for the nature lovers. On another front, Keonjhar district is home to the maximum mineral resources including iron ore and manganese, highest perhaps in the country. It was a princely state during pre-independence era and the district's own deity, *Maa Taarini,* with the main temple in a place called Ghatagaon (literal meaning is a village amidst hilly terrain) about 45 kms from Keonjhar town, makes it nationally famous. My father who did his law education in Bhadrakh, moved to Keonjhar in mid-1940s to establish his law practice and soon established his grand reputation with all his extraordinary qualities, making not only large number of friends in the social circle but even becoming a close friend and confidante of the then King of the princely state, close on the heels of Indian independence.

As I mentioned earlier, during my entire childhood, the family atmosphere was Heavenly for me. However, considering the lack of development and urbanization, lack of higher education and in the absence of high degree of modernity and contemporary lifestyle, ideas like *Yoga, the Third Eye, and the Seat of Soul* etc. were French and German to this small town Odisha boy. But after several years of study and experience, I could begin to correlate the phenomenon that I observed with something that is taught by the *Brahmakumaris* and other spiritual groups and leaders. I am also very sure; everyone on the Earth can see this *White Light with Golden Edges* if they try to see it within themselves in a state of total calm, peace and serenity.

Who is swinging my leg?

The first time it hit me was when I was in my first year of college, after passing out of Higher Secondary School Board examinations. The year would be 1979.

On a Wintry Sunday afternoon, I was sitting in an arm chair and relaxing in the Sun, outside in the verandah of our house in Keonjhar. This used to be a usual practice since the afternoon Sun felt very pleasant during the peak of the cold season. Most of our family members used to enjoy an after-lunch siesta, either sitting in chairs in different postures, or by lying down on a mat. My legs were crossed, right leg above the left. I was feeling calm, peaceful, as I basked in the pleasant Sunshine. And incidentally there was no one at that particular moment with whom I could have engaged in conversation. There was an absolutely peaceful atmosphere outside, with hardly a vehicle or two on the main State Highway alongside which our house was located. Overall, there was absolutely no distraction to my mind. I was quiet and contemplating.

Suddenly, I noticed something which I never had earlier. My right leg was rhythmically swinging in a jerky fashion from the place around the knee up to the toes. It was literally swinging of its own accord, to a distance of more than an inch! It really caught me unawares because, in my peaceful and calm state of mind, I could easily see that I was not deliberately instructing my leg to swing at all, nor was I trying to move it that way either. I checked it again; whether there was some intentional or deliberate effort behind this apparently automatic swinging of my leg. Alas, there was absolutely no way I could say that I was giving any conscious instruction to my leg. I wanted to reconfirm by being even calmer, and after watching the leg in silence, I found that it was actually the same sort of reaction along all parts of the body associated with the pumping of the heart!

The beats were then closely observed at various other locations in the body and it was concluded that my own mind was not at all involved in the entire process, although there was good synchronicity. I was quick in making some calculations in the mind. It was the blood pumping machine, the *heart,* in its effort to supply blood to all parts of the body including the legs and toes that was doing its job silently without even waiting for any instruction from my *conscious mind*!

So who then was instructing the heart to carry on with its job? Was I, the person people knew as *Pradipta Kumar Das*, involved in this mysterious action? If someone - my friend, my sibling or my parents - asked me if I, Pradipta Kumar Das, had instructed my heart to do the job it had been doing since my birth, obviously the answer is a big NO. So who was it? When I am riding a bike or driving a car, if someone asks me who is responsible for the movement or displacement of the bike or car, the answer would be unequivocal. However, in this particular case, it was not me as I knew myself.

Obviously when our logical minds fail to get answers to such questions, the only one responsible for all this would be all-pervading God. In fact, as I moved along, I could see that in every bit of life on Earth, be it animal or plant, there was something unexplainable about what was moving everything. In *meditative contemplation,* or so called *neutral emotions,* one can easily comprehend what I mean in the above paragraphs.

Look deep inside you and meet your own God

When we hear someone saying something, we try to weigh their statements against our intellect and get to know the veracity of these statements through the scientific perspective that is latent in each one of us. The human brain is generally inquisitive and we often realize that, even though the statements may come from souls of the highest-level, they may not find acceptance with us. In some corner of our being, we might disagree even with the opinions or views of the most venerated saint on earth. We see TV snippets showing Mother Teresa writing in her diary that, towards the end of her life, she believed

God did not exist. Swami Ramdev Baba says that most things western are bad. I cannot accept either of these statements because we forget that we all are human beings and have evolved in a similar manner, at least bio-physically and biologically if not culturally, over time. A man of western civilization, of a few hundred years ago, did have similar characteristics to a man of eastern civilization during the same age now. The only difference might lie in the speed and form of the technology that has taken root in that part of the world. Who has told us to believe that God exists outside of us? Even if someone has said so, why take it at face value? Especially when, after so many years and decades of spiritual journey, we have come to the conclusion that this is not the case?

There have been clear-cut instances wherein every religious thought or philosophy has outlined a myriad of forms for the expression of God and that there is no one way in which God can be represented. It depends on how one perceives His presence. The reason we do not agree with someone else is because God actually does not reside anywhere outside of the human body, but rather in every human being's body, mind, heart and soul. He resides in every cell of our very being. The DNA constitutes a part of it within itself - so deeply spiritual, and hence unexplainable, particularly in physical terms. We need not try to find happiness by trying to correlate with the experiences of someone else. Nor do we have to act according to someone else's observation to remain happy. The very seeds of happiness remain within our own souls. It is our outward interpretation that creates doubt, skepticism, and fear about the things happening around us. The deepest part of us contains everything that any human has to offer and if we try and go very deep, we can realize that what others observe, see and experience can actually be seen, observed and experienced by us as well. Of course, all these things need conditioning and some guidance, but if we make ourselves amenable to such ideas and feelings, what we are expecting today will get fructified tomorrow. This is the law of the world.

We have to protect our own good self from destruction by the environment

Every one of us is endowed with good and bad. The way we handle the attributes pertaining to the good and bad within us makes us a man of reckoning because the distinction lies in how well we apply our mind in filtering the good from the bad in our thoughts, actions and habits. Whatever we do, we do according to what our *inner conscience* tells us to do. This is what is ascribed to God, the all-powerful, the Almighty. And it is dependent on our past Karma. Now, there is internal fear within us all. Lord Krishna has said in the *Gita* that it is extremely important to discriminate between what we should fear and what we should not fear, what we should do and what we should not do. He then advises that it is the greatest attribute *to see good in bad* and *bad in good*. This may appear to be contradictory to an ordinary soul, but there is great meaning in this. One should be capable of understanding what is good and what is bad and what a good deed is and what a bad deed is. In doing so, there could be even extremes like sacrifice of one's own life for a cause. We have numerous examples of such sacrifices during wars or for social causes, the most famous of them being the examples of Jesus, Mahatma Gandhi etc. One should be capable of realizing that social structure, social laws, have been framed and built over centuries of human struggle and that they need to be protected - and that the only way to do this is through selfless and yet selfish means. This again might sound contradictory, but it is like this: when God has created us, He had a purpose, and we need to be both sensitive and strong enough to realize that purpose. Wherefrom God will provide us with the necessary strength is His domain and should not bother us much - except with regards to our preparedness to learn from our experiences continuously.

When we are born, as said above, we are born with the greatest human attribute that is worth emulating. For example, the Dacoit Ratnakar had been a dacoit for most of his life and either looted or murdered people for his own survival and for the survival of his family. But a certain turn of events changed the course of his life and he was transformed into who history now remembers as Valmiki. He converted himself from the dreaded dacoit to the holy and pious Valmiki who wrote the '*Ramayana*'.

Then there is the more recent example of a drug dealer who shot to fame after writing his own life story. The story is based on his own experiences in Mumbai's underworld. It goes on to suggest that somehow, at some point of time, we get motivated to fall into bad hands, a bad track or bad habits, even though we might be endowed genetically with all the divine attributes from the very beginning.

The division of the world into good and evil, a distinction so clear that the world sometimes looks like a black and white picture, has been the bane of all such problems. The reinforcement of this traditional viewpoint by the actions of ordinary people aggravates the problem rather than solving it. The flexibility with which we operate helps us to visualize the picture in a better fashion. The world is not always black and white. There is gray and there is even colour. There are the seven shades of the rainbow and in computer terminology, colour gradations by mixing different percentage of basic colours in different permutations and combination can take it to literally infinity. This helps us to philosophically visualize the colours of life, the essence of life.

There will be continuous attempts by an environment full of disgruntled elements, rogue elements and fallen souls that will try to impinge on us all, and shake our faith to a great degree and cause turbulence in our lives. It is our inner resolve which will help us keep our strength in such cases. Inner strength of character particularly, if it remains undisturbed, will help us in the long run.

God wants us to keep our inner conscience undisturbed and as refined and shining as ever. And so we need to tread carefully but steadily trample everything in our paths that come to disturb our peace and serenity or inner conscience. There should not be any politics because politics is known by God and He understands. We may experience temporary weakness, but weakness of character should not be there under any circumstances. That will help us during rain, thunder, natural calamities, and all kinds of other disturbances, both natural and manmade. This is what our guiding light should be.

We should not allow ourselves to be hurt so badly that we generate negative feelings and thoughts. They may not be unfounded, but why should they be allowed to fester when we know they will only create weakness in us and hence largely reduce our capacity to progress and develop in a wholesome manner?

It is God who has provided us with different skills and attributes to protect our good selves, the divine souls within us, and to fight the world so as to bring in eternal peace, joy, happiness and cheer to our surroundings and to ourselves. There will be occasional hiccups because we are human, and we need to equip ourselves with the divine attributes of strength and resolve to thwart all so-called evil forces, conquer them in the long run, and achieve permanent success, peace and happiness. Sometimes, God reveals Himself in the form of these forces through other souls and we need to pick up the reins and march ahead in a similar manner, without fearing consequences. Faith on God will always prevail over all adversaries.

The late Dr. Kabi Prasad Mishra, a very reputed cardiologist at the Apollo Hospital in Chennai and later at Apollo, Bhubaneswar, was a great human being with education and experience from both India and the US, great oratory skills and elevated spiritual knowledge. He has written many books on cardiology, as well as on general spiritual subjects. His book '*Twenty two Steps*' is a bestseller and has been translated into many languages also. He writes in detail, in this book, about the sequence of events leading to his heart attack and subsequent heart operation. He recounts his thoughts on the eve of going into the operation theatre: 'Lord, I have everything in life and I am quite satisfied with what I have been graced with. If You think that the purpose for which I was sent has been fully served, I will have no regrets if You take me away from this earth and I surrender before You.' These thoughts from a highly advanced soul indicate what the *purpose of life* should actually mean to us. Dr. K.P.Mishra went on to serve humanity for nearly another two decades after his successful heart operation. The library at Apollo Hospitals, Bhubaneswar has been named after this great soul. Mahatma Gandhi has also recounted similar feelings about his own life. He used to wait for God's *diktat* before taking up any cause, so that his ego would not get in the way! Human life is basically meant for service to mankind. Right from the moment of our birth, where we had no control, it is somehow destined and guided by *cosmic intelligence*. Although we know that the human soul has almost all the ingredients that constitute the Universe, the ways and means of interaction between the human soul and the Universal Soul still remains a mystery and I believe humanity will enjoy bliss if that mystery takes a romantic form that is symbolized by 'all-encompassing love' tending towards 'merging with Thee'. It is only 'love' which lies at the root of *Bhakti* which as Lord Krishna says in *Bhagawat Gita*, the highest form of Yogic practice (Chapter 12).

We are the highest species, let us together justify that

Two incidents are etched in my memory. I was discussing the issue of vegetarianism versus non-vegetarianism with an Indian research scientist during my stay in Australia, during 1997 to 2001. I heard a statement from him which I heard again, many times, from my other Indian friends later as well. He said; 'If we do not eat goats, sheep, hens, cows, pigs etc. then their numbers will increase such that the world will become full of these animals and hence uninhabitable for humans. Therefore non-vegetarianism is what God wants!' I had raised the same issue with another European friend of mine while in Australia; about the natural inclination of the human species to be of a nonviolent nature and that hence all humans should be vegetarian. He was quick to rebuff me saying; 'No, I do not think so because humans living in the cold tundra areas, or in the Polar Regions, would need meat to sustain themselves and to save themselves from the wrath of the cold climate by maintaining the required body temperature. Hence, human beings are physically built by nature to be non-vegetarian.'

There will be millions of others who will also come up with their own arguments. They might say that eating vegetables and fruits also involve taking a life, even if the life in question is that of a plant's and not an animal's. There will be arguments like; 'Look, in nature, animals like tigers and lions prey and live on the meat of other animals, they hunt lower animals like deer and so on. Big fishes eat the smaller fishes in water. Hence both land and water based animals live on the meat of other animals.' Then there might also be an outcry from those in the society who are thinking about the livelihood of the millions who live on the trade and business of meat and meat products got from such land and sea animals if someone prophesises a future world devoid of non-vegetarianism!

I have been trying to find a reason for the wars wherein we, the human species, fight our own brothers and do not hesitate to kill them. This unfortunate behavior of humans gets tremendous affirmation in the two of the most sacred Hindu scriptures: The *'Ramayana'* and the *'Mahabharata'*. While the *'Ramayana'* (set in the *Trettaya Yug*) deals with the battle between Godly humans with Devilish humans, the *'Mahabharata'* deals with the battle between blood relatives including brothers! Even the setting for the *Bhagawat Gita* is just before the epic battle of Kurukshetra where the two groups of brothers are facing each other with their daggers drawn. In fact, millions of Hindus and other Indians who have been fed with the cultural learning from The *'Mahabharata'* do not lose a moment in saying; 'Whatever had to happen happened, and even Lord Krishna Himself was not able to stop the bloodshed!'

While I love this scripture with all my heart, I have been trying my best to find at least one way by which humanity can dream of escaping from the same bloodshed which was the setting for the greatest scripture on earth. Is it possible that our penchant for eating meat, which obviously involves the pain and suffering of these creatures, gets reflected back at us by a much greater force which indirectly motivates us to vie for the blood of our own brethren such that That Greater Force quenches its hunger for human blood in either same or multiplied scale in return? One needs to closely observe the moment when an animal is being prepared for religious sacrifice, or the moment when an animal is about to be slain for its meat for sale or further processing. With a compassionate eye, one can easily see the kind of fear, helplessness and anguish that the animal goes through the moment it senses that it is to be sacrificed for a religious ritual or human consumption.

I have been a meat lover myself and the idea that it could be bad never occurred to me until the time of my mental crisis in Australia during May 2000 to August 2001. I recall a very prominent religious or spiritual leader of international repute visiting Adelaide and, in the Ganesh Hindu temple premises, giving a lecture sometime in early 2001. With the very long beard and orange robes that are usual for our spiritual leaders, he started by thanking the Christian community's highest leader in Adelaide for attending a Hindu gathering (organized by the small Indian community of Adelaide) and spoke only very few sentences. The entire speech, which lasted less than ten minutes or so, was directed at how non-vegetarian food was despicable. He asked a question and answered it himself. 'What do we do with our dead brothers and sisters?' he asked. 'We either bury them or cremate them. But see what we do with the dead bodies of animals from which mutton, pork, chicken or beef are made. We bring them from the market and keep them inside our fridges so carefully.' The words had a powerful effect on me. At the time, I was still a meat eater, but I had developed an inclination to drop meat from my diet over the past few months, ever since my hospitalization in July 2000. After the meeting, I went close to the spiritual leader and asked him politely; 'Guruji, I have been asking my wife to abstain from non-vegetarian food, but, while I have made up my mind, she is not prepared to drop the habit.' To this he said; 'Do not worry, I have another meeting tomorrow afternoon here in the city. Bring your wife there and we would discuss.' This meeting did not happen for us but I began to abstain from non-vegetarian food from December 2001.

However, when tragedy struck me in the form of a serious illness, tuberculosis, in the month of July 2002, I was scared that perhaps stopping all non-vegetarian food was the reason for it. Perhaps my immunity had fallen so low that it left me prone to tuberculosis. I was determined not to include pure meat like chicken and mutton back into my diet, but I started eating fish again. While I had taken out meat altogether from my diet since December 2001, I stopped eating all non-vegetarian food starting from Ram Navami Day on the twenty-eighth of March 2015.

I know that if each one of us starts thinking along this line incrementally at least, while it may take some hardcore non-vegetarian people a few births to get rid of the habit totally, we will at least be making a start. And the world can eventually be freed from such senseless killing. Imagine this simple fact: if I could desist from consuming two hundred and fifty grams of meat every week (the usual routine in our household was to have meat curry on Sundays) over the last fourteen years or so, then I have consciously helped save the lives of at least ten to twenty middle-sized goats on Earth! Not a small achievement considering that I am otherwise incapable of *creating* a single goat on Earth!

Sportspersons are the ones who need meat to increase their physical strength. But the practice has now been entrenched so deeply in our psyche, that it is now difficult to imagine a world free from a non-vegetarian diet. However, we know that some of the great Indian sportspersons, in different fields, have been pure vegetarian. I have at least half a dozen examples from various sports where Indian players have reached the international level. I know that Indian achievement is miniscule in the field of sports, but one cannot ignore the fact that such things can happen. Elephants are the strongest land animals and deer are the fastest; both are vegetarians. Nature has provided us with such beautiful examples of how to increase both strength and speed. The justifications from the sports fraternity for consumption of meat can be outweighed if serious scientific research is done in such areas.

I have a strong feeling that until and unless the majority of the world becomes vegetarian, the penchant for human blood - both individually and collectively - will not go away from this earth. The motivation for war and killing generally orchestrated by a political brain emanates in such a way that an ordinary eye will not be able to see how it works. I was told once by a very senior retired Indian government official that Mother Teresa, who was the epitome of peace and love, was also a non-vegetarian. Some people claim Adolf Hitler was a vegetarian. See the contrast! Ordinary human brains will be caught up in a vicious circle of trying to justify non-vegetarianism by quoting such contrasts between world leaders who were and are in opposite domains of human emotions. Someone who would like to argue in favour of non-vegetarianism while repudiating vegetarianism will always quote these two examples of Mother Teresa and Hitler to prove his or her point. However, if we restrict our judgmental capacity and futuristic vision about the world to quoting few individuals from contemporary or ancient history, then perhaps, the kind of innovations in every field we see today both in scientific realm or otherwise, would not have been possible. The subtle way in which the killing of animals for human consumption adversely affects the *Total Balance Sheet of Compassion of the Universe* and how such effects are neutralized or compensated for in the overall *Universal Harmony* is yet to be understood fully either by science or spirituality anywhere in the world in easily conceivable and comprehensible terms. I believe that the pain and anguish generated by the souls (in the absence of a better word) of these lower animals owing to such mass killing, or even the accumulation of individual killings that are simultaneously happening all over the globe, creates an indirect means of triggering hatred and anger in one human being against another or others, based on religion, history, geography or just over natural resources. Until we have hard scientific proof, it is better to rely on the metaphysical plane for such arguments. It is not difficult to visualize such a thing.

Just imagine the statements about goats, sheep, hens, cows, pigs etc. that our approach to life has sustained with regards to balance in the eco system! No one ever imagines that hundreds and thousands of lower level species are getting extinct almost every day. This scientific phenomenon explains that species which are resilient in form and complexity are less likely to be extinct whereas the weaker ones will slowly become extinct. Nature lovers, animal lovers and environmentalists are now working tirelessly to help save lower species, but the most fundamental approach seen in the two ancient Indian concepts of *Vasudhaiba Kutumbakam* and *Sarve Bhavatu Sukhina* can really go a long way to help achieve such a target by the global community.

The Upanishadic teaching *Vasudhaiba Kutumbakam* indicates that the whole world is just one family. This is a very ancient Indian concept which prepares the platform for wholesome development of the world. Internet today and the economic model that is shaping the modern world can safely be said to indicate at least partial success towards the achieving of the global family concept.

The Vedic mantra that characterises the richest form of human aspirations is as follows:

"Om sarveshaam swastir bhavatu, Sarveshaam shantir bhavatu
Sarveshaam poornam bhavatu, Sarveshaam mangalam bhavatu
Sarve bhavantu sukhinah, Sarve santu niraamayaah
Sarve bhadraani pashyantu, Maakaschit duhkha bhaag bhavet"

Meaning:

Auspiciousness (swasti) be unto all; peace (shanti) be unto all; fullness (poornam) be unto all; prosperity (mangalam) be unto all; May all be happy! (sukhinah) May all be free from disabilities! (niraamayaah); May all look (pashyantu) to the good of others! May none suffer from sorrow! (duhkha).

Imagine a situation wherein we include the entire animal kingdom into our fold and start behaving towards it in exactly the same way, as if humanity extends to the whole of the animal kingdom, at least in terms of the violence meted towards it. We generally stop at the level of human beings, but it is conceivable that in a future world, we can include the entire animal kingdom as well. But to achieve that, nothing short of a global-level transformational movement taken up by students, teachers, workers, executives, managers, employees, researchers, scientists, technologists, politicians and so on, will suffice.

Our goal is to spread peace, love and compassion

I was casually talking about Indian life and Australian life to one of my friends, who was an Australian citizen of Indian origin. This was sometime in late 2000. He was working as a top research associate in one of the three international standard Universities of South Australia in Adelaide. Our discussion moved to this intriguing question: *what is the purpose of life?* This family friend of mine was quite knowledgeable and we shared very common interests. But what he said that day still rings in my ears. He said; 'There is no specific purpose to life.' I was bit shocked and did not argue too much because it would be a pointless argument, trying to convince each other of our viewpoints.

Is it that our sole purpose is to just be born one day and then die one day? Had that been the case, then we would not have moved out of the caves and forests! Even the language we communicate with, which gives rise to words like 'purpose', would then be purposeless. In fact, most of us miss the thread when we extend our philosophical imagination to one extreme. The purpose of a river ends when it meets a lake or ocean. On its long journey, it does perform great acts. One of them is to even create *fluvial reservoir sands* that can hold hydrocarbons as pools which might be discovered and used by humans millions of years later. So 'purpose' has a connotation and context which should never be disconnected from any discussion on the subject.

No one can dispute that the human soul yearns for peace, love, happiness, compassion and, ultimately, bliss. When one knows inside that there is a spiritual hunger which is much beyond the hunger

231

of bodily senses, one should not confuse the two things. Lord Jesus and Mahatma Gandhi have personified the epitome of all these attributes right through their lives. The easiest way to test such a claim is to observe internally the traces of ecstasy that come from being loveful and compassionate to fellow beings, during the other person's time of need. This suggests that the purpose of human life is to see God, meet God. And the surest path to achieve that is to be loveful, peaceful and compassionate within and to share the same with other fellow human beings.

CHAPTER 11

WHAT ARE THE TOOLS THEN?

Are there any skills or tools, and do we need to practice them?

During a regular TV programme broadcasted by a prominent Indian news channel every weekend, the founder of Isha Foundation, India, Sadhguru Jaggi Vasudev, normally took questions from highly reputed Indian citizens - including industrialists, entrepreneurs, bankers, artists, actors, sportspersons, doctors, social activists, journalists and philanthropists. In one such interview, the internationally acclaimed heart surgeon, Dr. Devi Setty, founder of Narayan Hridayalay, a chain of specialty hospitals providing cardiac care in India, asked about an intriguing observation saying; 'Sadhguru, I was a martial arts trainer during my college days and I used to teach many young boys. I used to feel that a few of the boys who showed exceptional talent in the art form had everything going correct for them - shape of body, physique, stamina, sharpness, agility and mental skills. I used to think they would go on to become black belts very soon and perhaps go even higher. But, almost unfailingly, what used to happen was that some of the boys whom I considered to be average, or less than average even, would ultimately go on to acquire very high skills in the trade - whereas those with apparent inborn talent would wither away, and even drop off completely after just six months.'

This has been an intriguing question from time immemorial. Children who possess perhaps lesser inborn talent scale great heights generally because they follow the simple three-four-five principle of three P's, four C's and five D's. *Passion, Patience &, Perseverance* (three P's); *Commitment, Concentration, Confidence and Courage* (four C's); *Determination, Diligence, Dedication, Deftness and Devotion* (five D's).

These are essential to succeed in any endeavor of life. Perhaps all of us notice this in our surroundings. Even if we have the access to the best of schools, best of teachers and the best of training materials and resources, unless we have these attributes, we will never succeed.

Imagine a situation wherein one has been afflicted by depression or anxiety for a prolonged period and reaches the stage where medication becomes absolutely necessary. But in spite of medication, he seems to be out of sync with holistic feeling inside. He thus reaches a stage where he just begins to harbor thoughts of "quitting life". What would be his choice? Does he have any standard tools? Does he need to develop some specific skills and practice them? The preceding paragraphs emphasize the importance of practice and this cannot be overstated even in the case of martial art skills.

I have gone through my midlife crisis and was able to overcome it. There was a time, when I was going through the peak of the crisis, when I was pretty much at the mercy of the environment, having lost my self-control. But somewhere there was a feeling in my subconscious brain that it was all linked to some choice or the other that I had myself made along the way. I was almost one hundred percent sure that, if I was instrumental in making the choices which ultimately caused my dramatic mental health crisis in Australia, then it was all the more in my power to undo the damage, provided I was careful and prepared to amend myself and make new choices.

Few months after my return from Australia, I consulted a very highly qualified mental health specialist (with several degrees) in Dehradun, India, to ensure that I was okay and my decision to discontinue the small amount of medication that I had continued for nearly one and half years by now would not cause any serious problems for me in future. To my surprise and to my disappointment, the doctor advised me that if I did not continue medication for the rest of my life, then there would be a constant danger that my problem might resurface with a vengeance and force me to take a much higher dosage later on. This was the threat lurking in the background, but somehow I was pretty convinced that the entire problem was of my *own doing* - and that it was up to me, hence, to *undo it* again.

Although, at the peak of the mental health crisis, I had to resort to mild medication for a period of about a year and half, I was hesitant to believe that medication was necessary for me. I was determined to bring my health back to normal by my own conscious efforts, and I was pretty confident that I could do that. I was also confident that I actually did not need any psychiatric drugs any further which fortunately for me, went exactly the way I thought out to be. However, to achieve my goal, I tried to do a series of things consciously, and tried to put into practice a few age old tools. I just reinvented and rediscovered these tools which had been around for humanity to use for centuries. While I was going through the rebuilding process, I was inclined to think that my whole experience would perhaps be beneficial for anyone afflicted with such mental health issues. Problems arising out of stress and anxiety these days are so ruthless that even right thinking individuals will not be spared from the associated risk. Summarising, I will sequentially put down my entire experience and piece together the specific skills and tools that are vital in such a crisis. I encourage the reader to feel completely free and experiment in his or her own style, to suit their needs. There is no hard and fast rule for the step-wise application of the tools I am putting forward. Adapting to them as per individual need is the key.

In terms of short term, medium term or long term crisis, the tools and procedures to handle the problems and come out of them would be the same. Most of us are aware of the bits and pieces of all the requisite measures, through our early learning in schools and colleges, building a repository of valid information or knowledge, but the ability to put them into practice is what matters. However difficult the problem may be, the human soul has the *Power of the Universe* ingrained within it, well coded but sometimes undecipherable, to face any challenge that life throws at us head on. The ease of success comes through the fact that great souls have appeared on Earth before us and have put their lives out as open books. These are the revelations of God's messages through millennia of human civilization. In terms of religious connotations, human civilization has grouped all this knowledge and wisdom into our scriptures and holy texts. Spiritual leaders of all ages have been messengers and carriers of God's messages which, if decoded, actually point to a simple fact. How human civilization progressed so dramatically, from ordinary animal-like ancient cave dwelling, forest trekking hominids a few millennia ago, on this Earth which is actually 4.5 billion years old, to today's stage, where almost each of the seven billion people on this planet is interconnected not only metaphysically but physically as well through mobile phone and internet, and hold together a common cause and bonding.

When a crisis or problem besieges a person, threatens to derail his entire thought processes and lead him to illness, if one is guided by the steps that are described herein, then there is no reason why one should not be able to not only face the crisis but also successfully come out of it. I have managed to personally experience the emotions associated with almost all the steps that are discussed below and can vouch for their efficacy.

Accept the problem, the responsibility and the reality

Accepting the fact that there is a problem is the most difficult task. Often we fail to notice the subtle changes that start occurring when long term stress builds up within us due to various factors. Irritability, loss of appetite or sometimes too much appetite, loss of zeal to work, continuous fatigue, drastic reduction in productivity, sleep disorder, an increase in blaming tendency and finger pointing, loss of focus, attention disorder, violent thoughts, suicidal thoughts, thoughts of helplessness and hopelessness are some of the warning signs. In spite of such signs, we tend to believe that everything is alright and that it may just be a short term issue that will go away on its own. The reality is that, in most cases, these untreated problems result in the accumulation of so much anxiety and stress that it leads to serious mental health problems needing urgent medication and even hospitalisation. This is when one needs to accept the situation and the problem.

Whether it is because of genetic propensity, or too much ambition, or circumstantial pressure, or physical ailments, or some influence of planetary positions, or even by accident, the fact is that it is likely that a person will go through a period of such crisis in this materialistic world unless he maintains a balanced approach to life, with full awareness and wisdom, which is not always easy. The mental health problems are such that the very core of a human being, which is responsible for day to day functioning, gets jolted badly and the mind fails to grasp the typical reasons that lead to such a problem in the first place. However, it is essential that once the problem manifests with physical symptoms, one accepts full responsibility for the same. There will always be a tendency to find fault with the system, to blame others including the spouse, children, life partners, family people, friends, colleagues, coaches and bosses, and even doctors and teachers. This is quite natural. The conscious part of the brain normally tries to find solutions outside of the body. But the subconscious part of the brain, our most fundamental genre or seed because it is related to conscience, which I term as the spiritual being, knows exactly where the fault lies. The *soul* has the extraordinary wherewithal to know the fundamental root of the problem. Once the person who is afflicted with such a mental health crisis reconciles to the fact it is his *soul* which is responsible for the problem, the subconscious brain starts giving the necessary instructions to the conscious brain to undo the damage and help come out of the crisis.

Responsibility means ability to respond. Once a person in a crisis accepts the problem and takes full responsibility for the same, then finding solutions becomes easier and certain. Until one accepts the problem and takes full responsibility for it, he or she will be beating around the bush and may attain temporary reprieve through the help of doctors, family and friends, but a long term and permanent solution can only be possible when the person takes full responsibility inside and decides to take action to change the situation.

Murphy's Law states that '*If you are feeling too good, do not worry; that will also pass.*' In reality, anything and everything will pass. If you are feeling too bad, then it is all the more certain that it will also pass.

Human sufferings are created by humans. If I am not happy with my state of being, be it my physical health condition, financial health, social health, job life etc., then I can definitely make a turnaround. It is only a matter of time. All it needs is a conscious effort directed towards the goal, which is to correct the situation and come into a healthier state.

Take a break

The apocalyptic whispers that rang inside my head, and later led to my hospitalization for a week in Adelaide, were a warning to me, a signal that it was time to act. It was time to act on the entire repository of knowledge I had – the knowledge that I'd derived consciously from my own actions and experiences so far, the metaphysical knowledge I'd derived from scriptures, and the knowledge I'd learnt from history books and the stories of modern day leaders but had not experienced. I decided I had to withdraw. This was the first step; using the power within to withdraw. The power for taking such a step lies in the fact that we can feel detached and be an unbiased observer from now on, without getting too bogged down by the burden of the crisis. This also helps in another way; it frees us from the swirling storm around the vortex of the crisis which we have put ourselves in. It is not easy to understand early on, but slowly, with time, this power to withdraw and detach brings a much clearer perspective to the whole problem wherein the brain gets uncluttered and becomes free to think of solutions.

After getting out of the mental hospital in Adelaide, during the most severe crisis of my life, I decided to take a break for two weeks. A friend of mine who was staying in another city of Australia (Sydney) reinforced the notion in me by saying that it was the right decision. I switched my brain off completely from the PhD research work that I was engaged in. I turned my attention to recharging my drained out batteries. I knew that I had succumbed to the drying up of positive emotions, and hence perhaps the brain chemicals responsible for happy feelings were in very short supply. But I had this intuitive feeling all along that if my body, mind and heart, which were all working pretty fine few months back, enjoying all the small and beautiful pleasures of life, could somehow be directed down this ominous path through mental stress arising out of unfounded anxiety, then it would also be possible to regenerate these same positive emotions and hence the chemicals associated with it. To start with, I consciously decided to hire videos of happy family dramas (mainly in my own mother tongue, Bengali), and a few light comedy based movies etc. I knew I could consciously work towards enjoying myself by watching these relaxing movies and in the process start developing a better and more realistic perspective of life. After all, the world was not going to come to an end just because I'd not completed my PhD project on time!

With this new routine built into my schedule, I increased the number of social visits I made to family friends in Adelaide and also to the two Hindu temples located in different parts of the city. Simultaneously, I started spending entire days with my family, taking my kids to nearby parks, shopping malls etc. much more frequently than I used to before. The morning walk regime was restarted, now with additional time. Spending time watching TV and reading good inspiring books was something I packed into my schedule for these two weeks. I was pretty sure that my drained out batteries had every likelihood to be recharged substantially so to help the 'car' that was my life, which had almost come to a halt, would start its auto-ignition, or self-start as we call it.

I recall another incident where a worried father asked the famous Indian spiritual leader and founder of the Art of Living Foundation, Sri Sri Ravi Shankar, during a question-answer session at a large public meeting: 'Swamiji, My son is very naughty and not at all serious about his studies and his preparations for the Board examination that he is to appear for and the competitive examinations for different engineering colleges that will come after. All my efforts to change his behavior are not making any headway whatsoever.' The Swamiji said; 'Why are you so worried? Also, you are forgetting that the more you are worried, the greater the adverse effect will be on your child. After all, performance in an examination is not everything in life.

What is the most that can happen? He might fail in that examination and that is all. He will definitely not lose his life!"

It is this attitude that should be the starting point for recovery and rebuilding. Imagine the situation to be zero and that it is from here that one needs to rise again.

People who suffer huge losses in businesses, agriculture or industries and become badly debt-ridden often feel they are at their wit's end and contemplate taking their own lives, as if that would solve the problems once for all. The simple thought that *sufferings are just lessons for an eternal life, and rich fodder for the soul's growth,* can dramatically alter the perception. There are solutions to every problem conceivable on earth. I recall having a conversation with a friend of mine in Australia sometime in 2000, after my release from the hospital, during the worst crisis I have ever faced. My friend too had similar feelings in Australia and was advised to take antidepressants, but he felt as if he was being used as a guinea pig for the testing of all such medicines. I, on the other hand, had already been through my most severe mental health crisis, having been hospitalized because of the ill effects of such medication. I was still continuing medication, but this time of a different composition. I thought to myself and then said to my friend; 'Okay, if Lord Jesus and Mahatma Gandhi could sacrifice their lives for the good of society, it is alright for the medical industry to treat me as a guinea pig if some good result is ultimately going to come out of it. Also, I know at the back of my mind that every drug that comes to the market normally goes through human trials first, and such human beings are just like me.' This single thought of total surrender to the Collective Consciousness could take me to the most basic level of the survival instinct which life builds itself on and allowed the creation of a situation wherein I was not so scared that I would not allow medication when it was necessary.

This world is actually a fascinating place to live in and the human soul is a wonderful medium to experience it through. There are bits and pieces of everything that any human soul can long for in this world and there are bits and pieces of every conceivable enjoyment that one can wish to experience in his lifetime. It is all there for the soul to experience and enjoy.

If we take the example of the struggles and victories of people like John Nash (a schizophrenic patient struggling to overcome his disease and later winning a Nobel Prize), Hellen Keller (the blind woman who set up a global chain of noble societies that work for the visually handicapped), Stephen Hawking (the physicist who overcame motor neuron disease to later become an illustrious physicist of the contemporary world) in the twentieth and twenty-first centuries, we can easily see what any human soul is capable of. There are numerous such examples, like those of Mahatma Gandhi and Anwar Sadat, and these tell us about this simple truth.

The problem I had with the uncertainty of completing my PhD may look trivial to many readers who might be thinking that their problems are much more serious. But it is not the scale of the problem which is the issue here. The processes and steps are important. The brain's neurons and neural network are fundamental to everything. The capacity to produce neurons may not be feasible, but it is definitely possible to create new neural pathways through conscious efforts. A relaxed mind, one that is free from anxieties and worries, is capable of creating fresh neural networks with optimism, hope and faith - the three most important driving forces for generating positive energy. A break does help to first douse the raging fire within. The relaxing hormones generated from good pastime activities during a long break rejuvenate us. This is nothing new. But it is important to deliberately cut off the stressful hormones and replace them with pleasant hormones.

Do not consider it to be 'the only life'

I have heard many youngsters, teenagers, saying unequivocally; 'You have only one life; enjoy it to the fullest.' These people generally tend to enjoy (or at least imagine they're enjoying) all sorts of things, including things that are normally not sanctioned by civil society on the basis of moral principles or ethics of society. What happens is that, sometimes, the stress arising out of a continuous and severe workload, or from physical diseases, or from accidents or from continuous anxiety, guilt or anger, can cause such enormous pain and suffering, or even mental damage, that we start asking; 'Why me?' This question is directed by a person at his Maker. When people try to extract too much from one life, thinking that it is "the only life" that they have been blessed with, and that they may never be born again, it may land them in serious mental health problem one day.

Nowadays, it is quite convincingly proven that human beings are not creatures with only one life. There is conclusive proof of rebirth, although many people might still question the fact based on some fishy conflicting arguments. The abject run of materialism and the chase of sensual pleasures and comforts of life, simply because we believe that we live only once, can be so devastating that it could lead to serious mental crisis at some point of time.

The best approach for someone who meets a dead-end (like a severe mental health crisis) is to first get back to thinking that it is not "the only life". The pain and suffering that one might come across in life can be mitigated by thoughts of the Karmic principles of life. Our souls are on their own individual journeys. We should not compare one with another. Each journey is different. It is okay to learn from others' lives so as to strengthen our own inner resolve to face the world, but each soul's journey is different. Such a thought helps to relieve, to a great extent, a lot of the built-up stress. Often a person may ask 'why me?' when he undergoes the pain and suffering caused by a dreaded disease like cancer. But a person who imbibes the fundamental teaching of the human birth and rebirth cycle will have a much stronger footing with which to deal with the problems of the superficial world.

My daughter was around eight years old. During a holiday sometime in 2002, we had come from Assam to our home state, Odisha, and were living at our in-laws' place. I recall quite vividly how, on the evening we reached Bhubaneswar, I had just switched on a TV channel, incidentally a news channel, and the conspicuous images of a train accident were being beamed live on to the TV screen. My daughter was jumping on the bed which was near the TV and when she saw the images of the accident site, where around fifty-two people had died; there was some sort of a quick mental rebuttal in her mind when she shook her head in a reflex. Immediately after that I heard her uttering; 'Oh, so many people died. It is alright, they will be born again!' I was stunned by what she said. She was so young that she'd hardly had any opportunity to have been taught about life and death by anyone, nor was she mature enough to understand and speak about rebirths.

In fact, we can learn greatly by watching small children. I reflected on how the sensitive human soul, which is so fresh inside a child's body, can remember the true nature of itself when I saw my own daughter, hardly eight years old, saying something which pointed towards the fact that we are not experiencing our first ever life as human beings. A similar incident happened again, in Assam. We were moving towards Shillong, from Guwahati, in a Tata Sumo vehicle. Members of my extended family had visited me in Assam in December 2004 on the eve of Christmas and we were making a holiday trip to the hill station of Shillong. There was a hilly patch with curvilinear bends with high gradient along the way. At one such bend, there was a huge memorial by the side of the road and when our vehicle crossed the spot, my son - who was just five years old at the time and who was sitting on my lap in the front of the vehicle and so could clearly see the memorial - remarked, on his own and without my prompting; 'Papa, what is that structure?' Without stopping the vehicle to see what exactly was written on the memorial, I just said; 'It is perhaps a memorial'. To this he asked; 'Papa, people who have died here must have been born again?' A five year old asking about rebirths!

These two incidents speak highly of the fact that even though, in the realm of bodily consciousness, we might feel as if we own our children, it is actually not so. They were all born earlier elsewhere and have had a long past and have been born again with their inbuilt wisdom - but only with our physical genes for this one life. Obviously, we are not going to have "only this one life" to "live fully".

Such an understanding can empower us enough to imagine a lot of possibilities.

In this connection, I shall describe one small story about which Dr. Sam Parnia has written in his book, *'What happens when we die'* which I find so intriguing but quite obvious from a Hindu perspective. Dr. Sam Parnia writes about a man from New Zealand who had been involved in a road traffic accident once reported to him, 'When I came to, someone was holding me down on the road and I was having a lot of difficulty breathing....I lapsed into unconsciousness again and revived partially once more in the ICU....I realize now that this must have been very soon after the accident. I knew I was in a different existence and in my unconscious state I remember thinking, "So this is dying". I never thought it was so easy. It was like taking off your coat....The one thing that stood out was that my spirit moved separately from my body....In some strange way, however, it was still part of me'.

First, why I find it obvious is because most of us in Indian culture believe so strongly about the concept of rebirth or reincarnation. The most sacred scripture the *Bhagawat Gita* teaches this concept explicitly, 'Just the way human beings change their old clothes and put on new ones in their place, similarly souls also move from one container to another'(Shloka 2.22). Why I find the above story intriguing is because the man from New Zealand is expected to be brought up in a very different culture dominated by Christian beliefs but here, what he says finds exact similarity with what Lord Krishna was preaching to Arjun in the Kurukshetra battlefield. There are some history books which suggest Lord Krishna lived in ancient India around 3192 BC, almost 5200 years ago and what is written in the scripture finds an echo in one of the most thoroughly scientific book of Dr.Sam Parnia written in 2008!

Get help from every possible quarter

When we lose sight of the track and fall into misguided paths, either by our own ignorance or because we are much too gullible, God is always there to put us back on the right track. It is necessary that we ourselves become alert to this reality. When our ancestors opined that God exists in every human soul, they actually meant it. It is folly to not believe them and not follow their ideals. When we are in real distress, help comes from extremely unexpected quarters, and this leads us to believe in God's grace. The sort of healing that can happen to our physical, mental, social or spiritual beings is unimaginable, provided we all have faith and confidence in that single entity, the all-pervasive God.

A friend of mine met with an accident one day, while alighting from a bus and moving swiftly towards the Chennai Airport so as to catch a flight to Mumbai. Help from many unexpected quarters came to his rescue right from the moment he met with the accident and was lying unconscious on the middle of the road. And it continued to come; right up to his getting the best medical attention at one of the topmost hospitals in the city of Chennai. He was almost at the brink, close to death (One passerby even contacted his wife in Mumbai by mobile and told her he was dead!). After prolonged hospitalization and excellent medical treatment, he fought his way back brilliantly to normal health. Although we sometimes tend to believe that we are predestined to face such crises (astrologers analyse birth charts and horoscopes and confirm such events, either before or after the occurrence, depending on the situation), the events that followed in the case of my friend's meeting accident and his recovery, which was aided by the help coming in from many quarters, were nothing short of a miracle. What I saw during this particular case convinced me that help will always arrive from unexpected quarters if one simply surrenders himself at the altar of God so as to be able to receive His grace through angels of many kinds.

To achieve this objective, one needs to open up completely. He must talk with family, friends, well-wishers, doctors and - most importantly - discuss his feelings openly with people who have some experience in the relevant field. An anecdote here and a story there, from any quarter, can make a big difference. Books are the best friends and guide. Spiritual masters are of the greatest help during such a crisis. The chemical imbalance inside the brain may not get corrected directly by these factors, but indirectly the soothing effect on the brain unshackles the neural networks responsible for creating the stressful condition that is causing the mental health crisis.

The feeling of loneliness during a mental health crisis is a very common phenomenon and a very dangerous sign. The least that one can do is create a bond with at least one other soul on earth - be it with past acquaintances, friends or family - during the worst stage of a mental health crisis. The idea is to share all stressful emotions with this person which in turn helps release pent-up feelings. In the absence of such relationships, one needs to think of creating a bond with a completely new person, if the situation comes to such a stage. Skepticism and suspicion are the general offshoots of a mental health crisis, but in order to avoid getting pulled into the deeper crisis of self-doubt, one needs to unequivocally start trusting at least one person with whom the physical vibrations of his heart start sensing some resonance. This first step starts working like a lubricant, in such a way that the soul in distress will pick up momentum and start shifting to higher gears and speeds by helping in the creation of newer friends and well-wishers.

Together you win

Just break down the word 'Together'. *To-Get-Her*. In a philosophical sense, to get 'Her', the Goddess, Mother Nature, or to merge with Her can be profound. During times of mental health crisis (or in any activity today for that matter), it is said that two brains are better than one brain, three brains are better than two, and so on. What it means is that if the person in question takes the help of and moves together with another, he or she is sure to get a better result. While moving along in this fashion, by first taking help from another person and then adding it to the list of helpers, one can slowly go on to attain enlightenment.

Mother Nature appears so balanced. The Sun rises in the east every morning and sets in the west every evening. Day is followed by night which is again followed by day. Night skies with thousands of stars are visible to the naked eye and appear with the fall of darkness. The moon appears, grows to become full, and then wanes slowly and disappears from the sky. Seasons change cyclically. These are so routine, so fixed, that we do not usually notice them internally. As individuals, we get up from bed in the morning, do our chores, eat, drink, do work, relax, and then go to bed again. And the routine continues until the day a mental health crisis creates a bitterness and irritation towards everything around us, even towards those purely routine natural things happening around us. Everything around us starts looking imbalanced and out of place!

'To - get- her' means to get that balance in life back again. One by one, we can try to get her, get back the pleasure in the mundane and routine things. I took the help of my wife during what was possibly the worst situation I'd ever faced, while in Australia, in the minutest of minute things. My interaction level with my spouse was deliberately increased manifold over during the fateful one and a half years towards the last phase of my PhD stay. This was done with clear intentions to release my stress bit by bit, to improve my understanding of my own fluctuating moods and feelings, to take as much moral support from her as possible, to open up my intellect and to see things from a different perspective i.e. from my wife's perspective so as to gather a different contextual meaning to any small issue arising during the day, day after day. Because mental illness sometimes restricts our visionary powers so much that we miss out on the ability to view things from different angles. And the neural network that we build while interacting with our environment can appear and feel very biased unless we broaden our horizons. Many people suggest; *'do not compete, just cooperate and see the result'.* If it is spouse today, it could be a friend or colleague tomorrow. Ultimately, with such a step by step approach, we can keep winning and moving together.

In a professional field, during times of mental depression, one feels so disempowered that he or she loses the minimum strength required to do some activity, take some risk or try new things. He or she may even get scared of doing the routine things. A person who would otherwise be deft in handling a machine, software or tool may lose confidence in himself such that he or she would be scared to even attempt to handle it again. This is the time one needs to be clear about the need to seek help. He should forget all fears of feeling humiliated and not hesitate to ask for help from family, friends, colleagues, neighbourers, club pals and so on. The energy of the system grows if we seek help from our environment, be it from family, friends, neighbours, colleagues etc. And together we win.

Let go

The negative emotions that are the root cause for all problems need to be disowned so that the bad influence of these negative emotions will not continue to bother us. In the face of a major crisis, due to which all of our thought processes may have become negative, this first step, if successfully carried out, will definitely lead to a position wherein one can start freeing himself from the clutches of the negative emotions that have been plaguing him or her. The power of intention is most vital here.

Give up the excessive greed, the excessive ambition or the excessive attachment. The root for all impending future problems is excessive greed and passion. The natural offshoots of this greed and passion are anger and hatred, and the associated feelings of fear, anxiety, frustration and bitterness. All of these stifle the intellect. All of it leads to nasty actions which could create terrible guilt within us and may also haunt us. *'Every saint has a past and every sinner has a future'* should be our guiding light during times of such crisis.

There are other emotions that plague us when we are in a crisis. There will be acute tendencies to blame people around us including our spouse, close family members, friends, colleagues, customers, vendors, bankers, government agencies and so on. It is important not to lose sight of the equality of the system that Collective Consciousness or God always holds. At one point of time during the peak of my own crisis, I began behaving violent towards my spouse, thinking that it was her decisions that had led me to such a crisis! How childish it was! Then there was finger pointing at a few of my family friends, and even research colleagues in the institute, as if it was their fault I'd gotten into such trouble! These are manifestations of a mind totally derailed. The key is to first try and bring back sanity in the thought processes. Each one of us in the system enjoys the same rights and privileges before God and it would be futile to cast an aspersion on anyone, either individually or as a group, and try to get away with it. Hence, it is better to delink such thought processes from our minds to help address our own problems in a much more wholesome manner rather than in a biased manner.

Our tendency to be monotheistic has projected human imagination onto the Supreme Power, the Omniscient, Omnipotent and Omnipresent God. Any deviation in our pursuit towards ultimate good causes a flutter and it is then stirred up as some negative emotion like guilt, and this can be overpowering. One needs to understand that we are all human and do make mistakes. We should be prepared to forgive ourselves as much as we would others. It is wiser to learn from mistakes than to allow the repeating of mistakes to ruin us.

Don't be angry or guilty; have faith in the greater design of God

Whenever mental health crisis strikes, two very potent and dangerous negative emotions start working against you. Anger at everything around you first, and then slowly at yourself as well. Similarly, guilt is another extremely negative emotion which can kill a person unless we understand the root cause behind such emotions. Getting out of the Queen Elizabeth Hospital in Adelaide in July 2000, after my one week stay during the worst health crisis of my life, the first thought that came into my conscious mind was to blame everyone but me and I would get angry at everyone and everything upon receiving the slightest stimulus from the environment. The subconscious brain is generally powerful enough to travel back to the moment when it all began. There would be a logical analysis inside the brain continuously and at several junctures, our conscious decisions with whatever input data available at that moment of time that we took could be viewed as wrong by the current state of conscious mind. It is the tendency of the conscious part of the brain that tries to find faults with itself. When one reaches this stage, apart from becoming angry at oneself, guilt also sets in. This process is peculiar and intriguing to those who do not understand very well the mechanics of how our minds behave.

I recall the way I tried to dissipate my stress by talking to people, including my brothers and sisters back home, through letters (Those days, India was not so advanced that all households had PCs and internet as it is the case these days). In one letter, my eldest brother expressed his consternation on how I could land myself in the terrible mess of such a mental breakdown when my job was only to study and do research for my PhD. Until then no one could have anticipated that I would face such a terrible crisis in the far away land of Adelaide. And my eldest brother was skeptical because he knew my capabilities in studies and also had full confidence in me. However, his doubts were not at all unfounded when he learnt about my hospitalization to a mental health unit. Around the time my wife had gone back to India for the delivery of my son, I was left all alone in Adelaide for a period of about six months. It was during this period that I drifted a bit and was running after a female PhD student at the institute, perhaps in an illusory love affair! I wrote back to my eldest brother, admitting that there was a small mistake on my side. However, the guilt I was beginning to experience was, to a great extent, dispelled by what my eldest brother had written in the second part of the same letter. He advised me not to regret the decisions I had made without even knowing anything about what sort of activities I was engaged in, apart from PhD research study! That advice from him was powerful enough for me to be relieved, slowly but steadily, of my guilt over running after a woman when my main focus should have been to study. After all, since my father was no more, my eldest brother's words carried fatherly weight for me during that period and I derived much strength from them.

Similarly, my younger brother wrote to me after getting to know of my problem. By this time, he had vast experience in dealing with mental health issues because he was under mental health treatment for quite some time. My younger brother always had special attachment towards me and had almost infinite respect and love for me. When he came to know of my condition, he soon wrote; *'Accept everything'*. These two words are very powerful and find echo in scriptures like the *Bhagawat Gita* wherein it is suggested that total surrender to God is the path to salvation. These two things may appear to be different, but essentially they are the same. When we allow our minds to accept everything, it means that whatever pain and suffering that may come to us during a mental health crisis are better allowed to pass without much resistance from our conscious brain. The healing that happens when we surrender to the Collective Consciousness cannot happen if we remain angry and guilty and do not allow our brains feel the relaxation that comes with total surrender to God. The technique takes us back to the initial moments of our birth process where the sperm from the father moves towards the mother's egg under the influence of *Cosmic Intelligence* alone i.e. without any conscious influence of a human being. It is not easy, but it is not impossible to abstain from anger and guilt at such times of mental health crisis. It may be difficult in the beginning, but with practice it becomes easier.

The last part is to have total faith in God's greater design. Atheists and agnostics may have problems with these statements, but at the time of mental health crises - like depression, anxiety, stress etc. resorting to such faith is a sure way of getting healed quickly. What actually happens by this process is a bit winding. Our inner or latent desires, which take birth at some point of time of our lives, take our conscious brains down a path without fear until such a time it gets obstructed by circumstances - leading sometimes to mental health breakdown. This is similar to how reckless driving meets with a road accident! The injury could be physical in the latter case while it may be mental in the former case. But when, with all efforts and care, we come out of the problem, it is quite common to come across feelings of wonder about the greater design that God had in creating those obstructions and the problems along the way because this is the only way our souls can learn about God, Collective Consciousness or Cosmic Intelligence. Many a times, we observe that opportunities for growth and expansion multiply when we come out of the problems and crises. This is because the soul also does get expanded by wisdom and experience.

You are already a winner! Just maintain the status

We all know quite a few things about our planet, the solar system and the Universe. We also know quite a bit about the ages of each. Earth is around 3.8 - 4.5 billion years old and the Universe is about fifteen billion years old. We also know that human beings are the latest, most advanced and sophisticated animals roaming the planet earth. Several higher order animals, including lions, tigers, elephants, cows, goats, pigs and marine animals exist as well. But we also know from paleontological evidence that humans or homosapiens came to this earth around 2.5-4.5 lakh years ago. Although there are various estimates of when the first humans roamed on earth, that is the general consensus. Now, within this period which is a miniscule length of time compared to the age of Universe and even the age of the planet, we have been progressing rapidly in all dimensions of knowledge - be it scientific, physical, emotional, spiritual or sociological.

Regarding the birth of humans, it is well established by science that the fertilization of the egg of the mother by the sperm from the father gives rise to the birth of a baby. We now know that the average sperm concentration today is between twenty and forty million per millilitre in the Western world (having decreased by a percent or two every year from a substantially higher number decades ago). The global average of sperm concentration is said to vary between fifteen million to three hundred million per millilitre.

The fact that each one of us exists on earth today is because we have somehow been ahead of all our competitor sperms, inside the mother's womb, just before fertilization. Human fertilization is the union of a human egg and human sperm, usually occurring in the *ampulla* of *the uterine tube*. The result of this union is the production of a *zygote*, or *fertilized egg*, initiating prenatal development. Scientists discovered the dynamics of human fertilization in the nineteenth century and it is now quite clear that only one sperm out of the concentrate stated above, i.e. the fifteen to three hundred million per millilitre, has succeeded in moving towards the egg for union. Is it not the *race of all races* that each of us has already won, although none of us ran the race in a conscious manner, using what we define as our conscious mind? While astrologers will ascribe such a phenomenon completely to celestial influence, spiritual leaders will bring Karmic influence but is there anyone on earth who can deny the fact that the very process of fertilization which created us was not of our own making at all? All these details have been discovered only in the last two hundred years of modern science.

When such a fierce competitive race, in which the odds stacked against the ultimate winner is so huge, has been won at the time of fertilization itself, is it not going to be relatively easier, in this beautiful world, to maintain this winning position of ours which has already been decided by no power less than God? And that without resorting to the unnecessary rat race in later life that might leave us prone to stress and danger? Hence, whatever mental stress, worries or anxieties are being perceived or felt, they have more than a one hundred percent chance of being melted away provided we are a little more cautious, listen to our inner voice, make some changes in our lifestyle, take the necessary medical help as and when required, have faith in the Collective Consciousness or God, lead a balanced healthy life and move ahead in life.

Discern and Discriminate

It is an established fact that our mind has the ability to visualize, through the power of imagination, certain things that are yet to occur in our lives. The essence of the book *'The Secret'* by Rhonda Bryne suggests that just by the power of positive thinking, we can attract anything in this world towards us. There is however a small amount of myth attached to this concept. It is okay to be ambitious, it is okay to harbor dreams and desires, but it is not okay to become despondent because of failures, or because ambitious goals or desires go unfulfilled.

There is another aspect of visualization. While growing up, we have all come across very beautiful and pleasant memories of our own successes, of the toil and hard work behind each of these successes and of the occasional lucky draw wherein the alignment of the forces of nature are in our favour such that we land up achieving far more than we imagined. These situations record two extreme positions on our path to success. One path is that of pure hard work and the other is the path of so-called divine intervention. Great sports personalities across generations have both these elements well recorded within themselves. Sachin Tendulkar, who is often and fondly called the "God of cricket" in India, and who has scored a century of centuries in international cricket, had an uncanny habit. Every time he scored a century, be it in Test cricket or in One Day Internationals, he would throw both his arms wide open, and turn his head upwards and stare at the Heavens with reverence, holding his bat in one hand. The scene is akin to *raising a toast to the Divine*. While no one knows better than Sachin how much hard work and focus, both during practice sessions and during the course of every match, goes behind each success, he also knows that in sports, as in life, divine help has its place. Although we intrinsically always recall the sweet fruits of our hard work, the forces of nature that conspire to make such success possible do contribute their own share.

While not taking anything away from each such outstanding effort, we all know that cricketers, and all sportspersons for that matter, benefit from the lapses of their opponents at critical junctures. Sometimes, batsmen may enjoy what is called *'life'*, which are basically chances dropped by fielders. They take advantage of such misses and go on to hit hundreds, double hundreds and even triple hundreds. This is applicable to each and every batsman in the world as well as to any other sportsman. An international tennis player, a grand slam champion, may have a bad day and make umpteen numbers of unforced errors, including double faults, when otherwise, on a good day, he would never have made such mistakes. These are just a few examples of how, apart from our own efforts, *divine intervention*, or *chance factors* as rationalists call them, also operates to decide our destinies both in the short term and long term.

With such a backdrop, we can record these sweet memories of success and derive power from them during future endeavours. Such incidents happen in everyone's life at different levels and in different situations, but nevertheless they are important. If we can make use of the power of visualization, then we can inject some power of faith into our goals which would help in our achieving success. Goal setting is only one part of the story, but if we can back it up with the power of visualization of the successful achievement of goals, half the job would be done.

Panic attacks are not natural occurrences but aberrations. The tremendous stress that is built up within our mind and body, and which arises out of our overly ambitious targets or unfounded fears and anxieties, is the root cause for such panic attacks. Now, through the power of visualization, if we can recall the sweet memories of success, the happy and pleasant feelings of past, then we will be able to activate our memory cells in such a way that positive energy is generated. This will help tremendously in healing our mind and body.

Once a person is in a diseased mental health condition, it might become difficult for him to *discern and discriminate* between what is right and what is wrong, what is good for him and what is bad, because the conscious brain is badly weakened. However, the subconscious brain remains strong as ever. During such a crisis, if a part of the decision making process is relegated to the subconscious brain, then it augurs well for the person. Here, the "subconscious brain" mostly means the heart and feelings. The heart has its own way of functioning, thinking and taking decisions which, when combined, I term as the subconscious brain. The conscious brain is made up of the mind alone and hence, to discern and discriminate properly during a crisis, it is better, for a few days or weeks, to give the steering wheel to the heart.

I shall give a few examples of how we make stupid mistakes as fellow human beings on earth due to our racial bias or communal bias or even our gender bias. Racism has been around in this world ever since human society took a structured form. And I can safely visualize how gender bias has been ingrained in society for centuries. Simply because we have failed to understand and discriminate between nature's longing for a clear-cut distinction between male and female, we have exploited the physical weakness of the female body (weak when compared to the male's) and built an entrenched gender bias towards women. The beauty in the creation of distinctive traits as well as physical features of male and female is not only a matter to be respected, but cherished too. Instead, degeneration in society due to lack of control over our senses has permeated across all sections of the world. With education and understanding, individuals and societies overcome such shortcomings. The Indian caste system is another area where human frailty, in the form of racial bias, has reached its nadir. When centuries of discrimination are perpetuated against a whole community of people, in the name of caste, the resulting social stratification does no benefit to anyone. Many generations of agents of exploitation are the only output.

When Bhagawat Gita speaks of the four major divisions of society i.e. the four varnas - *Brahman, Kshatriya, Vaishya* and *Shudra* - it is very simple to correlate it to the way human intellect should be utilized. The four divisions respectively point to thought leaders, political leaders and warriors, business leaders and the common followers who serve these leaders. There is absolutely no incongruity if one can visualize this system in any age, or generation, or stage of development of society, without resorting to a branded caste based on birth and death alone. This system was mainly created to enable smooth functioning of society, based on intellectual power, education and training with relevant skills along with attitudes and the inclination towards different type of activities. Lord Krishna has indicated quite emphatically that those who are greedy for the results of their actions (*Sakami Yogi*) can never attain Brahma and those who are not greedy for results (*Nishcami Yogi*) can attain Brahma (shloka 8.23). These verses from the Lord Himself suggest that the four divisions are actually indicating human attributes and attitudes and do not have anything to do with caste or creed. It was because of human follies that society has degenerated into such divisions based on caste or class, where clever people start exploiting their fellow men in the name of caste or class. There is another instance where Lord Krishna has tried to dispel the belief in the supremacy of two varnas, Brahman and Kshatriya, over the other two, Vaishya and Shudra. He says that the two varnas branded as "lower" in society (by ignorant people) will attain Moksha or liberation through their devotion and surrender (shloka 9.32) whereas the two varnas that consider themselves to be superior will be bound by the illusion or Maya of family bondage and social bondage and hence be stuck in the vicious cycle of birth and death without getting liberated (shloka 9.33). Thus, when the human mind becomes shortsighted, it fails to measure up to the high ideals described in scriptures and tries to justify selfish gains through all sorts of misinterpretations. Hence, over the centuries, what actually happened is there for everyone to see in the badly entrenched caste system of India because the tendency of human beings to exploit others has been there from time immemorial. The caste or varna system of Hindus which was product of evolution of society with a noble aim in the beginning got hijacked by the overzealous upper castes leaving behind a trail of massive exploitation, misery and deprivation. Leaders like Mahatma Gandhi understood this malaise in Indian society and worked tirelessly to improve the system.

There are many claims by scholars who quote the cycle of the four Yugas, *Satya Yug*, *Trettaya Yug*, *Dwapar Yug* and *Kali Yug*, and, according to some, *Brahmagnyana* says that the four Yugas correspond to four varnas; *Satya Yug* with Brahmana varna, *Trettaya Yug* with Kshatriya varna, Vaishyas with *Dwapar Yug* and Shudras with *Kali Yug*. Again, the four varnas are differentiated based on the presence or absence of positive and negative attitudes. While the Brahmana represents both positive and negative attitudes merged into one, the Kshatriya represents the separateness of the two attitudes, the Vaishya represents only positive attitude and the Shudra has no attitudes. This sort of discrimination or division between two groups of human beings or even two individuals, backed by all kinds of logic related to celestial motion and positions for Yugas and human attitudes, are difficult to accept without any hard scientific evidence. One needs to exercise his own power of reasoning to deduce an interpretation that appeals to him internally such that he or she is in harmony with Nature. After all, all human beings have the same DNA and modern genealogy might at best indicate some tendencies towards certain attributes in certain human beings, but the scope for transcendence by conscious efforts can never be overlooked. In fact, study of the Bhagawat Gita in true perspective and in a holistic manner can dispel all doubts that arise in mind and such a scope for transcendence for each human being towards not only attaining higher qualities within one life span itself but also prepare oneself for salvation has been elegantly described in the Gita.

I recall one annual meeting of our village deity and temple committee held every year on the Ekadashi (eleventh day), the day after the immersion of idols of Maa Durga in the river Salandi after celebrations of the Durga Puja festival are completed. Actually, we have three small temples popularly called Radha-Krishna temple, Laxmi-Narayan temple and Shiva temple. Generally, during such meetings, village elders discussed the management of the temples and take major decisions regarding the welfare of the temples and the do's and dont's for the *sevayats* (devotees). The year of this particular meeting was perhaps 1986.

My village, Boudpur, about three kms from the Bhadrakh town, is my most favourite place in the world and the place closest to my heart. It is a small and beautiful village on the banks of the Salandi River where, legends say, few Bengali families from the Bardhhaman district of West Bengal migrated and settled down around three to four hundred years ago. The childhood memories of my village where we used to go during Durga Puja festival every year without fail, are still fresh and sacrosanct. I do not know why, but in spite of the fact that none of the eight siblings except the eldest of our family being born there, the attraction to go from wherever we are, during the holy Durga Puja festival, for each member of the family even today is so magnetic that it defies logic. Perhaps, the loving closeness amongst all the village folk which manifests freely in the stress free atmosphere during about one week long festival creates such a gel amongst all Boudpurians, young and old, male or female, rich and poor, that the bondage has become very deep rooted in our psyche. I recall talking only last year to a very young boy of our village, actually a far related nephew of mine. He was working in Switzerland at that time and he was describing the mental pull he experienced for somehow coming over to this sacred village of Boudpur, so that he would not miss anything during the festival period. The anecdote that is tagged with our village is that ours was actually a *Vidyanagari* (city of knowledge) for the fact that every member of almost every family of our village was highly educated, perhaps the minimum being a graduate. Doctors, engineers, scientists, administrators, defense officers galore in our village. The reputation of the village is widespread across the entire state of Odisha for all the good reasons.

During one such annual meeting of the management committee of our village deity, I discovered some peculiar traits amongst generally the old in the village. One highly placed government officer from our village proposed at this particular meeting that the temple be opened to people of all communities and that the restriction against lower caste people that was then prevalent be removed. Being a senior governmental officer, he knew quite well the fallacy of the caste system and was trying to implement government policy of equality in his village temple. It was a genuine and sincere attempt. I was relatively young at the time, and there was an unwritten restraint on very young people on voicing opinions at such village meetings where elders were deliberating on important issues. But I vividly remember the kind of opposition and protests that many of our elders expressed against this proposal. Being such a highly placed government official, he had to find a way to escape the humiliation he was facing. He then asked whether our village temple was a private temple or a public temple, knowing perhaps fully well that everyone knew the exact status of the temple. It was built on a piece of land donated by one of the village families and with funds donated by the village people who mainly consisted of our ancestors. To this question, there was a chorus of voices saying that it was a private temple meant only for the village people and not a public temple. I was witness to the processes of how human beings can get carried away by the traditional bias that runs in societies even in a place where so called modern education have brought in social status to almost all. Although it is perfectly within the democratic rights of a group of people to use one of their private places of worship with limited access, what I found intriguing, as a normal human being, was that we allowed such discriminations in the first place and also allowed our children and grandchildren to perpetuate such practices.

Similarly, I recall seeing another incident on a TV programme almost twenty-five years ago. The apartheid system in South Africa had just been officially abolished and Nelson Mandela was the first President of the predominantly black country, coming into power immediately after the end of apartheid. In this particular TV programme, a white man being interviewed about his experiences in the pre- and post-apartheid regimes of the country. He was speaking very innocently; his innocence was quite visible in his face and his voice. He was saying; 'Beating for petty crimes, the torture and even the killing of black people never created a ripple in my mind. I thought it was so very mundane and nothing abnormal and not the least inhuman.' The kind of innocence he was speaking with points to a grave danger that the human community is facing. The danger of social evils getting so badly entrenched through generations of practice anywhere in the world, be it India or South Africa, and of human beings losing the compassionate feelings for even their own species! They behave like animals of the jungle and not even like social animals anymore.

Divisions in society on the basis of caste, colour and creed have always bothered me. Taking birth into a certain family need not be made the criteria for recognition in society. It is a person's Karma in his or her present life which should decide that. Instituionalising a birth and death based system is contrary to democratic ethos which otherwise forms the most viable form of social development as of date. There is one more incongruity that is noticed in such a discriminatory system. If we take protection of the Bhagawat Gita, written perhaps around 3100 BC, more than 5000 years ago for justification of the four varna system, and project that to the present generations, it will be a gross undervaluation of the most sacred scripture of the Hindus. If we go through the scripture carefully, we will notice that towards the end of the scripture, in last eighteenth chapter (shlokas 18.42-18.44), Lord Krishna has tried to summarise what is meant by these four varnas. The intriguing fact that the first two varnas, described in the first two shlokas (18.42 & 18.43) as above, enlist more of a set of subjective attributes or attitudes which personify the Brahmanas and Kshyatriyas, apart from prescribing passingly religious rituals, study etc. for Brahmanas and fighting and administration for Kshyatriyas whereas the next shloka (only one!) (18.44) describe the other two varnas slightly differently, specifying mainly the type of jobs or in other words indicating their professions directly. Agriculture and commerce for the Vaishyas and all round service to the other varnas by the Shudras. This division has baffled me all along. Obviously something else is hidden here which to my mind points to the future. Today, during the age of modern science when we are trying to find out the most fundamental unifying theory that explains everything, including gravitational, electromagnetic, strong and weak forces and in the process, discovering the most fundamental of sub-atomic particles, to think of a social stratification based on any rigid birth based theory or diktats would be counterproductive for humanity.

However, past Karma might be responsible for someone's taking birth into a particular family or varna, but it should be restricted to that alone. The Karma of the present life should be given maximum value in this modern world where access to education, training, resources etc. is promoted equally for all sections of society by most of the democratic governments all over the world. I can imagine that the system which divided Hindu society into four varnas as per the ancient Hindu belief systems can now be easily correlated with the modern way of life. The manufacturing sector involving cutting edge technology and research can be safely correlated to

Brahmanas, the defense sector to Kshatriyas, the agricultural sector to Vaishyas and the services sector to Shudras. I believe that even in the *Dwapar Yug* that was Lord Krishna's time, a similar logic would have gone into categorizing social activities. But due to the power of the thought leaders, generally associated with the Brahmins, there was a deliberate corruption of the pure intentions behind the formation of such a nice and stable system and it was turned into an institutionalised exploitative system in later centuries. It was leaders like Mahatma Gandhi and Dr. Bhim Rao Ambedkar who could visualize the implications of such an entrenched system and how destructive it would be for nation building. If we just undertake some statistical analysis today, the above four sectors of the economy will have people from many different castes or varna based families in any given sector. However, there are claims by many biased writers and thinkers still, mostly from the so called higher varnas, that there would be a tendency in group statistics, the prevalence of bias of the original qualities and attributes of respective varnas! It is literally strange to proclaim that human frailties will occur less in a particular varna based community and more in the others unless there is an artificial restriction deliberately created for whichever purpose. Also, minute observer or researcher would agree that genetic mixing within a particular type of people restricted through social customs will obviously result in the above statistical bias which therefore has a scientific basis. In this fast changing world of science and technology which is breaking all barriers, which have even reached Frankenstein proportions of going towards cloning of human beings, it is simply dangerous to carry such a mental bias of varna based superiority or inferiority any further. It is not unlikely we'll find Brahmins in all four sectors of the economy - either directly or indirectly related to them. Manual labour and mental labour are two different things, but to characterize this as the basis of division of society is once again naive. Peasant movements and labour movements are just manifestations of human beings' cry for dignity, and this has happened periodically in all parts of the world. It is perhaps for this reason, some have attributed four parts of human beings representing four varnas. Brahman being the top most part of the body including neck and head, hands and shoulder area representing Kshyatriya, middle part of the body representing Vaishya and the leg downward is Shudra. The head which houses the brain including the main four sense organs, is capable of doing what Brahmins are supposed to do, hands protect the body parts, middle part digests food, supplies all vital nutrients to body, doing as if the service for all the parts of the body and the lower most part bears the entire burden of the body and the mind. I have always believed that human civilization has gathered knowledge and wisdom in a collective manner and never by an individual manner. Be it science or spirituality, no single human being can ever be considered to have contributed every bit of knowledge in any particular field. This applies to all fields of science or all sects of religions around the world. Application of knowledge and wisdom is meant for each individual on earth.

Sometimes, people born into certain sections of society are humiliated and exploited based on varnas or any such categorisation. This causes them immense mental agony and torture that may also lead to mental health issues unless one is very clear about his or her ideas on social stratification and the root causes, weaknesses and strengths of such systems. The idea is to be alert to such issues, effectively discern and discriminate, so that they do not cause unnecessary anguish in the mind. Dr. Brian Weiss has been working on *past life regression therapy* and has somehow concluded that when a soul takes birth, it comes with a specific level of knowledge and wisdom. And when it makes its journey of life, it is as if it is moving through the different classes in a modern education system. According to his research, some souls may have reached the nursery level, some of them primary school, some high school, and some realized souls may be at graduate level. What it means is that, without getting too affected by the mental health crisis that hits you at some point of life's journey, it is essential that the soul feels assured and uses it as a lesson, or a chapter, or a subject, learned over the course of that lifetime and so acquire a little more wisdom. Because soul has infinite power for learning and growth. Each social custom built over centuries can be understood if one uses his or her intellect properly in a logical manner. The fact that human species is hardly 2.5 lakh years old and is still evolving gives him the assurance that his own contribution in terms of understanding the customs and trying to bring in improvement for the overall good of the human species can still be immense.

Feel content and feel grateful

We have a tendency to forget the little help we receive along the way, while climbing our ladder to success. Subconscious part of our brains are powerful enough to record each and every bit of help that we get. In the same way our brains record small obstacles and the pain and suffering caused by others (as we perceive them), the acts of kindness also get recorded. The *Karmic Cycle of Life* can explain almost all the paradoxes in life. Sometimes we ask why, out of two siblings, one is more gifted. Sometimes we ask why one is not behaving as perfectly as the other. This is the closest that two human beings can get. And the same logic can be extended to compare two friends, two classmates, two colleagues, two partners; any two travellers on this journey called life.

Contentment is the key to bliss. There are cases of the poorest of the poor feeling happy and content in spite of poor living conditions. It is quite obvious that such a person's soul knows very well what to expect from this journey of life, even though he is born poor. And on the other hand, there are cases where the richest of the rich feel miserable in spite of having everything (outwardly at least) at his disposal. Once again the reason is simple. The concerned soul does not know what this life is all about. In terms of *"the soul's class"* in this beautiful journey of life, the former soul may be at a high school level whereas the latter could be at the nursery level only. This sort of understanding is of great help in rapidly overcoming the mental health crisis one is going through.

The moment we recall the acts of kindness extended to us by an individual or a group, instantly, the vibrational energy created by the very thoughts of gratitude can bring transformational changes within us. The person we hate now, if we can just make a small forceful and deliberate effort to recall an act of kindness of his, the help rendered by the same person in the past, in a different situation, we can suddenly see our hatred towards that person just melting away. It is just that the power of anger and hatred can be overpowering and blind us from such positive and satisfying thoughts. But, with practice, this is absolutely possible.

Spouses fight over trivial issues. These fights create negative emotional energy in our bodies and minds which are neither healthy nor helpful. Sometimes, such small fights accumulated over a long period of time can make us feel allergic to the very sight of the other person, just the way our bodies feel allergic to any other extraneous agent. This can kick-start the process of draining our energy because nothing positive comes out. Such an attitude is the beginning of another mental health crisis. In a marriage, it does not emanate from one side just like that. It is a thought that originates in the mind and generally arises due to our failure to look at the acts of kindness of the other person, or feel the gratitude we owe them. Therefore, whenever such negative thoughts occur, it is quite effective to recollect, with a sense of contentment and gratitude, all the help rendered by the spouse - or any person for that matter. By doing so, one can neutralize the ill effects of the negative thoughts that crop up in relationships. Constant feelings of gratitude towards fellow human beings can do wonders and gratitude to God works miracles. I have personally applied this technique to great results.

Adapt & adopt Halt-Rewind-Meditate-Grow (HRMG) model

From infancy, we grow in different environments depending on our family background and the conditions of the rural or urban life that we are born into. The term 'family' includes parents, siblings, and the relatives and social friends that visit them. Apart from that, the economic status, the deep rooted beliefs, traditions, religious rituals etc. of all the above people, in the close community, influence the infant's mind. The prevalent socio-political and socio-economic situation does affect the mind as well, depending on how well or how badly the events around the family, be it in rural or urban background, get filtered or passed on into the infant's mind.

The story of Gautam (Buddha) or Siddhartha is well known and taught in schools. It is about how, as royal child, Gautam, even after growing up surrounded by a royal family atmosphere, gets disillusioned with life due to influences both from within the family and from the surroundings. He starts his personal search for the answers to life's many questions until he attains spiritual enlightenment. It is said of Buddha that, as a child, his *'kundali'* (horoscope or birth chart) was verified by the royal astrologer who predicted that Buddha would either turn out to be a great and powerful King or a renowned and respected monk. Hearing of the chance that his son might get to the stage of renouncing all worldly pleasures, his father, the king, made sure that his little child was debarred from seeing anything bad or painful, from seeing any kind of suffering in the world. It was as if the world was just full of pleasures and there was nothing wrong in the world! This was maintained very strictly until Buddha was crowned king. One day, as the king, Buddha desired to be taken for a ride around the kingdom, to see the condition of his subjects. While travelling through his kingdom that day, his entourage encountered three scenes that altered the course of his life. The first was the sight of a very old man with almost total infirmity who was not able to walk properly and was being neglected on the road by passersby. The second was of a very poor man begging for alms, and the last one was that of a family following the procession for a dead man and crying over the departed soul. These three painful scenes of suffering jolted the innermost being of Gautam Buddha who then started asking questions from his subjects and, upon not getting satisfactory answers from any quarter, began his own journey. He denounced everything- including his wife and small child, his kingdom, and all the worldly pleasures associated with them.

The story of Mahatma Gandhi, similarly, tells us how a character built up over the course of a particular situation during childhood, and later adulthood, gets transformed due to prevalent political situations. Mahatma Gandhi, early on in his life, behaved with strong morality when confronted with a situation where he could either copy and be at par with his class friends and appreciated by the visiting school inspector, or not copy and face the humiliation of poor performance and being branded a fool. Another situation was when he challenged the power and strength of the train officials in South Africa, who were white supremacists and tried to dislodge Mahatma Gandhi from the first class train compartment for which he had a valid ticket. There are hundreds of such stories for our own enlightenment.

My own search for a powerful tool culminates with this model which I call the *HRMG model,* the acronym for *Halt-Rewind-Meditate-Grow.* I believe that use of this model in the modern world is both idealistic and practical at the same time. Those who sarcastically term anything good as too idealistic and utopian fall into the trap of hankering after the same goals that appear to them as utopian in the first place. Till one does not suffer defeats, one is inclined to believe he or she is unconquerable. Any suggestion to him to include some amount of idealism in his goals for achievement generally falls apart because of the tendency inside to vanquish the opponents in the next attempt considering the lucky successes tasted so far. But the moment one gets the taste of his first defeat, reality strikes and he tries to complain against his opponents looking now for the same idealism in his opponents which he once overlooked as too idealistic. One needs to be very minute in order to be successful in observing such tendencies in leaders or anybody for that matter.

Each human being is endowed with several fundamental instincts. The basic needs are to live and survive, the next needs are to love and be loved, next is to learn and satisfy the ego through acquiring power and position and the final need is to leave a legacy through the path of self-actualization and even transcendence. But if we deeply study any of these human need theories, we will find that the final and ultimate choice of any human being is to follow the path of spirituality, the path of sacrifice, the path of unconditional love, the path of total commitment to the highest goal of human life - which is to serve the community, that of total mankind. Each one of us is born with the instinct for self-gratification through worldly pleasures, for ambition, for the desire to enjoy lives to the fullest. But, at the same time, we are born also with the fundamental instinct of helping ourselves and others achieve higher goals of life, apart from satisfying the basic needs.

At the time of a crisis, if we analyse, we will find that the cause of it will be related to one of the four parts that make up a whole human being: body, mind, heart and spirit. I believe that, as a human being, the problems of life affect us in this order i.e. in the order of body, mind, heart and spirit. Any crisis can progressively lead to either temporary or semi-permanent damage of any of these four parts and hence may be viewed as a disease both to the victim as well as to the society. The effect will always be complimentary and may lead to a vicious cycle unless treated properly. There will be situations wherein the person concerned might lose complete control of himself. Initially untreated or wrongly treated problems might have to be dealt with by another - a family member, or a friend, or some other member of society - in the worst case scenario.

Any small crisis can be dealt with if we attend to the problem in accordance with our model; *Halt-rewind-meditate-grow.* It should be applied in progressive phases, in steps, to the body, the mind, the heart and the spirit – and in that order. Generally, a problem affects the body first and hence, if we just step back and introspect, we will find that there could be valid reasons for any problem, big or small, and we can tackle the problem accordingly. I shall illustrate this with a personal example.

The *panic attacks* which I experienced during the period from 2000 to 2001 were most severe. In the time from 2002 to 2006, the frequency and intensity of these *panic attacks* went down drastically. However, one day the problem reappeared. It would have been around September 2006.

After a very hectic day followed by hardly any rest in the evening, straddled with a few energy-sapping domestic arguments, I went to attend an official meeting the next morning. My mouth started feeling dry. It was a feeling of total fear, similar to a *panic attack* but a little different because it had been long time now since I'd had that feeling. I could sense that there would be problems, but I could not decide. One of my friends, a colleague, who was sitting just beside me at the meeting, suggested that I check my BP with our doctor. It turned out that my BP was high, but the doctor said that it was not a cause for worry and that it was mainly due to some deeper anxiety - and I could sense that the anxieties that had built up inside over the last twelve hours or so were the cause.

I quickly recalled my own theorized model - *Halt, rewind, meditate and grow* - and put it into action. I knew that it was a smaller problem, but it needed exactly the same treatment as the bigger problems of life. I rested and relaxed the whole day (*"halted"*). Modern medical research says that rest heals the body much faster and allows faster recovery for any patient. I used that technique. I immediately took myself away to a remote corner inside the office complex, into a room that was not used much, and relaxed on the couch there for few hours. Then I *"rewinded"* myself to think about possible causes for the recurrence of my *panic attack* problem and whether there was really any threat to my life. I concluded that it was because of the physical and emotional exhaustion of the previous day combined with my own inner sense of insecurity. Then I *"meditated"* by resting fully the whole afternoon and early that evening and came back fresh the next morning. I could conclude that every problem of life could be tackled with this model. The moment the mind and heart sense a crisis, both should direct their attentions to this beautiful model and instruct the body first and mind later to take a full break and relax. This would give sufficient scope for settling down of the disturbance and an opportunity for reinvigoration. The last part is *"Grow"* - which actually means that these small events of success can be inbuilt into the subconscious in such a way that the whole body-mind-heart-spirit system can absorb the feelings and keep them intact for retrieval in times of crisis. The other advantage of "Grow" is to share this experience with others so that they can also benefit.

Power of the Universe lies within you

While knowing fully well that the thought processes that pass my mind and try to take root inside my mind from time to time, are always not pure and divine, I have however always tried consciously to apply a filtering process to separate them into two groups; good, positive and divine in one group and bad, negative and devil in another. There is always a struggle inside the mind by one group trying to overpower the other and my conscious efforts have always been to allow the group that is good to be provided some extra energy for sustenance such that the ill effect of the other is overshadowed.

One day, perhaps in late 2007, I had a feeling inside me, a burning desire to contain and reorient my life in such a way that all my actions, words, thoughts and behaviour should be directed towards some sort of sacrifice for the benefit of at least one human being or a collection of human beings in different situations. During my hour-long *Pranayam*, that evening, it struck me that I should consciously pray to God or for Heavenly intervention to transform these ideals into my life, interweave them into my whole *being*. While lying down with a posture of my back on the floor, head towards the ceiling, all of a sudden, when I was metaphorically looking for blessings from Heaven to shower me with all the strength and courage needed to maintain such magnanimity, I got a feeling of strange sensations inside me, as if the Heaven was telling me from above; *'Hey, do not look at me. Everything is there inside you. Try to find everything that you are searching for within yourself. I have given you everything already, built it into your soul. You do not have to look to me, every time you get into difficulty, for peace of mind and freedom from worries. It is all there already within you. You just have to pull that pearl out from underneath the deep sea of life that is within you.'*

It was a great calling for me. I tried to visualize that and I felt perhaps for the first time in my life that yes, it was the Truth. All these years of my life, what I had been scientifically thinking, mentally believing and spiritually experiencing had all converged into the above sermon of life from Heaven. I thought that I must at least begin exploiting the message and proceed further along the path.

Slowly I began to believe in how true that one statement was. Fear is developed when the mind is not in unison with one's own soul - which is nothing but the replica of the universal soul, or at least a part of the replica of the universal soul. The moment one is in alignment with the universal soul, fear disappears. The universal soul is nothing but our crude interpretation of God. When we start to realize that our birth, and our growth from birth through every passing moment of life, is basically guided by the intricate network of the universe, the universe in which every being and creature, small or big, and every material thing in different form, basically influences the divine force that interplays with our souls right from the moment of birth. It is just our own understanding and how we translate that into our material lives on Earth that is important. For example, I have a strong belief that if I do not cheat anybody on Earth, I will never be cheated. If I do not harm anybody on Earth, no one will harm me. If I extend help to the needy, I shall get the help I need, if not from the people I helped but certainly from different quarters. If I work hard, I am bound to get good result and if I am lazy, I will have to suffer. If I am careless and negligent, I will have to pay a price for it and so on.

Engage yourself till you make it a habit

My friend and senior colleague once told me a story of how a gentleman once thought he would confront Gautam Buddha. He used to travel far from his village to listen to Gautam Buddha giving his discourses. The man, out of curiosity, asked after a month of attending the discourses whether he would really ever benefit from what he was hearing from Gautam Buddha. He felt that he had not benefited in the past one month, so how was he going to benefit in his life time?

Gautam Buddha asked where he was coming from. The man named his village and described how far away it was from there. Then Buddha asked him if he thought that anyone there had been told

271

about the path leading from their village to this place, and if, by just knowing about the route, anyone could reach that place without stepping out from his house and actually treading the path. The man realized his mistakes and went home, satisfied with what Buddha said. Buddha's discourses would remain discourses only unless one follows the advice, teachings and the principles of life as suggested by Buddha. Unless we tread the path to a certain desired destination, we will never reach there just by knowing the route to the place. This is exactly what Stephen Covey means too when he says that to know the path and not work on it is as good as not knowing the path at all. Similarly, to simply learn the techniques and not practice them is no better than not learning the same. Habit makes life's jobs much easier. It is sometimes very difficult to imagine how to cultivate a habit. But there are subtle ways and expressions of God's grace through which one can achieve this difficult goal of transforming some practices into habits - after thorough practice for several weeks and sometimes even months. It is the prerogative of each individual to test the universal and timeless principles, such as how *habit makes a man perfect.*

It won't be easy at all, but the easiest way is to surrender one's ego at the altar of God and allow Him to charter His aims and desires through your actions, however small they may seem to be. Because, in a broader perspective, all such small acts that may appear to be humiliating now in fact, when combined, give rise to the full realization of a noble path or goal. The frustration or hopelessness vanishes the moment the individual suggests to himself that it is just God's desire he is fulfilling, and that the only desire within him should be to devote himself totally to the service to others - to mankind in general, and to individuals, family, groups or the larger society in particular. The moment one does that, he derives immense strength and a sense of purpose from what comes to him and is brought to him. Mahatma Gandhi experienced this when he said clearly that, in a state of egolessness, he just picked up his cudgels whenever such a call came to him.

Go back to your hobbies

Many people miss out on the subtle importance of hobbies. As human beings, each of us is born with some talent which looks for expression and which, if we get the opportunity, blooms to become a hobby. Hobbies can vary widely. Gardening, painting, sculpting, cooking, recitation, dance, music, drawing cartoons, writing satire, astronomy or star gazing, astrology, reading or writing poetry or prose, games and sports, rearing and caring a pet at home, chit chatting amongst friends, playing cards or carom or ludo or chess with family and friends, go to a temple or church and enjoy the company of like-minded people there, even go shopping, and the list can go on and on. The issue is not how well one can perform in that field. It is not important whether one is championship material or not. What is important is how passionate he feels about his hobby or the activity of his liking. These hobbies can only benefit our entire beings positively, and not just the mind alone. When one suffers from severe mental stress, it is more than possible that the person can get cut off from the flow of passionate energy he needs to enjoy a hobby or get associated with an activity. The mental stress thus gets into a vicious cycle, neither getting an opportunity to get released nor allowing even the physical body to help produce and provide stress reducing hormones into the brain, which is what gets maximum affected during such time of mental health problems.

Instinctively, one will observe that the subconscious brain points towards the drought-like situation in the area which has not got any attention for a long time in an attempt to run for only intellectual satisfaction or materialistic pursuits - which can be the root cause of stress. In times of such problems, spending time on old hobbies can be very relaxing, and can generate dopamine in large quantities to balance the chemical imbalance created in a stressed-out brain. What we saw in fifth chapter, *happiness is just a thought and emotion away!* Here, one should not be confused about happiness not being considered as an emotion. What it means is that the thought and associated emotion has to be somehow triggered. During mental health crisis, some of the fundamental knowledge which each one of us has gathered from our childhood, the most basic ones can be of immense help. However, the one conscious thought is vital to take the first step. Once the thought about deciding to engage in some pastime or hobbies is taken with a clean inner desire, howsoever feeble it may be, the energy flux is certain to start favouring to somehow release the blockade from the mind to take up such hobbies even when the mind would be tricking to make us believe its uselessness at the time of severest mental stress.

I recall how, when I faced my crisis in Australia, I made it a point to go back to sports in right earnest. I quickly made arrangements with a couple of my Indian friends and started playing tennis three times a week - something I had neglected to do so far in Australia. I joined a small Indian music band where I played Tabla, an Indian percussion instrument, and even performed on stage a couple of times during my last year of stay in Australia. I could derive immense benefits from such activities by balancing the stress during the last leg of my PhD research work including thesis writing.

Turn around to the Nature

Most of us fail to realize the power of human mind in receiving fresh vibrational energy if one focuses specifically towards observing the smallest of the small processes of Nature including physical processes like river flowing down the gorges cutting through large rocks and making its way down the slope of a hill, or meandering rivers eating their banks slowly in the sandy and clayey plains, flowing river making hissing sound, waves and tides never stopping to come again and dashing against the shore, wind blowing the leaves and branches of a tree, rain drops falling on roof top, hailstorms lashing at window panes, lightening and thunders making the atmosphere alive, and so on. They can be other things like small insects looking for their food and even bigger insects eating the smaller ones. It can even be ants making a disciplined line carrying their food and exchanging some message at each meeting point between two ants in a mysterious manner. We still do not know very well what exactly goes between two small ants when, while coming from opposite direction, they stop for some micro seconds, as if in an attempt to say how much still is left over from the pile of food they have decided to finish off for the day! Just watch this phenomenon and you will understand what I mean.

Birds chipping in the morning and evening during Sun Rise and Sun Set can generate one of the most pleasant feelings for anybody. Flocking of a group of birds returning to their nests at the fall of sunset, crows making the day break known to all, butterflies moving around from one flower to another, pigeons at the window side making sound or creating their nests or laying eggs and then caring their chicks, cows licking the body of the new born calf, calf taking milk from its mother cow, frogs making sound at the advent of rains, jackals making sound at a distance at the fall of darkness, ducklings moving along ponds and lakes, squirrel sitting on a branch of tree and searching for its food, the serenity of forests with its wild animals and birds, these are some of the examples from the Nature that can be so refreshing and reinvigorating to the mind and soul that one would not be able to imagine the impact unless one makes conscious efforts to engage in observing such activities. The vibrational energy associated with all such processes of Nature, both physical and those associated with animals, birds etc. can instantly bring in fresh energy into the depressed mind and gloomy heart. CDs and DVDs are made these days to recreate artificially a soothing and relaxing feeling inside the mind. These have less effect than the actual scenes from the lap of Nature. Nevertheless, one must understand the basic principle behind such a phenomenon. Sights of lush green paddy fields, greeneries in and around the neighbourhood, small and big trees and variety of flowers in a park etc. can be very refreshing. Modern stress does not get relief amidst concrete jungles, streams of cars racing along highways or machineries doing their jobs mechanically but rather gets accentuated. Throwing food items in a pond and watching hordes of fish trying to grab the same can be a very pleasant sight and relaxing too.

Be aware that weakness is not always a burden

Lord Jesus had said that; *'The meek shall inherit the earth.'*

Few perhaps have imagined that weakness can itself be a talent. Weakness per se may not be a talent, but complete awareness about our weakness can definitely be a talent. We make mistakes out of ignorance, out of negligence, out of greed and lack of control over ourselves, out of carelessness, out of overconfidence, out of our lack of sincerity, out of our lack of application or dedication, and above all because of our lack of commitment. Mistakes are the result of any of these failings, which may not be at the fundamental grain of our being, but still keep occurring. Mistakes make us sad and obviously throw our happiness budget out of balance. But a total awareness of such mistakes in our past, and the reasons leading to such mistakes, can unravel a world of so-called weakness grains in our own system. The moment we are aware of such weakness, a feedback mechanism can easily be built such that we bring back the power of our strongest attributes to safeguard our weaker ones. And the stronger the chain or loop we make, the better.

A deserter on a battlefield may personify cowardice to many, but it can actually be a virtue. Earlier, in the 1930s and 1940s, people ran after the blood of deserters, but the Cuban Missile Crisis of 1960s brought in a new concept. Cowardice can be a virtue then since nuclear war could cause unthinkable destruction and suffering and no one can predict the outcome of a full-scale nuclear war. Many people will consider the backing out from such a nuclear war like situation by any nation as signifying cowardice in the old school of thought. Also, this would violate the principles hidden in the apparent teaching of Lord Krishna to Arjun in the Kurukshetra battlefield to forgo delusional thoughts and fight his enemies. However, I believe, we have come a long way since the advent of that most holy and dear scripture. Can we imagine now a situation wherein the alter ego of Lord Krishna is advising Arjun to use logic and reasoning rather than actual weapons to win over the warring factions in the situation of such a nuclear war keeping the entire humanity in perspective rather than just a group or a community because during the period when the Bhagawat Gita was written, wars and battles would not have threatened entire humanity as they do because of stockpiling of nuclear weapons by several countries around the world. So in order to get the true essence of Bhagawat Gita in such a war like situation, it would perhaps be wiser to use the real philosophical meaning hidden in the Bhagawat Gita and not the biased, distorted views generally manufactured by some unscrupulous writers or thought leaders. Lord Krishna encourages in the Gita each human being to be enriched with all round wisdom, so as to be capable of destroying one's own ignorance (germinated not in the battlefield in the form of enemies but rather in the form of wrong concepts inside one's own mind) before carrying out any action thinking about the entire humanity rather than for any small group or nation.

Learn and relearn constantly

When we think of the goal post and attempt to score a goal that would bring us total happiness and joy, we take into account our total strength, plan our moves and outsmart our opponents before moving ahead to the goal post and finally scoring the goal. The dodging, the dribbling and the swift moves all are part of the process. Similarly, when we know our ultimate mission or goal, how we reach it will depend on the ability of the individual to encompass all the qualities of a goal scorer.

The human journey, if analysed, can actually tell us how we simply follow our predecessors, their wisdom and their knowledge, and take on the strings they leave behind and then proceed on our own journeys. We will face obstacles, impediments, on our way in the form of natural disasters, problems caused by unscrupulous elements in the society, uninvited diseases, sometimes our own genetic makeup and sometimes environmental degradation caused by our follies. We have to pass through these obstacles and how we do so depends on how strong our will power is and how we maneuver ourselves through the journey of life.

The wisdom of rishis, seers, philosophers are timeless principles and today management thinkers are exploring and discovering truths that have already been realized by pure souls before us. We need to pick up those pearls in our journey through the ocean of sand.

When we fix the goal post, we just need to be vigilant enough to pick up passes from our co players, which reach us in the form of these diamonds or pearls, and then carry on with the journey to the goal post by either dribbling through the mesh of opponents or perhaps passing to a better positioned or more talented player. The pearls can be pure scientific theories, management principles, life's golden virtues taught by religious leaders or philosophers, technological skills, wise ideas generated within our own souls (this is sanctified if it is coming from the deepest part of our own soul, which can stand the test of time and space as other principles have).

Reading is one of the most potent means of acquiring knowledge and learning skills to help oneself. It is therefore vital that, whenever the mind becomes too stressed, we get help from any source - and books are one of the best companions. The other easy method to bring back mental peace and stability to a derailed mind is by talking to trusted friends and relatives. Attending discourses given by spiritual leaders is another very good tonic that helps in faster recovery. Similarly, TV today has very good channels streaming spiritual knowledge and wisdom from different parts of the world. Since we have access now to various channels running spiritual discourses of many different faiths, one can find out certain tidbits that may suit him or herself from any faith. It is important to note that even though we can imagine ten thousand varieties of chocolate being manufactured and enjoyed by the human population around the globe, or a thousand variations in the way a dish of chicken curry can be prepared by different cultures, or a thousand ways a sweet dish can be prepared, only a few that may be of our liking. It is okay to relish only the ones we like. Out of hundreds of TV channels or thousands of books, the ones which resonate with our core being are the ones which should be stuck to in times of crisis. Too much variation not only confuses, but also creates unnecessary problems for a diseased mind. Till the mind attains full recovery, one should be guided by the dictum that he should prefer that which appeals to him or her. Actually, God reveals Himself in many ways. It is seen that hardcore believers of one faith, following some serious mental health crisis, actually benefit from some other faith's teachings. Since the human brain has tremendous potential to build new neural networks through available neurons in the brain, it is important that we keep our minds open to ideas from every source possible.

Immerse in Awe

This is a new technique to relax the brain muscles and the nervous system. A stressed-out brain gets plenty of healing energy from this method of allowing our entire self to get awestruck by the various creations of nature and the magical discoveries and inventions of humanity through civilizational history. Just look at the Sun, the mountains, the sky, the ocean, the rivers, the forests, the deserts, the wild animals, the birds, the insects, the worms, the breeze or anything else that appeals to the senses. We connect to a dream-like conscious state by just feeling the *sensation of awe and wonder*. We feel very relaxed. Nature is so vast and amazing that it is beyond the human mind's power to capture all creations in a logical brain. Sometimes, the surrender of all the senses to the wonderful and amazing power of nature, by just enjoying with awe and wonder each of the different creations and feeling that we are in in harmony with it, can speed the recovery process. Similarly, some of our own brothers and sisters have created amazing inventions and discovered many outstanding things in the last few centuries of modern science and technology and when we see them, feel them, we can experience blissful joy by simply thinking that one of our own species has created them. If the natural inclination of a human being to feel elated at someone else's achievement, which is generally hidden and suppressed by our egoistic jealousy, is allowed to blossom through a liberated brain in awe and admiration, the healing process's results are magnified.

In modern TV channels like National Geographic, Discovery, Animal Planet, History of the Planet etc., the sheer joy one gets by watching various instinctive activities of wildlife or observing the human ingenuity in creating wonderful and gigantic structures around the world both in the ancient past and present day, one can achieve both a quick as well as long term soothing effect on the senses and hence the mind. Some people enjoy cartoon shows on TV at any age. Kids generally like it everywhere in the world. The reason is that their innocent brains feel bliss when they see such cartoon shows. When these kids grow a little older, they start relishing family dramas more. This kind of intricate relationship between the human mind and what it likes or dislikes can be observed by watching kids grow from infancy into their teenage years. At the time of a mental health crisis, it is wise to go back to what we enjoyed in the past, even during our childhood, because these activities can give heartful good feelings.

The sports channels in TV can also be a source of immense help under this technique. World class sports persons, athletics, gymnasts, swimmers, players of different games perform at such a high level that the very sight can create a sense of awe and wonder in us. That happy feeling of awe and wonder at the feats of individual sportspersons can also be instrumental in giving soothing inspiration to the distressed brain.

Get involved and make others involved

It was during my PhD that a good Iranian friend of mine, on listening one day to my complaints that the supervisor did not show any specific interest in my PhD work, said; 'It is your PhD and you have to make your supervisor get involved and not the other way round.' This statement was very profound but my skills were too limited at the time to make my supervisor get involved more intensely in my PhD work. I can recollect, even in spite of getting my PhD in time, that I had only one or two meetings every six months with my supervisor with regards to my work. There could have been a dozen reasons for this shortcoming of mine, but ultimately the fact remains that I could not make my supervisor get fully involved in my PhD work, at least not to my satisfaction.

After nearly six years since the first incident. I was once again complaining, telling my friends at my parent organisation's work place; 'I can't see why I do not get the attention of our boss. He seems to have developed some sort of complex with me and whenever I say something, particularly in a technical gathering, he just brushes aside my suggestions or comments on any technical matter. Apart from doing my day-to-day technical job, I thought I was supposed to give my opinion in this manner, but the boss does not seem to want to listen to my good advice or suggestions." More than one of my good friends and well-wishers said at once; 'Look, it is your fault. You have to get involved more. As they say, what is the fun in owning jewellery and not showing it to the people it's meant to be shown to anyway.' Another said; 'You run the risk of losing your credibility and may lose all the reputation you have built up and accumulated with your hard work till now.'

You can now see how these two different perspectives were presented to me by my friends and well-wishers. In one occasion, some were telling me to involve others more (in my PhD work) and some were suggesting that I should myself get more involved. However, in both cases, my underlying problem was to derive more satisfaction and happiness in my workplace. If we analyse it more deeply, the solution lies in the understanding that we as individuals need to constantly look for both our own involvement and involvement of others to get results from our projects. Here our project, in simple terms, is to derive ultimate happiness in life. When Stephen Covey focuses on Quadrant II activities, in his highly acclaimed book, *'Seven habits of highly effective people'*, he basically means the full realization of the inner ability in us to plan, prepare, and prevent any fallout arising from the lack of the same. In the *'Time Management Matrix'*, Stephen Covey has defined Quadrant II activities as those activities which are important but may not be urgent.

I could not get my supervisor more involved because of my own internal fear and dread of more work, more confusion and perhaps my incapacity to meet the demands of my supervisor because, sometimes, it seemed to me that I knew better than even my supervisor! I believe that any individual on earth will develop such a feeling (which may be very real) when he delves very deep into a particular field of knowledge. There are hundreds of examples where we know that students have surpassed their teachers in some particular field. There is no harm in communicating with people concerned about the ability to do any job or lack of it in any matter. Whenever a company launches a new product, the campaign to reach the prospective buyers through various advertising media is essential. Similarly, the boss needs to be aware about the ability to do something or lack of it. I realized that just dreaming that someone would convince my boss on my behalf or tell him about my great achievements in the past - and hence my ability to achieve in future - would not be enough in this fast world.

I would like to summarise that getting involved or making others more involved needs the individual concerned to play a role and the interdependent entities around him to play a role as well, in every situation. So it is this interdependence and the internal ability to supply energy to this interwoven machine that is crucial for good results. The lessons I learnt through the above experience helped me later on in all my job assignments, when instead of complaining and doing nothing till the last moment, I started becoming more proactive in getting myself and other members of the team involved. This exercise is applicable in all situations; be it family life, school, college, workplace, sports team, management board, social group or any organization. One needs to decide his role in any group activity and chalk out a detailed plan for carrying out the responsibility assigned to him or her.

Pour love & affection and make the small family the best teacher and boss

I can explain my own understanding of how this works with the example of my own small family. I have carefully nurtured what I believe are the fundamental principles of life and tried my best to restrict myself and all my activities to these parameters. The resultant effect has been so wonderful that my family itself has been providing me with all the necessary ingredients for my own life's sustenance for nearly two and half decades now.

There was a time when I used to feel frustrated because I was not getting the kind of work environment that I was looking for in my organization. These feelings were somehow picked up by my two small children. I remember how, when I used to drop my son (hardly six years old at the time) at the school gate in Chennai, he used to remark; 'Dad, do good work at office.' That sight is vividly etched into my memory. It was such a proud feeing! I knew that his concerns were coming from his instinctive feelings to see his father happy. He used to mentally calculate that by doing good work at office, his father could remain happy himself and perhaps make his bosses happy as well! This is how even small children can be a source of enormous inspiration and the spiritual bosses for us all by making us more focused. To achieve this, one needs to pour love and affection into the family unit he builds.

On another occasion, when I was in Chennai, I was contemplating quitting my parent organization for lack of satisfaction and due recognition at the workplace. I was looking casually at an advertisement in a national newspaper, for a new opening, when my daughter, aged 12 years, who was studying in class VII that time saw me scanning the advertisement and politely asked; 'Papa, is your company a very bad company?' I was shocked, but I got a wakeup call nonetheless. I knew that my entire family was quite happy with the kind of family and social life I was leading with the remuneration, allowances and other perquisites that my current job offered, but somewhere I was failing to keep myself happy and motivated at my workplace due to the usual workplace politics and associated problems.

This innocent question from my daughter was basically indicating two intricate aspects of life. One: when everything was fine outwardly, why then was her father looking to change to a new organization? And was this satisfying her own internal assessment that perhaps her father was not doing the right thing by abandoning the organization which she herself was feeling quite attached to by now? She knew internally that her father's organization was able to fulfill all their family needs including basic and common luxury needs like housing, food, clothes, education, health, recreation, conveyance, holidays etc. My daughter who was beginning to understand the world knew all this and hence developed her own attachment to my parent organization. And so when her father thought of quitting the organization that cared so much for her entire family, she was naturally confused and shocked.

The other aspect was more subtle.

In *'Tuesdays with Morrie'*, an internationally acclaimed bestseller, the seventy-eight year old sociology professor, Morrie Schwartz of Brandeis University, who was dying from *amyotrophic lateral sclerosis* (ALS), communicates with his former student, biographer and author Mitch Albom one day. He says; 'Why is there this madness to be the number one? Why can't we settle with number two or even number three?' Acceptance, communication, love, values, openness, and happiness are the golden attributes espoused by Morrie for forging a culture of one's own to transcend the tyranny of popular culture of unlimited pursuit of materialistic pleasure.

To establish and reaffirm my daughter's faith in these finer aspects of life, I assuaged her feelings of hurt by saying; 'Sweety, I have got almost everything from my current organization, which is not bad at all. For that matter, no organization can be bad. Only the people working for the organization can sometimes behave in a bad and ignorant manner, and that can make things difficult. If we properly understand why human beings behave the way they do, we will perhaps never fall into problems.' I added; 'I have dreamt of working in two different organizations, and if possible in two different countries.' She knew that I had to work for four years in Australia for my PhD. She nodded, perhaps indicating her partial satisfaction with my reply even if, deep inside, she still remained skeptical. Then I tried to somehow satisfy her by citing the examples of a few of her school mates, who'd had to take Transfer Certificates on account of their fathers moving out to places like Dubai for new jobs. Such incidents go on to suggest how the small family unit can work like a watchdog against the folly of own pursuits in the direction of abject materialism and can create a balanced atmosphere.

On another occasion, again in Chennai, she asked me how my office days were going. I gave her a disappointing reply, said that it was not good. She asked me why it was so. I said it was perhaps because I was not able to do good work and hence my bosses were not happy. Hearing this, she became violent - if not in her behavior, then in her words and gestures. She said; 'Papa, if you do not do good work at office, forget about me working hard at school, which you always insist I do." That gave me the reply to my internal problems which made me silently smile. I had to gear up and put up a better show at office. Next day, when she asked the same question before her mom, I said that it was actually a good day. My daughter immediately said that at last her dictum had worked! My wife who was standing nearby could not understand and passingly remarked that it was the threat of my boss at office that made me do good work. But I promptly replied that it was more the threat of my daughter than the threat of my boss! That made my daughter remark wryly to her mother that she was a bigger boss than Thomas (name changed) who was my boss at that time. This story tells us how, for our lives, our little families can be the best teachers and guides and a source of real inspiration.

One simple statement can create imbalance in an otherwise peacefully running system. The family is the most fundamental unit of society and if it is in perfect order, the world will be in perfect order. If we create perturbations in the fundamental unit's potential field, we will see its repercussions transgressing into other territories quickly. To enhance the strength, the circle of influence, the power of the influence of this fundamental unit, one needs to maintain and strengthen the character of such a system. This is possible by clearly chalking out plans through mutual discussions and deliberations, limiting and delimiting each other's territories, defining each other's working needs, working resources, working aim and working mission, and then slowly making small and dynamic changes and adjustments to the set goals, objectives, mission etc. and proceed accordingly. If there is any lack of clarity in any of these, there is a likelihood of a roadblock, road jam or speed breaker. Understanding each other's viewpoints, understanding each other's strengths and weaknesses would help define clear-cut goals, objectives, activities to be performed, time schedules etc. If someone is failing to understand something, the reasons could be poor communication, poor transmission or even lack of maturity. A caring and compromising stand is necessary to overcome such a problem and keep the gap from widening.

An example will illustrate this further. In my anxiety to see my growing teenage son do well in his studies, I used to get very worried when he spent hours together playing computer games. The teenage years are such a vulnerable time that parents anywhere in the world will understand this. I knew that the potential of my son was far more than what his result cards in school reflected. I could vouch for this after I got excellent feedback about my son from his teachers at school. Now, I was facing a problem which I did not have any clue about. I tried everything including disconnecting the broadband connection at home so that he would be automatically barred from a very violent computer game he clearly seemed addicted to. I tried to reason with him saying; 'My loving Son, it is not good for you to be addicted to such violent computer games because neither are they good for your health nor do they help with your studies. Rather, your time is wasted because of such addiction and your studies are getting hampered.' But he would always come up with a counter-argument. He would say; 'Dad, you too are addicted to things like TV, tea etc.' Thus, the forcefulness of my statements used to get diluted by such counter-arguments.

I will describe an anecdote here. In a village, a mother was very worried for her son who used to eat too much *Gur (jaggery)*, a natural product of sugarcane. *Gur* is of a more unrefined form than sugar. It is a brown raw mass of sucrose which gets it color from other elements found in the concentration; elements such as wood ash and bagasse. The mother knew of a Sadhu (monk) who lived in one corner in the village and who was very reputed for his divine powers. He had a mass following because the villagers always benefited from his advice. The mother decided to go and ask for his advice regarding the problem with her son. When she took her to the Sadhu and told him what was bothering her, giving him all the details about her son's addiction to *Gur*, and requested him to do something to alleviate her fear and anxiety, the monk asked her to go home and come back to see him again after a month. A month passed and the mother took her son to the Sadhu again. This time the Sadhu affectionately called the boy to him and gave him a few tips and blessings. He then said to the mother; 'Now you will see your son slowly leaving his bad habit.' The mother was happy but at the same time baffled. She went near the Sadhu and asked; 'Guruji, I don't understand. What you told my son now you could have told him one month ago, when I first visited you.' To this the Sadhu smilingly replied; 'Mother, what can I do? I had no moral authority to ask your son to let go of his addiction to *Gur* because I had to first free myself from the same addiction!'

To approach someone with a humane face, with a loving and caring attitude, is the best solution. After all, we deal with human beings in their infinite possibilities, in their infinite variants, and hence there exists the possibility that there will be both stimulants and receptors ingrained within every soul to understand each other. Whether it is a small family unit where we pour our love and affection and bond through emotional energy, or any such unit in our day-to-day lives, it is important to be aware of the principles on which they work. If one is running a small business unit where he or she is the head of the unit, the principles on which the emotional energy of love and affection work will remain the same. In small social groups also, the rules apply in a similar manner. It is sensitivity which is necessary to pick up such signals from each individual in the close-knit group we are involved with, be it a family unit or a business unit.

There will be struggles, frustrations and disappointments, but these are nothing when compared to the beautiful moments of joy one gains through the closeness of the members of the family. The bigger the family, the bigger the charm and happiness enjoyed by all. This family could consist of people in a workplace where they share emotions, take care of each other, show empathy, and are compassionate to each other. They share joy and happiness as much as they share pain and suffering amongst themselves. This sort of caring and sharing gives the courage, strength, love and affection which are so valuable for a contented life.

Believe in infinite happiness

When I read the *'abundance vs. scarcity mentality'* idea of Stephen Covey, I see a very good resemblance between it and my own concept of infinite happiness. I have been grappling with the idea of how to bring happiness to the human mind and soul. And I have almost realized that happiness is an ingredient of the human soul and not linked in any way to outer dimensions like physical, mental or emotional. The moment we align with our soul, we feel bliss and happiness. Once an American earth scientist said at a public meeting addressed by Swami Sri Ravi Shankar where a discussion on modern day stress and its remedies was going on; 'Guruji, I find listening to music or even singing to be very relaxing.' Swami Sri Ravi Shankar replied that he would not stop there, that he would go beyond and prefer *silence* as the medium for relaxation. In fact, all forms of meditation lead to silence ultimately. Because, as the Swami explained that day, music needs some kind of action or expense of energy through the sense organs which may lead to some amount of stress. Hence silence is the best stress reliever. Now, we know that this kind of approach makes us believe that the true image of the soul is actually in motionless, action less silence. When we do some activity directed at achieving anything to meet our physical, mental or emotional needs, these activities can give us true happiness - if they all emanate from the root or seed of the soul.

Someone's happiness could be related to someone else's sadness in today's commercial world of trade, profit, give and take, vested interests, friend-and-enemy concept etc. We can visualize an array of hope in our mathematical concept of infinity. While infinity is a concept which is very well established in mathematical terms, and is taught right from school level, I can visualize that the world of the future (if not in the short term future, then definitely in the long term) can be guided towards complete happiness and that sadness can be removed from earth. We have made the world complicated with our scientific and technological inventions, but at the same time the idea of infinite happiness can be easily applied to bring the human soul back from the brink of frustration, depression, to a state of happiness through a well-crafted and charted path. Spiritual leaders do that on a daily basis and management gurus try to grapple with bits and pieces here and there. The *Bhagawat Gita* is one complete book that is sufficient to guide any human soul to a true state of happiness, if he understands the true essence of the *Gita*. I strongly believe that fundamental religious books or scriptures of all world religions, the most sacred ones, can easily help human souls find true happiness. If we can all believe that one can easily remain happy even in scarce conditions, then it is not going to be difficult for us to visualize a state wherein we can always think that this world is so big and vast that happiness can easily be achieved by connecting to the spiritual inner core of the being. The inherent infiniteness of the '*happiness budget of the world*' can be a source for providing each individual on Earth the happiness he is searching for, provided one is following the *true north principles* that his conscience guides him through. Many great thinkers like Stephen Covey have already discovered the same path, and have dwelt on true north principles in a detailed way and there is no reason why anyone who wants to follow the same principles would not achieve happiness in his life.

I have tried to experiment with an idea. The idea is: *When money is lost nothing is lost, when health is lost something is lost, but when character is lost then everything is lost.* Here, character is nothing but belief in the *collective goodness.* Once we lose that belief, we first feel victimized, and then we try to make victims of others and then ultimately become a threat to the common good. We literally become terrorists. All of us reach this state either in a full blown-out form, or in a very subtle form when we lose the belief in common good. When we encounter some temporary losses in our lives, in comparison to our fellow human beings, the only way to maintain the balance is to keep believing in that the collective goodness will always be alive. Hence, the common good is actually born out of the infinite happiness concept and everything else flows from it. The *happiness budget* of the world is infinite. As individuals, we need to trade with this infinite happiness at a very personal scale by one-to-one correspondence with God.

Behind each suicidal attempt, there are two major components. One of these is physiological underpinning and the other is extreme ambition mixed with greed. The physical and mental body we inherit is primarily decided by the DNA or genes of our parents, grandparents and great grandparents. At a very fundamental spiritual level of the soul, it is even claimed that a person who committed suicide in his or her previous birth might do so again in the next birth, if his or her learning from the action in the previous birth remains incomplete. Dr. Brian Weiss has found some evidence for this in his *past life regression therapy* cases. But this entire book of mine is just an attempt to explore these concepts further. There have been cases of mass suicides due to illusory thought influences in various parts of even the developed world. Large scale farmer suicides in many parts of India cause me consternation. Recently, a German citizen committed suicide by crashing his airplane into the Alps. The 9/11 terror attacks in the USA were pure suicides as are many other such terrorist attacks around the globe, with explosives laden around the bodies of misguided and disgruntled youths. These emanate from extreme religious views but then they also have roots in the ambitions of one or more human beings to establish superiority of their own religion or beliefs over others.

In a slightly different socio-economic situation, ambition mixed with greed causes many people to become too burdened by debt and, when they fail to handle the stress caused by such debt, they tend to kill themselves. It is important that one checks his or her activities in such a way that even if a major crisis arises due to one's own follies, at some point of time, he or she can still apply the earlier described HRMG model - through which one can definitely reorient his or her life and come out of the crisis to lead a stable life. The two most fundamental fears, *fear of death* and *fear of loss of prestige*, can be scientifically and logically found to be the roots of problems like anxiety, stress, depression and ultimately desperate feelings. It will take time to correct the imbalance generated by misguided thoughts, but it is possible by just imagining that there always was, there always is and there always will be an *infinite happiness budget* available to us in the world created by God for all his seven billion children today and all the new children who will join us in the future. We just need to plug into this infinite source of everything positive - hope, trust, belief, faith, help, love, compassion, fellow feeling, empathy, gratitude, devotion, happiness etc. - by the power of our thoughts and start allowing those much needed resources flow into our lives for benefit and sustenance. If we connect to the collective consciousness arising out of the Cosmic Intelligence slowly but steadily, a time will come when, out of the deepest morass, one can start relishing faith in humanity and enjoy life again. If a person as ordinary and average as me could do this, then anyone else can do it, provided he makes some conscious efforts towards the same.

Prioritise through Child-Adult-Parent Continuum

Quadrant II prioritizing means *not scheduling your priorities but prioritizing your schedules* as Stephen Covey has so succinctly put it. It is a profound statement, and to achieve this state takes immense experience. Thomas Harris in his book *'I am OK, You are OK'* has clearly outlined the three components of the human brain: *the Child, the Adult and the Parent*. These components actually try to work in tandem in our day to day interactions with others depending on the core of the being, which is again the balance between the conscious and subconscious brain. The three forms of child, adult and parent are actually manifestations of the human being in the ways and means it interacts with the environment. Every human being is endowed with three basic parts - *creativity, maintenance through survival instinct and the power to destroy itself.* Right from birth, these three parts get to blossom in different ways and means depending on how the newly born is allowed to grow both in the immediate family environment and in the surroundings. Some analysts believe that the Child represents creativity, the Adult represents maintenance through survival instinct and the Parent represents the power to destroy. Interpretations of this by the human mind can know no bounds, if the mind is allowed the freedom. I have sometimes believed that the concept of a Trinity, *Brahma-Vishnu-Maheswar, Generation-Operation-Destruction* or *Creation-Maintenance-Destruction,* all have a similar connotation. When modern students of science (Thomas Harris and Eric Berne) bring out the psychological underpinnings of the human mind through concepts like P-A-C (Parent-Adult-Child), I always feel that the Cosmic Intelligence can find expressions in this fashion in different places and during different eras of the world.

Lord Krishna has categorically said in the *Bhagawat Gita* that even if the physical body of a human being is destroyed, the soul does not get destroyed (Shloka 2.13). He also says that, just in the way the physical body moves along the path from childhood to adulthood to old age, the soul also progresses in a similar fashion. This means that the soul as a *composite of wisdom* also moves along a path, from a raw level to an adult level and then to a highly matured level of growth. And when Dr. Brian L. Weiss said that he has found, through his technique of *past life regression therapy,* that human souls on earth simply represent different levels of knowledge and wisdom attained through repeated births and deaths (and that all of these souls have reached nursery level, primary level, high school, UG or PG level) we can see the correlation between the two schools of thought. Each human soul has the power to learn and move from a lower class to a higher class, just the way we progress in our modern education system.

By the time one becomes a teenager, he has seen all the different aspects of life and experienced them to some degree in different environments like the family environment, school, the neighborhood and the larger society in general. These inputs get processed and reprocessed in our brains to consolidate what we think our conscious and subconscious brains should look like. For example, during my teenage years, I always felt the need to excel in every field I participated in and longed to be the darling of all. I dreamt of being a leader, leading the way for everyone in the group through personal example and sacrifice. Also, I always felt an inner urge to immensely appreciate someone else's contribution to the society or I was always thinking and dreaming of how I could contribute in a similar measure to society as well. Although my achievements might not be as big as I dreamt but I have never stopped dreaming big.

I've always had two major goals in life since I understood implications of having such goals. One, to continue living my life to its natural end with all its perturbations, and two, to follow to the best of my ability, and in harmony with the environment, the fundamental principles and tenets of the Hindu philosophy of *Brahmacharya, Grihastha, Vanaprastha and Sanyasa* - the four well known and well researched stages of the Hindu way of life. Human life is so very precious. We sometimes make mistakes and spiral downwards into the dangerous zone. It is our individual duty and responsibility then to maintain such a balance that God's gift of life is guided normally to its logical end. Diseases, pain and suffering and accidents are a part of the natural process, but that should not jolt our core being to such an extent that we lose hope and faith in life itself. The very fact that we are breathing should be construed as a gift of God; it is so precious and divine to be able to breathe!

Of the four stages of human life, *Brahmacharya* or *Celibate Student* is a period of formal education. It lasts until the age of twenty-five and during this time the young male leaves home to go stay with a guru and acquire both spiritual and practical knowledge. During this period, he is called a *Brahmachari,* and is trained for his future profession, as well as for his coming family, social and religious life.

We all know that, physically, it may not be possible for everyone to go back to ancient times, but with modern facilities like residential schools and colleges, these concepts can be universalized for a richer society.

Grihastha or *Married Family Man* is a period which begins when a man gets married and undertakes the responsibility of earning a living and supporting his family. At this stage, Hinduism supports the pursuit of wealth (artha) as a necessity, and indulgence in sexual pleasure (kama), under certain defined social and cosmic norms. This *ashrama* lasts until around the age of fifty. But in modern society, where the average lifespan has increased dramatically, the retirement age is pushed further for each subsequent generation and hence this age can now be much higher.

The *Vanaprastha or Hermit in Retreat* stage for a man begins when his duty as a householder comes to an end. He has become a grandfather; his children are grown up and have established lives of their own. At this age, he should renounce all physical, material and sexual pleasures, retire from his social and professional life, leave his home, and go live in a forest hut, spending his time at prayer. Although, in the modern age, it is not feasible literally, metaphorically each of these aspects can very well be enacted.

Sannyasa or Wandering Recluse is a stage of renunciation and one where a person is supposed to be totally devoted to God. He is a *sannyasi;* he has no home, no other attachment. He has renounced all his desires, fears and hopes, duties and responsibilities. He is virtually merged with God. All his worldly ties are broken, and his sole concern is attaining *moksha*, or release from the circle of birth and death. This stage is attained by few in today's society but idealistically, aiming to reach such a stage is not impossible.

Whatever I do must be anchored to these two most fundamental goals of my life. And it is these two goals which I see running through all other goals as a common thread. Somewhere in my growing years, these two main goals, as outlined by social customs and traditions, have clung to me as eternal pursuits. To be more explicit, I will go into further details about how these goals have become my anchors in life. Once, in a television adaptation of the *'Ramayana'*, the great Indian epic set in the *Trettaya Yug*, Sage Vasishta was seen teaching King Ram that when one is born into this world, he comes with several debts. Primary among these is to give birth to at least one progeny for the sake of humanity and its continuity, and thus repaying the debt to parents as well. But in the *Bhagawat Gita* of the later *Dwapar Yug*, Lord Krishna has outlined different paths to salvation; two of the major ones are *Gnyana Yoga* and *Karma Yoga*. He has also outlined that *Gnyana Yoga* is only applicable for the *Sannyasins*. Hence, it is quite clear that if we can bring about a synthesis of these two philosophies, anyone who is born into this world can adopt the four stages of the Hindu way of life and meet the requirements outlined during both the *Trettaya Yug* and *Dwapar Yug*.

Similarly, when the Sankaracharya of Kanchi Kamakothi Peetham was addressing a large public gathering at Dehradun, during an event inside our organizational complex, he argued that the four stages of Hindu life are the best solutions for all problems in the modern world. If all human beings understand the deeper meaning of the four stages and reorient their lifestyles in such a manner that each individual enjoys the entire gamut of all worldly pleasures conceivable on earth and at the same time develops himself stage by stage to finally reach the rich state of a liberated soul, it will help relieve stress from human beings at an individual level as well as at a society level since rabid materialistic pursuit is the bane of the world today. Although many people will find it difficult to go through the rigidly interpreted later two stages of life, *Vanaprastha* and *Sanyasa*, conceived few millennia back, to my mind, it is not very difficult to stay back at home but live a life of renunciation of all worldly pleasures, devoted to divine thoughts and actions of selfless service to mankind, meditative contemplation and prayer to the Almighty.

In the modern age of TV and internet, what is required is just mass awareness and education. The signs are already there when we can see the richest Americans of the twentieth century devoting most of their post-professional lives to charity work. The Rockfeller,

Kellogg and Ford Foundations of the past and the Bill and Melinda Gates Foundation of recent years are the pioneers in large scale implementation of this trend worldwide. In India also, the trend has set in at a massive scale. Most of the large business houses like Tatas, Birlas, Ambanis, Goenkas, Jindals, Mittals, Mahindras including those of the new age IT sector firms like Infosys have all started supporting charity through various Trusts and Foundations. Their work is mostly in the field of education and health. The four stage Hindu way of life was conceived in the fifth century BC. It is good to see that two thousand and five hundred years later, modern science and technology has sort of come a full circle when it helps in bringing the virtues of the ancient concepts to the fore.

Whenever one is going through a severe mental crisis, one needs to prioritise his goals in such a way that the onward journey of the soul, which appears to be derailed temporarily, is brought back on track whilst keeping the ultimate goals of life intact and in sight.

List out long, medium and short term goals and mark the calendar

Many books have been written suggesting ways to improve our quality of life and one of the major themes includes how to plan out detailed break up of our goals of life. Concepts like *mission statement* (Stephen Covey), dividing our activities into *four quadrants* (Stephen Covey); *goal book*(Jack Canfield), *to do lists*, are quite useful when mind is functioning normally and it needs just a bit of discipline to implement such concepts and reorient our lives for higher achievement and success. But when the chemical imbalances in the brain cause serious depression, anxiety and psychosis, such concepts need to be applied with a bit of caution. In times of crisis, human beings instinctively aim for survival first with all their physical and mental resources and might. Thus overall, the *goal book* should be turned upside down unlike the diktat of *'thinking from the end'*. It is more important during such crisis to concentrate first on the short term goals, and then slowly move towards medium term and long term goals.

During my worst mental crisis of life while doing my PhD study in Australia in 2000-2001, I literally began for a couple of days with the lowest denominator, i.e., with the *ability to breathe*. The confidence level for a mentally ill patient is the worst affected. Leaving everything in the back burner, I then moved to the short term goals, i.e. to do my daily chores properly, do all domestic chores including helping the family of wife and two children do their daily jobs in a timely manner like bathing, cooking, eating, sleeping, going to schools, going to market, cleaning, taking family to park etc. Having achieved such short term goals within two to three weeks with relatively greater confidence, I moved to medium term goals which included completing remaining research work for my PhD and finally doing the write-up of the thesis. The last stage of any PhD work is the most daunting which anyone who has gone on this path knows very well. I mustered enough mental strength to write down in details the '*to do list*' in a notebook day wise, week wise and month wise. I had just about twelve months to go for completing my PhD work before leaving for India.

The long term goals during this period were consciously relegated by me to the back. Generally, one loses the mental power to conceive long term goals effectively and hence the long term goals, encompassing a period of about a decade or half which were in the subconscious mind were left as they were. Thus the mental health crisis that struck me in Adelaide, Australia did not dislodge my long term goals of life but I could revive them once I became absolutely normal again. Interestingly, one of the major long term goals which were conceived while I was inside the Queen Elizabeth Hospital, Adelaide, immediately following my hospitalization, that is to write a comprehensive book on my unusual experiences of life, was never taken up in right earnest during my last twelve months of Australian stay. Of course, my initial efforts towards writing the book, were discouraged and diverted quite appropriately and effectively by my consultant psychiatrist Dr. Jo Lammersma.

Listing out the long, medium and short term goals of life, preparing the *to do lists*, marking the calendar for all such jobs and goals have thus to be carefully taken up considering the mental strength one achieves stepwise at the time. The beauty is that once such a calendar is prepared and if such a calendar is referred to regularly for balancing between the target and achievement even during the worst mental crisis, the power within the subconscious brain helps navigate the conscious brain mysteriously for obtaining ultimate success. Happiness which eludes mentally ill patients temporarily can thus be brought back to life. I recall how I could complete some hard research analysis work still pending during my last year of stay, collate all the results systematically, put them together chapter and sub-chapter-wise and completed writing of the thesis even before the deadline I had set for myself. This resulted in timely submission of the PhD thesis within the stipulated time defined by the University and my parent organization and to top it all, could squeeze a three day family holiday-break at Bangkok on my return journey to India!

Choose the path to happiness

'Happiness is like a butterfly; you try to catch it and it eludes you. You remain still and do not notice when it sits over you.' Happiness is a state of bliss. Can we train ourselves to attain it? To a great extent, yes we can. There have been great saints, philosophers and thinkers, leaders in different fields, who have realized their life's goals through consistent effort and who have also noted their feelings during their journeys. We can learn from their stories by listening to their achievements and journeys, by reading about their lives or going through their works and achievements.

The greatest happiness that one can get is when he is respected not for his material possessions, but for the power of his words and thoughts that strike a chord with others and reverberate amongst his fellow human beings. It is when a person is appreciated for his spirituality (which actually encompasses the highest form of elevation) and not his physical possessions. You can conduct a self-test on this concept. Many people might have appreciated your own personal achievements, generosity, kindness, any help that you may have extended in terms of material aid or through the sharing of emotions, a piece of advice that might have worked etc. You will notice that lasting memories will be associated with the non-materialistic help rather than the materialistic help you extended and which someone might have appreciated you for in return. The reason for this is the connection between souls rather than bodily connection. Soul consciousness transcends many lower order planes and the inspirational energy that one gets when the soul's power emanates from someone gracious and wise is much more lasting.

These thoughts and words, when they emanate from the very core of our being, radiate a kind of energy and shine that automatically attracts those around. There will always be people who will remain skeptical and not easily fall to the influences of such energy radiation, but over a period of time, when everyone else falls in line with the words and thoughts of such great persons, the last skeptics would also join the bandwagon. However, for the world to move through reasoning and scientific beliefs, it is mandatory that alternative thought processes are generated simultaneously - ones that do not nullify the effect of the previous domain, but try to develop along with it a different path for maintenance of the balance. This is where the contribution of realized souls to help humanity becomes powerful. But in our attempt to woo a following, we sometimes adopt ways and means that are not quite tenable.

It was soon after the Gujarat earthquake of January 2001 that I was attending a gathering of devotees of Divine Life Society in Adelaide where the famous spiritual leader Swami Sri Ramswurapanand was giving a lecture to an audience of around fifty people in a private place. News of the quake had spread far and wide and I recall that when the spiritual leader spoke of the earthquake, trying to answer his own question put to audience, "Was God angry to kill so many people at one go?', he brought in a weird concept saying that it was something similar to the human action of trying to rub the back after a mosquito bite wherein the interaction between the hand and the back would kill many microorganisms! Although the news of all the pain and suffering in Gujarat had hit one and all, including this spiritual leader, in an attempt to keep common people from losing faith in God at such a time, he was trying to draw a parallel between us humans killing so many microorganisms when trying to massage by hand the area of mosquito bite and God's hand just waving and rubbing in this incident in which thousands had died.

I could not take this kind of weird explanation and opposed it then and there saying that we should not bring God into this discussion at all. I knew, being a student of earth science, that earthquakes like these were part of the Earth's natural processes, that this was simply due to different crustal plates moving on the mantle, stress being built up until such a time that fractures or joints or zones of weakness inside the Earth's crust crumble, creating massive fault planes which led to earthquakes and the associated devastation. This had been happening since the time of the birth of the planet, when human beings were not even in existence. To a student of geoscience, Wilson cycle represents ocean opening and closing, all caused by such processes of crustal extension, rifting, crustal break-up, mid-oceanic ridge formation, ocean widening with drifting of crustal plates, collision of plates and subduction of oceanic plate below continental plate etc. before another cycle begins. To this, the spiritual leader changed the tone of his explanation and said that geological events were indeed behind such happenings. However, he emphatically added that each one of us present there should commit to helping in whatever they could to those affected by the earthquake. I believe that *this* is where God should be brought in. *Natural disasters are the greatest opportunities for the human species to change their course of life.* We shall continue to have natural disasters around the globe and it is better for humanity to divert all their innovation and energy away from war preparations to mitigate the sufferings of humanity caused by such natural disasters anywhere in the globe, particularly when we are all so very well interconnected and communication between different parts of the globe has now become almost instantaneous! This is actually what God wants us to do; not fight amongst ourselves and prepare ourselves incessantly for future conflicts.

Human beings are the highest order of animals, having been endowed with the most vital component of their being: *Conscience.*

Perhaps *self-awareness* exists in other forms of the animal kingdom also, but *Conscience* is the greatest attribute so far. This attribute helps human beings sense the power of something higher and bigger than themselves. It allows them to visualize the difference between good and bad from a moralistic standpoint and also help them to go deep into the soul of another being. Other animals perhaps do not have the ability to delve into what others could be feeling through conscious imaginary power. Whatever these lower animals do is through their inbuilt instinctive mechanism. However, human beings are endowed with this unique ability to decipher the meaning of the stimuli and responses, both in themselves and in their fellow human beings.

Material possessions can make life comfortable physically, but for mental or spiritual peace and comfort, one needs much more than physical or material possessions. The spiritual dimension is characterized by elements like the ability to help others, to share in the pain and suffering of others, to share in the happiness of others and to sacrifice one's own happiness and joy for the benefit and happiness of others. Lord Jesus who sacrificed His life for others eulogizes the kind of joy one gets when he sacrifices his time and energy for the benefit of others, for the upliftment of others, for the poor and the downtrodden. The reason for such a feeling lies perhaps in the fact that self-sacrifice is the surest way for salvation of human beings. Honesty, integrity, truthfulness, kindness, sacrifice etc. are the qualities, which resonate with the Divine and hence bring us instant bliss. There will be attempts by people to mimic such acts for influencing public opinion, but so long as it is not a true and honest feeling from within, one will not attain perfect happiness.

Sometimes, in the daily struggles of life, small obstacles disturb us so much that we keep blaming one another. We blame the neighbour, the driver, the washer man, the housemaid, the grocery person, the electric repairman, the car workshop man, the tuition teacher of the child, the school authorities, the games coach, the manager of our business, the office peon, the boss, and - if we fail to satisfy ourselves with this - we start blaming our friends, our own family, the parents, the siblings, the children, the relatives and almost everyone else that can come to mind. And if even that does not help, we blame politicians, the government and sometimes even nature - the rains, the heat, the cold, the snow and whatnot. Blaming is an inherent tendency of an inadequate or incomplete mind. Most of us indulge in such blaming activity, but what matters is how aware we are to overcome such inherent lacunae and come to terms with reality and learn to adapt to circumstances.

In the shadow of such a blame game, we instantly get carried away by a small rebuke from another person, by some criticism or comments from another person. On many occasions, we will notice that the very criticism or rebuke might have worked wonders for us. For example, kids nowadays get irritated easily when asked to do certain things like study or behave in a disciplined manner etc. If by some chance, the subconscious minds of these kids pick up the signal and they do what their parents are asking them to when they're growing up, then much later they will smile when they see how the rebuke or chiding of their parents proved to be beneficial in the long run. The touching account given by Rajesh Prabhakar Patil in his book '*Maa, Mun Collector Heli*' about how his mother used to be very strict with him in his childhood, to an extent of getting sticks for his naughty and dirty tricks, and how those strong disciplinary measures helped in a big way to shape his later life to achieve one of the greatest successes of life, qualifying in one of the dream examinations namely, IAS (Indian Administrative Service).

Similarly, we may miss the good hidden in the rebukes of our elders, or the criticism we get from our peers, bosses, fans or from the media etc. But they may inspire us to improve further in our work and our approach to life. I have observed that a moment of wrath caused by a personal rebuke from someone sometimes has worked wonders for me by making me more energetic, alert, non-complacent and proactive, and has pulled me out of laziness and slumber. What could have degenerated into a personal ego clash, and deterioration of a relationship, instead got me to work harder. In this way, one can easily notice subtle goodness hidden in almost everything if we try to anaylse the reactions of people to our words or actions.

Some genuine leaders therefore keep critiques in good humour by encouraging them to voice opinions against their actions so that they get an opportunity to know the areas they could improve upon and increase their popularity.

Revisit the fundamental scripture

The *Bhagawat Gita*, which is actually a commentary on life delivered by Lord Krishna to Arjun on a battlefield, which we can refer as symbolizing the *battlefield of life*. In fact, I believe that the depression-struck mind, a mind which does not find any interest in anything worldly, can derive solace from reading the *Gita*. The *Gita* can reach the deepest part of the mind when the world is akin to an unreal vision *(Maya)* to a real mind or vice versa. It is similar to the dichotomy arising between the emphasis on the physics of pure matter and the realm of quantum mechanics. *Bhagawat Gita* has the power to slowly teach this mind which is in a state of depression, which is a frustrated mind suffering on the brink of hopelessness, helplessness, purposelessness, and directionlessness. Though the teachings of Gita seem to be directed at only one individual, it can actually be extended easily in the form of a collective goal or direction if the proper scaling is done. The *Gita* appears to consist of sermons to an individual soul to help him first get rid of his hallucinations, help him get rid of all kinds of illusory thoughts, all kinds of wrong notions about life, and to then help him embark on a path of renewal and sustenance, a path of fight towards survival, a path towards victory with courage, and ultimately to salvation.

As far as my association with the *Bhagawat Gita* is concerned, it all started in high school, Dhanurjay Narayan High School, my Alma mater at Keonjhar. We had this morning prayer session in our school which we used to start our day with. The prayer consisted of a few shlokas (verses) from the eleventh chapter of the *Bhagawat Gita*. I was curious to delve deeper into the *Bhagawat Gita* because, as a school going kid, I found it bit intriguing why we would use some verses from a religious book as our morning prayer in the first place! It was not a very melodious *Bhajan* (religious song) which could have diverted my attention otherwise and thank God, it was only a few Sanskrit shlokas. To satisfy my curiosity, I bought a copy from the market during the summer holidays, immediately after my final class XI - Board Examinations were over. But during the morning Puja (prayer) hours, when I tried to read a chapter or a few shlokas every day, I could hardly understand a thing. Most of the ideas espoused in the scripture were French and Latin to me for a very long time, even after I became a professional and a married adult with children. I had this habit of reading almost a chapter a day if time permitted, or at least few shlokas every day, as a ritual. I enjoyed the habit, but understanding the true meaning of the text happened only a long time after, while I was in Australia. When I went through my mental health crisis, the inner meaning of the entire text started becoming very clear to me, as if veil of ignorance being removed peel by peel from my mind.

There was another twist to the story. Although I used to carry a copy of the book as my permanent companion wherever I was transferred, during the period leading up to my mental health crisis in Australia, I had become extremely irregular in going through the text for want of time, and perhaps carelessness. At one point of time, under the influence of the modern westernized world, it crossed my mind that the power of the mind was all one needed to achieve everything in life and that one did not need any support from religious rituals! Few will believe that from the moment this thought crossed my mind, for whatever reasons, and by whatever permutation and combination of planetary positions and their influence on my life, it took perhaps six months for events and circumstances to unfold around me which ultimately landed me at the mental health hospital!

The first thing I decided, therefore, when I was hospitalized for my problem in Australia, was that I would immediately go back to my fundamental scripture, the *Bhagawat Gita*, which works as the greatest support, friend, philosopher and guide for all the Hindus in the world. It is such a powerful scripture that, although it took me time, I ultimately made sure that I came out of my deadly crisis with considerable help from the sacred Gita. Such fundamental scriptures are sources of infinite power and wisdom and they provide sustenance during times of crisis to all of humanity.

I have a strong belief and faith in that, regardless of the religion or cultural traditions that one is born into, there will be a few such fundamental scriptures and the knowledge of them will be running in the family they are born into. For Christians it is the Holy Bible, for Muslims it is the Holy Koran, for Sikhs it is the teachings of the Holy Guru Granth Sahib, for Hindus it is the *Bhagawat Gita*, and so on. It is essential that one realises that if one is struck with a mental health problem at any stage of life, one of the greatest support systems they can hope for is their own fundamental scripture – just like how I found my solace in the *Bhagawat Gita*.

The path of virtue as expounded by the *Gita* is applicable as much to an individual as to an organization. The tenets of *Karma Yoga, Gnyana Yoga* and *Bhakti Yoga* can all find expression in our thought processes as well as in our actions. These Yogic activities and practices however should be directed in a holistic manner such that it could take the form of self-renewal in line of a continuously changing and dynamic world. For example, if we think of the root cause for the birth of any organization, say in case of an oil and gas refining unit, the original need for it by a country was to supply hydrocarbon fuel energy to the economy. Now, with modern thoughts and technology improving every day and changing every day, a time will come when the world will no more rely on oil and gas to drive the engine of economic growth. Evidence for such a possibility is seen from the environmental concerns, rapidly depleting hydrocarbon reserves, development of alternate energy sources etc. And then the very purpose for which such an organization, the oil and gas refining unit, came into existence would vanish in this ever-changing dynamic world. There will be no reason left to validate or argue in favour of the existence of such an organization anymore. The tacit shift therefore would be to align ourselves to changing scenarios such that we can exist in harmony with nature forever. There is a saying that goes; *'The stone age did not end because we ran out of stones.'* Similarly, the oil and gas age will not end because we will run out of oil and gas. Modern alternative energy means are being developed every day and it is very possible that, in a few hundred years, the oil and gas industry will vanish altogether.

The smooth transition for such renewal through a proper understanding of the environment requires deep knowledge that is normally not available to common people. There will be a fight for a market share in this materialistic world, the constant fight between dominance and meekness. But the power and prestige associated with a dominant position, both for an individual and an organization, have their advantages and disadvantages. History has told us how European powers wanted to dominate the world through the political maneuvering, unscrupulous politicking and brute military strength and power, but they have all disintegrated over time. It is in the welfare and interest of every citizen of the globe not to allow any community or nation to go back to such a stupid and ignorant experiment again. It needs to be understood that only *love* can sustain the world. The Hindu religion or philosophy, perhaps being the oldest of all, has taught these methods well and other world religions, having appeared much later, are learning from hard struggle and experience. Perhaps religion tries to forge ahead with associated power to dominate, but ultimately godly benevolence triumphs. These godly characteristics are enunciated well in the *Gita* - which needs to be applied both at an individual level and group level so as to meet the requirements of an individual or a group.

Engage in some holy rituals

Prayer is one of the most powerful ways to connect with both the inner core of our being and with the all-pervasive God outside of the body. Through prayer, one can elevate one's state of bodily consciousness to a state of soul consciousness. Devotional songs are a practical means to express oneself in prayer. Going to temples or churches or mosques to offer prayer is a way of surrendering one's ego at the altar of God. Making a ritual out of such daily or weekly visits can be highly uplifting because these places of worship are actually abodes of peace and tranquility and it is easier to connect to our original core of love, peace, beauty and harmony through such visits with a pure heart and a mind free from any materialistic desire. The Hindu ritual of paying obeisance to God four times at home and at temples is a means of connecting to the God within and the God without. Bhajans and Kirtans (music-based prayers to the Gods) are powerful practices that elevate the Spirit within and have a tremendous healing power for those who have been afflicted with mental health problems. I have used these techniques quite effectively during my own crisis.

Some atheists or agnostics may not like the idea of a public show of emotion, but they may be attracted to activities like social service. They would rather believe in the philosophy of *'Service to mankind is preferable to service to God'* and engage in such activities that directly benefit common people. Services offered to the blind, the deaf and dumb, the handicapped, the elderly, the homeless, the hungry and to orphans all come under this. Actually, these practices have a holy nature inbuilt into them. The essence of such activities is to purify oneself from inside out by offering selfless service to people. By such activities, the Holy Spirit is also awakened in us considerably.

Live in Hope

In the third chapter, I have recounted the story of the miracle that happened in my life through the incident in which my one year old son played a key role. The *'Live in Hope'* paradigm is a most potent one, particularly during the time mental health crisis strikes a person. I believe, the interaction between the human soul (consciousness) and the Super Soul (Super Consciousness) happens in a mysterious manner when a person is afflicted with such a deadly crisis. Cosmic Intelligence acts in tandem with human intelligence and not everything can be explained by ordinary physics, chemistry, mathematics and biology. Some modern day management gurus and inspirational leaders view *hope* to be an equivalent of begging and prefer instead to use *faith* in its place. It is quite easy to miss the tree for the woods because, at the time of serious mental tribulations, *faith* per se gets completely destabilized and disturbed if not fully destroyed. I recall that my usually lovely feelings of wholesome peace, love and happiness while entering Hindu temples was so badly bruised after I was struck by my mental health crisis that I developed some sort of distaste. Extremely bizarre thoughts came into my mind during visits to temples in the aftermath of the crises for several months, arising out of the frustrated anger I felt towards my own beloved Gods whom I blamed for not preventing my mental breakdown! There must be neurobiological reasons for all these bizarre reactions in a human brain during the immediate aftermath of a mental breakdown which needs further dedicated research. But I was determined to bring my health back to normal and I had to finally bank upon the most sacred Hindu fundamental scripture the *Bhagawat Gita* to bring my derailed engine back on track.

Lord Krishna has prescribed the *Bhakti Yoga*, the highest form of Yoga, while advising Arjun by saying that if he could surrender his mind and body at the altar of the Lord, then the Lord would set everything right (shloka 12.8). And if by chance Arjun could not concentrate, then Lord Krishna advised a rigorous or habitual practice that would help straighten things out (shloka 12.9). In the event when even that was difficult, then he advises a simple routine of a rituals of nine steps glorifying God: listening to God's name, chanting God's name, mentally remembering His name, proving by reasoning the glory of His name, feeling His name in the heart, donating one's life to God, acting like a friend of God, acting like a slave of God, and finally totally surrendering to God (shloka 12.10). Lord Krishna has not stopped there. He goes on to the last and most powerful and effective step. In case all the steps enumerated above fail, He has advised that, since it is the desire for success and attachment to the fruit or result of actions that creates a problem then, by denouncing that completely, if one surrenders to Him, then He will certainly listen to the call of the distressed soul (shloka 12.11).

One can easily find that, in an attempt to achieve success, when a person goes on accumulating stress and reaches a point of no return, and the problem becomes insurmountable for him, then the very purpose for the building up of that stress i.e. the desire for success, needs to be sacrificed in the hope that the Lord will save him. The power of faith actually works best when the brain chemicals are balanced and the divinity is back in the body and mind such that the conscious brain is capable of moving in tandem with the subconscious brain. When the brain chemicals are imbalanced, the pain and suffering that affects the conscious brain makes the person so distraught that the signals of divinity from the subconscious brain are not easily accepted. But through the systematic efforts that have been described above, one can incessantly work towards achieving a state of mental peace and stability and free himself from the burden of hopelessness and helplessness.

Create a safety network and nourish it for your own help

While growing up, we make friends within the neighborhood, in school, in college, at the university, at the ancestral village, in the place we work at and so on. By having two-way interactions with them, many of these friends become very close to us. We share our emotional feelings with many such close friends during times of both joy and sorrow, during good and bad days, and during times of success and failure. Our bond with these friends is such that, at times of emotional turmoil, we can look up to them or rely on their unconditional love and empathy. Someone who leads a balanced life, without resorting to rash decisions in his or her activities, and who follows standard social norms is less likely to face any crisis. But one who is not so balanced runs the risk of meeting a dead-end at some point. It is during these times that emotional upheavals can be very unsettling and may create extraordinary stress for a person.

Man is a social animal, and thus the sharing of emotions at such critical periods can help a person in a big way. The sharing of personal pain and suffering with family and friends comes in very handy because, whenever one goes through such a stressful period, a period full of fear, anxiety and depression, he can calm his nerves drastically by opening up to fellow human beings. It is important to look for people who have gone through such problems themselves, share our feelings with them and then try to learn the coping strategies utilized by such friends. Well-wishers have a great role to play. When one who knows the people whom he or she can bank upon, it is advisable to immediately open up a channel of communication with those people. In this way, new people can also be found to create an effective network along with old friends. The wider the network, the better it is. The letter from my younger brother at a critical juncture of my mental crisis in Australia with an advice of just two words *'Accept everything'* worked like magic for me. My younger brother had a long history of mental illness and his advice would be practical knowledge. When I combined this practical knowledge with the theoretical knowledge I had from the teachings of the Bhagawat *Gita* wherein it is suggested that total surrender to God is the path to salvation; I could slowly get back my mental balance which was otherwise in a complete mess.

Relish the speed breakers

With the slow progression of time and maturity, we tend to develop lines of logic ourselves and then tune them to our internal and external system in the hope that we will achieve our goals. Goals can either be broad, or long term and short term. An often quoted Chinese proverb says; *'Any big task can be divided into a large number of smaller tasks.'*

I shall describe a personal anecdote here. I used to wash my clothes and press them from a very early age, as a routine, even without being asked by my parents or the elders in the family. I do not recall from where I learnt this habit. However, my father saw me one late afternoon washing a big bucket full of my clothes. I must have been in class VIII or so. What he said to me at the time has stayed with me ever since. "Do not wash all the clothes on the same day. Try to do it in two or three installments; it will be easier for you", he had said. Whether it was a father's feeling pained at watching his son's hardship (we had couple of maids working at home those days) or whether it was a proud father's timeless wisdom coming to me, this remark created a lasting impact on me and I have used this simple concept in almost every major task that I have taken up in life so far. Time management calls for looking at all the tasks at hand and weighing the pros and cons of these being attended to and achieved. It is these two things together that make the final outcome possible.

Whenever a major crisis strikes, the mind becomes so stressed that to think of solving even small problems becomes very daunting. Similarly, in such a situation, minor obstacles in the way create too much frustration because of the imbalance in brain chemicals. The tendency towards despondency is accentuated because of the inability to think clearly. In these circumstances, the best approach is to break any major task into smaller ones. At the peak of my health crisis, I used to give preference to carrying out the most mundane and mechanical of jobs, the ones for which I would not need too much mental resilience. The advantage is that even small successes and the achievement of taking tiny steps bring in positive energy into the system, facilitating improvement in the interaction and level of brain chemicals. The English proverb *'Journey of a thousand miles begins with one step'* is a corollary to the previous statement. When depression and anxiety are severe, the vigor to carry out any major task is reduced. But the problem with such a mental state is that it comes with another bit of baggage: procrastination. As we all know, *procrastination is the thief of life.* The best solution in such a condition is to somehow take the first step towards finding a solution to the problem, or to complete a major task. The step may be very small, but it is essential not to lose sight of the ultimate goal and be prepared to congratulate ourselves for even such a beginning. Self-praise is a very powerful tool. One can derive support from his own memory bank. Before a major mental health crisis strikes, each one of us must surely have achieved something in life however trivial or small it may seem. The mind has a unique way of reviving and reinvigorating itself if some good mental tonic is deliberately fed to it by self-analysis and recalling these small successes of the past.

The tasks that we set for ourselves are guided mainly by two components. One of these is internal need and desire and the other is the external environment. This balance between the internal and external systems is crucial because sometimes things happen that are not within our control. For example, some social problems like strikes, dharna and riots, or disasters like fires, earthquakes, hurricanes, tsunamis and war, which are either guided by much larger forces like the natural or political environment, can upset our schedules so much that becoming stressed is a very real possibility unless one understands the dynamics well enough. I always wondered what the chairman of Tata Group companies, Ratan Tata who relentlessly pursued his dream of bringing out the *Nano*, the iconic car on Indian roads at a cost of less than one lakh, would have felt when the plant at Singur in West Bengal faced tremendous political turmoil in 2007-2008. Against so much adversity, Ratan Tata never budged from his principles which included among others, complete safety and security of his employees as the top most priority. It was a matter of providence that the then Chief Minister of Gujarat and the current Prime Minister of India, offered him the land for his plant to be shifted from Bengal to Gujarat. Ratan Tata had categorically declared in the back drop of so much disturbances that he would not hesitate to shift the plant even if it meant incurring a huge loss of fifteen hundred crores of rupees at that time. Similarly, in political field, we see the example of Prime Minister Narendra Modi who in spite of being the chief minister of Gujarat for four consecutive terms had to face tremendous political opposition from every possible quarter including foreign powers. But the spiritual power within him never made him lose the dream of thinking even bigger and he came out with an unprecedented victory in the general elections of 2014. Thus the bigger the goal we set up, the greater the chances that we will be subjected to opposition and hence stress. But it is also true that unless we set bigger goals, we cannot achieve anything significant in life.

When we set our targets for a day, a week, a month or for a year, there arises the likelihood that we will be able to achieve the greater percentage of those targets at least. We can systematically evaluate our targets and carefully adjust and change ourselves accordingly with periodic evaluation because everything in this world is dynamic in nature and changing continuously. Failure happens only when the mind is rigid and too stiff to accept sudden changes. The mind needs to be ready for sudden adjustments depending on the kicks it gets from the environment - which includes the immediate family, children, friends and relatives apart from those at the workplace. The beauty lies in the fact that one needs to be qualified and intelligent to modify the call of such changes in such a manner that nothing is really jeopardized and everything will still travel along a track which has its ultimate and fixed goal. The rumblings and tumblings that come on the way, the obstacles that come up, are merely impediments that need to be overcome as they appear on any of our journeys.

It is very important that we take care of our own internal needs as well as the needs of our surroundings. The highest efficiency will be achieved if there is a considerable amount of flexibility attached to our mindset. What appears to be an obstacle today could turn out to be a boon later because of the experience it provides to our soul and mind in the form of acquired practical knowledge. If we can manage to remain unruffled when an obstacle comes in our way and do what is essential to overcome that obstacle, then it will be easy for us to get back to our original plan and get back to our unfinished agenda. If however we get stuck up and murmur and grumble that our progress has been hampered, and start blaming either ourselves or our loved ones, it is sure to result in disaster, either on a minute scale or a large scale.

Whenever there is apparent derailment, we should go back to the original plan and see whether smaller components of the larger task can be achieved. We must at least begin so as to set the ball rolling. *If there is a mountain to be climbed, waiting does not make it smaller.* Unless the sheer zeal with which we allow thoughts and dreams to take root in our mind is followed up with proportionate enthusiasm and action, no major achievement is possible. I recall the TV commentary for a cricket match that was being played in Australia wherein the commentator was heaping praise on Anil Kumble, who as it so happens, in spite of not being the best turner of the ball in modern cricket, had achieved dizzy heights in the field of bowling. The commentator was expressing genuine amazement saying; *'Anil just keeps coming!'* Anil Kumble used to keep trying variations in speed, arm ball, flight of the ball, googly and so on. It was his patience, perseverance and the zeal with which he kept coming back at the batsman at the other end which ensured that, in spite of being hit for a four or a six, his enthusiasm for the next ball never got diminished. This is the key. But in times of mental crisis, when the zeal is at its lowest, the solution will be to try to do at least *one percent* of the amount of work we used to do earlier. Slowly, over a period of time, this one percent can be increased until one reaches his original hundred percent efficiency. It will take time, but no matter what, ultimately, one will be able to reach it.

I must reiterate here that, during the deadliest days of my mental crisis in Australia, I started with the lowest possible denominator, which was my ability to breathe, to do my work! I became happy at one moment, one day, that I could at least breathe! Then I moved to the next step for a couple of days which was the ability to do normal chores like washing my face, going to the bathroom, putting on my dress, eating by myself, making my bed etc. After a few days, I congratulated myself when I started doing additional tasks like taking my child to school, taking my family to the nearby park, going to the market for daily usables, helping the family in domestic chores etc. Over the next few days I concentrated on simply staying at the University for the whole day and enjoying reading some inspirational magazines. Next, I started doing my usual research work - initially for few hours and later on for the full day.

This way, step by step, I moved on until I reached a stage where I was moving at full throttle again.

Add just one more layer to your soul

It is normally a momentous occasion when a child is born. Scientists, researchers and philosophers have been thinking and trying to derive the meaning of every happening on earth - be it driven by nature or by man. The continuous process has actually resulted in man questioning everything that comes his way. He tries to find answers to every such query that arises in his mind and then records it for the benefit of posterity. This has not only happened over the last few thousands of years, but it has been happening in an indirect fashion throughout the evolutionary process by which the highest level of animal, man, has been formed.

Spiritual leaders try to connect the meaning of the birth of a human being to the long and arduous process of the soul's journey and I recall one article that I read in Adelaide. The article was on Jain philosophy which suggested how the human soul was formed and how it accumulates thousands of layers of wisdom and experience with each birth. Scientific thinking, particularly the votaries of Darwinian theory of evolution by natural selection, would then entail that if the evolutionary process has actually brought the human soul to earth, then perhaps our souls were those of a lower animal's before it became a human's.

The above stated fact would then point to the wisdom and experience that human civilization has gained in each and every field of activity - politics, economy, science, religion, spirituality. And it would then make us believe also that the world a new born comes into, the existing world, is actually the product of millions and even billions of similar creatures born on earth before him.

'*Rome was not built in one day*'. What stands today, as the Italian capital city, is actually a product of not one day's worth of work but some millions of years' worth of work, first by nature itself and then by the efforts of human civilization - from its inception, prehistoric times and through modern times. Similarly, each and every thing that we see today on this beautiful earth including the creations of human ingenuity are products of ongoing work both at the thought level as well as the execution level. Human spirit has also evolved accordingly and this is born out of the fact that modern humans are progressively born with extraordinary talent so as to help civilization grow further. Conscious efforts in this direction can also help the individual soul to grow in a similar fashion.

Whether we talk of a school, a college, a hospital, a club house, a University, a road, a building, a playground, a garden, an organization, an industry, a society or even a family, it has taken decades or at least years for them to come into existence. Similarly, if we want to achieve something, short term or long term, what we must understand is that it needs careful study, planning and formulating of the mechanism needed to achieve the desired goal. Irrespective of the goal in question, it involves the same process of first a desire or dream, followed by careful planning at both macro and micro levels, and then execution of the plan according to set norms and regulations.

The ultimate success however depends on our fate to a great degree. But that fate is guided to a large extent by studied and carefully thought out plans and actions. If, say, we want our children to be a good technocrat or bureaucrat or scientist, or an economist or industrialist, or a good player or sportsperson, then we need to concentrate on the nitty gritties of how to achieve that. We need to choose good schools and colleges or training centers, and then carefully spare time for their proper education in the relevant fields. We have to also provide a congenial atmosphere at home and outside for the child to get the freedom to think and work on the stated goals. Similarly, if we want to build a company, we need to arrange first for a blue print of the functionalities in the system, arrange for land, a proper office building, a production facility if it is a manufacturing company or a chain of trading points, if it is service company, arrange for working capital, finance for operating expenses, selection of vendors and suppliers, selection of relevant staff to man the offices and production facilities, proper procedures for marketing and distribution of finished products, warehouses for raw material and finished goods etc. Unless one does macro and micro level planning, no business is going to succeed. This applies to any project. We will succeed definitely if a proper foundation is built. Proper thoughts and actions go into the functioning of a company. The success will depend on the mission statement, the goals that we set for ourselves, the roles that we chalk out to achieve the goals, and how well we execute our responsibilities in discharging our assigned roles.

The whole project may be thought of as an immortal tree or soul that, when implanted with good zeal and purpose and the best of intentions, will keep running until its own natural death and will also deliver offspring to the earth to carry on the torch that is the laid down principles and policies which could be dynamic with respect to changing times and changing needs. The need to adapt and adopt to change arises primarily due to advances in science and technology, growing population, depletion of exhaustible resources on the planet. The project could have short term and long term goals which can then be divided into micro level plans and goals so that each can be taken up for completion and achievement of the overall goal.

Have a two-way switch ready: from within or from without

Out of utter helplessness and hopelessness, many ordinary people have at some time contemplated killing themselves. But through some mechanism, which is the theme of this sub-chapter, they have not only come out of their crisis but have either remained carriers of hope and faith while apparently looking ordinary outwardly, or they have risen to become famous public figures who command awe and respect from the general public. There have been such instances in each and every society. The reasons for such a phenomenon lie in the understanding - or the lack of it - about the purpose of life.

Buddha had said; 'Those who have worked towards the Truth have missed the purpose of living.' And Swami Sivananda had said; 'Your sole business in life is to attain God realization. All else is useless and worthless.'

In this fast changing technological world, it is naïve to expect human sense organs to remain undisturbed by the impact of the brazen display of materialistic forms of energy. Unless proper care is built into our internal systems, it is highly likely that the process of internal growth through the cleansing of dirt from the purest form of our souls will be hampered. The attraction, the greed for ego driven materialistic gain in various forms, will tend to derail the natural growth cycle of the soul which the Lord has spoken of in the *Bhagawat Gita* (The work of all our sense organs is to derive *Sattwic* pleasure and not *Rajashik* or *Tamashik* pleasure meaning that the natural state of our being is to either maintain a state of egolessness or attain a state of complete egolessness with the progress of time). Failure to achieve fulfillment of materialistic desires leads to a vicious circle of more greed and hence slowly but steadily it leads to self-destruction. There will come a time when the soul will set off an alarm, having reached a state of total hopelessness or helplessness. This alarm bell should be enough to revitalize the internal system such that the soul takes over from the ego (the mind becoming soul conscious rather than body conscious) and slowly guides itself back to its actual path, which is God realization. Some people who manage to cling to the deepest part of their souls, in times of severe crisis, when they are drowning in the ocean of hopelessness, allow the seed of Divinity in them to take charge when they need to come out of a crisis.

I once had a two-way switch in my bedroom in Chennai. I could turn the light and fan in my room on and off with the help of the two-way switch located right next to my bed. The above metaphor 'From within or from without' is similar to this. When all is going well in life, you can work out your resources *from within* - and these are partly mixed with materialistic manifestations of the world, just like how the form of your body is a materialistic expression of the spiritual energy within you. You need food, shelter and clothing for the upkeep of the physical body. All other technological innovations that humankind has brought in till today are basically meant for the upkeep of the mental being. Basic needs for the body are met from food, clothing and shelter whereas the higher order needs are mainly mind driven. If I needed to cover a distance, I could just walk. But I have invented cars to take me places if I need comfort and save valuable time. It could now be just for the sake of ego satisfaction that I own a car. Hence, the pleasure that you derive from maintaining a healthy balance between false ego and actual need keeps you physically and mentally fit.

But when there is derailment of this whole process because of the onslaught of ego on your daily life, the system collapses or begins to collapse. There will be definite signals and alarm bells pointing in the direction of derailment. It is our sensitive soul that must decipher and then wage a strong battle against the ego; it must overtake the ego and take charge.

Once that happens, the smooth process of normal growth happens and this is when we will be assured of the good results which will lead us to life of satisfaction, happiness, peace and bliss. When we allow our soul to take full charge of our lives, it gets connected automatically to the Collective Consciousness which is acting *from without*. Right from the time the desire took root in our parents to commingle or have a physical union, the all-pervading Source or all-pervading Creator guided our destiny, right from the time the male sperm fertilized female egg and a new foetus was created which then grew inside the womb. We never imagine that, right from the moment the desire originated in the minds of our parents, to this day where I am writing or you are reading this, perhaps not much was in our own control. It was pure destiny and we seem to be totally blind to it. But the all-pervading *Cosmic Intelligence* that we define as God has always been acting, *'acting from without'*. The more we realize this phenomenon, the lower the chances of feeling helpless or hopeless or separate from feeling at one with God. This basic understanding is perhaps the only way to glue ourselves together with the Universal Soul, the Universal Consciousness. And we should do this sooner rather than later for the sake of our own spiritual growth - meaning the path to happiness, peace and bliss.

Look from the end to when it all began

The concept of *'thinking from the end'* is explored by both Stephen Covey and Wayne D. Dyer in their books. When we do this, our subconscious mind is what contributes to conceptualizing and formulating the end. The power of intention/intuition as suggested by Wayne Dyer, or the power of conscience as I put it, both have one thing in common which is the power to imagine. The power of imagination has the greatest strength, the longest vision, the greatest power, when it is emanating from the very core of a human being, from the innermost level of its conscience. This helps in formulating the end and its associated elements - which is again a reflection of what destiny has in store for a person. When one thinks from the end, it means that conscience and intuition stretches the limits of his imagination to extents that an ordinary conscious mind cannot easily capture. And so it becomes hard for other human beings with whom he is associated to visualize the effects of this idea, this thought, from the end. This is very personal and derives maximum power from the conscience. If we can keep our conscience clean, and keep it clean for as long as possible, we will be able to achieve miraculous things that would not be easily conceivable otherwise to our own conscious mind - to say nothing of friends, colleagues, family etc.

The interesting thing, as Maharishi Patanjali has remarked, is that once we are driven by great ideas or thoughts (which is something similar to thinking from the end) then things will begin to happen in such a way that everything will look like it is falling into place. The entire universe then conspires in such a fashion that this great idea or goal that we have thought of will drive everything systematically towards the achievement of that goal or fulfillment of that idea.

Stable homes and matured parents normally provide the early background for a happy life. Childhood memories will hold happiness for one if, during his or her early life, the parents managed to provide an environment of love, peace, happiness and joy through the examples they set and through their own hard work and the fruits thereof. Regardless of culture and place, if a newborn child is reared in a careful manner, with all the different ingredients that make up a full life, then the mental growth and maturity of that child is almost assured.

Basically, life consists of a few simple truths. There are components which require man to work first for the satisfaction of his basic needs, and then his social needs, his ego needs, and finally his self-actualization needs. Although they may look like they are arranged in a vertical manner, it is not so. When we analyse our daily lives, we find that we cannot live without food and shelter and so on. This means that no one need is removed completely from the others. There can always be some amount of flexibility which can allow one to accommodate any change, whether drastic or gradual, depending on the forces that cause it. For example, in times of emergency, such as during natural disasters, accidents, social crisis and war, the mind has an inbuilt mechanism to accept some major or minor changes in the daily routine and can often absorb stress to varying degree. But if such changes in the schedule are forced upon for a long time on one's psyche for some reason, either knowingly or unknowingly, then it starts building up stress - which will lead to health problems and other associated problems.

We all are gifted with a physical body with sense organs and with a mental body to process information and work accordingly for survival and growth. We are also gifted with intellect, which helps in the envisioning of the future, and finally with some spiritual intent - the degree of which can vary from person to person. Some persons are naturally inclined to help, serve and sacrifice. Some less so. Some have leadership qualities; they can understand the environment and accordingly exploit the situation so as to bring benefits to the masses and hence command a following. There are others who are happy to remain within their own family circle and be content with that.

There are seeds of anger, hatred, distaste, frustration, jealousy, unhealthy competitiveness and other such negative attributes in all of us which try to assess us as well as our surroundings, and make a superficial analysis that gives our mind some kind of balance through satisfaction of the ego - resulting in apparent happiness, peace and tranquility. However, these will not be lasting because they are the result of negative emotions rather than positive emotions. If one is predisposed to constant nagging, complaining and dissatisfaction with his surroundings, then there is a chance that he will fall sick sooner rather than later.

Happiness is a state of mind which we all constantly try to reach every moment. The reason why mind tries to reach this state of happiness is that there is a substratum of happiness, as Swami Chinmayanand has said. Suppose we have decided to work towards achieving some kind of successful career for the sake of our children, while we may work towards it with all our might, if there are minor hiccups along the way, we feel disheartened and think that it is perhaps the end of the world and we will not be able to achieve the desired goal. But that is not true. Because, in one corner of our mind, we nourish desires for a brighter future for our children and, in another corner, we nourish the desire for a brighter career for ourselves. Both desires may not be complimentary or supplementary. There can be balance and adjustment and some flexibility between both desires. This is achieved by our intellect and wisdom. If for some reason there is a setback to some of our goals in the short term, there is always scope for taking corrective measures and bringing the progress towards achieving long term goals back on rail. Similarly, if there is a major long term setback, there is scope in this ever-expanding world of opportunities to adjust and reorient our goals both in the short term and long term so that they align themselves according to our ultimate objective. This is where our imagination and intellect and power of vision come in. They will guide us in the right direction.

Usually, during times of mental stress, we get carried away by what lies before us. The imaginary goal we visualize and work towards achieving sometimes causes stress, but if we can also keep looking back at where it all began, it will be easy to keep a balance. Many a times, we achieve successes even greater than what we initially imagined for ourselves at some point of time in our lives. These are the key memories that will help us become stable again in case a mental health crisis occurs due to too much anxiety and depression.

Never allow your soul to feel like a burden

Right through several months of extreme mental health crisis during PhD study in Australia, I never allowed myself to think that my *soul* was to blame. The key to doing this lies in reflecting on the simplest truth of life: 'How was I born and how did I achieve so much till now? This has only been possible by God's grace and God's will and by God's will, my *soul* exists'. The close interaction between the soul's desire and God's desire manifests in the various truthful expressions of this universe. We are just mute spectators who record things through our sense organs. And if we detach ourselves, all the history of life will seem like a great movie. There is a hidden power in such a feeling of detachment.

The moment one feels heavy physically, he needs physical rest and the moment one feels heavy mentally, he needs mental rest. But one can never feel heavy in his soul nor he should ever imagine. The soul is ever expansive and ever expanding, ever growing. It can accommodate infinite possibilities; if we allow our soul to be in line with infinity, it can really accommodate an infinite number of things. And this means one is equipped with infinite power to be humble, to be intelligent, to be forgiving, to be kind, to be humane, to be loving, to be peaceful, to be content, to be happy, to be all kinds of Godly qualities. One can then overcome all the negative emotions that come in his way due to obstacles.

One of the greatest ever personalities in the game of cricket, Sachin Tendulkar, has outlined in his autobiography how he was twice lucky during his first test hundred - once in his thirties and later in his nineties. He has thanked God for that. Similarly if we analyse all the greatest achievers of ancient and modern times, we will notice their gratitude towards Heavenly help. This only proves that when even the most successful people depend on the luck factor, God; ordinary souls perhaps need it all the more. And this is possible if there is fine tuning between an individual soul and the Super Soul.

During mental health crisis, the body-mind combine generally feels drained and exhausted. This creates feelings of desperation simply because energy to do work is so low that optimism and hope start deserting. It then becomes a vicious cycle because, positive energy to do anything feels lacking while failure to do much causes further frustration in mind. In such a scenario, there is a tendency of the subconscious brain to throttle the conscious brain. Because when out of total frustration and desperation, the conscious brain creates too much pain, the subconscious brain loses its balance and attempts to silence it which can be really dangerous and fatal. It is at this time, there needs to be some divine intervention and it happens when the conscious brain leaves everything on God. Instead of complaining, one needs to surrender with whole body-mind combine to the Almighty to bear the pain with a prayerful stance. To achieve this end, the easiest method is to look around and keenly observe the pains and sufferings that millions of people go through daily. Even TV news over war ravaged areas, hurricane, flood, tsunami, earthquake affected areas, can sometimes trigger the necessary zeal to survive because we see extremely painful sufferings people go through which could be much more serious than one might be going through at the peak of own mental health crisis. This is not easy but it is possible provided one allows his ego to be totally surrendered at the altar of God and allow the God given survival instinct the chance to bloom again. Even real life accounts from books describing such painful stories can provide necessary feedstock because by doing an internal comparison, one would start feeling much lighter which would then trigger some positive energy back into the system. Thus it is important to ensure that soul is never felt like a burden because it has infinite power and wherewithal to come out of any crisis provided one is prepared to forgo his false ego or vanity.

Major causes of mental health illness, other than those which are afflicted since birth, are either due to distorted views about the world or due to chronic physical diseases that do not seem to be improving. This book is mostly about issues regarding distorted views of the world. Marriages fall part so easily these days. Sibling rivalries, jealousy in corporate world, breach of trust amongst friends, breach of trust among dating partners, unscrupulous dealings amongst business partners, too much libido driven activities etc. and too much ambition can all lead one day to serious mental health crisis. Too much of materialism and material pursuits is the bane of society now. But if one calms down his or her mind and opens up to free thinking, it is quite possible that one would notice that one's own problem of mental health would appear much more trivial compared to some of the worst case sufferings people go through in life. One needs to understand that human soul is so powerful that derailment due to temporary setbacks during conscious life journey can be reversed provided he or she is prepared to listen to the inner voice and act accordingly.

Follow a healthy diet and a healthy exercise regime

Most of the time, it is observed that mental health patients are oblivious to the impact of a good and healthy diet and healthy physical exercises. The human body is a wonderful machine. All the metabolic functions that can happen within an Olympic champion's body can happen within the body of a common man and even in the body of a beggar on the street. It is essential to understand that the saying *'we are what we eat'* is so apt for maintaining a healthy body and mind. In the face of a growing population, global resources are not equally distributed for various reasons. Deficiency in nutrition is rampant in different strata of the society and even amongst different members or families within each stratum. Lack of education and awareness add to the problem. Nutritious food is equally important to both the physical body as well as the mind and this cannot be overstated. Food and beverages can be a very important ingredient for keeping one in a normal state. I was telling my doctor one day, during the time of my mental crisis; 'Jo, I was sipping coffee one day and for few hours after that, I felt like I was having mild panic attacks. Is there any link?" Jo said; 'Caffeine can act as a trigger.' This reiterates the fact that, when such mental imbalances happen, because of the hundreds of different thoughts churning inside the brain, it is wise to be careful and avoid risky food and beverages.

Similarly the wonderful machine that is the human body-mind-heart system needs regular exercise to keep itself fit. I recall a PowerPoint presentation featuring animation on the heart's functioning made by a renowned doctor from Apollo Hospital, Hyderabad who compared the human body to a car. As we take regular care of our car, so should we take regular care of our body as well. Actually, the physical body is like the body of a car with an engine and the mind is like the driver. In a slightly different way, even the combination of the physical body and the mind can be compared to the body of a car and its engine, with the soul as the driver instead. The same way a car needs fuel to run, both our body and mind require proper nutritious food. Proper amounts of protein, carbohydrate and fibre should be present in the food that we eat daily if we are to maintain a healthy physical body. Eating enough vegetables and fruits is the minimum that any doctor prescribes as a healthy food habit. Reading good books, watching good spiritual programmes and discourses on TV and conversations with good and spiritual people all help in providing tonic for the mind. Maintenance includes servicing the body regularly as we would service a car. And it includes taking regular medical check-ups and adjusting the requirement of food and supplements.

Breathe your way to life

When I was first struck with my mental crisis, it was through the bipolar disorder, in response to the drug overreaction, I was not able to understand what was happening inside me when, at one moment, it was as if blood was flowing through my body, to all my organs and through my veins and arteries, and the next moment, it was turning into cold water. I could not comprehend anything at that time. It was midnight of the sixth of July 2000 in Australia. I tried to jump up and down in order to bring my blood flow back to normal, thinking that physical exercise is the solution to all bodily problems. Then, when this did not help, I was bewildered and suddenly a thought came to mind: how could there be cold water inside the body one moment and warm normal blood the next? This thought made it certain to me that there was something still flowing and that the entire system was working, driven by my ability to breathe! This thought came from my own brain, an impulse certainly provided by the subconscious that helped me back to normalcy slowly when I started reasoning with myself saying that there couldn't be anything seriously wrong and that I could bring myself back to normal.

Another incident: when I was deep into a severe health crisis in Jorhat, Assam. I felt a total sense of anxiety and helplessness after three or four months of fever, pain, high temperature etc., and had thoughts of almost certainly dying. Then suddenly, this thought about my ability to breathe reappeared. Ability to breathe is what life is all about. This fundamental ability to breathe is the most important process of the life-sustaining mechanism. If I was able to breathe, it meant that not everything was lost. I therefore believed that it could only be a matter of moments or months before I got healthy again through proper medical treatment etc. I started thinking positively again at a time which was the lowest point of my life and realised that the most fundamental source of life i.e. the capacity to breathe properly was still with me. This ability to breathe is actually not ours as such and though we are supposed to protect it with all our knowledge, actions, habits and treatments (if any), the fundamental ability is never in our hands and this fact needs to be kept in mind. This realisation will help all those who suffer unnecessarily in a depressed situation. Though it is difficult to crack this phenomenon, it is there in all of us.

Life will be full of challenges, difficulties and pain and suffering, but moments of joy, happiness, success, achievement and thrill will also be there. It is important for one not to lose sight of the positive side of life during a time of crisis. So, if any one of you thinks that everything is lost, I assure you that if you are at least able to breathe, irrespective of the degree of physical or mental pain you face, then not everything is lost. God is there with you. He is helping you through your ability to breathe and that is fundamental to life.

Since those two incidents in my life, I have been closely observing the human spirit which has been affected so very severely by tragedy, disease, natural disaster, incapacitation etc., but I have also observed in what a fine way the human spirit always keeps glowing inside, how the fire keeps burning. The *fire of eternal life* is burning inside all of us and this is the *Holy Spirit*. We must all embrace this Holy Spirit, day in and day out, and also wholeheartedly welcome all the beautiful things that are gifted to us - the ability to feel, the ability to think positive, the ability to fight back during times of adversity, the ability to perceive extraordinary help arriving from unknown quarters etc.

Yoga and Pranayam are the two most important and effective techniques that I have put my bets on, particularly after going through two major health crisis, first in Australia and then in Jorhat, Assam. Although I was aware of their efficacy, I never tried these techniques earlier in my life. The massive awareness raised by Swami Ramdev Baba through television and his week-long programme across the length and breadth of India came as a God-sent boon for me. I somehow held on to the belief that if I was responsible for the damage to my health, in whatever way and for whatever reasons, then it was up to me again to repair the damage and return to normal health. *Pranayam* became my most potent companion since February 2006, when I started the breathing exercise in a regular and focused manner. Millions are reaping the benefits of *Yoga and Pranayam* around the world and millions are joining each day. There are similar ancient systems like *Reiki, Pranhic healing, Vipasana meditation, Raja Yoga meditation* etc. which are also drawing large numbers of followers everywhere in the world. For getting quick relief from the pain and suffering caused by a mental health crisis, these ancient systems can add immense value to any medical rehabilitation programme.

I have made a habit of doing *Pranayam* for about an hour and of brisk walking for about thirty-five to forty minutes every day. The Pranayam usually consists of at least five breathing exercises including *Udgeet, Bashtrika, Kapal Bhaati, Anilum Vilom and Bhramari.* Although there are days when I fail to keep to schedule due to various preoccupations and my hectic routine, I make it a point to do at least one of the two, Pranayam or brisk walking every day in the morning, not as exclusive to each other but as complimentary to each other. I know people who maintain excellent health because of such strict adherence to yoga and pranayam with light exercises. Fifteen years since my deadly mental crisis, I have come a long way - and these two routines have certainly contributed to my wellbeing in a substantial manner.

Cultivate laughter into your life

Generally, a person under mental stress can't laugh easily or often. However, the fact that there is a drought of laughter during times of mental stress is something to seriously take note of. Conscious feelings leading to laughter may be hard to come by during a mental health crisis, but subconsciously we all know the benefits of laughter. It is generally believed that *laughter is the best medicine*. Laughter causes the dilatation of the inner lining of blood vessels, and increases blood flow. Other cardio protective properties of nitric oxide include reduction of inflammation and decreased platelet aggregation.

Laughter also leads to reductions in stress hormones such as cortisol and epinephrine. When laughing, the brain also releases endorphins that can relieve physical pain. Laughter also boosts the number of antibody-producing cells, thus leading to a stronger immune system. Laughing lowers blood pressure, helps in toning the tummy, improves cardiac health, boosts T cells, triggers the release of endorphins and increases the overall sense of well-being.

It is thus very important that efforts are made to bring laughter back into our life through conscious practice. The Yoga camps conducted by Swami Ramdev Baba promote forceful laughter even in the absence of any particularly funny stimuli. I have personally experienced, at one such camp that I attended in Chennai in 2006, that by just taking part in such a mass laughter programme, the benefits generally associated with laughing are perceptibly felt. There are *laughing clubs* which have sprung up based on this theory and members of such clubs make deliberate efforts to fill their lives with laughter as much as possible. Conscious efforts to join such a club will bring immense benefits. Nowadays, there are so many cartoon channels on television that one has ample sources and triggers for laughter. It may look odd in the beginning, to just laugh when there seems to be no trigger for laughing, as is instructed in Yoga camps, but I have observed that laughter is actually contagious. Jokes are another way to create stimulations for laughter. A depressed and anxious mind may find it difficult in the beginning, but one can train his or her mind in such a manner that the subconscious wisdom takes over and directs the mind to enjoy bouts of laughter. With practice, this can enhance the sense of general well-being and can lift the depressed mood to a normal state.

Heal through meditation and visualisation

Modern research has proved that the effect of meditation and visualization techniques on diseases and healing has been phenomenal. There are intensive experiments conducted on patients afflicted with diseases like diabetes. According to some detailed reports, after just two weeks of disciplined change in food habits, exercise habits and lifestyle, along with meditation and visualization, there has been a seventy percent improvement in the blood sugar level of patients.

There are actually three steps to the process. The first step is the generation of thought. We must increase our awareness through conscious thoughts on certain ailments. For example, we all know that if we put excessive stress or pressure on the heart, it will start malfunctioning. The arteries will get choked by the deposit of cholesterol in the blood vessels. At the thought level, we must first tell ourselves of this fact, acknowledge the involvement of our own selves in the creation of such a problem. Then we go to the level of feeling. Once we accept responsibility, we can generate compassionate feeling towards our heart as an organ which has been put under excessive stress by our indiscipline or ignorance. The next step is the visualisation. We visualize that we will make conscious efforts to keep the heart relaxed, be very compassionate towards it, and derive divine energy and power by connecting to God through meditation. The focused meditation will allow God's grace to fall upon us, which will ultimately heal such heart ailments.

There have been many research studies to see the impact of meditation, how it improves functioning of various organs of the body like pancreas, kidney, heart etc. For example, a group of researchers in Brahmakumaris' Headquarters at Mount Abu have found a drastic reduction in the blood sugar levels of about fifty diabetes patients. The initial preparation involved meditation to raise self-awareness from *body consciousness* to *soul consciousness*. The technique works well when we can go very deep into the soul and make ourselves as one with the Universal Spirit.

The patients are first made to visualize the carrot-like pancreas which has become hyperactive and, by conscious thought processes, are asked to feel relaxed. The pancreas is then visualized to release sufficient insulin, so as to lower the blood sugar level. The visualization is more effective when the patients can first generate belief and faith in the procedure. The simplest example that can be quoted to draw a parallel here is the fact that our mouths generally tend to water when we see some very tasty food being prepared or served. When our minds can generate saliva just by the sight of food, the same logic can be applied to other organs, by conscious thought processes and through the visualization technique.

When I was going through the worst of my panic attacks, suffering from serious depression, anxiety and psychosis, I had the very subtle feeling that it was just a manifestation of my conscious mind. The subconscious mind or my inner voice was always telling me that I would be well one day. I believe this is one of the most powerful elements in our healing process. Each one of us is endowed with this *power within our soul*, but due to the overreaching influence of the conscious mind, this inner voice of the subconscious mind gets masked. Modern medicine definitely helps in bringing back a normal chemical balance in the brain to some degree, but the power within can work wonders if we listen to our inner voice. The best way to visualize a normal healed body and mind is by going back to the past, look into our own memories of times when we were quite fine. This visualization itself can provide feedback hormones or neurochemicals to our brain and improve the healing process. Visualising a future healed body and mind may not be easy at the peak of the crisis, but with help from doctors, care givers, family and friends, and spiritual gurus, even this is possible. Meditation is the most effective way to ensure sustainable and rapid progress in healing. It is therefore essential for one who is struck with a mental health problem to resort to such practices of visualization through meditation. Meditation, in recent years, is getting the most attention in medical research. Yoga and meditation actually helps remove all the *bikaras* or *negative feelings* from the mind and connects the soul with all-pervading Thee.

Rewire and recover

We have seen that our brains maintain plasticity well into old age, contrary to the popular myth that it becomes static during early adulthood. Apart from physiological problems or bodily illness (which needs specific medical treatment) we are sometimes affected by mental health problems also. Most such mental health problems, if not all of them, and especially the ones which start during midlife crisis, need similar medical attention in the beginning, but to get back to a medication-free normal life, one can attempt various *coping strategies*. We have already discussed how our brains function, how important the interactions amongst neurons and the resulting neural pathways are. In a time of crisis, the tendency of negative neural networks that get created is to pull the person repeatedly into the problem, to a stage where it almost has a debilitating effect. But there is hope and optimism and good news from modern neuroscientific studies. We retain almost an infinite potential for creating new neural pathways to avoid these very problems that incapacitate us.

Just the way we avoid the cardiac problems arising from a blockage in the arteries by bypassing the blocked passage and creating a new passage for blood flow through surgical intervention, we can visualize avoiding the disturbing and nuisance-making neural pathways by simply creating new neural pathways through positivity, creativity, hope and faith in the benevolence of God. The spiritual potential within remains intact and we can take the help of such spiritual power to generate optimism and hope and deliberately create new neural networks - slowly at first and later in leaps and bounds. Thomas Harris has written in *'Staying OK'* how brains maintain the power to create new neural network to circumvent the trouble-creating neural pathways. What happens by such processes is that the brain does not sink into depression, anxiety or psychosis as it often used to during the peak of the crisis. Slowly, the mind gets positive nutrition and begins to feel good, positive, reassured and gets reinvigorated with optimism and hope. Thus, the mental energy available to face the hardships, to face the world, improves dramatically. Obvious result is faster recovery.

Activate the dormant feel-good old circuits in the brain

All of us have sweet memories from our past. Starting from childhood till the moment you are reading these lines, each one of us would certainly have had sometimes very good memories of fun, frolic and pleasure associated with small successes of ourselves in various fields, whether studies, sports & games, social events, cultural programmes and competitions, neighbourhood activities, organized protests, charity events, family unions or even romance. The interesting thing about the collective functioning of our brain, mind and consciousness is that the thoughts and feelings created during such moments of pleasure are well recorded in our memory cells to an extent that they can be relived. They remain like old and dormant circuitry inside our brain. The very experience of happy feelings caused due to any pleasant event in the past in our lives has the potential to be recalled by deliberate efforts and imaginative thought processes if we chose to. There are many such stored memories which were created following such successes and celebrations in the past. Personally, I have innumerable such memories inside my brain-mind-consciousness combine which I am sure every reader would also similarly have of their own. Couple of such memories, I shall describe here.

I vividly remember the result declaration day of our annual examinations of class VI. Large number of students, all products of different primary schools from all around the district headquarters town of Keonjhar (my hometown) used to study at D.N.High School, considered to be the best high school of the entire district those days. Very recently a high school friend of mine commented about the glorious past of our school, "During our times, dream of each parent was to put his child in our school and if he somehow could not cope with the studies and used to fail, only then he used to look for other schools". After completion of primary education, I thus moved from Mochibandha Primary school to this high school. In spite of being the topper of the Primary School all through, I was very nervous when I entered the big high school where very large number of students from different parts of the town as well as from adjoining rural area schools also had arrived. Quite expectedly, I felt drowned amidst so many talented boys in the school and started feeling whether I could compete with such smart boys. Results of the quarterly and half yearly examinations were generally graded amongst students of each section, there being four sections in each class (A, B, C & D). My position in the section however, to my good luck, was within best three in all these examinations.

Finally, time came for the annual examination result. The tradition in the school those days was to declare the annual examinations result in a common gathering where students of each section and each class would be present, making respective queues for each section. After declaration of results, there would be declaration by the Head Master of the school regarding ensuing long Summer Holidays. Naturally, an opportunity arises to go with a high for such a long holiday break with good results from the annual examinations. There was at the same time a possibility of heartburn at the less than satisfactory results. The moment arrived. When the declaration of the combined result for all the four sections of class VI was made and the concerned teacher read out my name as the topper of the entire class of VI, my joy knew no bounds. I could not believe myself for few moments that I could beat everyone in the entire class! I remember to this day, the scene, how we were standing in different queues, the location on the verandah where the teacher was standing and reading out the result, and how I felt. After all, D.N.High School being the best of all, where all the good students from almost the entire district studied, clinching the top most position was akin to topping the entire district! I naturally felt very proud.

The second incident was around the same time, or may be a year earlier. I was the captain of our neighborhood cricket team. We were playing a cricket match with a nearby neighbourhood team in the Park Grounds about five hundred metres from my home. Our team was batting second and we were to score some one hundred twenty odd runs to win the game. We lost two quick wickets and I went at number four. Although we lost couple of more wickets in the game, I batted for an unbeaten half century and we quite easily won the match. It was a captain's knock and naturally I felt very proud. Memories of that afternoon are still fresh in my mind.

Such *feel good memories* can be from other sources also. Dr. Sam Parnia recalls in his book *'What happens when we die'* how tasteful they had baked a delicious Swedish bread one morning during a research trip to Sweden and how he relished that for years. He claims he recalls even after a decade, the happy feeling he generated during that trip. Such sweet and positive memories can be of any kind and can be from any situation. What is important is that our brains are capable of storing such *feel good memories* for almost as long as we want and the specific neuronal circuitry in the brain associated with these memories can be switched on at a later time. Every one of us has experienced peacefulness and happy feelings when certain past pleasant memories are either discussed or rerun in the mind at a later date. The neuronal circuitry involved during creation of such memories will definitely create similar feeling of happiness and bliss second time around. The intensity may not be as strong as in the first instance, but it would definitely be felt.

During times of mental health crisis, when one loses the power to think and act positive instinctively, one need not worry too much about losing such a capacity for ever. Actually, the imbalances in brain chemicals deter us creating such positive attitude in an automated manner. However, all the dormant *feel good memories* of the past can be recharged and relived by consistent and deliberate efforts, by plugging into the infinite source of energy of the all expansive God, the Almighty. The advantage of such a visualization procedure is to lift the internal strength of the neurons and neurotransmitters to produce and transmit brain chemicals responsible for lifting the mood of such a mental health patient. Regular practice of activation of dormant feel good old circuits in the brain through such visualization can help empowering the mind and the brain in a positive way.

You may not like everybody but you can certainly love all

Margaret Atwood had said, 'The Eskimos had fifty-two names for snow because it was important to them; and hence there ought to be as many for love' perhaps thinking that love is important to us. Actually love is an emotion which transcends all other emotions. Love is infinite and a finite number of names would be insufficient to describe it - just like how Eskimos try to define the seemingly infinitely extending snow around them through fifty-two expressions (One perhaps for each of the fifty-two weeks of the year!).

The basic essence is that each moment we live here on earth is actually an expression of love, if we can visualize it as an expression of the love of God for humanity. There are thefts, burglaries, cheating, betrayal, murder, wars, killings, hurricanes, tsunamis, earthquakes, floods, accidents, famine, diseases, natural tragedies and industrial accidents, but while all these are happening, there will be some miracle unfolding somewhere else. God expresses Himself in such miracles. I recall a sight I saw on TV, more than a decade ago, in which, during a massive flood in Mozambique, there was a rescue operation wherein a Helicopter was saving a mother holding a baby in her arms who was on top of a tree three fourths of which was already submerged under the flood waters. There are thousands of such cases of miraculous survivals from the tsunami affected areas and hurricane affected areas. We hear of survivors coming out without a scratch from the most wretched and messy accidents, from underneath the debris of building collapse by an earthquake etc. All such instances reiterate that each moment, even while I am writing these words, somewhere around this world, lives are being saved miraculously. How is it happening? People either through government sponsored rescue efforts or otherwise, are going out of the way, even risking their own lives, and trying to save lives. The motivation one gets to carry out such tasks can never be imagined by an apparently heartless or loveless human being. Therefore, these are nothing but pure expressions of all-encompassing love from the all-pervading God, flowing to the human species, through some of their representatives (rescuers at the appropriate moment) which are actually God's own replicas to a large extent.

The reason why our initial dislike for someone grows into hatred is simple. Depending on our upbringing, the behaviour of a person may not suit our tastes. Sometimes, our genetic design causes a sort of misalignment. Genetics after all is conditioned over several centuries, if not millions of years. This seed of hatred is the root cause of mental agony, right from the small scale initial violent thoughts to large scale war. And all this can be stopped when whatever we try to do is aligned with our inner voice and conscience. The best examples before us today are the sacrifices of Lord Jesus Christ and Mahatma Gandhi who laid down their lives propagating messages of love and peace.

The beauty lies in scientifically thinking that we can together create a world that will only be full of infinite peace and happiness. There is a simple truth; the moment we are born into this world, we must acknowledge the basic fundamental fact that there will always be something in common between two human beings. The moment we accept this, we shall be able to rejoice in the fact that there must be something apparently very fine and subtle, something apparently invisible to the naked eye and naked senses, which is common to two human beings. It is our duty and responsibility to search for the common thread, and then settle down to build on that common platform and work out differences, if any, thrashing out the problems that may crop up.

If we can try to visualize this truth of life, that there is always something in common between two human beings, either by seeing it easily or by finding out after a careful search, then we can fall in love with each other. It is at this stage that two human beings get connected to the Infinite Source and then act according to the Divine will.

The primary aim and goal of life should be to fall in love with someone at first sight or at least to try harder and harder to discover common ground and start loving! Human nature is infinite dimensional because human intellect is infinite dimensional – and both of these stem from spiritual roots. It is only when we focus our energy and connect to the power of God that we can harness this energy, either to reshape the world or beautify it.

The path to reaching commonality is not easy. However, it becomes easy if we open ourselves up and start believing in the inner self and the outer Self. The celebrated author, M. Scot Peck, believed that there must be something common between two human beings, and to develop faith in a doctor he was visiting, he kept an open mind. Once while he was waiting to see this doctor, he saw the books and magazines lying in the chamber outside. Through these, he was able to identify an interest they both shared! This sudden linkage can be achieved anywhere if we simply let go of our *ego* and *surrender to that omnipresent, omniscient, omnipotent God*. He will then express Himself by tallying our vibrational rhythms with those of the person we want to pair with.

By combining the intention of a peaceful and happy world within and without, all of us can together start creating such a feeling from this very moment. I have a belief and faith that God will help propagate the seed of such a thought which has arisen in my mind of which I am not only aware but quite confident too. This may happen when God, whom we imagine in infinite number of ways, in His own way, creates the so called *Satya Yug* like conditions, when the entire human race comes in contact with this thought and appreciates. I am sure that this thought does not belong to me alone because *Morphic Resonance* has been proven to exist beyond a doubt. This is a case in which the same or a very similar thought (either purely scientific or philosophical) may be crossing two or more human minds on earth at the same time. It is a matter of time the reverberations get amplified amongst human race.

What takes shape as a thought ultimately materializes and the advent of *Satya Yug* is within our reach if some people do not believe that it has already arrived. I have tried to reason out elsewhere that the Hindu belief of cyclic phenomenon of *Satya Yug* being a distant dream (in terms of lakhs of years away) as propagated by some self-proclaimed astrologers can be refined through the same great attribute of Hindu belief system which encourages free human thoughts and no rigid or dogmatic thinking in many other cases. Mahatma Gandhi said, *'Be the change you seek'*. I strongly believe that *Satya Yug* has already arrived. And I am sure such a thought would have already crossed the minds of several others by now, if I have made sense in my arguments in the book starting from origin of earth, origin of the Universe, expansion of earth, expansion of Universe, origin of human species, evolution of human species and finally evolution of human society. It is just a matter of time until such a thought reaches a scale that results in a large part of the population of the world, and not just India, which propagates the concept of *Satya Yug*. Once that happens, there is every likelihood that such thoughts, at least metaphorically, can then be consumed, digested and then reborn through similar thoughts and subjected to rapid recycling in exactly the same manner in which, some of the so called entrenched belief systems have taken very strong roots in human psyche so far. Such a belief is being propagated by the *Brahmakumaris* themselves. They have devised the concept of *tipping point theory* which suggests that the stage of the world will turn into *Satya Yug* from the current *Kali Yug* after a certain number of people start believing in the concept and start acting accordingly. Those who think that the scale of cheating, forgery, murder, killing, sexual abuse, racism, terrorism, violence against women and children and exploitation of people has grown manifold by seeing the reporting of such events in the media should hold their breaths and meditatively contemplate on what their own inner voices are saying about their real feelings. I have always been of the view that to see in the world what you want to, you must first create the same within yourself. The rest will take care of itself. Interestingly, the ideas of *'Satya Yug has already begun'* and this previous idea that *'we see in the world what is there within us and hence we must first create within us what we want to see in the world'* came to my mind without any prompting either from what I have seen, heard or read. Many may not believe, I came across the often quoted statement of Mahatma Gandhi as above much later which signifies that every one of us in this world has the potential to realize such Truth.

Dr. Brian L. Weiss has reported on hundreds of cases of *past life regression therapy* and concluded that *'only love is real'*. This is not a small achievement in terms of realization of Truth. He has even personally guided two patients, who were completely unrelated in their present lives, through *past life regression* to discover how these two patients were actually closely related in one of their past lives. The two souls were in love with each other during a previous lifetime, but they could not fruitfully and completely enjoy their conjugal lives for some reason, and were hence back on earth. It was the great *theoretically-always-believed-but-finally-scientifically-proven* skill of Dr. Brian Weiss which helped the two souls become engaged again by entering into another blissful marriage in their current lives. Dr. Brian's book, which is dedicated to this real life story, is such a wholesome treat! This example proves that souls are loveful and that they keep coming to earth until they experience all the *infinite dimensions of love*. Love is a feeling that can be experienced through some conscious efforts even if we dislike someone because of his or her habits, attitudes or even background.

One of the easiest ways to get inspired is to closely watch highly advanced and realized souls who have an immense following as revered spiritual leaders of the public at large. If contemporary human beings, in the skin of spiritual leaders, can achieve *universal love towards all their fellow citizens of the world*, then it is possible for any common person - provided he keeps an open mind and heart and does not discriminate between two human beings, at least at the level of divinity in the mind's substratum. This may be difficult to attain, because of the *Karmic Account Balance* one carries from previous birth, but it is definitely not impossible, at least to create a positive thought about its possibility. The usual tendency of people is to say;

'I am not a saint, so do not expect such attitudes from someone like me.' The very thought and statement that 'No, we are all same and, even if born different, we have that potential to be same in the long run' is so powerful that anything can be achieved with the power of such a thought. Actually, each soul on earth will progressively rise ultimately to the state of a realized soul. The only thing that will remain to be seen is the number of births that he or she will need, and this depends upon how much *Karmic efforts* he or she is prepared to put in each birth.

Recollect and reinforce all your successes of the past

This entire book is intended to help those who have lived happy, contented lives for a sizable number of years - until their early teens, or late teens, or early adulthoods or late adulthoods. Those who are born with mental ailments right from birth may not be benefitted as much as those who, due to some stroke of bad luck, have gravitated to a serious mental health crisis.

There was a time during my own crisis in Australia when I thought to myself; 'I am still breathing and hence able to do some work - considering the act of breathing as the work I was capable of then. Slowly and steadily, I will increase the types of work that I can do and load my work schedule with activities that will include my own daily chores at least.' In a few days, I included higher order activities like taking my daughter to school, bringing her back from school, going to the market for vegetables, going to the supermarket for groceries etc. I also included other activities like taking my family for a stroll across the road to a nearby park where I could watch my two children enjoying rides and having fun. And I did all this while I was supposed to be going to my research institution to do research and complete my project. But I had relegated all those objectives and goals of life to the back of my mind and concentrated on doing menial work first, in a determined manner, for the first few days of the crisis. This way, bit by bit or brick by brick, I built up my confidence - which had hit rock bottom after the acute psychotic episode that forced me into hospitalization for about a week in Adelaide.

During these times, my subconscious was very active, reminding me that all those things that I had been able to do and accomplish in the past were there to be taken into account. It was certainly not the end of the world when I came out of the hospital, feeling awful as I did. And I never allowed myself to become despondent by thinking that the temporary breakdown was in any way going to ruin my future. I focused on deliberate attempts to remind myself of the small and big successes that I had already achieved in life and there were quite a few of them already. Such a process actually helps in creating new neural pathways in the brain that will be associated with the happy feelings of victories, successes and achievements. The association of neurons, buttons and synapses with such thoughts will then register in the brain, helping in recovery from the deadly low, depressive, anxious or even psychotic feelings that may be overpowering us during the time of a serious imbalance in brain chemicals.

Each one of you, whether you are a teenager or an adult, irrespective of age, gender, geography, culture, religion, family and social background, has achieved some success already in the past. For example, it could be a primary school race you won, or a competition of some sort related either to academics or extracurricular activities. But right now, because of some deadly mental health crisis, your conscious brain has been so jammed and blocked that your whole world appears to be plain, simple and dark without any sign of hope. I urge you then to simply try to activate your subconscious brain, where all past memories are stored, and recall the happy thoughts you felt during the time of that past victory or win. It can even be some small act of compassion, some help that you might have extended to someone on the street, such as extending a hand to help a blind person cross the road. These small successes contain exceptional energy in the memory cells of the brain and the moment you activate these, it can create new beautiful neural pathways that will provide you with immense confidence, courage and conviction that yes, it was you who achieved that in the past and that, hence there was and still is, within you, everything that is needed to recreate such successes now and in future. You may feel skeptical, wonder about how these things are related, since the problem at hand might appear as daunting as Himalayan whereas your achievement in the past will seem to be a small pitiful thing. But the hidden power in taking small steps towards recovery, by reminding ourselves our smallest of small successes in the past, can ultimately do wonders. Actually, it is very similar to the way a two or three-storied building stands on thousands of individual bricks stacked systematically to support the structure. Any large goal can be achieved by accumulated small successes, in due course of time. I have achieved amazing results by this very process and there is no reason why anyone else cannot achieve dramatic results.

Keep challenging your own bias and widen the horizon

Modern research in neuroscience and neuropsychiatry has clearly brought out simple facts how our upbringing plays a huge role in the making of our personality. In an abusive atmosphere, a child will develop very different behavior compared to a situation wherein he grows up in a calm, serene and peaceful environment. A child who grows up in an environment rich with intellectual stimulations in his growing years, be it through parental guidance or extended family interactions, will have a very different capacity as compared to one who grows up in the family of a drunk or drug-addicted or poorly educated person. Orthodox beliefs are another area which influences young growing minds. Mythological and Puranic-based stories can sometimes influence young brains in such a way that they become almost blind and closed to anything that modern science and technology brings in. For example, when we see natural calamities happening, we try to connect them with something mysterious and unknown. But most of the broader scientific discoveries have helped humanity remove the veil of ignorance which our previous generations of ancient past suffered from. There is another extreme wherein belief in astrology can sometimes make one lazy, lethargic and devoid of enthusiasm to work harder for achieving his goals by simply saying that everything in his or her life is pre-ordained or pre-destined.

There can be other extremes also. Social customs can sometimes be deadly. Elders sometimes say 'Look, that woman did not bear any child all her life; must be a cursed woman.' or 'That man could not feed his children properly and threw away opportunities to make lots of money by refusing bribes. He should have at least fed his children properly!' or 'Look, his parents died a sad death because their child could never hold a top rank even though he was so brilliant in his younger days'. If, when he is growing up, the young innocent mind of a child is constantly exposed to such stuff, there is every possibility that a wrong belief system will develop inside the brain of that little child. He might end up thinking that a woman who is incapable of childbearing is worthless and does not deserve to live. Or he may start believing that bribe-taking is a virtue and is much preferable to trying to change his vocation, or to developing other skills that will help him earn more, or to even working harder to earn more so as to lead a better life. And, with respect to the last case, the child could start believing that any position below the top rank in school, college or the workplace is absolutely worthless and this could lead to the child's growing up to be a nervous wreck.

If we analyse our lives properly, starting from early childhood, we might notice that many of the notions and belief systems that we have been carrying with us from childhood - due to our upbringing - have no relevance in the modern world. Although science and technology have been rapidly progressing, so as to help humanity, one still needs to be alert as to where to draw the line. Supposing a couple has failed to produce a child after many years, and in spite of embracing several modern technological developments in childbearing like IVF, artificial insemination and surrogacy, does it not sound prudent for the couple to go for adoption and raise a family instead of being obsessed with producing a child of their own, and even through repeated attempts might be endangering the health of the would-be mother? All these wrong ideas about worthlessness owing to failure to bear a child have deep roots in our mindsets, born out of social customs and traditional belief systems. These need to be challenged and sensible steps should be taken in order to lead healthier and more content and peaceful lives.

There is vast scope for every human being who comes to Earth to not only eke out a living but also to make a place for himself in society. Nowadays, there are examples of extraordinary human beings who have overcome serious disabilities in their lives and achieved great heights in almost every field - including education, research, industry, sports, art and music. The greatest help one gets is through the media, be it print or electronic. There are thousands of books, both autobiographical and biographical, depicting such great and inspiring stories. They help in providing us with the inspiration to challenge the established myths that are handed down to us by previous generations.

It is quite obvious that today's problems cannot be solved with yesterday's knowledge or wisdom. We need to fight ignorance with wisdom to solve any problem of today. And we cannot fight ignorance with ignorance. Some of the social traditions that have been causing immense pain and anguish to human beings can never be eradicated by applying yesterday's knowledge. Someone's ignorance, be it of any form, cannot be handled by another person's higher order ignorance. The answers to all problems therefore lie in the simple fact of challenging the age old customs and traditions, if they have outlived their useful expiry date and are causing more nuisance than help. Beliefs are okay if they help us grow, but if they pose impediments to the path of progress and growth, it is high time we get rid of such beliefs or at least tone down our faith in them. I have personally experienced how a few age old customs and traditions have a damaging influence on our relationships and hence spoil our mental peace and stability.

Human ingenuity, which lies in the ability to challenge every old concept and replace it with a new and better concept in every field, has helped mankind so far. One cannot solve a problem of today by remaining at the level he was when the problem was created. Even in case of personal problems, this principle applies. One has to rise to a higher plane to attempt solving a problem. It is not easy, but it is not impossible either. No one ever thought that DNA could be changed, or that neurons could be generated, or that earth could be expanding and so on. Conventional wisdom is also subject to change because of the rapid pace at which scientific and technological change is occurring around the globe. It is always better to challenge the bias that could have crept into our thought processes due to wrong teachings during our early childhood. By doing this, one can certainly widen the horizons of one's thought level.

Give and Live

At the time of my mental health crisis, such a concept never occurred to my mind simply because the diseased mind was so overburdened with stress and anxiety that to even perceive such a possibility was beyond its capacity. But there is a beautiful phenomenon involved here. The *Brahmakumaris* have refined this idea brilliantly. One who gives actually receives. God's grace falls on every being equally and it is wiser to allow such grace to pass through an individual soul to another, thereby helping the first person to be ready to receive further grace. People should not confuse this with materialistic gain alone. It includes all the basic ingredients of God's grace; love, peace and compassion.

Connecting to God or the Universal Soul through meditation means plugging into the infinite source of power, love, peace, compassion, happiness and beauty. And once we successfully plug in, it is only a matter of time before the individual soul starts receiving the power, love, peace, compassion, happiness and beauty. It is in the best interest of the individual also to share the same with fellow human beings. This is how God chooses us as a medium to transmit peace, love and compassion and helps us receive grace as well. Hence 'to give' means 'to live'. The lives of great souls, starting from Lord Buddha, Lord Mahavira and Lord Jesus, to even our leaders of contemporary history like Mahatma Gandhi, teach us this simple philosophy. To what extent or percentage we can achieve the level or standard they have set before us is in our hands.

Leave your legacy: Dad, Mom and You

My whole journey till date has been pivotally guided by what I have learnt from my parents and everything in them that still inspires me, guides me, encourages me to move on, everything in them that makes me proud, makes me what I am and makes me work harder to leave the same kind of legacy - albeit a little fine-tuned with the edges smoothened and a little more attuned to the changing environment and dynamics of this ever-evolving Earth.

My father loved education and always cherished the fact that his children were highly educated and had built themselves up to be strong men and women who were of help to the society. Everything he did in his life was directed at achieving such a goal, and hence it is easy to imbibe such things from father. He was also very religious and a disciplined devotee to the Hindu Gods and Goddesses, followed the practice of praying to Gods with *Kirtans* twice daily.

My mother was a pious lady who always believed in God, in the efficacy of God in her life. She measured everything by her faith in God and it was a sight to see how she got solace from God. She used to immerse herself in thoughts of God, particularly towards the final stage of her life.

Every frown on the face of my father used to signal to me some kind of life lesson that had to be learnt. His frowning or shouting at anything used to get captured in my mind as a piece of wisdom, a gem that I could learn from and refine my life with. His words, particularly those words which matched his uncanny habit of *living by example*, greatly influenced my life.

For example, he used to wield the wood cutter himself and head to our backyard to cut the bigger pieces of wood/logs that the firewood sellers used to dump in our backyard, for the fireplace. Those days, our cooking and heating were all done using old-style fireplaces fuelled by firewood. My father's habit of killing two birds with one stone created an indelible impression on my mind. He made it a habit to get some physical exercise as well as help the household in whatever way he could, whenever he could. These sights of such an ideal family man were so moving to me, particularly since we all knew he was one of the three leading lawyers of the town, if not the best. To his children, siblings, close relatives and trusted juniors of course, he was the best in the town. The best lawyer, the best senior advocate and the best father.

There were other instances which made a similar impact on me. His going to the market everyday on his old bicycle (he'd used it for perhaps fifty years) to buy fresh vegetables and then sitting back on the verandah to cut the vegetables for lunch etc. was so moving to our young brains that it remains my ultimate goal to reach. There were several other instances which would thrill any ordinary middle class family person and make him proud of such fatherly attributes. My father would pull out all kinds of implements from around the house and sit down and try to repair small articles like umbrellas and kitchen appliances with some minor defects, small pieces of wooden furniture which needed a bit of attention etc.

The Kitchen garden was his favourite. He also grew a variety of flowers in some parts of our backyard garden. And this in addition to trees likes guava, mango, bel or golden apple, jackfruit, banana etc. all planted inside our large campus. The memories of it are so humbling and profound, that I feel so bad when I compare it with some of the present day city-apartment living and lifestyle. He used to spend his early morning and evening hours in the kitchen garden, tilling the land with his small implements, weeding, watering and even harvesting the vegetables he used to grow. Those memories are really profound and so very natural. Anyone can be taken very close to nature and create an ocean of peace and happiness if they try to go on a similar path and imitate a similar lifestyle.

Apart from such things, he would cook food for us, manage transport, even carry us to different places on his bicycle if the need arose - such as when I had my phimosis operation when I was in class X. He took me on his bicycle to the doctor who suggested the operation. He stood there all day and brought me back from the hospital and also arranged post-operative dressing and care - through his friend Doctor Shri Braja Kishore Mishra - and helped me recover fast. I could attend school one week after the operation. I vividly remember his caring attitude. It gave me strength at the time. And his feeling that it was not a big thing but only a minor operation (to his knowledge) also helped me recover and get back to my normal life very fast.

My father had an uncanny attitude; he loved sports, he loved fishing and hunting, he loved taking risks. He loved music; he played musical instruments and he used to sing at gatherings, particularly at religious gatherings in our village of Boudpur during the Durga Puja festival. He loved making friends and his social circle was very large and diverse. He was so adventurous that he tried almost everything in life. He was good at hockey and played at the inter-college level. He was extremely good at football and he used to tell stories of his football acumen. He was the champion in bridge. He opened and closed several businesses over a span of two decades during his prime life. He was the first government advocate in the district court, an honour engraved in the annals of the court history. He was the uncontested President of the Keonjhar Bar association and the first President of the Lions Club of Keonjhar. He even contested State Assembly elections!

Mom on the other hand was so loving that no one who visited our house would leave without getting a warm reception. There were always guests at our house and both my parents entertained them all with warmth. Many of our cousin brothers and sisters were invited by my parents to stay with us whilst studying at the college of our town which was very reputed those days. The affection showered by my parents on them was a real lesson for me during my growing years, showed me how one can really keep an absolutely loving state of mind. I have been immensely fortunate to be born to these two great souls and raised in a highly elevated environment.

Each individual born on this Earth receives the love and affection of his or her parents to a great extent. The spectrum may range from sometimes abusive parents to extremely affectionate and learned parents. Depending on the physical, mental, social and financial condition of the parents, each child will be exposed to different levels of care. But there are thousands of examples wherein we see children born into extreme poverty, and who are otherwise deprived of all the good things of life, have been able to excel in their lives and establish themselves in society. These are inspiring stories. In case one's childhood is not that good, I believe that, historically, we have had so many thousands of examples of great souls who tell us that it is possible to emulate them and follow a similar path to emancipation. The human mind follows the trajectory depicted so well by Stephen Covey through his four processes: live, love, learn, leave a legacy. Irrespective of the kind of upbringing one has been lucky or unlucky enough to get, there is always something one can finally do to leave behind a legacy that he or she will be proud of.

One recent statement sums it up so well. The small boy who once sold tea in a railway station, and rose up to the highest position of Indian government that of Prime Minister, Shri Narendra Modi remarked while condoling the death of another great contemporary soul, that of ex-President and Bharat Ratna awardee Mr. APJ Abdul Kalam, "India has lost its true Ratna. Shri Kalam who once sold newspapers as a boy to support his family, achieved such great heights and rose to become the people's president and today all the newspapers in the country have filled their pages with his eulogy and praise." Ex-President Kalam has in his latest book *'Transcendence'* mentioned about how he was influenced by his childhood memories of his father, an Imam in the mosque and two senior religious leaders from Rameswaram including the local priest of the famous Rameswaram temple and the Christian Church leader of Rameswaram used to discuss about problems facing the local community and their possible solutions. The way the three elders from three different faiths converged at his house and harmoniously blended into one with a common objective had a remarkable influence on Kalam which he has proudly mentioned in his book. He goes on to say that eight decades of his life's experience only proved to him the words and teachings of his Imam father. Such is the true testimony to the concept of *'leaving the legacy of parents'.* This is generally the case with most of the great men those who have graced this world.

Similarly, some common and ordinary people will be happy enough to leave behind disciplined offspring who are trained almost in the same traditional mould as they were trained by their parents. It is no mean achievement in this fast-changing society to do even this successfully. Some people will learn so much from their struggles and sufferings that it would be prudent for them to record their experience in some form so that humanity can benefit from the same.

It is not always necessary to leave a progeny behind so as to satisfy the intrinsic human urge of procreation. Although it may be desirable, in cases where it is medically difficult and so on, the legacy can take any form. Even adoption would be an option to help satisfy all the desires that human beings generally possess, i.e. to live, to love, to learn and to leave a legacy. We can learn from our parents, from the environment, from great seers, we can acquire some new knowledge, and finally pass on this knowledge and wisdom to our own progeny or adopted children and leave behind a better world than what we inherited. In this extremely scientifically and technologically developed digital world, a world that is interdependent, this is the least that the highest species, human beings, can be expected to give back to the world where they all originated to begin with.

****

BIBLIOGRAPHY

The journey of my life so far has been enriched by many books of outstanding quality. Some of the ideas perceived by me at different times might have resonated very well with the authors of these books. I have referred to some of these books in places. Sometimes I have directly quoted lines from them and sometimes I have not. Those which have not been quoted directly are sincerely acknowledged here in this bibliography.

Similarly I have been an avid listener to spiritual discourses, interactive sessions, interviews with spiritual leaders of India and overseas telecasts by various TV channels. And I have learnt many finer aspects of life that may have been filtered through my own perceptions and then been mentioned in this book. Teachings on spiritual knowledge through TV channels like Aastha and Sanskar and TV programmes by *Brahmakumaris* are the most important TV programmes that I have imbibed from and have used profusely in my book.

Apart from all these, some of the material have been taken directly from the free internet based *Wikipedia* and through *Google searches* and have been modified suitably for the book.

Following is the list of books that have shaped my ideas before embarking on such a project of writing the first ever book which is partly autobiographical.

A Brief History Of Time: From The Big Bang To The Black Holes by Stephen W. Hawking. Introduction by Carl Sagan, illustrations by Ron Miller, Bantam Books, a division of Transworld Publishers, 1988.

An Intimate Note To The Sincere Seeker: Sri Sri Ravi Shankar, Volume 7 complied by Bill Hayden & Anne Elixhauser, Vyakti Vikas Kendra.

An Intimate Note To The Sincere Seeker by Sri Sri Ravi Shankar: Volume 2 compiled by David L.Burge, Art Of Living Foundation.

An Autobiography OR The Story Of My Experiments With Truth written originally by M.K. Gandhi, Navajivan Publishing House, 1925. Translated From Gujarati by Mahadev Desai,

Autobiography Of A Yogi by Paramahansa Yogananda, Jaico Publishing House.

Baisi Pahacha (Twenty two steps) by Dr.Kavi Prasad Mishra, Mahavir Books, 2005.'

Being Indian: The Truth About Why Twenty First Century Will Be India's' by Pavan K.Varma, Penguin Books, Published by Penguin Group, 2005.

Bhagaban Sri Raman Maharishi by Dr. Kavi Prasad Mishra, published by Mahavir Prakashan, 2010.

Bhagawat Gita by Basudev Nayak, 1978.

Circulation Problems by J.A. Gillespie, Guideway Publishing Ltd, London.

Code Name God: The Spiritual Odyssey of a Man of Science by Mani Bhaumik, published by Penguin Books.

Denial Of The Soul: Spiritual And Medical Perspectives On Euthanasia And Mortality by M.Scott Peck, Harmony Books, A Division of Crown Publishers, New York.

Depression and Anxiety by Dr. Arthur Graham, Guideway Publishing Ltd, London.

Feeling Good: The New Mood Therapy (Revised and Updated) by David D. Burns, Avon Books (An Imprint Of Harper Collins Publishers).

First Things First : To Live, to Love, to Learn, to Leave a Legacy by Stephen R.Covey, A.Roger Merill and Rebecca R.Merill, Simon & Schuster UK Ltd, 1994.

Games People Play: The Psychology Of Human Relationships by Eric Berne, Published by Ballantine Books, 1964.

Galileo's Daughter by Dava Sobel published by Fourth Estate, A division of Harper Collins Publishers, 1999.

Health In Your Hands: Acupressure and other Natural Therapies by Devendra Vora, Gala publishers.

Holy Basil Tulsi (A Herb): A Unique Medicinal Plant by Yash Rai, Navneet Publications India LTD.

How To Enjoy Your Life And Your Job by Dale Carnegie, Published by Pocket Books, A Division of Simon & Schuster Inc, A Gulf Western Company, 1970.

How To Win Friends and Influence People by Dale Carnegie, published by Pocket Books (a Simon and Schuster division of gulf and Western Corporation), New York, 1940.

How to Stop Worrying and Start Living by Dale Carnegie, published by Simon & Schuster, 1948.

How to Get from where you are to where you want to be by Jack Canfield, published by Harper Collins, 2005.

I am OK You are OK by Thomas A Harris, published by Harper & Row, 1969.

Illusions: The Adventure Of a Reluctant Messiah by Richard Bach, published by Dell Publishing Co., Inc, division of Bantam Doubleday Dell Publishing Group, Inc. New York, November 1989.

Intuitive Creativity by B.K.Banerji; published by Avon Books, London, 1998.

Jesus Lived In India: His Unknown Life before and After Crucifixion: Holger Kersten, Penguin Books, 1986.

Linda Goodman's Sun signs by Bantam Books published by arrangement with Taplinger Publishing Co, Inc, 1968.

Mahabharata by C.Rajagopalachari, published by Bharatiya Vidya Bhavan, 1958.

Maa!, Mun Collector Heli by Rajesh Prabhakar Patil(translated from original Marathi by V.S.Jogalekar), 2014.

Many Lives, Many Masters: The true story of a prominent psychiatrist, His Young Patient, and Past-Life Therapy That Changed Both Their Lives by Brian L.Weiss, A Fireside Book published by Simon and Schuster, 1988.

Messages From The Masters: Tapping Into The Power Of Love by Dr Brian Weiss, Piaktus, An imprint of Little, Brown Book Group Hachette UK Company, 2000.

Messiahs Don't Die by Lalchand K.Nichani, Maya Moon Publications, Chennai, 1998.

Miracles Happen: The Transformational Healing Power Of Past Life Memories by Dr Brian Weiss and Amy E.Weiss, H Hay House Publishers, 2012.

Mister God, This Is Anna by Fynn (Pseudonym Of Sydney Hopkins) Illustrated by Papas, Ballantine Books, New York.

Modern Man In Search Of A Soul by Carl Gustav Jung, Routledge (Imprint Of Taylor and Francis group).

My Unforgettable Memories by Mamata Banerjee, The Lotus Collection, an imprint of Roli Books, 2012.

Numerous TV programmes by Brahmakumaris and religious channel programmes of Aastha.

Only Love Is Real: The Story Of Soulmates Reunited by Dr Brian Weiss, An imprint of Little, Brown Book Group Hachette UK Company, 1996.

Out Of My Mind: A Flight Into The Realm Of Thought And Spirit by Richard Bach, Sidwig and Jackson, an imprint of Macmillan Publishers Limited, 1999.

Prakriti Ro Dano, Rashmi Prabha Publication.

Raja Yoga or Conquering the Internal Nature by Swami Vivekananda, published by Advaita Ashrama.

Rich Dad Poor Dad: What The Rich Teach Their Kids About Money-That The Poor And Middle Class Do Not! by Robert T. Kiyosaki with Sharon L.Lechter, published by A Time Warner Company.

Sachin Tendulkar, Playing it my way, My Autobiography with Boria Mazumdar, published by Hodder & Stoughton, 2014.

Secrets Of Happiness by Tanushree Podder, Pustak Mahal, Delhi 2003.

Spouse: The Truth About Marriage by Shobha De', published by penguin books in 2005.

Sri Sri As I Know Him: A Collection Of Personal Experiences and Anecdotes: Compiled and edited by Dinesh Kashikar and Sharmila Murarka, Published by Vyakti Vikas Kendra, India 2000

Staying OK by Amy Bjork Harris and Thomas A.Harris MD, published by arrow books in 1995.

Tuesdays with Morrie by Mitch Albom, Doubleday, 1997.

The Art Of Happy Living by G.D. Budhiraja, Pustak Mahal Publishers 2006.

The Laws Of Scientific Hand Reading by William G.Benham published by agreement with Putnam & Co LTD, London.

The Power Of Intention: Learning To Co-create Your World Your Way by Dr. Wayne W.Dyer, Hayhouse, Inc.

The Power Of Positive Thinking: A Practical Guide to Mastering the Problems of the Everyday Living by Norman Vincent Peale, A Universal Publication Arrangement With World's Work (1973) Ltd. Reprint 1987

The Road Less Travelled: A new psychology of love, traditional values and spiritual growth by M.Scott Peck, M.D A Touchstone Book published by Simon and Schuster.

The Speed Of Trust: The One Thing That Changes Everything by Stephen M.R. Covey with Rebecca R.Merrill, published by Simon & Schuster UK Ltd, 2006.This Edition first published by Pocket Books, 2008, imprint of Simon & Schuler UK Ltd.

The 7 Habits Of Highly Effective People by Stephen R. Covey, First published by Simon and Schuster UK Ltd, 1989.

The Nectar Of Instruction by His Divine Grace by A.C. Bhaktivedanta Swami Prabhupada, The Bhaktivedanta Book Trust.

The Quick and Easy Way to Effective Speaking by Dale Carnegie and Dorothy Carnegie, published by Pocket Books, a Simon and Schuster division of Gulf and Western Corporation 1977.

The Ramayana by R.K. Narayan, published by Chatto and Windus, 1973.

The Secret by Rhonda Bryne, Atria Books, Beyond Words Publishing. A division of Simon and Schuster, Inc, 2006.

The Test Of My Life :From Cricket to Cancer and Back by Yuvraj Singh with Sharda Ugra & Nishant Jeet Arora, published by Random House India, 2013.

Through Time Into Healing by Brian L.Weiss, A Fireside Book published by Simon and Schuster, 1993.

Turning Points: A Journey Through Challenges by A.P.J Abdul Kalam, Harper Collins Publishers India a joint venture with India Today Group, 2012.

The Kingdom Of God And Peace Essays by Leo Tolstoy (Graf) translated with an introduction by Aylmer Maude, Rupa Co. 2001.

The Autobiography Of Benjamin Franklin: Introduction by Lewis Leary, A Touchstone Book, published by Simon & Schuster, 2004.

The World's Greatest Comebacks by Robert A. Schuller, Orient Paperbacks, A Division of Vision Books Pvt Ltd, 2001.

The Monk Who Sold His Ferrari: A Fable About Fulfilling Your Dreams And Reaching Your Destiny by Robin S. Sharma, Jaico Publishing House.

What happens when we die by Dr.Sam Parnia, Hay House, India, 2008

Why I assassinated Gandhi by Nathuram Godse and Gopal Godse, Farsight Publishers and Distributors, 2015.

Wings of Fire, An autobiography by A.P.J.Abdul Kalam, published by Universities Press, 1999.

ABOUT THE AUTHOR

Pradipta Kumar Das was born in May 1962 at Keonjhar, Odisha as the seventh of the eight children of his parents. His father, Late Ambika Pada Das and mother, Late Biraja Rani Das were originally from the village Boudpur, about three kilometres from the town of Bhadrakh in Odisha. He went to Mochibandha Primary School and D.N. High School at Keonjhar for his primary and secondary education respectively. Graduating with Physics, Mathematics and Geology from Keonjhar College in 1982, he then moved to I.I.T Kharagpur to do his Masters in Exploration Geophysics.

He has worked for the National Oil Company of India, ONGC Limited for more than three decades now and is still working. He obtained an MTech degree in Petroleum Exploration from I.S.M, Dhanbad and a PhD from the University of Adelaide, Australia while still working for ONGC. The stint for four years in Adelaide from July 1997 to August 2001 was not only very successful in terms of his research in petroleum geophysics, but certain events during the same period dramatically transformed his whole perspective about life itself. Making numerous friends whilst being in Australia, he still maintains a sweet bond with Australia. He has travelled widely in India and abroad. Among his numerous achievements and awards; the best technical paper awards in two international geosciences conferences, one in Australia in February 2001 and one in India in January 2011 are most dear to him. He also fondly remembers the first prize for his short story in Odiya language in a state-wide competition conducted by YMCA when he was in Junior college.

He has been happily married for about twenty-four years now. He currently lives in Bhubaneswar with his wife and two children. Apart from his research interests in the latest trends in hydrocarbon exploration tools and technologies, he shows an inclination towards subtle metaphysical and philosophical aspects of life in general and the teachings of the *Bhagawat Gita* in particular. He writes essays, short stories and commentaries for local journals and newspapers. He is currently working on his first book on fiction, *'Recycled Souls'*.

Printed in the United States
By Bookmasters